Missions in Conflict:
Essays on U.S.-Mexican Relations and Chicano Culture

Cosponsored by

UC MEXUS
Center for Chicano Studies
University of California Santa Barbara
and Johannes Gutenberg-Universität Mainz

Renate von Bardeleben (Managing Editor)
Dietrich Briesemeister (Consultant Editor)
Juan Bruce-Novoa (Consultant Editor)

Missions in Conflict:
Essays on U.S.-Mexican Relations
and Chicano Culture

 Gunter Narr Verlag Tübingen

E
184.
.M5
M56
1986

CIP-Kurztitelaufnahme der Deutschen Bibliothek

Missions in conflict: essays on US Mexican relations and Chicano culture /
Renate von Bardeleben (managing ed.) ... Cosponsored by UC MEXUS,
Center for Chicano Studies ...– Tübingen : Narr, 1986.
 ISBN 3–87808–721–7

NE: Bardeleben, Renate von [Hrsg.]

© 1986 · Gunter Narr Verlag Tübingen
Alle Rechte vorbehalten. Nachdruck oder Vervielfältigung, auch
auszugsweise, in allen Formen wie Mikrofilm, Xerographie, Mikrofiche,
Mikrocard, Offset verboten.

Druck: Gulde-Druck GmbH, Tübingen
Verarbeitung: Braun + Lamparter, Reutlingen
Printed in Germany

ISBN 3–87808–721–7

Acknowledgments

The twenty-six papers collected in this volume were presented at the First International Symposium on Chicano Culture, July 5 to 7, 1984 at the University of Mainz at Germersheim. The conference had been organized on the occasion of the seventieth birthday of Gustav H. Blanke, the first holder of the chair in American Studies at Germersheim, and was generously supported by financial aid granted by the German Association for American Studies, the Johannes Gutenberg-Universität Mainz and private donors. The organizers hereby state their gratitude, which was also expressed at various times and in various forms before, during, and after the symposium by the participants. In addition, they wish to repeat that without the considerable private effort on the part of the participants this conference could not have been realized in its full scope. Therefore the support given by several home universities of the members must be acknowledged here as an important help. Thanks must also go to the Fachbereich Angewandte Sprachwissenschaft that housed the conference and lent all its facilities, especially the interpreting equipment, and to the technicians who did not mind working extra hours.

The printing of the contributions was made possible by further substantial support received from UC MEXUS, Center for Chicano Studies, University of California, Santa Barbara, and the University of Mainz. All papers were revised and are published here with permission of the authors. The editorial work was largely confined to the revising of the annotations, the correction of obvious errors, and the preparation of an index. This was accomplished with the assistance of Monika Hoffmann, Donald Kiraly, Hans Klinkhammer and Sabina Matter. The never failing patience of the secretary-typist Erika Scharrer-Wetterauer also deserves praise. Last, I would like to mention the commitment of those who in many minor, but indispensable ways helped to bring this volume into its present shape.

R. v. B.

Contents

VIII

Introduction

Renate von Bardeleben

In introducing his anthology *We Are Chicanos* in 1973 Philip D. Ortego stated, "Mexican-Americans have been the most shamefully neglected minority in the United States," and complained about the inaccurate and superficial image of the Chicano then current in literature and the media. It was in the same year when Ihab Hassan published his famed study *Contemporary American Literature 1945–1972* and devoted special sections to the Jewish as well as the Black contributions to U.S. American literature, but passed over in silence the Chicano, a situation that was to continue till the end of that decade, when the *Harvard Guide to Contemporary American Writing* appeared. This important handbook does not offer a chapter on Chicano literature, though it does on Black, and when a Chicano work is mentioned, like John Rechy's *City of Night*, the unsuspecting reader would fail to make the connection. In historical terms the situation was slightly better. Not only has the history of the American Southwest been treated by both Mexican and United States historians, the Spanish colonial travel and exploration reports, too, have found admittance to the canon of the renowned *Literary History of the United States*, first published in 1946.

Visibility was first achieved by the political activism of the second half of the 1960s, starting with the strike of the grape pickers in Delano, California in September 1965. The struggle for Civil Rights was accompanied, some say followed, by a burst of cultural production. To document the new political and cultural identity, the word Chicano, an in-group term of the turn of the century,[1] quickly began to supplant the older label Mexican-American, which had acquired derogatory connotations in everyday usage. The new designation was a handy term to underline the new awareness of ethnicity and the energetic character of the socio-political and cultural movement. As to the origin of the word, there is no unanimous consent. The most frequently adopted etymology links the term with *Mexicano* by a process of shortening and alteration.[2] Edward A. Stephenson in a three-page discussion in *American Speech* records its first printed appearance in 1947 and offers two derivations. He quotes a letter by Philip D. Ortego of October 6, 1970 who points to "Nahuatl origin, suggesting that Indians pronounce Mexicano as 'Me-shi-ca-noh'," thereby explaining the phonological changes. The use of this word thus stresses Mexican-Indian culture. The other explanation derives the word from *chico*, a young boy, by a process of suffixation, adding *ano*.[3] Rodolfo Acuña, disregarding the philological problems involved, links several important aspects in his definition by stating, "'Chicano' . . . was what the middle-class Mexican Americans called the grass roots or the poor sector — which formed the majority of Mexicans in the United States. Youth popularized the terms by stating that they were committed 'to the poor Mexican, to the *Chicano*'."[4] While it can thus be argued with certainty that the term gained popularity and was at first associated with the political actions of the young and the lower classes, its usage has been rapidly extended by members of the academic community who identify with it, "to apply to all Americans of Mexican descent regardless of profession, education, or political persuasion."[5]

It may be suggested here that other terms available to designate this ethnic group like Hispanics, Hispanos, Latins, Latin-Americans, Spanish-Americans were either too wide, or like Mexican-Americans had acquired a pejorative meaning. They also tended to stress only part of the multicultural heritage of the group.[6] Nor did any of the other terms correctly reflect the present linguistic situation. Even in physical appearance there is great variety. Armando B. Rendón sums up the multiracial traits: "Our people range widely from light-skinned güeros to dark-skinned Indios. Certainly we have our share of black blood from Negroes who escaped into Mexico, a free country, from the southern slave states, and even Arab-Semitic traces from the Moors."[7] The history of the Chicano therefore has more than one root. Different from all other American ethnic groups, the Chicano does not consider himself a transplanted minority, but points to his Mexican Indian past prior to Spanish colonization. As the people of Aztlán, the Chicano holds a claim to be a descendent of the Aztec civilization, the epoch of el Quinto Sol, the Fifth Sun. He also holds a claim to a distinct territory in which he has lived for centuries and which can be roughly described by the geographic area of the present American Southwest, the five-state area of Texas, New Mexico, Colorado, Arizona, and California. As Carey McWilliams phrased it in his pioneer study *North from Mexico*,[8] Mexican-Americans were very much a part of the landscape when the Anglo-Americans arrived, and as Rodolfo Acuña put it, "Anglo-Americans inherited a long tradition of Indian and Mexican settlement."[9] Three centuries of Spanish rule, formally starting with the conquest of Tenochtitlán in 1521 and formally ending with Mexico winning its independence from Spain in 1821, left an indelible imprint on the region and its inhabitants. Though small in numbers, the Spaniards were able to transmit their language, religion and legal system to the native peoples as a unifying force. Mixing with the native population was an important factor despite a discriminatory caste-class system, which distinguished between criollos (native-born Spanish), mestizos (mixed Spanish and Indian), mulattoes (mixed Spanish and black), and zambos (mixed Indian and African), with the peninsular (Spaniard born in Spain), the Indio and the Negro representing the unmixed portion of the society. Spanish whites held the important offices in church and government, but the aspect of society was determined by the numerically dominating mestizos.

During the short period of Mexican rule, Anglo-Americans entered the region of California, New Mexico and especially Texas. These new immigrants who received land grants or worked as merchants proved difficult to integrate. Centralizing tendencies on the part of the Mexican government provoked the Texas Revolution in 1835. When Texas joined the United States in 1845, this was not only the starting signal for the U.S.-Mexican War of 1846—48, it also marked the beginning of a new minority group, the Mexican-Americans. The Treaty of Guadalupe Hidalgo, ratified in 1848, became a landmark in Chicano history: the Mexican Northwest was signed over to the U.S. and became the American Southwest. For a period of one year the population was given the choice of "returning" to Mexico or of remaining and "at the proper time (to be judged of by the Congress of the United States) to be admitted as United States citizens."[10] The border that was thus established was an open frontier until the 1920s. Due to its approximate length of 1,900 miles from Tijuana to Brownsville, it was hard to control and encouraged illegal crossing. Its comparatively recent nature, the common cultural heritage, and the lack of a linguistic barrier further contributed to its uniqueness. Rudolph O. de la Garza and Rowena Rivera in "The Socio-Political World of the Chicano" state that, "particularly in South Texas, many Chicanos and Mexicans have never recognized the existence of the border and cross it almost at will."[11]

Immigration, on a minor scale in the nineteenth century and on a major scale throughout the twentieth with peak periods from 1911 to 1930 and from 1950 onwards, helped to reinforce common bonds. Figures available on the number of immigrants remain unsatisfactory on account of the high number of undocumented immigrants, but they reflect well the general tendency.[12] One pull factor, family and kinship ties, served to further increase the number of Chicanos living in the traditional centers of the Southwest, while the other pull factor, demand for unskilled labor in the fields and factories, contributed to spread Chicanos all over the United States, especially in the Midwest and the Northwest. As a result the former regional minority has become a national minority people. A recent investigation reports that there are presently an estimated 17.6 million Hispanics with roughly 60% tracing their ancestry to Mexico.[13]

The additional promise of further growth by unflagging immigration and a birth-rate above the national average has imparted a new sense of stability to the group. Group identity, though, continues to be challenged. The move from Mexico to the United States in many cases was combined with a move from rural to urban surroundings. Thus between 1950 and 1980 the share of urban dwellers rose from 66% to 90%.[14] This fact by itself means a severe threat to traditional value patterns of a formerly predominantly agrarian society. The annual trip to Mexico, as Rendón pointed out, may also work in the opposite direction by breeding a cultural ambivalence rather than a cultural equilibrium.[15] The consciousness of alienation from Anglo-American society is coupled by a feeling of alienation from Mexican society. Both Chicanos and Mexicans sense the difference, Chicanos identifying Mexicans as *nacionales* and Mexicans referring to Chicanos as "señores norteamericanos."[16] The counteractive forces of the traditional Mexican culture and U.S. culture probably exert their greatest pressures upon the young, and this is the majority of the Chicanos, since the median age ranges around 20, considerably below the national American average.[17] The young Chicano, who has not yet made his political, social, economic, and cultural choices, is confronted with conflicting demands of loyalty and contradictory sets of social behaviour rules. The resultant struggle has become a dominant theme in Chicano literature where it has been treated both as an ingroup and as an intergroup experience.

Immigration and the specific border situation did not only contribute to cultural continuity, but also supported language loyalty. Language maintenance was especially easy in the barrio situation, where Spanish remained the primary language, used not only at home but also outside in shops and by the local media services.[18] With the younger generations leaving the barrios and dispersing all over the United States in search of better job opportunities, the question of whether to maintain the use of Spanish became a choice similar to that of preserving cultural values. Bilingualism in the younger generation can now often be interpreted as a conscious decision. The use of Spanish, standard as well as its various regional varieties, signals family ties, friendship and group feeling. Code-switching between English and Spanish bridges the spheres of influence and conveys subtle shades of meaning. This linguistic reality is reflected in the theater, in poetry and in fiction. Rolando Hinojosa, one of the best Chicano writers, describes a typical case, his own:

> I decided to write whatever it was I had, in Spanish, and I decided to set it on the border, in the Valley. As reduced as that space was, it too was Texas with all of its contradictions and its often repeated one-sided telling of Texas history. When the characters stayed in the Spanish-speaking milieu or society, the Spanish language worked well, and then it was in the natural order of things that English made its entrance when the characters strayed or found themselves in Anglo institutions; in cases where both cultures would come into contact, both languages were used, and I would employ both, and where one and only one would do, I would follow that as well; what dominated, then, was the place, at first. Later on I discovered that generational and class differences also dictated not only usage but which language as well. From this came the *how* they said *what* they said.[19]

The use of two languages has for a long time prevented the awareness of a literary continuity. When the first studies appeared, the cultural production was viewed as a contemporary phenomenon of recent growth, a literature of living poets. The label Chicano was assigned to the literary output since 1965. Some, though, with some misgivings on account of the assimilationist tendency of the book, let it begin with the publication of José Antonio Villarreal's *Pocho* in 1959.[20] One of the early anthologies, *El Espejo — The Mirror*, which saw five printings between 1969 and 1972, spans only the years from 1967 to 1972 and its editors claim: "This literature may be young in terms of history, but it has a full right to exist."[21] Philip D. Ortego's anthology in 1973, *We Are Chicanos*, though mainly consisting of literary materials copyrighted between 1960 and 1972, includes some earlier selections from the decade between 1930 and 1940, which make up 17 percent of the entire book. In the introduction he proposes a still wider historical perspective: "And properly speaking, Mexican-American literature begins in 1848, the date the United States acquired the Mexican land in the Southwest . . . ."[22] Ten years later, in studies published in 1982,[23] Luis Leal, Raymund A. Paredes, and Charles M. Tatum agree on an even further extended view, and see the origins of Chicano literature in the sixteenth century, when the Spanish started to explore and colonize the region that is now the American Southwest. Finally, the aboriginal heritage has to be considered with a rich oral tradition of myth and folklore dating from pre-Columbian times. Luis Leal's and Pepe Barrón's concept of four periods deserves critical attention. They distinguish Pre-Chicano Literature (to 1848), the Literature of Transition (1848–1910), the Emergence of a Group Consciousness (1910–1943), and the Literature of Confrontation (1943–1981) using the historical events of the Treaty of Guadalupe Hidalgo in 1848, the beginning of Mexican-American mass immigration in 1910, and the Zoot Suit Riots in 1943 as literary landmarks.[24]

In the early centuries the transplanted Spanish cultural heritage was quickly Mexicanized. Paredes points out: "the types of folksong that took root in the region — the *romance, copla*, and *décima* . . . — were Spanish forms modified by Indian and mestizo influences."[25] Thus when Anglo-Americans entered the Southwest, they encountered what has to be properly termed an indigenous tradition. The turn of the century marks the beginning of the dual language use. Miguel A. Otero, for example, recorded his experiences in English as *My Life on the Frontier*, while others, the majority, continued to write in Spanish. The twentieth century saw a gradually growing number of authors who composed their work in English. The publication in English for a while meant consciously addressing the Anglo-American audience, a situation which changed in the sixties when both Spanish and English, or a mixture of the two, became an acceptable medium to address a Chicano audience. In the wake of this development it has been argued, that the language choice also implies the choice of a literary tradition, works in English following the Anglo-American literary models and works in Spanish being under the impact of Latin American writers. Apparently no such clear-cut distinction can be established, since there is hardly a contemporary Chicano author who can throw off the influences of his Anglo-American environment nor escape his Spanish-Mexican ancestral consciousness. In negative terms this is categorized as cultural ambivalence, in positive terms it can be viewed as a particular sensitivity for — often conflicting — cultural value patterns.

> But we didn't return to Mexico; we didn't have to; we were Borderers
> with a living and unifying culture born of conflict with another culture
> and this, too, helped to cement further still the knowing exactly where
> one came from and from whom one was descended.[26]

The essays collected in this volume are a tribute to the impressive growth of
scholarship during the seventies and early eighties.[27] They show that the pioneer
days are over and that the investigation of Chicano topics is now based on a solid
rock of research. Anyone who has followed the rapid development of the last
two decades cannot help feeling elated at the prospects that are now unfolding
in this area of study.

The first section of this book provides the reader with general perspectives.
Assessments by European scholars are balanced by the insider's view, the voices
of Chicano poets and critics. Gustav H. Blanke opens the discussion with a survey
of the situation of ethnic America vs. mainstream America by paying special attention to the traditional ideological concepts that helped and hindered the acceptance of those defined as the "others" by the dominant group. Sergio D. Elizondo interprets the concept of Aztlán as the real and as the spiritual homeland
of Chicanos and extends the meaning of the term Borderlands much in the
manner of Tomás Rivera's poem "The Rooster Crows en Iowa y en Texas." He
analyzes the historical forces, that made for cultural conflict, the sense of mission of the Spanish as well as the later Anglo-American conquerors, and he traces
the process by which Chicano socio-cultural values were preserved in spite of
growing assimilationist pressures, concluding with a final note of hope for the
present where he sees "a factual attenuation of conflict between our two cultures." José Montoya's representative personal statement manifests the strong
national consciousness in contemporary Chicano art. He establishes the link between political activism and creativeness, and conveys a feeling of the isolated
position of the artist who is either rejected or appreciated for the wrong reasons
by Anglo-Americans, Latins, and even Mexicans. Marcienne Rocard discusses the
alternate uses of Spanish and English as a mode of self-expression. Tension shaped
into oppositions, she argues, governs the thematic as well as the linguistic choices
of Chicano writers. Alurista, whose poetry furnishes major examples for Rocard's
thesis, ends the general section with an analysis of the functions of culture and
of cultural nationalism as the source and mainstay of the literary production of
the Chicano Renaissance.

The next section centers on the Mexican impact. Juan Bruce-Novoa crosses the
Border and by inquiring into the deeper recesses of the Mexican mind, he studies
the meanings and implications of the image of the "mexicano-yankee" forged by
Mexican writers. Juanita Lawhn studies the subtle ways in which Mexican
(-American) women were manipulated in their consciousness by the highly influential newspaper *La Prensa* that for over fifty years held up a Hispanic tradition in Texas and the neighboring states. She then proceeds to examine the

female symbolism in the poetry of Bernice Zamora by placing it against this anti-feminist background.

Section III, partly overlapping with section II, is devoted to the theater. Jorge A. Huerta reverses Bruce-Novoa's approach by investigating the image of the Mexican on the Chicano stage. Selecting the figures of Mexicans, real, archetypal and stereotypical, from plays by Valdez, Morton and Trambley, he studies their representative functions as parent, dreamer, comic character, and revolutionary. Nicolás Kanellos reviews the development of the Hispanic stage in California and the Southwest from the middle of the 19th century to the Depression era. He refutes John W. Brokaw's denial of an early political motivation for the theater of the past and illustrates his point by a long series of very successful plays that deal with the clash of culture, that directly or, more often, indirectly criticize Mexico and the U.S., and that prepare the political and social organizing of the group. Geneviève Fabre interprets the various uses of the mask in Valdez' plays, from the actos to the mitos. She explores their functions as stereotypes and archetypes, uniting past and present experiences, and she stresses the harmonizing force which amalgamates symbols derived from Mayan, Aztec, Indian, and trans-planted European Christian cultures. Annick Tréguer compares the didactic uses of the corrido (a narrative ballad developed as a formtype in the 19th century) and the theater, both serving as a kind of historical repository for the Chicano people, and she illustrates the considerable thematic variety of the corridos. Dieter Herms, for his part correcting some of the older Marxist interpretations, evaluates the ideological implications of the recent changes in the Teatro Campesino, especially the professionalization from playwriting to performance. He thinks that while the confrontation of Anglo and Chicano cultures cannot be denied, the "perspective from below" is the more important aspect.

Section IV takes up poetry. Expressly excluding any attempt to deal with the political message, Yves-Charles Grandjeat proposes a new approach by using Alurista's statements about the therapeutic effectiveness of literature. Applying the interpretative device of the Shaman's symbolic journey, Grandjeat offers a careful close reading of the imagery and symbolism. Wolfgang Binder tackles a very specific, but prominent theme in Chicano lyrics, the motif of the mother and grandmother as a carrier of basic Chicano values and traditions. The section closes with an annotated reading by Melba Boyd of her poem *Song for Maya* which mythologizes the merging of three cultures in the prophetic utopian figure Maya-Meridian and her son Joaquín.

Section V examines leading contemporary Chicano writers. The arrangement here follows a thematic, not a chronological order. Fred Jung concentrates on the major regionalist motifs in Anaya's writings like the conflicting lifestyles of farmer and cowboy, the curanderismo, the llorona figure and the tortuga, and traces their relative importance in novels and short stories over a decade from 1972 to 1982. Even more strongly rooted in the Spanish folktale tradition,

Sabine Reyes Ulibarrí's *Tierra Amarilla* (1964) contains earlier examples of New Mexico regionalism. Donaldo W. Urioste selects three stories, "Mi caballo mago," "Juan P.," and "La fragua sin fuego," as samples of the costumbrista mode and proves that the writer is able to go beyond the traditional descriptions of locality, manners, and quaint characters and to arrive at universal lessons about human conduct by introducing the innocent critical perspective of a child protagonist-observer. László Scholz deals with Hinojosa's *Klail City y sus alrededores* (1976). He shows how the collage-like structure is an essential device by analyzing in detail the spatial and temporal fragmentation of the work. He proves that all the novel's parameters point to the one decisive characteristic: fragmentation. Though Scholz calls it a rare device in Chicano literature, it had been made use of already in Alejandro Morales' *Caras viejas y vino nuevo* (1975), which is treated by Francisco A. Lomelí as a fine example of what he terms the Isolated Generation of 1975 with Morales, Ríos and Arias and which he sets apart from the Quinto Sol Writers like Rivera, Hinojosa, Anaya and Mendez. Lomelí focuses on the structural techniques such as the reverse order, fragmentation of time and space, multiple point of view, analyzes the neorealist mode of presenting barrio life, and deals extensively with Morales' aesthetic of violence and ugliness. To do justice to Oscar "Zeta" Acosta's autobiographical novel *The Revolt of the Cockroach People* (1973), Horst Tonn claims, it has to be read as a piece of New Journalism. He rejects a simplistic unilinear ideological interpretation by demonstrating how the author purposefully mingles fiction and reality to create a pattern of meaningful ambiguity and unresolved conflict. José David Saldívar also questions a one-dimensional reading of Chicano texts. Using Frederic Jameson's post-modernist concepts of the ideological and the utopian, he offers a dialectical reading of the political as well as aesthetic dimensions of Rivera's . . . *y no se lo tragó la tierra* and Arias' *The Road to Tamazunchale*. Section V closes with a discussion of a prominent example of *literatura chicanesca*, John Nichols' *The Milagro Beanfield War* (1974). Discounting the biological part of the definition, Heiner Bus challenges the appropriateness and validity of such a classificatory label on aesthetic grounds.

The last section is given to further aspects of Chicano culture. Carol Pfaff's and Laura Chávez' detailed investigation of Spanish/English code-switching serves as the connecting link, since the textual corpus for the study was chosen from Chicano drama. The general introduction to the basic types of code-switching is followed by the linguistic analysis of two major varieties, texts basically written in Spanish with code-switching into English and texts basically written in English with code-switching into Spanish. Though generally in agreement with the linguistic data on code-switching in natural discourse, the authors are also able to show several significant differences which are partly of interpretative relevance to the literary text. In the next essay, also language-related, Hartmut Lutz addresses himself to the problem of the educational advancement of the Chicano. He describes the experiment of self-determined Deganawidah-Quetzalcoatl University, near Davis, California and offers two interesting case-reports from his own experience as an instructor. The subject of minority teaching is continued and internationalized by Manfred Zirkel's observations on multicultural educa- tion on the elementary school level based on a current project sponsored by the European Cultural Foundation, Brussels. He compares and evaluates the situa- tion of joint education in Germany, Britain and the U.S. and reflects on the necessity of achieving what he terms an intercultural identity. The final essay of the collection is a reception study by Lia Tessarolo Bondolfi, in which she reviews the situation of Chicano Studies in Italy. Though limited to one country, her findings can be considered representative for the publishing sector as well as academic study in Europe.

It is deeply regretted here that it was not possible to print the highly instructive discussions which followed the presentation of the individual papers. For the interested student though, the tape-recorded debates are available in the archives of the Department of Applied Linguistics at Germersheim.

Notes

[1] Carlos E. Cortés, "Mexicans" in *Harvard Encyclopedia of American Ethnic Groups*, ed. Stephan Thernstrom (Cambridge, Mass.: Belknap Press, 1981), p. 697.

[2] e.g. *The Random House Dictionary of the English Language* (New York: Random House, 1981), p. 255.

[3] Edward A. Stephenson, "Chicano: Origin and Meaning," *American Speech*, 44 (1969), 225–226.

[4] Rodolfo Acuña, "Freedom in a Cage: The Subjugation of the Chicano in the United States," in *The Reinterpretation of American History and Culture*, ed. William H. Cart- wright and Richard L. Watson, Jr. (Washington, D.C.: National Council for the Social Studies, 1973), p. 131.

[5] Stephenson, p. 227.

[6] Armando B. Rendón, *Chicano Manifesto: The History and Aspirations of the Second Largest Minority in America* (New York: Macmillan, 1971), p. 13, writes: "The word Chicano is offered not merely as a term of differentiation ... but also as a term of iden- tification with that distinct melding of bloods and cultures."

[7] Rendón, p. 15.

[8] Carey McWilliams, *North from Mexico: The Spanish-Speaking People in the United States* (New York: Greenwood Press, 1948. Repr. 1968).

[9] Acuña, p. 117.

[10] Article VIII; see Rendón, p. 72–73.

[11] Rudolph O. de la Garza and Rowena Rivera, "The Socio-Political World of the Chicano: A Comparative Analysis of Social Scientific and Literary Perspectives," in *Minority Lan- guage and Literature: Retrospective and Perspective*, ed. Dexter Fisher (New York: MLA, 1977), p. 53.

[12] See Joe R. Feagin, *Racial and Ethnic Relations* (Englewood Cliffs, N.J., 1978), p. 290:

Decade	Number of immigrants
1881–1900	2,884
1901–1910	49,642
1911–1920	219, 004
1921–1930	459,287
1931–1940	22,319

1941–1950	60,589
1951–1960	299,811
1961–1970	453,937
1971–1975	319,179

See also Cortés, p. 699, 702–704.

[13] George J. Church, "Hispanics: A Melding of Cultures," *Time* (July 8, 1985), 28–31. Figures on the total number of Chicanos vary considerably. The 1980 census used a system of self-identification, in which persons of Spanish/Hispanic origin or descent listed themselves in one of the following categories, Mexican, Puerto Rican, Cuban, or Other Spanish/Hispanic origin. In the Current Population Survey (CPS) persons classified themselves in the Spanish origin categories as Mexican-American, Chicano, Mexican, Puerto Rican, Cuban, Central or South American, or other Spanish origin. 1980 data are not always comparable to earlier census reports, since there were some important modifications in census procedures from the 1970 to the 1980 census. For details see *Statistical Abstract of the United States 1985: National Data Book and Guide to Sources*, 105th Edition, ed. U.S. Department of Commerce (Washington, D.C.: Bureau of the Census, 1985), p. 3.

[14] Church, p. 29.

[15] Rendón, p. 20.

[16] Garza and Rivera, p. 53–54.

[17] Cortés, p. 699, quotes a median age of 20.2 years for Chicanos in 1970, Church, p. 28, a median age of 23 for all Hispanics.

[18] The strikingly high percentage of Spanish language loyalty is evidenced by the data of the 1980 Census, repr. in the *Statistical Abstract of the United States 1985*, p. 36:

NO. 43. CURRENT LANGUAGES OTHER THAN ENGLISH SPOKEN AT HOME: 1980

[As of April 1. Based on a sample and subject to sampling variability, see text, p. 1 and Appendix III]

CURRENT LANGUAGE SPOKEN	PERSONS 5 TO 17 YEARS OLD		PERSONS 18 YRS. OLD AND OVER		CURRENT LANGUAGE SPOKEN	PERSONS 5 TO 17 YEARS OLD		PERSONS 18 YRS. OLD AND OVER	
	Total (1,000)	Difficulty with English [1] (percent)	Total (1,000)	Difficulty with English [1] (percent)		Total (1,000)	Difficulty with English [1] (percent)	Total (1,000)	Difficulty with English [1] (percent)
Total persons	47,494	(x)	162,753	(x)	Chinese	114	20.9	516	31.6
Speaking a language					Greek	66	5.2	336	17.0
other than English	4,568	14.0	18,492	19.4	Philippine languages	63	8.9	411	9.4
Spanish	2,952	15.4	8,164	27.6	Portuguese	68	10.3	284	31.6
Italian	147	5.4	1,471	14.0	Japanese	34	18.7	303	19.6
French	223	6.8	1,328	7.2	Korean	60	17.0	207	32.4
German	192	6.2	1,395	4.7	Vietnamese	64	36.0	130	38.7
Polish	41	5.7	780	10.6	All other	544	12.3	3,167	11.2

X Not applicable. [1] Persons reported as speaking English "not well" or "not at all".

Source: U.S. Bureau of the Census, *1980 Census of Population*, vol. 1, chapter C (PC80-1-C); and unpublished data.

[19] Rolando Hinojosa, "The Sense of Place," in *The Rolando Hinojosa Reader: Essays Historical and Critical*, ed. José David Saldívar (Houston: Arte Publico Press, 1985), p. 23.

[20] See the introduction by Ramón Eduardo Ruiz to the 1970 edition of *Pocho* (Garden City, N.Y.: Doubleday, 1970), p. VII–XII.

[21] Herminio Ríos C. and Octavio Ignacio Romano-V., "Introduction," *El Espejo – The Mirror* (Berkeley, Cal.: Quinto Sol Pub., 1972), p. XIV.

[22] Philip D. Ortego, *We Are Chicanos: An Anthology of Mexican-American Literature* (New York: Washington Square Press, 1973), p. XVIII.

[23] Luis Leal and Pepe Barrón, "Chicano Literature: An Overview," pp. 9–32, Raymund A. Paredes, "The Evolution of Chicano Literature," pp. 33–79 in *Three American Literatures*, ed. Houston A. Baker, Jr. (New York: MLA, 1982). Charles M. Tatum, *Chicano Literature* (Boston: Twayne, 1982).

[24] In *Chicano Literature: A Reference Guide* (Westport, Conn.: Greenwood Press, 1985), p. 463–471, Julio A. Martínez and Francisco A. Lomelí roughly follow the same pattern, but prefer to further subdivide and to rename the periods. Their classification comprises:

    I. Southwest Antecedents,
       A. Hispanic Period, 1539–1820;
       B. Mexican Period, 1821–1847.
   II. Transition Period, 1848–1910.
  III. Interaction Period, 1911–1942.
  IV. Adjustment Period, 1943–1964.
   V. Renaissance Period, 1965–1982.

[25] Paredes, p. 34.

[26] Hinojosa, p. 20.

[27] See for example Ernestina N. Eger's *A Bibliography of Criticism of Contemporary Chicano Literature* (Berkeley, Cal.: Chicano Studies Library Pub., 1982).

I GENERAL

Major Myths of the Mainstream Society and the Concerns of the Ethnics

Gustav Blanke

Since colonial times Anglo-Americans have found it difficult to accept the others, the ethnics, especially those with a darker skin.[1] Indians and Blacks, Orientals, Latin Americans, Chicanos, and various other ethnic groups with different religious and cultural traditions have encountered contempt, discriminations, hostility, and violence. The white Anglo-Saxon Protestants who believed and "rationalized" that they were doing the Lord's work in a new land, expected the others to accept their dominant role. Some of them who had reasons to be concerned, resented this attitude and criticized the "WASP society." But the optimists among the strangers in the land were confident that the oldtimers would overcome their prejudices. One of them, the French immigrant Jean de Crèvecoeur, celebrated "the American" in 1775 as a "new man" who had left ancient "prejudices" behind and acted upon "new principles." Since oldtimers and newcomers had equally been "received in the broad lap" of the virgin land, good Americans would see to it that "individuals of all nations" would be "melted into a new race of men."[2]

The "Anglos" liked this appraisal and rephrased it on many festive occasions. The words fell in line with what the Founding Fathers were claiming for the new society. It was a "model" society where "all" were said to be "created equal" and possessed certain natural and God-given "inalienable rights to life, liberty, and the pursuit of happiness." But in the minds of many New Englanders and of those Americans who accepted the spiritual leadership of New England, these "enlightened" words were mixed with solemn Puritan notions about a divine mission to Christianize and civilize "other", inferior peoples and to combat those who refused to be guided by "God's elect." These "visible saints" were convinced that "the eyes of all people" were fixed on the "city upon a hill" (John Winthrop, 1630), the "new Zion" which "anticipated the New Jerusalem" (Cotton Mather, 1702). The Enlightenment watered such Puritan concepts down somewhat, but in their secularized form they remained very effective in the minds of the dominant group, and their public spokesmen were very active to add new elements to the rhetorical pattern, because the national ideology with its persuasive mythical notions was a powerful, useful, and necessary cohesive for the cementing of a new national society.

On every Fourth of July hundreds of orators reiterated and paraphrased the rhetorical pattern which can be traced back to the Puritan divines: Patriots were supposed to renew the sacred "covenant" of the true believers with one another and with their God; pious patriots were supposed to act together as brothers and sisters and be guided by one heavenly father; their forefathers had been "commissioned" by God to formulate "their own articles" (Winthrop) for the model society which was predestined by providence to be mankind's last and final "antitypal" Israel; the Lord of hosts expected his "children of light" to be ready for battle against the "children of darkness"; their model society would grow and grow, and become more powerful until the chosen people in God's country would defeat Satan at "Armageddon" and inaugurate the perfect and everlasting realm of peace; the ideal land of promise would realize the most precious dreams of all mankind; "the later Eden planted in the wilds" would eventually guarantee freedom and equality to all people, and the humblest man would stand level with the highest in the law.[3]

After 1776 these myths were often called self-evident "truths." The orators did not think it wise to call them "myths" or "dreams" or "propositions" or "declarations of intent" or binding "promises." They also thought it best to use very general terms with powerful connotations which evoked consent and did not induce people to ask irritating questions.[4] But the presence of slaves was felt to be awkward. In his first draft of the Declaration of Independence Jefferson pronounced the abolition of slavery. But the clause was brushed aside because it endangered the signing of the entire document. Jefferson put up with it, but in 1782 he wrote: "I tremble for my country when I reflect that God is just; that his justice cannot sleep forever; that . . . a revolution . . . is among possible events."[5]

Such a premonition was not rare, as we know from the history of the abolition movement and from the history of dissent.[6] American patriotism was mixed with a suppressed sense of guilt, especially with regard to slavery, which Timothy Dwight called a "curse" and "first guilt, first woe, first infamy of man" (Greenfield Hill, 1794). The many references to the "great and foul stain upon the North American Union" (J.Q. Adams, Diary, 1820) which led to the "irrepressible conflict" (W.H. Seward, 1858), indicate that we are not dealing with a nation of hypocrites who combine clarity of mind with an unscrupulous intent to deceive others with the help of clever rationalizations. Edmund S. Morgan has pointed out that the early Virginia planters of the time of Governor Berkeley and Bacon's Rebellion were hardly aware of the fact that the gradual substitution of indentured servants and freedmen by Negro slaves allowed them to cherish and emphasize "the inherited privileges of Englishmen" until they could finally be made out to be "natural rights" which did not include the rights of Negro slaves. "The rights of Englishmen were preserved by destroying the rights of Africans." This was an "ugly matter" which became part of the "American para-

dox."[7] The gradual development of a patriotic rhetoric and of a national literature which operated successfully within "the magic circle of a myth" (Northrop
Frye) helped to cover up the discrepancy between the humanistic message of the
hallowed words and the moral ambiguities of the Puritan myth, the discrepancy
also between the egalitarian words of the Declaration of Independence and the
unwillingness of the dominant society to act accordingly. It took the Americans
a very long time before they began to realize that they were victims of an ancient
prejudice whenever they used ugly "ethnophaulisms" like "nigger," "dago,"
"wop," "greaser," "kike," "chink" etc. In the widest sense this prejudice is part
of the belief that God's "American Israel" is surrounded by "less blessed" and
by "cursed" people who are unable to see that it is in their interest to be assimilated into the society of the "children of light" or to undergo a period of guidance, tutelage, and patronage under the benevolent eyes of the morally superior
Anglo-American society and of their mature and model government. The "American dilemma" is bound to last, until the mainstream society drops the idea that
there are second-class democrats and second-class nations in need of guidance by
the "blessed" ones.

It is not easy for me as a German to say this. The Old World in general and Germany in particular have been guilty of many crimes committed under the sway
of ancient prejudices. But after what we have experienced under Hitler, we are
perhaps more aware of what can be achieved with the help of propaganda,
patriotic rhetoric, and mythical ideas. A sober detachment from myths and
patterns of patriotic rhetoric is needed. All shapers of public opinion who employ such dangerous instruments have a special responsibility. It is the concern
of all liberals, and especially of the liberals among the ethnic minorities who
have suffered from the divisive elements of the major myths, to bring this matter
into the open and to subject it to an enlightened study.[8] Members of the consensus school of historians are apt to deny the value of this approach. They like
to connect the criticism of the American system and the finding of shortcomings
with a lack of patriotism. The renowned Daniel Boorstin raised his voice against
those "hypochondriacs" and "dissenters" who deal with the negative aspects of
American society. Why talk so much about the "exceptions from the rule," and
why cultivate Ethnic Studies and promote cultural pluralism? Does not the
American system allow all people "to keep as much as they want" of their
special heritage, or are there any American laws which "compel" people to
abandon precious cultural traits?[9] Boorstin and other historians of this school
of thought expect people to be "pragmatic" and put up with the "givennesses."
The American system works best, they say, if all individuals and all groups accept a small "unavoidable" amount of separatism and console themselves with
the thought that a greater amount of assimilation, integration, and national
unity is "merely a matter of time."[10]

Fortunately many sociologists take the concern of the ethnics more seriously and present critical analyses of the social situation. Milton Gordon e.g. came up with this estimate and scale of assimilations: So-called "cultural assimilation" is encouraged by the mainstream society and granted to all ethnic groups. An additional "structural assimilation" which approves of equality in certain cultural areas like sports and entertainment and disapproves of it in other areas like big business and banking is conceded, especially in respect to groups which can be associated with partially approved European traditions. "Marital" or "genetic assimilation" is discouraged and often denied when a dark skin is involved. "Cultural pluralism" is frowned upon, and many overt and covert methods are employed to prevent undesirable results of the melting pot.[11] At certain occasions the covert prejudices come into the open. At the time of the Johnson Act (1924) for instance, Professor Henry Fairchild felt free to express and to spread the opinion that unrestricted immigration of certain ethnic groups would "insidiously" eat away the very heart of America and destroy everything that is noble in the American system.[12] This attitude is reminiscent of many similar utterances made by nineteenth century "nativists," "vigilantes," and "Protestant crusaders": "If this nation is to be both a refuge for the best and a home for select people, immigration must be controlled."[13] As late as 1969 the Ku Klux Klan made use of the ancient argument that God helped man to differentiate "the children of light" from "the children of darkness": When Noah "cursed" Ham, God took his side and punished Ham's descendants with a dark skin. Therefore, "a white lady can never marry a descendant of Ham. That is God's law. You cannot overcome God."[14]

Courageous spokesmen of several ethnic groups have always responded to such attacks on their dignity and peoplehood. Their experiences have also made them aware of the pressures involved in the process of the "melting pot," "smelting pot," "seething pot," "fining pot," "crucible," or "cauldron." These metaphors link the Americanization procedures with a metallurgical process, and they suggest that undesirable ethnic features can be "melted," "smelted," and "burnt away," while the rest are "fused" and "amalgamated" in such a way that the "Anglos" can be satisfied with the result. It is interesting to note, however, that these verbs are usually avoided by patriotic orators and writers because their negative connotations violate the American myth. Instead, verbs like the following are preferred: "to mix," "to mingle," "to blend," "to compound," "to merge," and "to unite." They seem to lend themselves more easily to the rhetorical rendering of the idea that America has an unlimited capacity to absorb peoples from all countries. When poets like Longfellow or Emerson spoke of the "blending" and "compounding" of all cultural traditions, they also concluded that "the blood of all nations" would be "mingling" with the blood which was already there.[15] Horace Bushnell even spoke of a new society of "reborn" and "regenerated" people who, by becoming citizens, experienced a "naturalization

of the soul."[16] This type of unrealistic rhetoric can turn the American nation
into a christlike "mediator." Edward Steiner made use of this idea in his novel
"The Mediator" (1907). The idea caught on and gave more strength to the popular saying that "God hath made of one blood all nations of men." It also
strengthened the Christian belief that converts are "circumcized in the spirit."
According to St. Paul, the newly born "put away the old man" and "put on the
new man" (Col. 3: 9–11; Eph. 2:14–15). It is interesting to note that the word
"ethnic" in English originally (OED 1375) referred to the spiritual and social
results of the sacrificial death of Christ, namely to the destruction of the "partition wall" in the Jewish temple and to the obliteration of all distinctions between "Jews" and "gentiles," between those who "belong" and "the others",
the "ethnics" (Gr. "ethnikos").

Woodrow Wilson, who liked to be looked upon as the "Savior-President," took
his departure from Steiner's novel, when, on April 20, 1915, he called America
"the mediating nation of the world."[17] His immediate concern was the restora-
tion of peace, but he was also engaged in strengthening American patriotism
with the help of the concept of mission, in particular of a world mission of
regeneration. When he described America as a nation which was "compounded
of the nations of the world," "mediating" their blood as well as their traditions,
he simply ignored the "partition wall" which still existed in the "American
temple," as well as the pressures used in the "Americanization schools" of his
day, and the unkind words about "hyphenated Americans" which patriotic
orators used in their speeches on "Americanization Day." The "new race" which
Wilson and the patriotic orators were celebrating, had "descendants" who believed in the ideas and principles of the mainstream society. They did not have
"roots" or "ancestors," and different cultural traditions to be cherished, culti-
vated, and maintained.

The discrepancy between the myth and reality has always been there, but is has
always been played down, because most Americans, being pragmatists as well as
idealists, shy away from dealing consistently with "the alien in our midst" who,
"although physically present in, and interactive with, the American scene,"
embodies attitudes and tendencies felt to be partly unassimilable by the mainstream society.[18] The pragmatists are likely to ignore the fact that "the alien in
our midst" has been operating continuously throughout American history.
Whithout the native Indians, the imported Negro, and other "undesirables" the
American "experiment" would have failed. David F. Bowers realized this in
1952, when he suggested and initiated the study of the "Foreign Influences in
American Life." The initial studies, he felt, had to be limited to "certain selected
ethnic and national groups . . . as have affected the national life in a decisive
way," which meant, that certain groups like the Chicanos were "not touched on
at all." His study was helpful, however, because it drew more attention to the
fact that most "native Americans," i.e. native-born Americans of North-European

and Middle-European descent have always reacted negatively to certain "foreign" impacts and were determined "to do something about the offending element," if it was felt to be "an active threat" to their own "vested interests." It was merely "unavoidable," if a "policy of exclusion" was preferred to a "policy of assimilation" in dealing with "the problem of adjustment," that nativism, loyalty to "native" traditions, and chauvinism would grow. The mere act of "defending" some native value often led to the exclusion of other values. In order to strengthen the mainstream society, its spokesmen would characterize the "others" as "inherently inferior," "not ready for assimilation," and not to be entrusted with full social responsibility. By segregating an alien group, its various skills were "drained off." Constrained to move only in certain areas or circles, "the minority's economic opportunities were curtailed." A "sense of bewilderment and instability" resulted from having to accept a lower social status. The final product was the rootless "marginal man" who belonged nowhere and often became a victim of internal strife.[19]

Spokesmen of undesirable ethnic groups who insisted upon the equal value of their roots and traditions could also get into trouble. Their endeavor to promote different cultural identities could be ostracized as an attack on the psychological unity of the nation. It was "alright," if spokesmen of the mainstream society preached "jeremiads" and published an occasional book about "betrayals of the covenant" or "transgressions" of the national ethos, but it was anathema if a spokesman of an ethnic minority took it upon himself to "unmask" the gulf between promise and fulfillment. When David Walker published his "Appeal to the Colored Citizens of the World" in 1828, he was told that he would not last long, and this prophecy soon became true. The former slave Frederick Douglass also got into trouble when he undertook it on July 5, 1852, to expose the Fourth-of-July oratory as a "sham" and a "mockery," when he characterized certain features of American liberty as "unholy license," and when he chastised the excessive drive for national grandeur as a "swelling vanity."[20] Dissenters belonging to certain ethnic groups have always experienced various types of persecution. The most famous case is that of Martin Luther King, whose main offense was his insistence upon the thesis, that the "dreams" of the ethnics ought to be an American reality.[21] This concern of the ethnics about their civil rights and about the need to "open the door of the promised land to all of God's children," has turned into a great service to the American people. It has become the chief function of the ethnics to serve as "the vanguard in the struggle for liberty and equal justice for all."[22]

This concern about carrying forward the humanistic struggle may also have an effect on America's foreign policy. Success on the home front may improve the chances for playing "a leading role in the universal struggle for peace and international understanding."[23] A prerequisite seems to be the abandoning of certain elements of patriotic rhetoric. Critics of American foreign policy have observed that the stereotyped emphasis on "uniqueness," the contradictory claim of being a "model," and the assumption of being "superior" to "the others" are countereffective for the promotion of international understanding. The sometimes bloated sense of mission, especially in regard to Latin American, Asiatic, and African countries, has produced condescension, patronizing, and a readiness to intervene. In regard to Western Europe it has sharpened the encounter with the rivaling ideology of world communism, and the assumption of having been commissioned "by God and history" to act as the defender of world freedom in its "final war" against totalitarianism has produced a powerful rhetoric of intransigence.[24]

Spokesmen of several ethnic groups have expressed their misgivings about this "style" of foreign policy. They have joined the ranks of the revisionist historians and of the dissenters in general, and they have pointed out that the style smacks of an attempt to extend Anglo-conformity to the global level. No amount of mythical and missionary rhetoric can turn America's modern "Atomic Diplomacy" into a prelude of a "diplomacy in Eden."[25] It is unwise and presumptuous to claim, as Alexander Haig did in his Berlin speech, that "America alone" is fighting for a democratic "idea of man," which honors "the diversity of man," and that it is America's "unique privilege – and a compelling obligation – to promulgate her own revolutionary doctrine throughout the world."[26]

Certain ethnic groups cannot help to be concerned about the fact that Alexander Haig preached against "pluralism" in this speech, while stressing the "diversity of man," on the ground that pluralism was a "selfish" way of various ethnic groups to advance their interests at the expense of "the common good." Haig also said that their "excessive introspection" would paralyze the will and thereby "threaten the peace." The ethnics tend to believe that people like Haig are not honoring the American idea of man which includes the diversity of "men." They feel that American foreign policy as well as American literature ought to affirm the idea that the United States "share" with other nations the responsibility for solving the problems which confront our world. Ethnic writers have, therefore, taken the lead in the rejection of ethnocentricity, tribalism, ideological chauvinism, missionary zeal, exceptionalism, and imperialistic globalism.[27]

A more immediate effect of the ethnic concern for the humanistic tradition in American culture can be seen in the field of American literature and of American Studies. Until the middle of the last century the body of American literature contained not a single masterpiece which did not look on American life "through the eyes of an Anglo-American." If ethnics were introduced, they were "reduced to a subordinate role and expected to furnish comic relief."[28] Today, many American critics encourage ethnic writers to discover their roots and to create images which add something to a broader American spirit. The hero of an American novel is no longer required to condemn or criticize his "alien" or "pre-American" past in order to be well received by "the Promised Land," as Mary

Antin suggested in her novel of 1912. Ethnicity as ancestry and as diversity has been discovered as an element which can produce powerfully moving images. No one has to feel "uprooted," and everyone ought to be encouraged to express his innermost self. The new emphasis on ethnicity may lead to a world-view which harmonizes the mythical image of the "new man" in a "new society" with the almost forgotten image of "ancestral footsteps" (Hawthorne). Ethnicity studies can bring us closer to the social reality. They are also very interesting to people everywhere, because every cultural "deep structure" reveals elements which are constant from one culture to another. American Studies of this type are another step to an all-embracing study of man. Our present knowledge of the contribution of the ethnic writers has already revealed one thing: They stress the concern for all humanity, and they assert the right of the "simple genuine self against the whole world" (Emerson).[29] Underneath all the interesting differences of ethnic groups is the "invisible man" who is "of the human race, a man at large in the human world, preparing a new man . . . , of no specific region (but) of the earth . . . of no particular class (but) of the human class . . . , of no special field (but) of the field of being."[30]

Notes

[1] "Ethnic" is used here in a more general sense to include "racial" with its emphasis on differences in color.

[2] Jean de Crèvecoeur, *Letters of an American Farmer* (1775, published 1782), in *American Life in Literature*, 2 vols., ed. Jay B. Hubbell (New York: Harper & Brothers, 1949), I, p. 180.

[3] These are abstractions from hundreds of election sermons and Fourth-of-July orations read in the Huntington Library, San Marino, Cal., and in the Library of Congress.

[4] Three publications by Sacvan Bercovitch are particularly relevant: *The Puritan Origins of the American Self* (New Haven: Yale University Press, 1975), "How the Puritans Won the American Revolution," *Mass. Hist. Rev.*, 17 (1976), and "The Rites of Assent: Rhetoric, Ritual, and the Ideology of Consensus," in *The American Self: Myth, Ideology, and Popular Culture*, ed. Samuel B. Girgus (Albuquerque: University of New Mexico Press, 1981), pp. 5–42.

[5] Saul K. Padover, ed., *The Complete Jefferson* (New York: Duell, Sloan and Pearce, 1943), p. 677 ("Notes on the State of Virginia").

[6] I merely refer to the excellent study by Lawrence J. Friedman, *Inventors of the Promised Land* (New York: Alfred A. Knopf, 1975).

[7] Edmund S. Morgan, "Slavery and Freedom: The American Paradox," in *In Search of the American Dream*, ed. Jane L. Scheiber and Robert C. Elliott (New York: The New American Library, 1974), pp. 170, 180, 183.

[8] G.H. Blanke, "The Rhetoric of America's World Mission and the Problem of Ethnicity," in *Festschrift für Karl Schneider*, ed. Kurt R. Jankowsky and Ernst S. Dick (Amsterdam: John Benjamins, 1982), pp. 337–60.

[9] Daniel Boorstin, "A Case of Hypochondria," in *In Search of the American Dream*, p. 436.

[10] Morris Freedman and Carolyn Blanks, eds., *American Mix: The Minority Experience in America* (Philadelphia: J. B. Lippincott, 1972), p. 3.

[11] Milton M. Gordon, *Assimilation in American Life: The Role of Race, Religion and National Origin* (New York: Oxford Univ. Press, 1964); James A. Geschwender, *Racial*

Stratification in America (Dubuque, Iowa: W. C. Brown, 1978), p. 54; Nathan Glazer and Daniel P. Moynihan, *Beyond the Melting Pot* (Cambridge, Mass.: The M.I.T. Press, 1963), pp. 314/15.

[12] Henry Pratt Fairchild, "The Melting-Pot Mistake" (1926), in *American Issues:* Vol. I. *The Social Record*, ed. Willard Thorp, Merle Curti, and Carlos Baker (Chicago: J. B. Lippincott, 1941), p. 784.

[13] Quoted by Perry Miller, *Nature's Nation* (Cambridge, Mass.: Harvard U. Press, 1967), p. 173; cf. Ray Allen Billington, *Protestant Crusade* (New York: Macmillan, 1938); Samuel Whelpley, *A Compound of History* (Boston: Richardson, 1825), II, p. 204.

[14] Matt Murphy, "Imperial Klonsel of the Ku Klux Klan (1965)," in *Black Tangled Path: Race in America*, ed. D. G. Anderson and R. L. Wright (New York: Macmillan, 1971), p. 273; cf. Winthrop D. Jordan, *White Over Black: American Attitudes Toward the Negro, 1550–1812* (Baltimore: Penguin, 1969); Ruby J.R. Kennedy, "Single or triple melting pot: intermarriage in New Haven," *American Journal of Sociology*, 58 (1952), 56–59.

[15] Henry, W. Longfellow, "The Question of a National Literature," in *American Life in Literature*, Vol. I, p. 524.

[16] Horace Bushnell, *Christian Nurture* (New York: Scribner, 1847), p. 100.

[17] Louis Filler, ed., *The President Speaks: From William McKinley to Lyndon B. Johnson* (New York: Macmillan, 1964), p. 106.

[18] David F. Bowers, "The Problem of Social and Cultural Impact," in *Foreign Influences on American Life: Essays and Critical Bibliographies*, ed. D.F. Bowers (New York: Peter Smith, 1952), p. 5.

[19] Bowers, pp. 7, 8, 12, 30–33.

[20] Frederick Douglass, "Independence Day Oration," in *In Search of the American Dream*, p. 237; cf. Melvin Tolson, "Egypt Land, The Red Sea, The Wilderness and the Promised Land," in *Black Tangled Path*, pp. 120–34; Roy L. Hill, *Rhetoric of Racial Revolt* (Denver, 1964), pp. 8–10; Irving Kristol, "The Negro today is like the immigrant of yesterday," in *Nation of Nations: The Ethnic Experience and the Racial Crisis*, ed. Peter I. Rose (New York: Random House, 1972), pp. 197–210.

[21] Martin Luther King, "I have a Dream" (Address at the March on Washington), in *In Search of the American Dream*, p. 411.

[22] W.E.B. DuBois, *The Souls of Black Folk* (New York: Fawcett Publications, 1903), p. 52.

[23] John Hope Franklin, *From Slavery to Freedom: A History of American Negroes* (New York: Alfred A. Knopf, 1948), p. 589.

[24] Morrell Heald, "Foreign Relations, American Style," in *American Character and Culture in a Changing World. Contributions in Americans Studies*, ed. Robert H. Walter, No. 42 (Westport, Conn., 1979), pp. 198–201; cf. Henry Kissinger, *American Foreign Policy* (New York: W.W. Norton, 1969), pp. 52, 92–93.

[25] Gar Alperovitz, *Atomic Diplomacy* (New York: Simon and Schuster, 1965); Bruce Kuklick, "Myth and Symbol in American Studies," *American Quarterly*, 24 (1972), 446.

[26] International Communication Agency, *Three Speeches. American Perspectives on Western Values, NATO and Nuclear Deterrence* (Washington, D.C., 1981), p. 2.

[27] Jay Martin, "National Development and Ethnic Poetics," in *The Study of American Cultures: Contemporary Conflicts*, ed. Luther S. Luedtke (DeLand, Fla.: Everett & Edwards, 1977), pp. 219–44.

[28] Howard Mumford Jones, "American Literature and the Melting Pot," in *Ideas in America* (Cambridge, Mass.: Harvard Univ. Press, 1944), p. 202.

[29] S.K. Aithal, "American Ethnic Fiction in the Universal Human Context," *American Studies International* (1983), 66.

[30] Jean Toomer, *Essentials* (New York, 1931), p. 100.

ABC:
Aztlán, the Borderlands, and Chicago

Sergio D. Elizondo

Some day, when an accurate, well-documented sociohistory of the Chicano is written, when historiographers have a poetic view of our past, it is hoped that scholars and writers will become more metaphorical so that the term *Aztlán* can take on a more complete meaning than it seems to have currently.

It is likewise hoped that at that auspicious time, we shall not be as fearful of ourselves to speak the truth in public more forcefully than we are at the present. At that time it would be more pleasurable to deal with the whole concept of the abode of our Hispanic and Amerindian ancestors. At that time, poetry, sociohistory, philosophy and indeed our very presence may be more wholly integrated as the *persona chicana* that many dream that we have become. For now, we hope for a more universal union of minds such as we hoped for two decades ago. Dreamers of a brilliant future free of ignorance and superstition would do well to anticipate more fulfilled lives for our descendants and possibly some respect from those who presently, as testimony of their decadence, continue to oppress us and many others in this land.

We have needed to know and understand our history better. We understand now the Border between the United States of America and the Estados Unidos Mexicanos; now we would do well to consider that Borderlands might be a more appropriate term to designate the entire area over which the Chicano people are spread in this country. In so doing, we would come also to understand that the mere physical extension between the U.S.-Mexico border and, let us say, Chicago, is a fact of human dispersion, and *not* a diaspora of the Chicano people. It is not static for us, but rather it has always been a dynamic and natural motion motivated by laws and processes common to all cultures. Our migrations north of the old historical border have extended the geography and social fabric of Aztlán northward in all directions; we have been able to expand our communal life and fantasies. Our Chicano society today has been able to function better communally because we share much knowledge about ourselves and use it more efficiently than in the past.

The term Borderlands carries an added meaning beyond the traditional term *border.* It connotes that we, as Chicanos, shall forever in our lives carry values that identify us as descendants of the modern and ancient cultures of Indian America, Mexico, and Spain.

The border between the United States and México is one of the longest between any two countries; it is some 3,000 kilometers long from Tijuana-San Ysidro to Brownsville-Matamoros. This line that divides the two countries was fixed after 1848 following the Angloamerican war of conquest of México; an adjustment was made upon the purchase of the Mesilla territory in 1852.

In our generation, however, there has been a series of events, changes, and a renewed interest in the interpretation of the culture of the area of this borderland.

It seems that for a proper view of this phenomenon one ought to recall the historical events that shaped the concept of the borderland in the past leading us to the present reality as seen by many writers: the latter period is the principal thrust of this proposition.

Moved by physical vigor and a well-motivated nationalistic and religious zeal, the Spanish, in the first half of the sixteenth century, having recently conquered and destroyed the material majesty of the *Mexica* "empire," sought to extend their hegemony north of the borderlands of Mesoamerica. They entered the most physically forbidding land of the desert north. It was a feat that befitted Spanish daring and sense of mission for God, king, and personal fame at a time when Spain also was at the peak of its political, military, and cultural renaissance. Traveling from the translucent valley of México City to the cool and beauty-filled highlands of the present day Santa Fe, was a journey that exceeded the distance between the royal city of Toledo in Castilla La Vieja to the kingdom of Naples (annexed by the Spaniards in 1504). It has now been nearly four hundred and fifty years since Francisco Vásquez de Coronado entered the dry lands north of the Río Grande del Norte. And it was along the elongated basin of this river that the Spanish conquerors, with the assistance of Tlaxcalteca natives from the environs of Tenochtitlán, founded their physical and symbolic settlements such as missions, *presidios, ayuntamientos* and laid out a traditional square plaza that imitated the urban plan of their possessions in México and in Old Spain.

The Spanish and their Mexican subjects moved into Alta California and Texas; two centuries later the Spanish settlements and influence all along the Río Grande, the Gila, and the sparsely-populated California territory became a fact. The Spanish-Mexican people did not grow much numerically, but their national language and forms of culture were firm. Native Indian customs did not really influence the strangers' own cultural fabric as happened in the more populated Mesoamerican lands with México City as their center. While the people of the northern provinces were far from being culturally homogeneous, their social, economic and national reality was not as diversified as that of their southern Mesoamerican relatives. We think that society on these extensive Borderlands was purely rural and idyllic where the *ricos* were the privileged few who would enjoy more of the finer stuff of life, a situation that might not differ much from that which prevailed in the wealthier south where the seat of real power developed figuratively upon the rubble and ashes of the former *Mexica* empire. One could well surmise that the quality of life generally did not improve during the early Mexican period of independence.

The loss of the northern borderlands was due in part to the failure of centralized power to populate, strengthen, and develop it. Also a very probable cause was the vision of the more 'ambitious,' 'aggressive,' 'materialistic,' 'zealous' Anglo-Americans who could so easily invade the borderlands. The 'idyllic' life came to an end owing to the defeat and humiliation of México in 1847 and the ineptitude of its leadership.

The new master's arrogance is well documented in the text of the *Treaty of Guadalupe Hidalgo*. This arrogance was well reflected in the messianic attitude of expansion that extended all the way to the Pacific Ocean. This has become so great a social and philosophical problem that it has affected negatively the behavior of some Chicanos and that of some American nativists who seem to believe that the entire goodness of the American nation was reserved for the ruling descendants of the ex-Europeans. It is not an exclusive Angloamerican prerogative, for it appears to occur wherever two contrasting cultural systems come into contact; a clash between adversaries decides the winner who imposes his dominance. He first destroys the very foundations of the conquered people, such as the power base, and then imposes his cultural apparatus through dominance of the autochthonous primary values, such as language, religion, and the economic means of support. While the *Treaty of Guadalupe Hidalgo* guaranteed specifically the freedom of religion, it promised nothing concerning the integrity of language use or the control of the roots of power, i.e. the economy. The Treaty set the stage for another phase of white Angloamerican imperialism that had been occurring during its movement west of the original national American territory after independence.

One ought to remember again that what is being said here is not new. The point that is stressed is that these are the foundations of cultural conflict involving the national, material, and ideological makeup of the Borderlands especially after 1848. This assumption becomes necessary in this view in order to point out the fact of the preservation of Chicano cultural values and its dynamics precisely within the dominating process that has attempted to impose its nationalistic determinism for six generations; it then redounds in the increasingly greater importance of the so-called Chicano Movement of the decade of the 1960s.

It is a known fact that the southwestern region of the U.S.A. bears the strong social and cultural characteristics of its Mexican Mestizo multicultural background, containing a plethora of values that have been filtered from the many different tribes of ancient and modern México. The Spanish peninsular background, through its language as base and the Roman Catholic religion as the catalyst, has given the Chicano a pluralistic identity of a biological, linguistic, and atavistic variety. One could say that those are reasons our skin coloration is varied and our multiglossia of the Mexican Spanish appears in many variants wherever Chicanos live. The vast territory of the southwestern Borderlands appeared to separate us politically and economically to the detriment of group unity; not so in the more lasting, transcendental customs and values. Religion has remained strongly Roman Catholic. The family, regardless of its extension, is an important factor for self-identity. And while language takes on many expressive forms regionally, it is still a source of relevant affective comfort.

The Borderlands in our day is still the mythical expanse of earth from eastern Texas to California, holding the treasured geological beauty that has been a factor in shaping the process of cultural development from the sixteenth century, a phenomenon that afforded Chicanos in former times to identify differently with the physical varieties in the immediate areas where we live, but without affecting the continuity of cultural recognition. The affinities among the Chicanos are now communally more recognized among ourselves than in the past.

Provincial attitudes aside, the Spanish Americans of New Mexico seem to be more like anyone else from the Aztlán Borderlands than the Franco-Americans of the northeastern U.S.A., or the Swedish-Americans of Minnesota, to cite only two general examples. We have spoken Spanish continuously since the middle of the sixteenth century.

The Borderlands we have known impressionistically through official frontier outpost reports, the literary images of non-natives, even early Spanish narratives, is here today. But the Chicanos no longer live in their "traditional" places along the Río Grande, as riparians along *arroyos* and other streams, not in the *barrio*, the segregated enclave, nor on the streets leading out from the *plaza*. The population of the Spanish-Mexican American Mestizo no longer is a footnote, officially or otherwise, recalled by the uninformed. We are now a nation of at least fifteen million people in the American nation, not counting an unknown number of undocumented Mexicans (and very recently Central Americans). This realization ought to be sobering to skeptics, and it should prompt us to ask for a new description of our actual physical presence, the extent of our cultural dimension, the atlas of our language use, and the limits of the Borderlands in view of the present concentration of more than five hundred thousand *Raza* in Chicago.

The presence of the Spanish in New Mexico since about 1540, the natural growth of its population for the next two centuries, the settlement of Texas and Alta California and the Pimería, the heavy immigration during and following the Mexican Revolution, and the apparent and continuing stream of workers from México from the early forties to the millions at the present; all such factors become of primary importance in an analysis of the Mexican-Chicano presence in the Borderlands today. That México now has a population of some 75 million might remind us that millions of its unemployed migrate north in search of work, in other words, it's a veritable humanitarian form of foreign aid.

Just as the Spanish and the Mexicans moved in as uninvited guests into the territories north from México, so did the Anglo-Americans in the Southwest.

Armed conflicts between the natives and the Spanish Mexicans ended more than one hundred years ago, except for the resistance of the Apaches who battled both the Mexicans and the Anglos until late in the last century. The frontier Borderlands has been free of armed clashes in this century. Struggles between the three cultural groups having ended, the people settled down peacefully to the task of developing the land, and a private racial and cultural consciousness became a natural course.

With the Spanish presence and its hegemony gone, the culture of the various regions began to look more Mexicanized beginning with the preservation of the many variants of Mexican Spanish, a family-centered Mexican Catholic religion with its Christ-Guadalupe bivalent form of official and familiar worship dating back more than four hundred and fifty years to the present (since December 12, 1531); the traditional close-bound-family life so plethoric of affective gratification and sentiment remains probably as one of the most unshakable social factors of ethnic identification at all social-typological levels. We remember this aspect of our civilization, if we are to understand the causal determinations of our intellectual and aesthetic forms of expression in all modes within the group. Chicanos, regardless of our feelings of personal self-identification as Tejanos, Mexicanos, Mexican Americans, Spanish, Spanish Americans, Americans or Latinos have the same cultural refuge.

Out of the ancient cultures of Spain and México a new and distinct *persona* has been formed, being neither "pure" Spanish nor Mexican, but *Mestizo*. One must understand this about us in order to comprehend the mythic of today's Chicano and Mestizo lifestyles in the present concept of Aztlán. Aztlán, the mythical abode of the ancient Nahoa tribes which wandered into the south to Mesoamerica to establish various kingdoms and cultures. After Mexican independence and the withdrawal of direct Spanish influence, the Mexican-Mestizo cultural hegemony was confronted for the first time by the new presence of the Anglo-Saxon people. In the new political and social systems, the Mestizo became a weak adversary facing the better-armed and greedier newcomer.

We could expect to see in future generations a greater influx of people from south of the Borderlands, a steady stream of immigrants divided into the documented and those who decide just to go north disregarding political boundaries, acts of legislation, and the vicissitudes encountered in a land that still does not readily accept "colored" people. But if numbers are not that important, one must reckon with the cultural influx that seems to revitalize language use as an immediate determinant in a culture, not to mention other equally imperative cultural baggage brought along by the newly-arrived *Mestizos*. Whether the person comes from México or Central America, it is all the same as far as the *Mestizo* culture is concerned.

Although the physical border has been Mexicanized for four centuries, what can we say of the further physical and moral Latinization of the Borderlands as far north as Chicago?

While we as Mexican-Chicano-Mestizos become more adept at understanding and publicly expressing our Latin American origins, we also now seem to understand much better those factors, moral and social, as Americans. We can now see in this decade of greater social and economic mobility that our destiny is inexorably tied to the past. It has been attempted here to demonstrate that there need not be a constant, forced state of aversion between Chicanos, especially if they are ethnically-culturally secure and included in the greater and dominant sector of American society, thanks to the mind-opening events of the past twenty years.

It can be affirmed that there have always been forms of cultural consciousness from the beginning of the Latinization process for more than four centuries. A motion that has not abated through the generations, but which has grown to accommodate, to integrate, to assimilate and to acculturate, less for reasons of survival than for natural forms of reformation in contact with an equally strong national social unit.

It could be argued that none were more surprised than ourselves as Chicanos when in the 1960s we confronted the established powers to realize how politically and educationally unprepared we were to face and to challenge one of the most monolithic and nativist modern nations in this century. Education, as one of the most critical issues of the struggle, quickly became the cause of our tactical failures precisely at a time when we needed it as a weapon of social liberation and economic advancement. But that aside, our primordial zeal filling us with pride and strength carried us from office to office to dress down, cajole, threaten, force, and shame the very fellow Americans who for *their* eight generations had been parroting the principles that guarantee equality for all. The so-called Chicano Movement fizzled out in less than a decade, but more transcendent aspects of human understanding prevailed as in the past, the most widespread being racial and cultural consciousness. This time those involved in it wanted more than the tokenism that establishment Americans had practiced for generations. The Chicanos demanded more of the good things for all *Raza*, and the Anglos gave, though grudgingly and never enough. It is evident that cultural consciousness is a relative fact of life wherever there are Chicanos today, and it could well be the most valuable piece of identification that has come out of the heroic period of Chicano activism in the sixties. Now we can expect all sorts of emergent opinions from social scientists and humanists in new research probably to reveal more scientifically than ever the merits and demerits of our social and economic mobility. These people who have been denied their opportunity for sustained progress by three powers — Spaniards, Mexicans, and Anglo Americans, at least since 1960, have been able to express the joy of gratification.

While the Chicanos are still a dispersed cultural, social, and political group, it is clear at this writing that the old seeds of resistance sown in the last century, the cowboys' and miners' strikes during the first half of the present, the surge of ethnic consciousness from the Second World War, the courageous contribution and integrity of César Chávez and the beleaguered farm workers, the angry revolt during the Chicano Movement, has given the Chicano-Latino-Mestizo the strength to mature as a collective *persona* and the strategies to hold what we have earned in contact with a racist, greedy, and xenophobic dominant society. It seems more certain now than ever that there is no turning back from the present. It is a good period of time to survive and live well despite the moral and social decadence of the patronizing cultural group.

Our ancient tools of survival, language, religion, and family, continue to sustain us. Our linguistic atlas is not any longer the discredited form of personal expression of former generations, for it is larger and more extensive than ever in our efforts to codify, define, and clarify it scientifically. We have also learned to be more tolerant of one another's dialectal variables, thanks to greater awareness of our multicultural diversity and having more formal education.

We watch with some degree of satisfaction as the English-speaking monolinguals approach our group to partake of our traditional foods and even our language resources albeit for commercial purposes. The Anglo is becoming Latinized.

While a progress report on attitudes by our own older generation still shows traces of nativist cultural conservatism, the vigor of our new generations overshadows the darkened mantle of ignorance that had been only too common among our ancestors. It is the idea of progress that has by now become more powerful than the doctrine of docility that has traditionally been promoted by the clergy, benign as their intentions might have been; nevertheless, such superstition and paternalism seem to affect us less than formerly. Though there is still a perceptible line of political, moral, and social conservatism among many, the impact of greater formal educational achievement carries more of the weight of progress than ignorance and superstition. This has brought degrees of mutual cordiality between Anglos and Mestizos, and we all gain much from it.

It seems that various results from the quiet after the storm of militant activism have contributed toward the emergence of spiritual, if not economic, cordiality. One of the most outstanding of these fruits is the phenomenal rise of artistic production and expression. The most serious and evident of these is the resurgence of literature since the publication of *Pocho*, a novel by J.A. Villarreal in

1959. The publication of such a novel initiated a prolific period of literary production in English and Spanish. Such best-selling works as Rudy Anaya's *Bless Me, Ultima* became a piece of written art that Anglos enjoyed and praised, thus promoting greater rapprochement between Anglos and Chicanos. It would seem that not enough is known about Chicano creative writers, or about our many young social scientists, humanists, and educators; their numbers, however, reveal a new presence in the nation. This is not to say that it really matters whether the established society accepts our scientific credentials, for the work of our learned *Mestizos* benefits our group immediately more than the dominant sector. However, our accomplishments belong to the entire nation.

There is not enough space here to enumerate all the progress the Chicano-Mestizo has made over two decades. Neither can we look back to the first half of the sixteenth century and give a detailed balance of all things of lasting value that have been produced. Let it suffice that a significant step forward has been taken by scholars recently as they propose that early Spanish narratives of exploration such as that of Alvar Núñez Cabeza de Baca, among others, are now considered as part of Chicano literature because their subject matter is *Aztlanense*. Its particular rhetoric becomes more Chicano and less Spanish due to the impact of the new images on the intellect and the sensitivity of the writer-perceiver. The concept of Aztlán as myth gathers depth of meaning, if one accepts the proposition given above, and the worth of such a cultural concept gains in reality for all of us, the contemporary and living descendants of all other *Aztlanenses* throughout the entire dynamic process of our history.

Every day we meet many different people in the community, and as it happens, we see ourselves in the many changing ways we are socially and linguistically, but the greater impact of institutions such as the Spanish language media immediately reminds us with its influences that we might not be as fragmented as we often lament. More so, the communications media in Spanish are growing and improving though slowly. The lag in the development of the television and screen industries as pertains the Spanish speaking people is due more to the marketing shyness of the moguls that control it than due to their social need. It may be a matter of time when the Chicanos themselves, probably with the support of the financially powerful, will see a greater presence on this important industry. This matter is brought up at this time in the belief that the media, when finally integrated to our social image, will serve to strenghthen our cultural consciousness.

But in order to realize our wish we shall have to exert an extra effort such as we have been able to put forth in many other sectors. The time for it is more propitious than ever, for we see a factual attenuation of conflict between our two cultures, probably more for reasons of private economic interest on the part of the powerful in the national culture than a lessening of subconscious fears of a "Mexican peril" in the minds of the Anglo people. At least this is what can be perceived at the present, but as Chicanos we would have a good reason to reserve final judgement with the awareness that a people's psychic defenses might re-awaken, let us say, in a time of economic or military crisis. American national dogma exists to this day in the dark corners of racists and others who would want the U.S.A. reserved for white, Anglo-Saxon Christians of all denominations. A note of optimism, however, may have already sounded in this decade of the eighties as someone out there has proclaimed that this is the decade of the "Hispanic." But substantial progress *in all* areas of human concern is, frankly, not seriously evident, except for the presence of *Raza* in the armed forces. That in itself is of no transcendent value except for those among us who still believe that militarism is a promising avenue to follow toward social and economic liberation. *Todo se vale*, there is a degree of value in everything we do, even through our large presence in the military.

While we have little power to influence national policy and social custom, we could agree, that as an established cultural minority with the dominant majority, forms of aquiescence could be tacitly adopted as many Chicanos, during the heroic period of the movement, did philosophically. We may still fear that during our generation, and a few more to come, the U.S.A. as a whole will not be ready to live up to the commitment of the constitution nor the eternal, universal presence of full and unequivocal enjoyment of human rights for Chicanos and other American minorities. Many believe that this realization is fair, neither offensive nor defensive, but communally present in our private existence. This proposition has been our primary and lasting source of personal integrity and strength as a culturally different group considering our regional differences in superficial modes of deportment, our multiglossia and changing socioeconomic condition for the time being. This is what our mythical condition as people of Aztlán may come to mean more clearly as time passes. Intellectual and emotional factors shape our personalities as we are rapidly becoming more *publicly* produc-tive intellectually, and as we appear more frequently in the realm of the national scence, a quantum jump from the days of "The Sleeping Giant." Emotionally-aesthetically, we have arrived, having developed our arts as best as we have been able with literature clearly ahead of all other forms of artistic expression. Ap-parently we have done this in a way that no other group has been able to do to this day, that is, in an ethnic language as well as in English.

Our small efforts in artistic expression, firm and disciplined as they are, are quite meager as compared to the commercial power of the established national cor-porations. For instance, our literary production is published almost exclusively by small presses, brave enterprises that manage to survive in a nation that does not eagerly tolerate small scale efforts in an industry that has been taken over by faceless multinational businesses whose human decision-makers care little for the ethics of fairness to all, or the aesthetics which is the central object of literary art. Our art has survived in the worst of times despite financial poverty, the early years in the business, and a rather weak Chicano reading market. No one can tell what the future holds for writers, but it would be hazardous to assume that Chicanos will not be writing for generations to come. If Hinojosa and Anaya are now being read in West Germany, can we not assume that others are in line for distribution in countries outside the U.S.A.? Again, time and the merits of artistic sense and discipline are sure to be factors which determine the durability of the art. Judging from the steady production of such consummated masters as Hinojosa, Anaya, Méndez and Gary Soto, then there ought to be little fear that our most developed art will be with us for a long time. Treated as an internal colony relatively uneducated and facing formidable odds, we are distinguished as a permanent nation within a nation, with a collective subconscious that has remained under public scrutiny. Now our artisans and scientists show our truer face before the world through a more correct reinterpretation of all aspects of our cultural character.

There is a new pace, a new determination to unveil a more complete image of our society. As it occurs, we may see ourselves as in a new mirror and what we see of ourselves indeed is more gratifying than formerly. As a surprise to the world here and beyond, we might well be satisfied that our progress has been achieved with little or no loss of the primary values of a profound faith in our religious background, an aesthetic sensibility, our adherence to family bonds and a commonly held *simpatía* through which we recognize ourselves as *Raza*. The historical process has bloomed after generations of dark images that threatened the suppression of all forms of our culture. We were able to take the worst this nation's most sinister weapons could inspire.

To conclude this rambling writing is to reiterate the obvious: it can only end on a note of optimism for us all as we take stock and summarize the factors that suggest strongly the imminence of our presence and expectation of times to come.

Despite satanic efforts of the powerful and privileged few in our society at the present, one can still perceive that our American community is more educated than ever to the point that a totalitarian government may not be established. Our language, Spanish, has not only survived but it perdures quite well. We have a growing *Raza* population. Formal education is on the rise as there is a perceptible attenuation of social and economic dominance. We are the owners of an innovative, serious, and disciplined literature; our provincialism has been preserved but not at the expense of the universalization of our cultural consciousness. This consciousness seems to be on the rise, or at least we know that "the lights changed back in the sixties," and while we still entertain degrees of local self-identification, we know that all of those names we call ourselves find solace under the same benign umbrella of brotherhood. The U.S.A. seems to understand us somewhat better now, as an attitude of increasing tolerance seems to be overshadowing the xenophobia and racism of earlier years. At least this particular social disease seems not to be as prevalent and unchecked as before. There is more cultural understanding now than only a generation ago as we, ourselves, understand, and reaffirm our own multicultural character and show less preoccupation than formerly with how White or Spanish we are. Only the most uninformed, insecure or vain among us hold onto such cultural fantasies of a purer Caucasian background. There is a continuous heavy immigration, the undocumented being the predominant sector, and this historical fact of social mobility into our population may well be assumed to be tantamount to a continuing process that nurtures our Mexican-Mestizo culture. To ignore this reality is to negate that Mexico, with its population now at 75 million, is static. The rise of our artistic expression in so many forms is only the beginning of an outpouring of our ancient aesthetic sense which formerly had been frustrated more by oppression and disenfranchisement than for lack of will or talent. Our resolve on this matter was initially rekindled during the 1960s, and we are still at it and improving with discipline and tenacity. We might momentarily reconsider the matter of Spanish-speaking immigration as an objective factor determining a greater degree of language use in all strata of our society, a phenomenon of flux and constant mobility that surely affects the permanent maintenance of the Spanish language. The greatest efforts to detain the tide of undocumented immigrants has been shown to be unworkable. There are signs that short, rash, or inhumane measures to interdict the millions of Mexicans and other Latinos from coming to the source of their prehistorical birthplace — an unthinkable occurrence, an unlikely thought — shall continue to have a strong current of cultural nourishment for generations to come, probably forever. If our cultural values have survived the worst forms of oppression, who are we not to dream that this country has yet to see the best of our cultural impact, a presence that is indeed a joy to conceive?

For dreamers and scientists of today, for all of us, regardless of the degree of information we have on hand, it is true, that the concept of the mythical Aztlán is very much alive in our minds and hearts. The mythical source of our *Nahoa* ancestors at the present still resides in the subconscious of all who proudly accept our nonwestern cultural background. We may see it in the present state of life more than ever. The concept of Aztlán, mythical, is the legendary and real component of our system of primary values that lay veiled until recently underneath the dust of our lack of awareness; it still is there, only now it glows.

Chicano Art: Resistance in Isolation
"Aquí Estamos y No Nos Vamos"

José Montoya

A country's greatness can be measured by its capacity to accommodate and recognize the new, the different, and the radically creative efforts of its culturally diverse people. In the United States today, Chicano art is radically different, radically creative; but, it is not being accommodated well. It is not being granted a respectable place aesthetically, philosophically, or politically within American society. In this sense, as well as others, Chicano artists have had to work in isolation and with a feeling of rejection.

Yet, even in spite of this, we Chicanos — we who have been colonized and oppressed in American society — continue to live and to produce our art with renewed vigor and determination.

We Chicanos have developed a national consciousness at two distinct levels. That is, while we are an integral part of the political nationality of the United States, we have our own distinct history of colonization and a common language that binds us into one mind. And, in this context, we have learned to use our art as an organizing tool to strip ourselves of the mental sedimentation of over three hundred years of colonization; our art reflects the emotional and sociological scars of our oppression.

Chicanismo is a basic concept which embodies both the Indio and the Spanish aspects of our heritage. As Chicano people we now accept the Indio side of our heritage. We somehow never had too much of a problem with our Hispanitude one way or the other. But to be considered an Indio! Now, of course, aware people that we have become, we feel differently about our European linkage, but we are stuck with it, and we are going to make the best of it. And all that we desire to be — all that we are striving for — is to be allowed to be Chicanos! Just as Mexicans can be Mexicans, and the Cubans are Cubans and the Nicaraguans Nicaraguans — or, for that matter like any of the countries in Latin America whose people are Indio-Hispanos. That was the *mezcla*, the mixture bequeathed to us by the conquest — and whether it be a malediction or a benediction is ultimately up to us. Some Latin American countries have already decided. We, as Chicanos, wanted to have the right to make that choice too, and we have. The realization of our Indianness — that side of our heritage we had not considered before either by choice or by ignorance — has given us incredible options with renewed energies. We are to be sure, very excited by our Chicanismo.

So why all the widespread frenzy about cultural identity? Confusion, plain and simple! Some of it self-imposed. Much of it, however, fabricated and directed at us to keep us from getting uppity! Briefly, let me elaborate by describing the other players in one of the most important and volatile human dramas of our time. You already know about the Chicano from the foregoing description. He is, as they say in literature, the protagonist. Now meet his three brothers: First, there is the Mexican-American. He grew up very close to his brother, the Chicano, and he finds himself torn between following him or remaining loyal to his hyphenation. It offers him so much . . . but he can't be sure. Yet, he doesn't want to betray his brother, so he decides he'll go with him, but only if he doesn't have to sign papers. Brother number two, on the other hand, has no problem deciding. He knows where his loyalties lie. He is American first! He is an American of Mexican descent. The third brother is a lot like brother number two, though perhaps a little darker, with straight, black hair. He used to think a lot like brother number two until he began noticing in the newspapers and on television what they were calling his people, and one day he made his declaration: He too, was American first! American of Hispanic descent! And we haven't even gotten to the villain, yet! But let me stop there. You have, at this point, perceived the tip of the proverbial iceberg regarding the complexity of this relatively new phenomenon that was begun when the Chicano people decided to become Chicanos.

Now, one would have thought that back in the fifties and sixties when the Chicano movement began to take form, such an incredibly exciting phenomenon would have been immediately acted upon by Anglo philosophers, or at least by the theologians — surely by the Anglo artists! But they let the opportunity go by. To add to our confusion and to compound our misery, it was the Anglo social scientists who were the first ones to act on it. And they in turn excited, or perhaps irritated, their Chicano students to get involved and there were only a handful of us in those early days. Unfortunately, of those few not too many survived the rigors of academia. Of the ones who made it through, only a smaller number yet came through ready for combat. The rest continued to study us and to define us using the same models and measurements of their Anglo mentors. The ones who came through with their minds unscathed are the creative Chicano anthropologists, sociologists, and historians that today are working with our Chicano artists and our Chicano philosophers and spiritual leaders at correcting the distortions promulgated by the Anglo social scientists and the effects those distortions have had on our Chicano people.

In retrospect, that the Anglo artist failed to take advantage of the emerging movement can be interpreted as a blessing in disguise. One can see now why he was incapable of acknowledging the potential of Chicano art. As he struggles in his own delirium of defunct, un-creative clutter he has little time and less inclination to take Chicano art seriously, let alone the sensitivities to understand our pain and our suffering. And spirited and defiant, avant-garde rebel he likes to think he is, he stubbornly refuses to admit how furiously he himself is hurting. His vision, or rather his creative madness, seems rutted solely on the tremendous, computerized wasteland that engulfs his existence. And to not avail. We have made efforts to help him — to save him, even — by saying to him, "Look, we bring fresh *visions* and dreams to share with you. We have a magic that is young and wise and vigorous, allow us to give you a lift!" A few respond. But the majority are too proud. And what nagging, mental conflicts they must endure! Because one assumes that as artists they must possess some measure of intelligence, and certainly a spark of inner vision worthy of being rekindled. But he would hypocritically transform that conflict into art forms that are archaic and devoid of humanness, or he continues to repeat vaguely disguised *isms* of the past. And the Anglo art critic, also being of some intelligence one assumes, balances his feelings of guilt with false powers of authoritarianism and glib jargon because it must be painful not to know precisely why one is being ignorant! Thus, both the Anglo artist and the art critic insist on seeing our artists as nothing more than folk artists. We certainly do not consider that an insult. On the contrary, we feel honored to be in the same company with that grand old craftsman, Don José Guadalupe Posada, or in the same league as our santero carvers and retablo painters; and our weavers; our ceramicists and our low-riders. But we do other types of art as well, and it is that art that the whites refuse to accept. But we persist in being uppity. We do superb murals and in our wall preparation techniques we have surpassed their own technology; and we are not afraid to employ computers to enhance our poster art. Frantz Fanon once said, "The people who take their destiny into their own hands assimilate the most modern forms of technology at an extraordinary rate." At the opposite end of the spectrum we have wood carvers that have respectfully deviated from tradition and are doing monumental works employing modern tools and a unique reverence for wood that rivals that of the older and respected maestros, the traditional santeros. The healthy activity that interaction produces, because it is respected, is very productive, not divisive as the Anglo art critics would have us believe. Incidentally, there is general agreement by Chicano artists that santos, including retablos and altares, and the tattoo art produced by our pinto brothers in the prisons are considered the two original Chicano art forms. There is also the insidious irony that these art forms are in danger because the Gavacho collectors and other pilferers have proclaimed them "high Chicano folk art," and they want them for their collections. Some would argue that this should please us except that, knowing too well the Gavas' penchant for romanticizing those things they consider exotic, they would go to great lengths and put out good money for that art. Thus, the most authentic and original of the Chicano art forms could go the way of the beads-and-mocassin commercialism that Anglo collectors inflicted upon our Native American brothers, a situation they are working hard to correct.

At this point in the proceedings, you must be saying, "What belly-achers and cry-babies these Chicanos are!" or "My, my, how terribly these gringos have treated you poor Chicanos!" Except that, with very few exceptions, Latin Americans, especially the intellectuals, haven't done much better by us. Not in the same vicious manner, to be sure. Their rejection has been mostly out of ignorance and arrogance.

The isolation of rejection has been further amplified by our own people, from the Mexicans in Mexico to the Mexicans living in this country. The results of critical issues that Chicano militants and community organizers literally spilt blood for in the sixties and early seventies are now bringing recognition to Mexicans in this country who, in those early days — and even to this day — detested Chicanos more than the Mexican-Americans detested Chicanos. There is a barrio park up in Northern Califas that is bringing the limelight to a group of Mexican-Americans because they were able to find the financial means to bring a statue from Mexico to commemorate that park — and they don't even know what the Chicanos had to go through in order to get a park built in the barrio in the first place — let alone the fight with Anglo governances to change the name of that park from one Gavacho military general to the name of Emiliano Zapata. Those two simple acts constituted revolutionary acts in the early days of the Chicano struggle and this committee doesn't even know what it took for that to happen. The Chicanitos and Mexican-American school children didn't learn about Zapata from their textbooks; the Mexican Americans didn't know about Zapata from Marlon Brando — it was the Chicano movement that brought Zapata to the United States. Every Chicano artist, from early on, used the image of Zapata in their murals, their picket signs and rally posters, and their banners. The images of Zapata, Che and the Virgen de Guadalupe comprised the trinity that spearheaded our Chicano struggle from the very beginning. We do not begrudge anybody the credit for bringing statues from Mexico or any other country. In fact we are grateful, and we thank the people of Mexico. Except that we have our own accomplished Chicano sculptors. Why aren't they being commissioned to do some of those works?

And the complexity of the Chicano drama continues. The biggest tragedy is that our own Chicano intellectuals and academicians have treated the Chicano artist rather shoddily as well. And here I would have to include some Chicano art critics and historians. From the above segment we have been labeled anarchists, profiteers, icon makers, copy cats and even retardants of "the revolution"! And others are genuinely fearful of us because they honestly think that our madness is induced by drugs and alcohol, that we're always drunk, getting loaded, and being promiscuous! How frustrated those poor brothers and sisters must be.

The most dangerous element in our complex fabric, however, has to be the one comprised of the opportunists, and they have existed and continue to exist at every level of the Chicano Movement. They are the ones that recognize, very precisely, the significance of Chicanismo and the by-products of that fresh and dynamic energy, and very methodically they set about to exploit not only the marketability of Chicano products, but also the movement for their own personal edification. The worst of these predators are the ones that pass themselves off as Chicanos. These always find a way of satisfying their voracious appetites by manipulation and by attaching themselves like leeches to every important segment of the movement. They are adept at changing their style to suit their means, from the beleaguered, obrero look one day to a three-piece suit and tie the next. Every embarrassing and damaging setback suffered by our Chicano leaders, from important position holders and top level political appointments to union leaders, has been orchestrated by these self-serving parasites.

Small wonder we have survived with enough energy left to produce the kind of art we have produced — an art that, in spite of all the contradictions, has gained a measure of international respectability for our Chicano artists. That acclaim, however small, has come from sensitive scholars in European countries as diverse as Germany, the Netherlands, and the Soviet Union. But to us, it is more important that our internationalism has also come by virtue of the art work we have executed for Third World nations struggling for liberation. And we even understand why there exists such an imbalance in the rate of reciprocity regarding our own struggle. It has to do, obviously, with the fact that those brothers and sisters have their hands full, and precious little time to worry about the struggle of the Chicano people. Thus, when Nicaragua or El Salvador resist, aid will come from Cuba, Algeria or Vietnam — and it will always come from the Chicano artists. Yet, it stings a little bit that when Chicanos resist, by and large, they resist alone.

In conclusion, I would like to leave you with two thoughts: One is that the statement made here today is not the statement of one Chicano artist. The statement conveys the sentiments of not only the Chicano artists but of the Chicano people. The few artists that would disagree would have to be the burnouts and those who have arrived at the conclusion that continued commitment to the Chicano struggle is futile and have become content to use their talents and their status as Chicano artists solely for commercial and monetary gains. But by and large, from the old, tired veteranos who are still active to the impudent young astro pilots of Aztlán (the restless new breed that even the wisdom of the old veteranos finds hard to contain), I feel confident they would provide me with backup regarding what I have shared with you here today.

No portfolio or slide demonstration could ever give an adequate representation of Chicano art today. It would be necessary to go into the streets and barrios (poor neighborhoods) of East Los Angeles and all throughout Aztlán where the art flourishes as we continue our struggle for self-determination. That brings me to the second important thing that I would wish you to remember about what I have said here today. And that is that I would hate for you to go away with the impression that only artists are activists in the Chicano Movement. Many involved and dedicated people at all levels — from the professional disciplines to the street organizers to our people behind bars — and many more are what make up that cultural task force. It is a collective of people acutely aware of the plight of all Chicanos — from the brave and struggling farmworkers to the pintos in the brutal and emasculating penal system that houses large numbers of our brothers and sisters. It is a collection of people worried about the neglect of our abuelitos and concerned about our children and the utter failure of the educational system, a failure that has been calculated to keep us in our place. The Chicano artists have been consistent in working with those determined to regain, retain, and maintain our cultural identity by instilling, nurturing, and cultivating that high level of "national" consciousness necessary to survive within our colonized nation of Aztlán. This is a full time endeavor, to be sure, that leaves no time for dabbling in the lofty pursuit of aesthetics, as most aestheticians would define that concept. That luxury may come one day, but for the time being, ours has been the more logical task of freeing ourselves from the shackles of ignorance and the stigma of poverty, two conditions that to our detriment have been considered synonymous by the self-proclaimed dominant culture. That we can find beauty in our squalid existence is an indication that we accept the contradictions inherent in our Chicano nature — a nature that, like our art, is as ancient as it is new, and in the realm of of our consciousness, infinitely exciting.

Note

This paper has been previously delivered in a slightly different form at a Symposium on Art and National Consciousness in Latin America at the University of California at Los Angeles, November 21 and 22, 1981. It is published here for the first time.

The Chicano: A Minority in Search of a Proper Literary Medium for Self-affirmation

Marcienne Rocard

The problem of minority literatures is achieving visibility (that is, finding an audience) and, at the same time, asserting their difference (that is, emphasizing their specificity). My study will not be a comparative one; my purpose is not to discuss how much of the American way of life Mexican-American culture has absorbed while maintaining its ties with Mexico, nor to show how crucially the trajectory of Chicano literature differs from the mainstream models of both Mexico and the United States. My study is less concerned with the thematic content of Chicano literature than with its form, its mode of self-expression, a mode which reflects the situation of the hyphenated writer within the dominant society.

The Mexican-American's visibility and mode of self-expression have evolved through the years. After the Conquest and practically until World War II, he remained all but invisible, linguistically, culturally, and literarily bound to Mexico. With a few notable exceptions (the books of New Mexico's governor Miguel Otero, Jovita Gonzalez' tales and some poems and short stories published in *Lulac News* and Southwestern magazines in the late 30s) Spanish, the vernacular language, remains the only means of oral and literary expression. An oral tradition of songs, poetry, and legend was kept very much alive, while the more sophisticated poets, Aurelio Gallardo in particular, in their written work, conformed to the neoclassical canons prevailing in 14th-century Latin-America. The Mexican-American's difficulty in adjusting to an alien culture tended to drive him into retirement from the American public eye to a more congenial, Mexico-oriented, Spanish-speaking environment. At the turn of the century there was no wide audience for works written in Spanish, because publication would be limited to local newspapers. To write in English, on the other hand, in order to be accepted for publication by Anglo-American publishers, required eliminating from one's literary discourse all traces of localism. The people continued to produce pastorelas and cuentos. Some of the corridos, however, a kind of narrative folk song created toward the end of the 14th century, reflect a new ambivalent attitude by explicitly referring to the situation of the Mexican-American poised between two cultural worlds. Not only do they introduce the theme of social protest but they point, by their satiric use of English, the vehicular language, to a frustrating but literarily fecund element of the Mexican-American experience:

> Y en tiempo de elección
> Y hay *aló* y hay *mai fren*;
> Ya passada la elección
> ya no hay *mai fren* ni hay *aló*. [1]

An "agringada," an Americanized Mexican girl, speaking: ". . . me no like Mexican men." [2] In some cuentos there is also a significant evidence of this linguistic use of satire, which foreshadows the language problem the Chicano writer will eventually have to contend with.

By the end of World War II, the Mexican-American had become fairly acculturated and familiar with the vehicular language. While the corridos remained the grassroots' cultural expression a first generation of writers, issued from the barrios, translated into English the Mexican-American migrant farmworker's experience, their parents' and their own. Their writings were essentially directed to an Anglo-American middleclass readership, as shown by the ironical manner in which Mario Suárez in his short stories deals with typically Mexican-American situations and José Antonio Villarreal in *Pocho*, the first Mexican-American novel, presents the immigrant's dilemma. Significantly enough, Amado Muro could then pass himself off for a first-generation Mexican-American and was considered as such for years. Effectively, Muro was really an Anglo, Chester Seltzer, born from a well-off family in Cleveland in 1915. [3] As if to deceive his readers even more, he added to the confusion by forging a biography and making fun of his own trick; thus, in the short story "Cecilia Rosas" he plays the role of the young Mexican-American, who pretends he is an Anglo-American, in order to win the love of the beautiful Cecilia Rosas. [4] There is a strong resemblance between the literary discourse of that self-made Mexican-American and that of Mexican-born Mario Suárez: both use the same linguistic medium (English) with equal ease, both keep ironically distant from their subject matter.

By aiming at visibility in American society through the medium of the dominant language the Mexican-American made himself heard but failed to assert his fundamental difference, since a clever fellow with a passion for all things Mexican could masquerade as an author of Mexican descent.

With the Delano strike in 1965 a new type of literature emerged, which was essentially aimed at a Chicano audience and marked a decisive rupture with mainstream literature. Not that all the literary production since the middle 60s has been disruptive but much of it is, on which we will focus our attention. A "minor" literature, that is the product of an ethnic or linguistic or social group faced with a dominant language, was born within the "major" Anglo-American literature. [5] The problem of minority literatures developing inside major ones was first posed by Kafka, a member, as a Prague Jew, of a small national group. [6]

A minor literature, he argued, has a political and revolutionary character: it is the expression of a collective consciousness and thrives on tension. Above all, he insisted on the problem of language, claiming that the Prague Jews were faced with three impossibilities: the impossibility of not writing, that of writing in German, and that of writing in another language.[7] Likewise the Chicano deems it impossible not to write and assert himself, as well as to write in American English, but, unlike the Prague Jew, he can write in another language, namely in Spanish. The mode of expression the minority writer resorts to in order to assert himself is "deterritorialized"[8] vis-à-vis the major language, it bears the mark of his irreducible distance from the "territory" on which he has elected or been forced to live. The German-speaking Prague Jew felt all the more uncomfortable in the language of the oppressive German community as he was excluded from it; likewise, the Chicano resents the supremacy of the English language and chooses to keep his distance from it.

"Collectively I am a spirit 'que es' explosive", writes the poet Abelardo Delgado.[9] This self-definition of the barrio best applies to Chicano literature born and nurtured in the turbulent Mexican barrios of the American Southwest.

Emphasis is laid upon the general experience, communal and social rather than individual and personal. Significantly enough, Tomás Rivera's central figure in *... y no se lo tragó la tierra* / *... and the earth did not part* remains nameless throughout the novel, as does Kafka's hero in *The Castle*; the former is consistently referred to as "he," the latter by the letter "K." Rivera's novel is to be considered as a paradigm of Chicano experience, not just as an autobiographical work relating the author's own predicament as a farmworker's son and his own maturing process as an artist; the writer presents a year in the life of Texas migrants, a fictive year which is meant to symbolize all the years in the life of this particular group of people. As Herminio Ríos notes in his preface to the novel:

> In his work, *el pueblo* becomes the central character. It is the anonymous and collective voice of the people that we hear. It is the collective voice that allows us to see events from a diversity of points of view.[10]

Therefore the anonymous "he" of the novel is to be viewed in terms of the farmworkers' community, not as an individual hero striving toward personal identity, but as a human being whose fulfilment is achieved through social commitment. By ambiguously merging both hero and author in the third-person narrative voice Rivera presents the unnamed protagonist as both a member and a spokesman of the community. After hiding from his boss, in the final chapter, and spending some time in solitary confinement underground, reflecting upon his past experience, the hero-narrator surfaces again: a novel about the plight of the Chicano farmworker was born:

"He had to come out ... He had discovered something. . . ."[11] The Chicano reader is to identify with the "I" in Rodolfo Gonzales' epic composition *I Am Joaquín*, or in Sergio Elizondo's *Perros y Antiperros. Una epica chicana*, or in Ricardo Sanchez' book *Canto y Grito mi Liberación*. Unlike *La chanson de Roland* Gonzales' Chicano epic does not indulge in hero-worship; it deals but briefly with the brilliant feats of a glorious figure of the past, namely Joaquín Murrietta; more like a Chicano *Légende des siècles*[12] the long poem portrays a people in the process of his gestation through the ages; it is not the epic of one man, Joaquín, but that of la Raza, performing as a sort of collective hero. The syntagm "I am" plus a predicate noun, either in the plural or in the singular, or plus a predicate pronoun in the third person designating a category of people, recurs like a leitmotif throughout the poem; the intentional confusion of person, gender, and number is meant to involve the Chicano reader, to force him/her/them to identify with the first-person narrator: "I am the black-shawled/faithful women" (p. 42); "I am the campesino" (p. 51); "I am her/and she is me" (p. 79); "the people/who I am" (p. 74); "I am the masses of my people" (p. 100).[13] The full title of Elizondo's work indicates that the reader is to view the author's personal quest of identity as an analogue of the Chicano community's journey toward self-discovery, while in Sanchez' book "I" significantly alternates with "we." By also addressing his Chicano readers as "carnales," brothers, the writer invites them to share in his own experience; a prisoner of his hatred, aggravated by months spent in jail, he shows his fellow-people how to liberate themselves from their own alienation, that is by singing and crying about it, as he is doing himself.

Chicano writing is no longer exclusively centered on the self because it would mean forgetting the minority's history and the struggle for survival; it involves the reader and becomes a political act as it confronts him with his cultural dilemma and awakens him to national consciousness. Like all ethnic literatures, Chicano literature is marked by tension, that is by a dialectical process of contradictions and opposing elements. Chicano poetry, prose fiction, and drama are dynamized by a number of polarities mirroring two antithetical views of life. The basic — spatial and spiritual — opposition between the barrio, the guardian of traditional values, and the dominant Anglo society modulates into a series of oppositions: the opposition between yesterday (the Mexican past) and today (the Anglo reality), between today (a grim present) and tomorrow (a hopefully better future), as expressed in Alurista's poem "When raza"; between farmworkers, Raymond Barrio's plum plum pickers, Luis Valdez' campesinos, and the agribusiness; the opposition, within the Mexican community, between those from "over there" and those born in the United States, between the vendido, the Mexican Uncle Tom, and the Chicano who refuses to sell himself; the opposition, within the family, between generations, depicted in Richard Vasquez' Bildungsroman *Chicano*; between two languages (Mexicanized English used by the parents and Anglicized Spanish, then standard English fluently spoken by the children); the opposition, within the Chicano himself, torn like the young schizoid hero of the novel *Pocho*, between two ways of life, between total assimilation and attachment to barrio values.

This overall conflict is best epitomized in Elizondo's epic *Perros y Antiperros*; confrontation appears in its very title; it gives the general orientation and sets the mood of the work; the latter is articulated around the two contrasting pronouns "we" and "they," facing each other as the two pages in Spanish and English; at the core of the poem lies the opposition between the deadly cold world of modern civilization and the human warmth of barrio life — maybe the Ur-theme of Chicano literature, the one which underlies all the others. Through a conflicting universe the Chicano poet has to find his own way toward identification and a proper mode of self-affirmation.

Tension is not only woven thematically into the fabric of Chicano writing, it also informs it by reflecting on the language.

As we said previously, the Chicano writer is faced with two — not three — impossibilities: that of not writing and that of writing in English. The Chicano must become visible but his visibility can no longer be achieved through the traditional medium of the dominant language, since speaking the latter means assuming an alien culture and, to a certain extent, adhering to an ideology responsible for his own alienation. Around 1965, with the Delano strike, began the process of questioning: which language, indeed, was to be used for expressing a non-Anglo reality and experience? A Chicano who speaks English is trapped in the language of the oppressor and "dissolves into the melting-pot," as Corky Gonzales puts it in his poem *I Am Joaquín*.[14] How then is he to mark his difference? To create a "language of difference"[15] in the face of the omnipresent Anglo-American cultural imperialism? Here I am using a concept that some critics applied to writing in today's Quebec; indeed, to a certain extent, Chicano literature, developing in a setting which is no longer Mexico, is faced with the same problem as New World French literature, which is not of France but resolutely part of the Francophone tradition.

Some writers, like Rivera, Elizondo, or Rolando Hinojosa, choose to publish their works in Spanish with an English translation alongside. Actually, Rivera, whose novel was originally written in Spanish and was published by a Chicano publishing house, made no secret of the fact that he felt more comfortable in his vernacular:

> I had published some of my writings before but they were in English and didn't reach into my subconscious mind because English is a learned experience for me. But when I learned that Quinto Sol accepted the manuscripts in Spanish, it liberated me. I knew that for the first time, I could express myself exactly as I wanted.[16]

Writing in his vernacular is, for the minority writer, one way to do away with the supremacy of the English words.

There is another, more subtle one, which consists in using the dominant language while perverting it by undermining, dismantling, exploding it. Thus, some American black writers, like LeRoi Jones and Ishmael Reed, create within the "major" language a "minor" language departing from the norm, by manipulating the English idiom, which to them has always been the vehicular as well as the vernacular language; while the West Indian poets integrate native Calipso rhythms into their English verse. Raymond Barrio, in some degree, in *The Plum Plum Pickers* and Alurista in *Spik in Glyph?* also create a "minor" language of their own, which tends to be "deterritorialized" vis-à-vis the dominant language.

Each, however, proceeds differently because their ends are different. Barrio is a novelist. *The Plum Plum Pickers* is the story of a migrant family in California drawing a negative picture of Anglo consumer society. As a novel proper, it is poor because the author does not deviate from the sociological point of view of the proletarian writers. What redeems the book, however, is the subversive operation directed against established WASP values through its language, that is through its use and misuse of English. The process of reification denounced through the themes of the novel somehow contaminates its very language. Affluent society and the dehumanization to which capitalism and industrialism inevitably lead produce a reified world. Barrio's text has somehow become a world of things, too. The writer manipulates the two key-words "agribusiness" and "dollars," both emblems of Anglo capitalism, as if they were mere puppets:

> all the glands of agricombines owned by holding companies holding their regular hoard meetings, engendering still more agriblob conglomerates up and down the agricoast, the ups and downs of the greedy agridollar coasters had also to be computed. . .[17]

He drops dollars along his sentences, using the sign by which the American currency is designated instead of the letter of the alphabet S. Elsewhere he plays with the names of the men and institutions that watch over the affluent society: Ronald Reagan comes out as Howlin Mad Nolan, the State House un-American Activities Committee as the State House un-American Festivities Committee etc. The text is glutted with words as the Californian fields are with plums; the surfeit of the fruit is both the symbol of the farmworker's plight and the instrument of his revenge on the agribusiness, since they will rot, unharvested, because of the strike. Barrio achieves a piling-up effect through the proliferation of words, alliterations, repetitions, enumerations; he hurls the English words like so many projectiles at the Anglo reader, confronted with the plum plum pickers, who had to work "from ding dong dawn to dusk."[18]

Barrio spills English with a vengeance, Alurista addresses the non-Anglo readers who "spik in glyph" and explores a new ferocious, iconoclastic way of tackling the English language. Alurista's text is a provocative one, indeed; the reader is called upon to enter a sort of reading/deciphering game as he goes through the artist's phonic de-compositions. Alurista is a poet, that is a maker of words; he, effectively, deals with words and under his magic wand, they dissolve (so to speak/spik?) into phonic fragments, like snatches of musical phrases, and modulate into all kinds of semantic possibilities:

> life throbs
> in the depths
> of the surfaced
> chaos and at
> times it rattles
> thunder
> . . . people won
> der often
> where to find
> noah
> no, a . . . ?
> si, a . . . ?
> c, i, a?
> questions
> re
> main
> while pots
> blossom
> and re
> volution
> volts, and revs
> and plots.[19]

The volume opens with thirteen pieces — thirteen "pieces of a Chicano mind," as Delgado puts it — numbered phonetically, regardless of conventional spelling: one=Juan, two=tu, six=seex, etc. The de-construction is carried on into the other sections of the book as well. We may wonder what the poet is driving at in this puzzling book of his, featuring on its cover page a woman, with her mouth wide open letting out the title inside a balloon, as in a comic strip. Through a jesting interplay of sound and symbol the poet does away with the magic value of English words; he blurs the relationship between the signifier and the signified as if to "scotch" and debunk the established idiom; he shows his non-English-speaking readers that, after all, the English language is but a set of bewildering glyphs, of symbols with hidden — and variable — meanings; a comforting relativistic view of linguistics, worth laughing at:

> some folk say
> say!
> wood u nut
> rather
> b

```
bean, being? be in
born than be
dye
in, ing? ang
s
t, angst?
ste, u us dead
usted. . .20
```

"as well" comes out as "*ass* well," and "two" modulates into "too," "tú," "to," etc.

Another strategy for survival is the systematic use – within the same work – of Spanish and English, the minor and major languages, whereby the American of Mexican descent expresses his difference from the dominant society and his duality:

> I have two words, Spanish and English,
> good at times
> at times not,
> but two, for better or for worse.[21]

Chicano literature is unique in that it places side by side, within the same scene, the same stanza, the same verse, the same phrase, Spanish and English words, thus translating the dialectical reality of the Chicano and carrying on the dialectical process of Chicano thought into the language itself.

As a matter of fact, bilingualism fulfils a double role: it prevents the minority language from being relegated to a secondary position, from being put, as it were, in parentheses, like French on the labels in Anglo-Canadian stores; secondly, by sandwiching Spanish words between English words, it checks the flow of the major idiom. The alternate use of the two conflicting languages in the Teatro Campesino is probably less disturbing than is its occurrence in poetry, inasmuch as the switching from one language to the other is accounted for by the respective origin and function of the speakers; the farmworkers stick to their vernacular, whereas the representatives of Anglo capitalism and power, including Don Coyote, speak English. Though the poems by Alurista, Delgado, José Montoya and Sanchez display no rupture of the basic structure of discourse, the combined use of Spanish, English, and Caló makes for an anarchic form, in which the language of the oppressed bursts out like the "que es" explosive of Delgado, as if internal tensions – reflecting external ones – had reached breaking point.

To Sanchez "the merging of languages, thoughts, feelings, and observations" is but the natural expression of people daily faced with dual perspectives.[22] H. Ríos thinks that "the violent switch into another system gives power to the poetic expression."[23] Does this mean that the language becomes autonomous, self-referential? Not really. Without being overly Cartesian, we can say that the respective use of the two linguistic codes is not totally gratuitous, that it very often appears to be dictated by the nature and origin of the referent. Sanchez insists on the inevitability of "dichotomies" and affirms that he cannot "traducir ciertas cosas" "en el idioma del gringo".[24] Elizondo gives us one key to this dichotomic approach:

> She
> She speaks English,
> she raps English,
> she reads English,
> she sits English,
> but she loves in Spanish.
> Dreams in Spanish
> thinks in Spanish,
> goes to church in Spanish,
> plays in Spanish,
> works in English,
> feels in Spanish,
> drives in English,
> caresses in Spanish,
> runs in English . . .[25]

As the aesthetic expression of a certain terrorism and the symbol of a people's bi-cultural identity, the combination of these two linguistic codes constitutes a political act; it also represents a factor of "deterritorialization" vis-à-vis mainstream American literature. Indeed, beside English *or* Spanish, "hay otra voz," Tino Villanueva would say, there is an extra voice through which the Mexican minority can best express its difference and specificity. However, the question of its visibility remains. By finding a proper means of self-affirmation has not the Chicano writer alienated himself from the national community? Will he make himself heard beyond his limited audience?

Considering the rise of the Hispanics in the United States and the predictions for the next millennium, it should be less and less "limited." And Alurista's defiant hope in bi- and multiculturalism should materialize:

> Now, ahorita define (di' fain?) tu mañana hoy."[26]

Notes

[1] "Viva Mexico," *Texas Folklore Archive*, p. 43–2.
[2] "A Una Niña de Este País," collected by A.M. Espinosa, in *Romancero de Nuevo Méjico*, No. 58 (1953), 264.
[3] *The Texas Observer*, 30 March 1973, pp. 1–5. Also see: J. Womack, "The Chicanos," *The New York Review of Books*, 31 Aug. 1972, p. 17: "The funniest, brightest, most moving, accomplished, and prolific Mexican American writer used to be Amado Muro, a veritable Isaac Babel of Southwest; . . . But Muro was really an Anglo, Charles Seltzer, and is now dead." As a matter of fact, Ortega was the first to find out about Muro's real identity.

40

[4] In *The Chicano: From Caricature to Self-Portrait*, ed. Ed. Simmen (N.Y.: New American Library, 1971), pp. 279–91.

[5] Gilles Deleuze, Félix Guattari, *Kafka: Pour une littérature mineure* (Paris: Editions de Minuit, 1975).

[6] F. Kafka, *Tagebücher 1910–1924*, ed. Max Brod (Frankfurt: S. Fischer Verlag, 1967), p. 150 ("innerhalb großer Literaturen"); p. 149 ("einer kleinen Nation").

[7] F. Kafka, *Briefe 1902–1924*, ed. Max Brod (Frankfurt: S. Fischer Verlag, 1966), pp. 337–38: "Sie lebten zwischen drei Unmöglichkeiten ... der Unmöglichkeit, nicht zu schreiben, der Unmöglichkeit, deutsch zu schreiben, der Unmöglichkeit, anders zu schreiben, fast könnte man eine vierte Unmöglichkeit hinzufügen, die Unmöglichkeit zu schreiben ... also war es eine von allen Seiten unmögliche Literatur, eine Zigeunerliteratur, die das deutsche Kind aus der Wiege gestohlen und in grosser Eile irgendwie zugerichtet hatte."

[8] Kafka, *Pour une littérature mineure*, p. 29.

[9] "El Barrio," in *Chicano: 25 Pieces of a Chicano Mind* (Denver, Colo.: Barrio Press, 1971) p. 20.

[10] Tomás Rivera, ... *y no se lo tragó la tierra* (Berkeley, Calif.: Quinto Sol, 1971), p. XVI.

[11] Rivera, p. 177.

[12] Victor Hugo's spacious epic poem evoking past ages of civilization.

[13] Rodolfo Gonzales, *I Am Joaquín/Yo Soy Joaquín* (Delano, Calif., Farm Workers Press, 1967).

[14] Gonzales, p. 52.

[15] "The Language of Difference: Writing in Quebecois," *Yale Language Studies*, No. 65 (1983).

[16] *Los Angeles Times*, 28 Jan. 1973, p. 66.

[17] Raymond Barrio, *The Plum Plum Pickers* (N.Y.: Harper and Row, 1969), p. 113.

[18] Barrio, p. 98.

[19] Alurista, "Life," in *Spik in Glyph?* (Houston: Arte Publico Press, University of Houston, 1980), p. 37.

[20] "Birth," in *Spik in Glyph?*, p. 17.

[21] Sergio Elizondo, *Perros y Antiperros*, (Berkeley, Calif.: Quinto Sol, 1972), p. 25.

[22] Ricardo Sanchez, "Dichotomies...," in *Canto y Grito mi Liberación* (El Paso, Tex.: Mictla Publ., 1971), p. 155.

[23] H. Ríos, *El Grito*, VII (March–May, 1974), p. 7.

[24] Ricardo Sánchez, "Stream," in *Canto y Grito*, pp. 81–82. On code switching see also Marcienne Rocard, *Les Fils du Soleil*, (Paris: Maisonneuve et Larose, 1980), pp. 420–24.

[25] Sergio Elizondo, *Libro para batos y chavalas chicanas* (Berkeley, Calif. Editorial Justa Publ., 1977), p. 63.

[26] Alurista, "When Raza," in *Floricanto en Aztlán*, (Los Angeles: Chicano Studies Center, University of California, 1971), p. 1.

Cultural Nationalism and Chicano Literature: 1965–75

Alurista

Culture and Nationalism

Although Chicano literature has been in existence since 1943, it is not until the 1960s that one can speak of the emergence of its modern form and content.[1] The production and accumulation of literary capital by the Chicano writers of the decade between 1965 and 1975 is ideologically rooted in cultural nationalism. That is to say that the literary products of 1965–75 sought to affirm a nationalism founded on the most ancient and pre-colonial cultural origins available to the *modern* Chicano writer. It was a search for the primitive (sic: pre-literate) communism of a society and a system of production which predated slavery – a slavery classically cast in the Roman definition of citizenry, a state of being prior to feudalism in its national and oligarchical form. A pre-mercantilism, which knew not gold as coin, was central to the neo-myth of the "newly born children of the sun." César Chávez and Luis Valdez are responsible for the "new awakening" to the "new colonialism," and its transnational monopoly capitalist infrastructure.

The movement and organization of farm workers, students, youth in general, and union labor at large, who identified with Aztlán as an anti-war, anti-racist, anti-ethnocentrist, anti-sexist, and an anti-class dominance posture, assumed national and cultural manifestations in the Chicano literary mode of production: "Because they realize they are in danger of losing their lives and thus becoming lost to their people, these men, hotheaded and with anger in their hearts, relentlessly determine to renew contact once more with the oldest and most pre-colonial springs of life of their people."[2]

Frantz Fanon's words are most appropriate in describing the precise stance and sentiment particular to the Chicano poets who emerged during the mid-sixties. In the face of flagrant institutional and personal racism and ethnocentrism Chicanos sought to redefine themselves in their own terms, that is to say in terms other than those prescribed by the Anglo-Saxon, male Protestant state to "keep Mexicans in their place." Much of the literature that had flowed from the pens of Anglo-American novelists, social commentators, journalists, and academicians since 1848 portrayed the Mexican in the United States as lazy, ignorant, criminally prone, and decidedly unworthy of trust. After many years and many generations of Chicano subordination to Anglo world views and values, the socialization process had clearly begun to take its toll, instilling in the hearts and minds of many children the notion that for some "divine" reason Chicanos were not quite as human as Anglo-Americans. Not being quite as human, the correlative notion that Chicanos did not merit the same treatment under the law, in employment, in education, in housing, was simply a logical extension of Anglo-Saxon, Protestant male supremacy. The need for the redefinition of Chicano identity was clearly at the core of the search for the historical self which predated the onslaught of the European colonizers on this continent. And it was a continental identity, to be sure, which Chicanos sought; well aware of the fact that "America was not a country, the United States was a country. America was a continent, a continent where mixed-blooded, Spanish-speaking people constituted the majority."[3] Identity was clearly a question that embraced at least two dimensions and a common thread. The common thread was clearly the historical dialectic which lent legitimacy to the other two dimensions:

(1) A cultural heritage which distinguished Chicano from United States culture and which clearly became a source of pride, a motivating catalyst, and a dynamic force of resistance; and

(2) A nationalist consciousness which differentiated Chicanos from other immigrants to the United States since it was, originally, the United States which came to Mexicans, occupying Mexican territory by the force of arms.

A nationalist consciousness which could unify the heterogeneous Chicano population in the United States was clearly a necessary dimension in the self-definition of Chicano identity.

Before proceeding with the analysis of some of the principal writers of the period in question, it is important to clarify the notion of "cultural heritage," the notion of culture as differentiated from custom. Culture is relationship, which may be said to exist in four kinds:

(1) Psychosexual
(2) Ethnopolitical
(3) Socioeconomic and
(4) Phenomeno-philosophical.

Each one of these kinds of relationship yields a particular contradiction which is, itself, the dynamic core of its historical dialectic. The first relation accounts for the subordination of women to the dictates of man. The ethnopolitical contradiction accounts for the subordination of all non-white races to the political will of the white state. The third kind of relationship and perhaps the determining and central contradiction, the socioeconomic one, subordinates those who work to live and live to work to the structures of social stratification engineered by those who own to live and live to own. The fourth kind of relationship, which in this essay is identified as phenomeno-philosophical, is the one which accounts for the subordination of all non-Western-Yankee-European world views to the ideological designs of a technocratic cosmovision particular to the United States, principally, and to Western Europe as its origin and extension. Culture, any culture, is then expressed with sexual, racial, class, and ideological contradictions, the dialectics of which constitute the core of their dynamic materialization across history and geography. Culture is not to be equated with its artifacts or its customs, ossified by time and ritual reproduction and repetition; culture is the dynamic adaptation of the human species to a set of ever-changing conditions; it makes for unity without casting out the inherent need for diversity. "Culture has never the translucidity of customs; it abhors all simplification. In its essence it is opposed to custom, for custom is always the deterioration of culture."[4] It is when culture began to be viewed in this contextual dynamic that Chicano culture became a force of resistance against the total assimilation and the consequent self-denigration of Chicanos in the United States. Language was, and is, clearly, the vehicle *par excellence* for this cultural resistance and, upon occasion, cultural offensive against the cultural imperialism of the United States — language, to be sure, is, by its very nature, dynamic, dialectical, subject to constant change over time and throughout geographical space.

Let us now briefly gaze at the second dimension which shaped the question of identity for the Chicano writer of the late sixties and early seventies: national consciousness. National consciousness presupposes the existence of a nation which in the classic sense has a common culture, a language of its own, a territory which has been held in common over many generations, an economy of its own and, to be sure, a sociopolitical structure crowned by a "state" (the seat of self-governance), which in turn is legitimized by the constituency of the nation in question. Chicanos in the sixties were well aware of the fact that they had a common — even though heterogeneous — culture, a common language (Chicano urban colloquial Spanish and English), and a common territory traditionally inhabited by Chicanos (the Southwest of the United States).[5] And, while Chicanos did not have an economy of their own, let alone their own state, Chicanos did share similar economic conditions set by a common oppressive Yankee state. All of these criteria differentiated Chicano people from mainstream United States society as well as from mainstream Mexican society. It was in this spirit that the metaphor which gave rubric to the Chicano nation was born: Aztlán. Aztlán, an ancient Nahuatl myth which described the prehistoric motherland of the Indians in the American continent had now become a contemporary metaphor for a nation in the making. The "Spiritual Plan of Aztlán," edited by the delegates to the First National Chicano Youth Conference held in Denver, Colorado's "Crusade for Justice," proclaimed the birth of the emerging Chicano nation: Aztlán. The Spiritual Plan of Aztlán, moreover, clearly stated that "Aztlán belonged to those who worked it" (not only to Chicano workers) and that no capricious frontiers would be recognized — an important point which, with the zealousness of an exclusivist narrow nationalism, was quickly overlooked and geographical borders were summarily delineated, that is, the southwestern United States, otherwise known as the states north of México. Clearly, without a "state" or a common economy, the notion of a nation with geographic boundaries was preposterous. Let it be noted that without capricious frontiers neither the agriculture and industries worked by Chicanos in non-southwestern lands were excluded nor were the Latin American republics' labor and resources left out of this continental metaphor. "Colonialism did not dream of wasting its time in denying the existence of one national culture after another. Therefore, the reply of the colonized peoples will be straightaway continental in its breadth."[6]

In order to shed light on the stated object of this inquiry — cultural nationalism as the root and sustenance of Chicano literary production during the decade between 1965 and 1975 — culture and national consciousness have been examined. We are now prepared to comment upon the codification of some producers of dramatic, poetic, and narrative discourse. In order to proceed from the popular to the more complex literary manifestations of Chicano cultural nationalism, we start with the simplest and most public of Chicano literary modes of production, Chicano theatre, and then examine the genre most saturated with cultural nationalist subjacency, Chicano poetry. The Chicano novel is the literary product which climaxes the literary and linguistic accumulation of the decade: for which reason it had better come last.

Chicano Theatre and Luis Valdez

In March 1966, the United Farm Workers' Organizing Committee headed by César Chávez drafted "El Plan de Delano." Luis Valdez, who was to become the leading force and personality in the development of the dramatic mode of literary production in national Chicano consciousness, contributed significantly in the drafting of this declaration. At one point the plan states: "Our revolution shall not be an armed one, but we want the order which now exists to be undone, and that a new social order replace it."[7] Clearly, the horizons which the farm workers traced for themselves called for protracted national struggle, and even though the "union" which Chávez proposed was not for Chicanos exclusively, the majority membership was, and is, undoubtedly Mexican. Valdez brought his theatrical tools to the level of a cultural organizing guerrilla. The Teatro Campesino became a central force in the recruitment and organizing of scab workers in the fields. This was not classical theatre nor were its actors professionals; the theatre performed its *actos* on flatbed trucks, in meeting halls, on the streets, etc., with no more props than cardboard signs to identify the characters and their social roles.

In the process of "almost spontaneous" dramatic production Luis Valdez started shaping his "ars poetica": "The characters and life situations emerging from our little teatros are too real, too full of *sudor, sangre* and body smells to be boxed in. Audience participation is no cute trick with us; it is a pre-established, pre-assumed privilege"[8] and further on:

> The nature of Chicanismo calls for a revolutionary turn in the arts as well as society. Chicano theatre must be revolutionary in technique as well as content. It must be popular, subject to no other critics except the pueblo itself; but it must also educate the pueblo toward an appreciation of social change, on and off the stage.[9]

Luis Valdez' forceful contributions to the dramatic mode of Chicano literary production came to a climax with the formation of *TENAZ (Teatro Nacional de Aztlán)*:

> ... If Aztlán is to become reality, then we as Chicanos must not be reluctant to act nationally − to think in national terms, politically, economically, spiritually. We must destroy the deadly regionalism that keeps us apart. The concept of a national theatre for *La Raza* is intimately related to our evolving nationalism in Aztlán ... Such a *teatro* could carry the message of *La Raza* into Latin America, Europe, Japan, Africa − in short, all over the world.[10]

Under the leadership and inspiration of Luis Valdez, Chicano theatre rapidly became a weapon in the cultural guerrilla of the Chicano nationalist mobilization of the late sixties and early seventies. Its form was simple: the *acto* (a short skit based on action, irony, and simplicity); and its content clear: self-discovery and definition, collective assertion of Mexican rights, unbending intent to nationalize Chicano life and consciousness.[11]

Five Chicano Poets

Rodolfo "Corky" Gonzales was the founder of the Crusade for Justice in Denver, Colorado. He was the host of the First Chicano National Youth Conference in March 1969 where Mexican culture and nationalism became central to the Chicano Movement. "Corky" Gonzales is the author of the Chicano "epic," *I Am Joaquín*. In this, his major and only work published to date, Gonzales sets on a historical journey that goes back to the indigenous origins of Mexican people and then on to the contemporary social conditions which Chicanos face in the United States. The historical dialectic of their struggle for survival is narrated in a forward, simple, declamatory style. While identity is one of its central concerns, *I Am Joaquín* leaves the question open in the sense that it includes all the terms used to describe the people: "*La Raza!, Mejicano!, Español!, Latino!, Hispano!, Chicano!* or whatever I call myself, I look the same, I feel the same, I cry and sing the same. I am the masses of my people. ...."[12] *I Am Joaquín* does, however, give a sense of universal identity while relating a singularity composed of a cultural syncretism that points to national self-affirmation within United States society. It is, as well, an affirmation of social struggle which "stirs the Revolution."[13]

Jose Montoya's contribution to Chicano literary production has been immortalized with his two well-known poems, "La Jefita" and "El Louie," from his collection *El Sol y Los de Abajo and Other R.C.A.F. Poems.*[14] Nationalism in the works of Montoya glorifies certain traditionally valued figures such as the Mexican mother on the one hand and the *vato loco* — heir to the *pachuco* lifestyle of the late thirties and early forties — on the other. His style is narrative, colloquial, bilingual, and very personal, almost conversational. It could be said that Montoya's brand of cultural nationalism is a blend of modern existentialism and contemporary Chicano folklore. He resorts to imagery of the Chicano past in order to affirm the authenticity of the ever-present here and now which Mexicans in the north must confront in order to build a future more suited to the humanitarianism which has, historically, characterized the Chicano. Montoya would quarrel with a cultural nationalism which would negate the right of other nations, cultures, and languages to be themselves. Unlike "Corky's" exclusivist nationalism Montoya would be willing to include other, non-Chicanos within his nationalist consciousness — in that respect he is very similar in tone to that of the farm workers' unionizing movement.

Abelardo Delgado's poetic production uses a traditional declamatory style which, often, does not rule out rhyme. His brand of cultural nationalism is inclusivist within a Christian superstructure which repeatedly asserts the equality of all men before God. His tone ranges from the humorously light to a mild angry indictment against the dehumanizing institutions which the Anglo-American state has formulated. The language of his literary production is most unassuming, colloquial, and usually bilingual. The world view which Abelardo's nationalism espouses has more to do with cultural artifacts and customs than with the dialectic dynamic of culture itself. He is perhaps best known for his poem "Stupid America" from his collection *Chicano: 25 Pieces of a Chicano Mind.*[15] His poetic call for action appeals more to a sense of moral and religious humanitarianism than to a socioeconomically based political activism.

In the literary production pioneered by Sergio Elizondo, cultural nationalism assumed the most "Mexican" (in the tradition of the Mexican Republic and its culture) of its manifestations. *Perros y Antiperros*[16] is perhaps one of the most dialectical — in a schooled sense — poetic literary products of the early seventies. It has been called an "epic" by some critics. The recurring affirmation of a proud Chicano inner self vehemently rejects acculturation and clearly points towards a rediscovery and redefinition of traditional Mexican culture: "Elizondo masterfully captures a people's expressive traditions: playfully mocks death, devalues machismo, satirizes macro-societies' attitudes. In keeping with this epic tone, language becomes progressively less formal into a variant of Chicano speech."[17]

Alurista, the fifth of the poets selected for examination in this essay, ". . . is the originator and main exponent of the Amerindian ideology of Aztlán, which synthesizes a Chicano identity, drawing from the Mexican indigenous heritage and the actual realities of *barrio* living in the United States."[18] His notion of culture is not, as some critics have asserted, monolithic, but is in fact and in literary form dialectical and dynamic. The tone of his work is often angry, but it is tempered by a tender respect for all life. Valdez, Elizondo, and Alurista deliberately discourse on sexual and class dominance, considering these matters central to the development of a national consciousness. The thread that seems to unify all of Alurista's works is the notion of an unbending will to be that which one determines it is necessary to become:

> our people to freedom
> when?
> now, *ahorita* define *tu mañana hoy*[19]

the conclusion being that what is necessary to be is: free; and that the time is: now.

Chicano literary production in the poetic mode, like Chicano theatre, brought its message to the people rather than wait for the people to pick up a manuscript and legitimize the birth of a new consciousness. Chicano poetry included its oral and public performance as an essential component of its literary product. It was not a closet poetry nor did its production occur in someone's attic but, on the contrary, in the thick of the mass mobilization and dedicated organizing efforts which characterized what we can, today, call "the cultural nationalist revolt" of the late sixties and early seventies, the decade between 1965 and 1975.

Four Chicano Novels

Cultural nationalism manifest in theatrical and poetic modes of literary production is rooted in the present (the decade in question, 1965–75), but the Chicano novel is set in different historical periods at different stages of economic production. The literary production manifest in the Chicano novel resembles the combined and uneven production of undeveloped nations dependent on transnational monopoly capitalism; it combines preceding modes of literary production and incorporates them at uneven levels to constitute a literary unit which is incomplete, fragmented, and open. Alienation comprises the subjacent narrative object, and irony establishes itself as the literary mediation through which

Mexicano reality is tranformed in its novelistic discourse. Language, as stated earlier in this chapter, is *"the* vehicle for cultural resistance and upon occasion ... offensive, against the cultural imperialism of the United States." The novels to be examined in this essay are those *not* written in English:

  (1) *... y no se lo tragó la tierra* by Tomás Rivera;
  (2) *Estampas del Valle* by Rolando Hinojosa;
  (3) *Peregrinos de Aztlán* by Miguel Méndez; and
  (4) *Caras Viejas y Vino Nuevo* by Alejandro Morales.

Sexual, racial, class, and ideological subordination embody a fourfold contradiction manifest, either by explicit discourse or its absence (novelistic silence), at this level of private accumulation of linguistic and literary capital: the Chicano novel.[20]

Rivera's novel, *... y no se lo tragó la tierra*, is without a doubt the most incomplete, fragmented, and open literary unit of the four in question. In fact, for quite a while critics debated whether or not it should be considered a novel. Its unity emanates from its chronological focus on a "lost year" since neither characterization, setting, or structure lend any unifying elements to its novelistic claim. It is incomplete through its most deliberate novelistic silences. Fragmented structurally into narrative vignettes and symbolic epigraphs, Rivera's novel remains open from beginning to end. The narration itself is set in the 1950–60 Texas-midwestern migrant stream, the Texas of that period already displaying the combined and uneven economic development characteristic of transnational monopoly capitalism. In his masterpiece, Rivera incorporates different modes of literary production (narrative, epigraph, and dialogue) at clearly uneven levels. A lapidary narrative establishes itself as the predominant mode, followed by ephemeral dialogue and epigraphic discourse. Alienation, at the most material level (migrant farm labor), is flagrantly evident throughout the novel which depicts living conditions well below any acceptable standards as well as the various tragedies which accompany such working man's odyssey. Irony, as literary mediation surfaces in Rivera's novel openly, often negating what the story appears to affirm or affirming what the story appears to deny. Irony in Rivera's work can perhaps be best exemplified in his use of the classically Mexican negation which affirms: "No pos sí"; or its reverse, the affirmation which negates: *"Sí pos no."*[21]

The women in his narrative discourse are classically subordinated to the mandate of the Mexican male. Chicano society is, itself, subordinated in terms of class, race, and world views to the corporate monopoly which agribusiness was already becoming in the Texas of the fifties. In Rivera's novel there appear to be no great complexities when it comes to depicting subordination; there are only two factors to each of the four equations: *Mejicanos* dominate *Mejicanas*, owners dominate workers, white Texans dominate Mexicans, and the Anglo world view dominates the Chicano world view through its socializing institutions: school, church, and state — and it is at this last level that "Chicano" consciousness is born as differentiated from *Mejicano*.[22]

The novelistic production of Rolando Hinojosa is exemplified for the decade in question (1965–75) with his prized work, *Estampas del Valle y Otras Obras*. Not unlike Rivera's literary production, his *obra* was debated in terms of its genre. Again, the reader confronted a fragmented, incomplete, and open work. Hinojosa's work is also framed in the forties and fifties, but instead of focusing on the Tejano (Texas-Mexican) migrant odyssey, it centers its discourse on the *Tejanos* of the great Rio Grande (south Texas) Valley, which — for the most part — are sedentary, constituting the labor force necessary for the constant capital formation essential in the developing agribusiness monopolies of *"el valle de Tejas."* The differing modes of literary production incorporated in his novel differ from those of Rivera's in quality as well as in quantity. Dialogue, familiar (in the sense of *familia*) and extended discourse, is the predominant mode, though narrative, portraiture, and documentary follow closely in quantity, in that order. Irony, as literary mediation, in Rolando's novel is manifest as satirical wit put into the horse's mouth: the *"raza"* from the great *"valle"* of Texas, including the *"bolillos."* Alienation is presented through more than two clearly distinguishable poles. The appearance in a "here-to-stay" fashion of a class between the *"trabajador"* in the south Texas valley and the rancher-farmer-"oilers to be" (Kingsville) is concretely depicted: a managerial and professional class — best exemplified in the teaching, law enforcement, and public health professions (*boticario* — pharmacist). The class aspect of the fourfold contradiction is more complex in *Estampas* than it is in *Tierra*; and understandably so, since Tomás focused on the "migrant stream": variable capital. *Estampas del Valle*, furthermore, exhibits the same quality when it concerns the sexual aspect of south Texas reality, only this time it is more generalized — it goes beyond *Mejicana* subordination to *Mejicano* rule — it pictures the subordination of women by men. This quantitative variant is due to Hinojosa's compounding of the racial aspect of subordination by the inclusion of bourgeois *Mejicanos* and proletarian *bolillos*. The racial aspect loses ground to the class and ideological manifestations of social consciousness. Culturally and linguistically, moreover, the "Chicanada" determines the "social" (if not the economic and political) milieu of the valley and it even maintains parallel socializing institutions (*"la escuelita,"* *"la iglesia católica,"* and the local *"caciques"*); all of these phenomena, of course, are concrete manifestations of the sedentary, emerging "professionals" amongst the Mexicans resettled in Texas after the Mexican revolution of 1910 and the ever-growing accumulation of "constant capital" ("old and hard money") by the Anglo-Texan carpetbaggers. The Chicano "persona" emerges in his *obra* as a concrete presence who witnesses the adage: "We told *them* that our house was *their* house, *they* moved in, and moved *us* out, now *we* watch through a window, and if *we're* lucky through the kitchen or from the garden. *They* now

50

control what used to be *our* house and we wait on their mandate."²³ The unifying element which makes Hinojosa's *obra* a novel is a particular historical period, a geographical stage, and the collective characterization of a distinct "brand" of Texans, the *"gente del Valle."*

As for the next novelist in this inquiry, Miguel Méndez takes the reader to the México-Arizona-Southern-California borderland through its *Peregrinos de Aztlán.* Méndez' novel is once again set in the forties and fifties (with the exception of its title which matches *his* present at the time of production), only this time the narrative, dialogical, and poetic modes of literary production are predominant, in that order, throughout its discourse. Characterization, setting, and linear chronology play the role of spinal column in the body-narrative of Miguel's work. Alienation is, once more, material and complex — that is to say the division of labor depicted goes even further than Hinojosa's discourse; Méndez distinguishes the different classes characterized in his *obra* through variables in the "parole." The classes depicted in his novel range from the "yaqui" lumpen — clearly marginal — to the in-house, aspiring, oligarchical, petty, "yori," bourgeoisie of Mexican social borderland-strata (which in Arizona are qualitatively and quantitatively identifiable). There again the racial aspect polarizes Anglo versus non-Anglo (even though within the Mexican population, a Mexican yori and yaqui polarity remains constant even if subtle). The Anglo world view and superstructure, as in Rivera's discourse, maintains its pervasiveness over the Chicano, the Yaqui and the Yori Mexican world views, while the sexual subordination of women in general remains constant through its novelistic silences as well as in its flagrant episodes of sexual exploitation. The novel cannot avoid, however, its incompleteness, fragmentation, and openness despite all the setting, linear chronology, and characterization. In fact, it is the unsealable border, as a silent character, which reiterates the *obra*'s open-endedness, its incomplete and fragmentary discourse. The "border" is for Méndez what the "Texas valley" and the "migrant odyssey" are for Hinojosa and Rivera. Irony is manifest in the novel more through tragic humor than through Rolando's satire or Tomás' unadorned reversal of true posture (classical Socratian irony).

With Morales, the *"barrio"* is the "border," the "valley," and the "migration." *Caras Viejas y Vino Nuevo* exhibited what perhaps can be called "grotesque irony off the asphalt jungle" as a literary mediation. Again, as in Méndez, characterization, setting, and linear time — deliberately disrupted in its Spanish version — Alejandro's novelistic enterprise consolidates the unity of his *obra* without "completing," "closing," or "filling all the literary silences" of its literary discourse. The different modes of literary production which Morales codifies are dominated by scatological urban dialogue, followed by interior monologues, and cinema techniques (such as the absolute focus on a part of the body as if it were autonomous and independent from the whole). The timespace embodied in *Caras Viejas y Vino Nuevo* is comprised by the southern — not borderland —

California of the fifties and sixties, particularly *"el barrio de Montebello."* By then, California transnational monopoly capitalism, in its agribusiness and tech-nocratic modes of material production, is rampant and pillaging the "third world," and pressuring the "old world" and the new "Soviet state." The "United Farm Worker's Unionizing Committee," the "anti-Vietnam-War-international-movement," and the *"Movimiento Estudiantil Chicano de Aztlán"* (MEChA) are present, or in the making. Violence as a response to external pressure on in-group relations qualifies the behavior of its protagonists – and the protagonist, again, to be sure, is multiple or collective. Alienation, as a subjacent narrative ob-ject in Alejandro's private accumulation of modern, southern California, lin-guistic and literary capital reaches out to the existential-materialist level which Sartre defined in his theoretical classic: *On Being and Nothingness.* Morales centers on "being-in-itself" with his metaphorization of the "stirp" (*la estirpe*), beaten to the core as a historical "stigma."

Notes

1 Luis Leal, "Mexican-American Literature: A Historical Perspective," in *Modern Chicano Writers*, ed. Joseph Sommers and Tomás Ybarra-Frausto (New York: Prentice-Hall, 1979), pp. 18–30.
2 Frantz Fanon, *The Wretched of the Earth* (New York: Grove Press, Inc., 1963), pp. 209–10.
3 I first heard these words on the lips of Luis Valdez in 1968 at a symposium on the Chic-ano Movement in UCLA.
4 Fanon, p. 224.
5 See Rodolfo Acuña, *Occupied America* (San Francisco: Harper and Row, 1972), partic-ularly chapters 9 and 10. Also see Armando Rendón, *Chicano Manifesto* (New York: Macmillan Co., 1971), particularly his chapters 1, 2, 9, and the appendix.
6 Fanon, p. 212.
7 See Rendón, *Chicano Manifesto* (New York: Collier Books, 1972), Appendix.
8 John Weismann, *Guerrilla Theatre* (New York: Anchor Books, 1973), p. 55.
9 Weisman, p. 56.
10 Weisman, pp. 57–58.
11 The Teatro Campesino later changed its technique and content and focus from the *acto* to the *mito*. A discussion of this transition is beyond the scope of this paper as it occurred towards the end of the decade in question in 1974. An excellent article on the matter was published by Yvonne Yarbo-Bejarano in *Modern Chicano Writers.*
12 Rodolfo Corky Gonzales, *I Am Joaquín* (New York: Bantam Pathfinder, 1972).
13 Gonzales, p. 20.
14 José Montoya, *El Sol y Los de Abajo and Other R.C.A.F. Poems* (San Francisco: Edi-ciones Pocho-Che, 1972).
15 Abelardo Delgado, *Chicano: 25 Pieces of a Chicano Mind* (El Paso: Barrio Publications, 1973).
16 Sergio Elizondo, *Perros y Antiperros* (Berkeley: Quinto Sol Publications, 1972).
17 Francisco Lomelí and Donaldo W. Urioste, *Chicano Perspectives in Literature* (Albuquer-que: Pajarito Publications, 1976).
18 [Juan] Bruce-Novoa, *Chicano Authors: Inquiry by Interview* (Austin: University of Texas Press, 1980), p. 265. Excerpt from Novoa's introduction to the interview.
19 Alurista, *Floricanto en Aztlán* (Los Angeles: UCLA – Aztlán Publications, 1971), p. 1.

52

20 For an extensive discussion of the writer's notion of the genre "novel" as literary capital, product and market in literary production, see *Maize*, Vol. III, No. 3 and 4, under the title, "El Capital y su Género: La Novela . . . Material, Instrumento y Dinero, Producto y Mercado," p. 23–41.

21 An excellent discussion of this point can be found in Joe Sommers' article, "Interpreting Tomás Rivera," in *Modern Chicano Writers*, p. 97.

22 For thorough discussion of the "roots" of Chicano literature and particularly the "transition" period, read Luis Leal's "Historical Perspective" in *Modern Chicano Writers*, pp. 18–30.

23 Anonymous.

II THE MEXICAN PERSPECTIVE

Chicanos In Mexican Literature

Juan Bruce-Novoa

In *Triga*, the Mexican poet Francisco Segovia included a poem inspired by his encounter with Chicano culture as he experienced it during a sojourn in Texas and in particular with Chicano literature. While the title of the poem, "La lengua y el gusto" (103), announces a play on language and food, it also promises, through reference to taste or *gusto*, a judgment as to value – good taste. Two epigraphs contextualize the brief poem and, perhaps, tell us more than Segovia's verses. The first, taken from Ricardo Sánchez, can be read as Segovia's perception of the Chicano situation: "it becomes imperative to pick up estoque and filero/ crying out the anguish of mi alma/ when you, bastard of the jive lenguaje . . . ." Segovia chooses to foreground as his synecdoche for Chicanismo the militant, even violent, protest typical of Sánchez' work. The epigraph also foregrounds the act of crying out in response to someone who can jive, that is misrepresent and fool others through the distortion of language. Sánchez' speech is, at the same time, interlingual, not only in its use of Spanish and English, but also in his characteristic leaps of diction from *imperative* to *bastard of live*, or *estoque* to *filero*. One might argue with Segovia's choice of Sánchez to represent Chicanismo, but this is not yet the place to correct his vision – my purpose is to interpret that choice first.

The second epigraph interfaces with the first. From Dante's *Inferno* Segovia quotes the transcription of Nimrod's unintelligible words cried out to Virgil and Dante when the voyagers come across the builder of the Tower of Babel chained among other evil giants in hell. Virgil first admonishes Nimrod not to speak, but rather to blow the horn hung at his neck. Then the epic guide explains to Dante that Nimrod's cries accuse only himself, for his evil idea caused the multiplicity of languages in the world today. Virgil closes ominously: "Let us leave him alone, and not speak in vain; for such is every language to him, as his to others which is known to no one" (46). Segovia's own poem will reach much the same conclusion, as we will see below. Here it is more pressing to decipher the intertextuality Segovia has created.

The verse from Dante establishes a context of the entire Western tradition of high-culture literature, from ancient to modern passing through the great summa of Dante's opus. Virgil can be read here to signify good taste – el buen gusto –

and Dante as the reader who has been brought face to face with the hellish creature in the form of Sánchez. Segovia can be seen as Virgil, in his role vis-à-vis the reader and Sánchez, but also as Dante inasmuch as Segovia himself wandered through the nether regions of Texas where he encountered Sánchez. Thus, hell equals the U.S. Southwest, and Segovia's sojourn assumes the significance of a passage through the inferno on his way to higher and more glorious things. Segovia's sustaining companion during his foray into darkness was the literary tradition of countless hero/narrator/survivors of epic wanderings. From that tradition Segovia gleans the wisdom of those defenders of the pure and noble canon of high culture, that is, forget Sánchez and his ilk, for to speak to him is to speak in vain, to waste time.

The reference to Babel and the biblical explanation of humankind's fall from the cosmic grace of social unity — symbolized in one language — into the chaos of multiple and mutually exclusive languages focuses our attention on the problem of cross-cultural conflict and the age-old search for a means of conflict-resolving communication. Sánchez' complaint expresses the same conflict and need for resolution.

Segovia adds one more twist to this intertextual frame by quoting Dante from Angel Crespo's translation. Of course, in one sense it makes no difference, because Nimrod's words remain the same in any translation. Yet Segovia achieves several things. He implies that translation from one language to another is the viable response to our post-Babel condition. At the same time, Nimrod's unintelligibility remains constant, implying that it, as well as its Chicano equivalent, defy translation because they are not a language. Thus, in the context of mutual understanding through translation, Nimrod's speech act — though it may attract our attention, perhaps even our admiration for its sonority and sensual beauty — remains pathetic, ultimately a lonely, isolated cry in the darkness. Translation signifies unity and a successful passage from one region to another, just as the text and the classical tradition have passed from Dante to Virgil to Segovia, writers of three different languages in three different epochs. Interlingualism, on the other hand, signifies detention between the earthly and heavenly lives, that is, the death and hell of unintelligible speech.

Segovia is not the first Mexican writer to pen a reaction to Chicano culture. Since the Mexican Revolution there have appeared numerous references to Chicanos in Mexican letters. What makes Segovia's significant is that it follows what we can see as a tradition formed by those texts, a coherent body of texts that allows us to extrapolate a Mexican high culture, or literary, view of Chicanos — and I emphasize *high culture* because what follows does not necessarily apply to popular culture expressions in Mexico. That view holds, in general terms, the following points. Chicano culture is a social aberration, revealed or signified through the synecdoches of language and food. Chicano culture is synthetic, hybrid, no longer Mexican, yet not U.S., and therefore negative; a degenerative as opposed to a generative-creative process. It is a threat to purity (Mexican) and good taste (Occidental). Chicanos are victims lost in and condemned by their geographical happenstance.

In their fictionalized autobiographies, Martín Luis Guzmán and José Vasconcelos recalled their travels in the U.S. Southwest during the Mexican Revolution. Like Segovia both authors resided for a time in San Antonio, Texas. There they were entertained by Samuel Belden, who appears in their texts as a personification of the Mexican/U.S. synthesis. Guzmán says of Belden, "abogado medio mexicano y medio norteamericano. . . [nos hablaba] en su español raro y difícil – ininteligible a veces –, español sin tercera persona ficticia y con sintaxis anglicizante. . . [la] manera directa y ruda de Belden nos lo hizo simpático a primera vista y nos indujo a tratarlo desde el principio con cierta amable familiaridad" (227). Guzmán, always the master of irony and finesse, subtly attributes to Belden a degenerate interlingual expression, at times Nimrodian in effect. Worse yet, for a man like Guzmán who addressed even his best friends in the formal third person, in Belden's speech and manners there no longer exists a social hierarchy. The result is a precipitous familiarity, which, although Guzmán modifies it as *amable*, must be read in the context of his high appreciation of formality and etiquette. Vasconcelos, always more caustic than Guzmán, dismissed Belden as a *"mexicano-yankee* . . . inculto como todos los que se crían en aquellos territorios" (785). Texas, for both authors, represented a hinterland of social degeneration, an inferno populated by half-caste monsters, into which they had been cast by the Revolution.

Just as Segovia does in his poem, as will be seen, both revolutionary writers also symbolize Chicano society in images of food. Belden took both of them to San Antonio restaurants. Guzmán recalls "restaurantes mexicanos – restaurantes patrióticos de cocina nacionalista sintética – . . . culto de los colores patrios y una misma efigie del cura Hidalgo . . . y en todos, por supuesto, comíamos unos mismos manjares sabrosísimos, tan sabrosos que por momentos resultaban de un mexicanismo excesivo o desvirtuado por interpretaciones demasiado coloristas de nuestro color local" (228). Guzmán ironically exalts the San Antonio Mexican cuisine to a level of inauthenticity attributed to hybridism and lack of subtlety – behind *sabrosísimos* hides *too spicy and unrefined*. In the process Chicano food becomes synthetic, superficially nationalistic. The result of this need to establish a clear identity with Mexico – a cry for recognition from within the nether region of U.S. control – is a food too rich and ultimately foreign to the authentic Mexican the author claims to be. In other words, Guzmán found Chicano food to be a Nimrodian feast.

Vasconcelos is, again, more direct. When Belden takes him to the best restaurant to eat steak, Vasconcelos is appalled at the huge slice of meat, served with no sauce. When one recalls the thinly sliced, well-cooked Mexican steaks, Vascon-celos' reaction to a Texas style one can be understood. Thus Belden almost assumes the image of a cannibal proudly offering the civilized explorer a hunk of human thigh. Later Vasconcelos, the man usually associated with the Raza Cósmica synthesis, also condemns hybrid Chicanismo through a reference to food. "No solo lo norteamericano, también lo mexicano se volvía absurdo, bajaba de categoría en la híbrida ciudad [San Antonio] que ha hecho negocio de revolver tamales con enchiladas, frijoles con carne, todo en un mismo plato" (786).

Although many Mexicans would find refuge in San Antonio, for Guzmán and Vasconcelos, guided in their wanderings by "good taste" and a strong sense of the inviolability of authentic Mexicanness and correct Spanish, Chicanismo spoke to them in Nimrod's voice. In their life both heeded Virgil's advise and continued their respective journey without wasting more time on useless dialogue with the repulsive, condemned giant.

Why are Chicanos so repulsive and despicable for Mexicans? Why, despite a few exceptions, do Mexican writers tend to view us negatively? In brief, because we undermine the protective wall of national separation between Mexico and the United States; we deconstruct the fictions of exclusivity necessary for Mexicans to go on seeing themselves in terms of a solidified absolute. We are a threat because we short-circuit their national self-project, so they must reduce us to less than equals.

If we borrow a construct from the Moscow-Tartu school of semioticians, cultures or ethnic groups perceive space as divided by a boundary into at least two parts: one, internal and organized, the space of We, a structured area opposed to the other disorganized and unlimited external space of the They. Jurij M. Lotman's examples of this opposition include: our nation/foreign nations, initiated/laymen, culture/barbarism, intelligentsia/masses, and cosmos/chaos (105). (Those familiar with my own work know that I prefer the last grouping and would add Mircea Eliade's sacred/profane configuration.) From the Mexican We perspective, then, Chicanos have ventured beyond the limits of internal space into U.S. chaos where they wander like lost children or frightful monsters. Lotman would say that Chicanos have *inverse orientation*, a *we* who focuses itself around the center of a space previously regarded as external; that is to say, that as a group Chicanos supposedly seek to assimilate to, or appropriate to themselves, the values or properties of an alien They. For the Moscow-Tartu school, the boundary belongs to either the inside or outside group, always marking "the break in the continuity of space, with the property of inaccessibility" (111). Therefore, the exceptional group that crosses the boundary struggles against, and puts into doubt, the inherent structure of the world; that is, it betrays the cultural fiction of inviolable unity, exclusivity, and cohesion.

To the primary, unitary text of Mexican nationalism – the texts, literary and non-literary alike, of Mexican identity in clear opposition to other national groups — Chicano culture is, in Lotman's terms, a secondary text in that it represents a violation of the tabu against crossing the forbidden boundaries established by the primary cultural texts. The Chicano text is superimposed on the Mexican cultural text as a violation of limits. In other words, Chicanos represent an ominous possibility of deconstruction through escape. The internal culture of Mexico depicts this as betrayal and prefers to force the traitors into the role of seeking complete assimilation to the They.

However, Chicanos, especially since the mid 1960s, refuse to fit these patterns. We insist on being, not those who have crossed an absolute boundary, but the active producers of interchange and synthesis between the would-be binary opposites. We construct the alternative, if nothing else on the ideal plane, of transcendence. On a lower, practical level we represent the disturbing revelation that the solid wall belongs to both sides — or even more horrifying, that it is actually an expanding organism with the perturbing capacity to absorb, discriminate, reject, retain and/or synthesize portions from the living space of either group without having to limit ourselves to one or the other. And if language is culture, our manipulation of it into hybrid forms is a metaphor of the boundary turned open, productive frontier, never static and thus continually in synthetic process never fully achieved. Chicanismo calls for a definition of culture as process, not as a static code of permanent characteristics. This, of course, threatens those on either side.

Octavio Paz saw this threat when he began his study of Mexican culture, *El laberinto de la soledad*, with an essay on the Pachuco.[1] Paz wants to see Mexico as the binary opposite of the U.S.; several times in the book he offers simplistic contrasts. The Pachuco, however, horrifies Paz because he is a hybrid who rejects the established national alternatives which Paz needs in order to orient himself and his text in the world. Paz must reject the Pachuco solution to preserve his own existential integrity. He must, then, destroy the Pachuco as a viable alternative. This he achieves, at least rhetorically, by interpreting Pachuco dress and behavior as a desire to be absorbed by the U.S. system if only as a criminal. Paz turns the Pachuco into an isolated shouter of unintelligible protest who finds his ultimate place — and meaning — in society as a prisoner. Paz turns the Pachuco into one more avatar of Nimrod.

Paz's desperate desire was to force Pachucos into Lotman's category of inverse orientation, because to entertain the possibility of the fluid continuity of intercultural space would deconstruct the fictional *We* of Paz's psychomythological historicism. Paz must first firm up the exterior walls of nationalism in order to eventually plunge into the ahistorical universals of Jungian archetypes. The stark reality of the hybrid, semiforeign Pachuco patrolling the ramparts is too much for Paz to accept.

Dean MacConnell's depiction of modern anthropology's relationship to alien cultures fits Paz's, and many other Mexican authors', reaction to Chicanos. "Once relocated in an alien culture," says MacConnell, "at the edge of their own world, their discipline requires ... a textual preservation of the core of cultural values, key symbols, and central themes they find there. Operating in this way, anthropology has built a bulwark around our civilization, a cultural equivalent to the Maginot Line or the Great Wall" (150). The imagery is appropriate. Paz reads Pachucos as aliens and notes their values and symbols. He does so not only to record them, however, but also to set them up as a warning against inauthenticity, an example of the fate awaiting those who wander beyond the limits of Mexicanism. In so doing Paz reaffirms Mexican core values and symbols and himself as their authentic voice, dug in behind the Cactus Curtain.[2]

Yet Chicanos more accurately represent what MacConnell calls the new approach of ethnosemiotics, "specifically a reversed polarity for anthropology which aims in the direction of a synthesis of center and periphery, [which], if accomplished on a historical and concrete cultural level, [promises] not merely the possibility for adaptation and survival but for transcendence, that is, the potential to develop new forms of society" (151). *New forms, synthesis, central value for the peripheral being, transcendence* – an enumeration of revolutionary, and thus threatening, terms for those who defend the old forms of centralized society, who will go to any lengths to prevent the transcendence of their status quo.

The possibility that the periphery might influence the center was hardly entertained by Guzmán or Vasconcelos. They dismissed Chicanismo as an aberration only deserving of humor or scorn. The decades between 1920 and 1950, with the advent of mass media, rapid mobility, and a surging Mexican immigration to the U.S. made the possibility a frightening one for Paz, who designed his book as a retreat into Mexicanness, first, and universalism second. Yet the periphery had already influenced the center in a decisive manner during the Revolution.

Friedrich Katz's *The Secret War in Mexico* has revolutionized our conception of the Mexican Revolution by highlighting the key role of Mexico's northern states as an area of U.S.-Mexican interaction. Vasconcelos denigrated this phenomenon by calling the northern strategy Pochismo, that is, the ideology of inverse orientation.[3] Yet, years later, but before Paz's *Laberinto*, Agustín Yañez, in *Al filo del agua* (1947), his novelistic analysis of Mexico on the brink of revolution, depicted as one of the catalysts the return of "norteños," who were actually Mexicans who had been living and working in the U.S. These workers, as Katz has noted, no longer respected traditional Mexican customs. Their behavior and language defined them as different, yet they were still Mexican – should we not say Chicano? Their presence became one of the main factors in the collapse of the Mexican government.

Carlos Fuentes, writing a decade after Yañez, created an updated norteño in the character of a Bracero in *La región más transparente*. The character's language, spiced with Anglicisms, and his aggressive behavior make him a threat to society. Yet Fuentes kills him off instead of letting him play out any positive role in changing society. Like Paz's Pachuco, Fuentes' Bracero finds his place in suicidal behavior. What Fuentes' and Yañez' characters share is the Chicano's characteristic of synthesis, of Mexican/U.S. hybridism, which places Mexicanness in doubt. They have crossed the boundary, survived in the chaos of hell, and returned to tell others about the possibility of change — not necessarily improvement on all fronts, but change.

The Chicano Movement itself has acted like a Yañez norteño, producing an increase in references to Chicanos in Mexican literature since the mid 1960s. *La frontera plural, estancias de un amor indocumentado* (1979), Miguel Alvarez Acosta's novel, promises much in the title; but good intentions aside, it adds little to Mexican understanding of Chicanos. If anything it betrays the author's less than profound comprehension of the differences among the several geographic areas along the border, each with its distinctive Chicano subculture. And in the end, for Acosta, to be Chicano means to want to really be Mexican, which of course makes the Chicano an inferior Mexican. Fiction by Federico Arana, David Ojeda, and Luis Casas Velasco satirizes Chicanos, seeing little of value or sincerity in Chicanismo. Casas Velasco's *Death Show* (1981), a grotesque parody of Horatio Alger fiction, offers as a metaphor of the Chicano synthesis a restaurant chain featuring cannibalistic meals in the guise of Mexican pre-Columbian rituals.

More positive voices have spoken, however. Vicente Leñero's references to Chicanos are succinct, yet highly significant. In his parody of the New Testament, *El evangelio de Lucas Gavilán* (1980), one possible explanation for St. John the Baptist's strange behavior is that he has spent time working with Chicanos — he has learned about God in the desert. And Christ saves money because he wants to go north to be with the Chicanos. Chicano culture, then, is both the rite of passage that produces Christian radical insights, as well as that part of humanity most in need, or perhaps most deserving, of God's presence.

José Agustín's satirical forary into the U.S., *Ciudades desiertas* (1982), can be read as a sojourn into Chicano territory as well. Near the end, through the eyes of a Mexican who has settled in New Mexico, Agustín offers the most accurate description of the regional subcultures in the Chicano southwest. Yet Agustín also calls on the traditional leitmotifs of language and food. In Iowa the Mexican protagonists find a Chicano couple who "ya casi había olvidado el español y servía una barbacoa aceitosa y hecha con carne de cerdo" (110). In the Southwest itself we are told that things are much better. One can find all the tortillas one desires and even speak Spanish, although it may be "de pueblito, vaciado, con truje, ansina y sus mercedes" (172). Yet the narrator finally realizes that he, as a Mexican, cannot adjust to the New Mexican synthesis. He must return to Mexico and his Mexican woman. It is highly significant, in this context, that the novel ends with one of the most blatantly macho, male chauvinistic scenes in recent Mexican fiction. The sojourner returns and, like Paz and others, through the semiotics of macho aggression and possessiveness reestablishes the clearly drawn borders of reactionary Mexican society.

Two short works begin with epigraphs taken from Chicano literature. The first, Florencio Sánchez Cámara's "Poly y el emparedado," is preceded by Alurista's poem "Mis ojos hinchados." The story is narrated by Pedro Vidales, the "primer mexicochicano an azotar las calles de Chicago con sus huaraches" (107). In the Chicago ghetto Vidales battles Blacks, Whites, and everyone. He marries a Polish woman and has a son who later attends college. Although he remembers Mexico as a glorious land, he knows that life there is impossible for the poor. And from all this he has gleaned an important philosophy of life, one that deconstructs the old national dichotomies: "todas las sangres salpican del mismo color. Esa fue mi cultura política" (108).

This quick historical overview brings us back to Francisco Segovia's poem, the second contemporary work to utilize a Chicano epigraph. Now we are better prepared to listen to the text itself, with its use of food and language motifs.

> Los dientes de sal
> como espinas secas
> del robalo
> la oniónica cebolla
> con los añales atados a la frente
> y el ajo gárlico
> ancestro
> de los ejércitos de árabes.
> La oliviada aceituna griega
> La gárlica rabia parda, curtida
> La violada lengua de la almeja
> en los duros arrozales del desierto. . .
> Pero nadie va a tener un paladar
> para probarlos.

We could leave it at face value, or more specifically, at Mexican face value, as one more negative commentary and rejection. Certainly the last verses imply a reaffirmation of Virgil's wisdom as conceived by Dante. Yes, Segovia echoes his high culture predecessors.

However, I propose that we reread it, this time from the center of the Chicano periphery. Nimrod's arrogant tower reminds me of Alurista's use of Icarus in *Floricanto en Aztlán* (12).[4] Like Nimrod, Icarus wants to reach the heavens and fails, yet both represent humankind's noblest urge to rise above its limits. To accept ground level has never satisfied the human spirit. Thus, Chicanos represent the desire to transcend; that is, we represent the best, not the worst, in human endeavors. The threat of chaos, raised by the Babel allusion, makes little sense to us now, living as we do in the midst of chaos itself in the guise of order. And perhaps the attempt to transcend is fated to fail, but after Camus, Adorno, Borges or Musil even assured failure must be read as the quintessential human situation, but always with the mandate to attempt the impossible with as much class as one can muster — a lesson José Montoya's "El Louie" bespeaks eloquently.

Segovia's verses allow even more interpretation. Chicanos are compared to Arabian armies, an image followed by the introduction of the Greek olive. Should we not read this as a reminder that the Moorish invasion of Europe not only produced a threat of chaos for centuries, but resulted in the creation of an order called Spain with its new language, Spanish. The periphery's invasion of the European center changed history and culture. And it was through Arabic texts that Greek civilization was passed on to Europeans who had no direct knowledge of it. And that process took place in the interlingual society of medieval Castilla. In this light the Chicano Nimrod threatens violence and change, but promises also a renovation of humanistic values, a reorientation of the dominant, but decadent, central powers towards the common lost origins of the highest ideals. After all, Nimrod cannot be understood because only he speaks the original human language. It behooves the rest of humankind to listen for echoes of itself.

Finally the question of language. Segovia, with Virgil and Dante, seems to condemn Chicano culture through the accusation of unintelligibility. However, the irony is that both Dante and Segovia undermine the surface message by creating examples of that speech which prove highly successful as communication.

"Raphel maí amech zabí aalmos," Nimrod's words, ring with echoes of the angelic spirit. Segovia, while not as heavenly, offers such phonetic and gastronomic delights as "el ajo gárlico" and "la oliviada aceituna." His interlingualism is minimal, yet it proves the process to be viable. And in the final analysis, Segovia contradicts himself — and Dante. It is Segovia's palate that savors the linguistic possibilities opened to him by the monster Sánchez. Segovia has tasted Chicano food and come away changed. His poem is a dialogue with Nimrod, even a translation of sorts offered to his fellow Mexicans. Perhaps Segovia intended none of this — probably not. Perhaps he really does side with Dante's Virgil — probably so — and seriously believes that Chicano culture will appeal to no one — surely wrong. But Segovia has chosen to speak to, and even for, Nimrod. And once having tasted la auténtica lengua of transcendence, can any mere Mexican seguir the same?

64

Notes

[1] For definition of, and bibliography on Pachucos see Bruce-Novoa, pp. 218–19.

[2] I have used this term, first coined by José Luis Cuevas in his essay of the same title, because, although Cuevas included Paz among those who supposedly were trying to open Mexico to the world, Paz's treatment of the Pachuco is a rhetorical drawing of a nationalistic curtain of sorts. The irony is deliberate.

[3] "Nortismos era, en realidad pochismo. Palabra que se usa en California para designar al descastado que reniega de lo mexicano aunque lo tiene en la sangre y procura ajustar todos sus actos al mimetismo de los amos actuales de la región [the United States]" (Vasconcelos, 782). Nortismo was attributed to the writings of Roberto Maytorena, whom Vasconcelos accused of inverse orientation: "Roberto era simple vehículo de ideas cuyo alcance le hubiera horrorizado si llega a entenderlo. Producto de aristocracia pueblerina y de sangre pura española, sólo la ignorancia peculiar de los medios en que se criara explica que anduviese propagando la doctrina enemiga; la destrucción de la cultura latinoespañola de nuestros padres, para sustituirla con el primitivismo norteamericano que desde la niñez se infiltra en los pochos" (782). Here the inverse orientation is unconscious, but perhaps for this reason more sinister.

[4] For a discussion of Alurista's use of the Icarus/flying motif see Bruce-Novoa, pp. 89–90.

References

Arana, Federico. *Enciclopedia de latinoamericana omnisciencia.* México D.F.: Joaquín Mortiz, 1977.

Alurista. *Floricanto en Aztlán.* Los Angeles: Chicano Culture Center of the University of California, 1971.

Alvarez Acosta, Miguel. *La frontera plural, estancias de un amor indocumentado.* México D.F.: Joaquín Mortiz, 1979.

Bruce-Novoa, Juan. *Chicano Poetry, A Response to Chaos.* Austin: University of Texas Press, 1982.

Cuevas, José Luis. "The Cactus Curtain." *Evergreen Review,* 7 (1959), 111–20.

Dante, Alighieri. *The Divine Comedy of Dante Alighieri.* Trans. Charles Eliot Norton. Chicago: Encyclopaedia Britannica, 1952.

Eliade, Mircea. *The Sacred and the Profane, The Nature of Religion.* New York: Harcourt, Brace & World, 1959.

Fuentes, Carlos. *La región más transparente.* México D.F.: Fondo de Cultura Económica, 1957.

Guzmán, Martín Luis. *El aguila y la serpiente.* In *La novela de la revolución mexicana,* T. 1. México D.F.: Ed. Aguilar, 1964.

Katz, Friedrich. *The Secret War in Mexico.* Chicago: University of Chicago Press, 1983.

Leñero, Vicente. *El evangelio de Lucas Gavilán.* México D.F.: Seix Barral, 1980.

Lotman, Jurij M. "On the Metalanguage of a Typological Description of Culture." *Semiotica,* 14, No. 2 (1975), 97–123.

MacConnell, Dean, "Ethnosemiotics." In *Semiotics of Culture.* Ed. Irene Portis Winner and Jean Umiker-Sebeok. The Hague: Mouton Publishers, 1979.

Montoya, José. "El Louie." In *Aztlán, An Anthology of Mexican American Literature.* Ed. Luis Valdez and Stan Steiner. New York: Random House, 1972.

Ojeda, David. *Las condiciones de la guerra.* La Habana: Casa de las Américas, 1978.

Paz, Octavio. *El laberinto de la soledad.* México D.F.: Fondo de Cultura Económica, 1959.

Sánchez Cámara, Florencio. *El notata y las mujeres mágicas.* México D.F.: Joaquín Mortiz, 1980.

Segovia, Francisco. "Poemas." In *Triga.* México D.F.: Universidad Nacional Autónoma de México, 1983.

Vasconcelos, José. *La tormenta.* In *Obras completas,* T. 1. México D.F.: Libreros Mexicanos Unidos, 1957.

Velasco, Luis Casas. *Death Show.* México D.F.: Joaquín Mortiz: 1981.

Yañez, Agustín. *Al filo del agua,* México D.F.: Editorial Porrua, 1963.

Victorian Attitudes Affecting the Mexican Woman Writing in *La Prensa* During the Early 1900s and the Chicana of the 1980s

Juanita Lawhn

During the early 1900s *La Prensa*, an international Spanish-language newspaper founded by Ignacio Lozano on February 13, 1913 in San Antonio, Texas, reported extensively on the Feminist Movement both in Europe and in the United States. This coverage and the reaction toward the Movement evident in issues during the first years of its publication demonstrate the Victorian attitudes[1] that subtly and subversively controlled and manipulated the consciousness of the Mexican woman. It is this same dominating, condescending, excluding, manipulative Victorian attitude toward the Mexican woman that is expressed by the Mexican man on the pages of *La Prensa* that is still undermining the literary accomplishments of the Chicana in the Chicano Movement.

As the Feminist Movement[2] in Europe and the United States gained momentum, *La Prensa* began its meticulous attempt to counter-act against the effect that the Movement might have upon the Mexican woman reading the newspaper. Many articles which documented objectively the progress of the international Movement appeared throughout the issues of *La Prensa*. However, these articles were published as if only to comply with the goals of the newspaper to be objective, for next to these articles would appear others that idealized the woman and affirmed the sanctity of the home or pieces that specifically described the education of a "respectable" woman. This education always included the training of young girls to be good wives and mothers. Furthermore, these articles, usually printed in the literary sections of *La Prensa* or in a section devoted to the home, never encouraged the Mexican woman to seek professional careers or to attempt self-realization anywhere other than inside the home or in occupations that were stereotypically acceptable for the woman – teaching inside the home, of course, was one of these "acceptable jobs." It may be this sort of encouragement and indoctrination that was the impetus for the emergence of many "escuelitas" throughout the barrios of the Southwest. On occasion, an alternative was mentioned for the educated, unmarried Mexican woman – starting a business. But the business usually would be a bookstore or some other enterprise run from within the home. If a woman decided to leave the home and enter the business world, then she was hired in "respectable jobs." *La Prensa* itself is an example. While both men and women worked on the Lozano enterprise, the men were the editors, journalists, and contributors to the paper, whereas the women worked as sales clerks in the Lozano bookstore. Furthermore, articles dealing with work alternatives never mentioned anything about the respectable woman who might feel emotionally and intellectually fulfilled as an unmarried working woman or as a woman who might consider matrimony and family only a part of her total reality.

Another way of subliminally manipulating the consciousness of the Mexican woman in the articles of *La Prensa* was the implied meaning of images on the printed page. For example, on September 15, 1915, an entire page was devoted to presenting the most distinguished ladies of San Antonio. However, in spite of the importance given these women, reasons as to why they were the most distinguished women in San Antonio were never mentioned. The oval portraits of these thirteen Hispanic women dressed in beautiful, high-collared, laced Victorianstyle dresses were placed symmetrically throughout the page. Delicate roses decorated the background of these beautiful feminine objects. On the bottom half of the page, a semicircular iron-latticed fence held together by iron rivets enclosed the rose garden. The beauty and delicateness of roses – traditionally synonymous with women – juxtaposed to the coldness and rigidity of the iron fence implies through images that women, like roses, were to be enclosed in gardens whose boundaries were to be set by an exterior reality. For the Mexican woman, that reality was comprised of male expectations and male norms. Today, the Chicana is confronting openly this image. For example, Alma Villanueva's latest book of poetry is entitled, "Women are not Roses." The cover design displays two beautiful red stemmed roses – one of which has the stem slashed and the rose is tipped over.

The Victorian attitude toward woman's sexuality is also evident in the pages of *La Prensa*. In fact, one way of *La Prensa* representing the "sexually pure woman" attitude is by using the Virgen de Guadalupe – an image familiar to the Mexican mind. La virgen is the counter-part to the "angel in the home" image that Susan Gubar refers to in her book.[3] For example, on September 16, 1919, the image of the Virgen de Guadalupe appeared for the first time on the pages of *La Prensa*. Although the newspaper had devoted a major part of the issues on the *Diez y Seis de Septiembre and Cinco de Mayo* to appropriate patriotic topics, September 16, 1919, was the first time that the image of *La Virgen de Guadalupe* appeared in conjunction with patriotic topics of Mexico. In this representation, a banner with the image of the Virgen, submissive and passive, was carried by a Mexican revolutionary. In the lower right-hand corner was a small portrait of Miguel Hidalgo. The appearance of the Virgen image next to Mexican heroes such as Hidalgo augmented the impact upon the Mexican woman's consciousness. Three months later, as if to reinforce the message – that the ideal woman was the sexually pure woman — the legend of the Indian Virgen was a feature story.[4] This image of the Virgen was also a prominent image during the Chicano Movement. It is as if during times of anxiety and anguish caused by social turmoil that bring about unknown, and, at times, unexpected changes, and take the woman outside the home that she must be reminded by a social code — verbal, written, or visual — to maintain her sexual purity, to be an "angel" in the Mexican home.

Consequently, it is no surprise that even though the Constitution of 1917 was a direct result of the Mexican Revolution[5] and that the Mexican *Soldadera*, like indentured servants, devotedly followed the Revolutionary into the battlefields,[6] equality was not automatically bestowed upon the women. Although in November, 1916, the Latin American Women's League met in Merida, Yucatán to discuss, among other topics, women's suffrage and later sent a representative to the Queretaro Convention of 1917 to seek the inclusion of the right of women to vote into the constitution, the right to vote was denied to the Mexican woman.[7] Other rights, however, such as the limitation of work hours and the protection of pregnant women in the work force were instituted into the Constitution of 1917.[8] Even these rights were insignificant, since Venustiano Carranza did not enforce the constitution of 1917.[9] This anti-feminist attitude was also prevalent in *La Prensa*. Thus while the feminist Movement began to emerge in Mexico, editorial essays against the Movement began to be intensified in *La Prensa*, and it was not uncommon to see anti-Feminist Movement articles with such titles as "Lo que pierde la mujer a cambio de su libertad" appear next to Vasconcelos' essays pleading for the equality of men.[10] This anti-Feminist attitude was also affecting the women writing in *La Prensa*. Even though most of the women publishing in the newspaper had not been prolific, works by women had been appearing consistently; now the appearance of their works began to diminish drastically. At times, eight to ten months would go by without the appearance of a short story, poem, or *epistolario*, written by a Mexican woman.

While not all Mexican women were confronting the Victorian attitudes that were apparent on the pages of *La Prensa*, Rosario Sansores and Maria Enriqueta, two Mexican exiles, did not hesitate to respond to the restrictive milieu that it produced. During this time, Rosario Sansores published "El Compañero,"[11] a poem depicting a relationship between lovers from a feminist point of view, and Maria Enriqueta, published an *epistolario femenino* that satirically confronted men who do not like romantic women who pursue men.[12] While Maria Enriqueta was capable of writing serious feminist poetry, as she had done in 1914 with her poem, "Para tus manos,"[13] her writings that were being published after 1917 were usually *epistolarios* — but this was also true of other women writers. Rosario Sansores often demonstrated the petrifying mental and emotional condition of women whose sexuality and intellectual growth were denied.

Maria Enriqueta, more direct and feminist than Sansores, confronts the hypocrisy of men and the destructiveness of love affairs or relationships that lose the spontaneity of movement and growth. Many images of death, decay, and disintegration appear in the poems that deal with relationships that are initiated, restricted, and controlled by men. However, it would be naive to assume that these women were constantly autonomous; in fact, their intellectual perceptibility vacillated between their feministic views and their Victorian milieu, but their literary contributions, although severely limited, are the foundation for the contemporary Chicana writer.

Today the Chicana is still being affected as Ruth Horowitz' documents in *Honor and the American Dream*[14], by a restrictive male-oriented attitude that predominates in the Chicano Community. For example, anyone studying Chicano literature will quickly learn that the first three Quinto Sol Prizes were given to three prominent Chicanos, but few know that Estela Portillo received the Quinto Sol Literary award in 1971.[15] Furthermore, a review in Bruce-Novoa's book, *Chicano Authors: Inquiry by Interview* demonstrates that during the twenty-year period, 1959–1979, very few Chicanas were being published. Their contributions were further restricted by the fact that many literary journals that emerged during this period were and are editorially dominated and controlled by men. Consequently, just as the Spanish-language newspapers had been controlled by men in earlier periods, so is the Chicano literary environment. Moreover, just as some Mexican women confronted their restrictive milieu of the early 1900s, so have the Chicanas struggled to publish their creative works in journals, chapbooks, poetry, short story collections, and in a very limited number of novels.

While in the 1980s there are many Chicanas writing and confronting the Victorian attitudes that still predominate in the United States, I will use Bernice Zamora's poem "Penitents"[16] to illustrate that she confronts the male-oriented society by reclaiming the woman's matriarchal, historical past. She is able to reclaim the woman's mythological history by using feminine symbols and images within the context of a religious, masculine domain that is the setting of the poem "Penitents." For example, the Holy Week environment of the poem had its beginnings in a matriarchal tradition. Originally, Easter was a "Springtime sacrificial festival named for the Saxon Goddess, Eostre ..."[17] Its pagan beginnings are further evident in the fact that its "dating system was based on the old lunar calendar. It is fixed as the first Sunday after the first full moon after the Spring equinox, formerly the 'pregnant' phase of Eostre passing into the fertile season. The Christian festival wasn't called Easter until the Goddess's name was given to it in the late middle ages." Zamora reclaims the matriarchal role by placing the woman in the center of a sacred ceremony which in modern times men have redefined to exclude women. For example, the "morada" that Zamora speaks of in her poem, "Penitents," was fenced-off with picket or barbed-wire fence to keep intruders out.[19] Just as a fence had been used to encircle the thirteen women that were mentioned in *La Prensa*, the fence, in this case, is used to keep women out of the Holy Week Christian ceremony. However, in spite of this attempt to keep women out, Bruce-Novoa cites that the men who have purposely excluded the woman from the ritual in *La morada* unsuspectingly bring her presence into the ceremony by their own selection of items – "type O Blood," rosary beads – that are needed to carry out the yearly ritual.[20] However, Bruce-Novoa did not go far enough. While Bernice Zamora's use of the serpent imagery is important in redefining woman's role, her skillful use of images and symbols illustrates that, while the physical body of the woman is not present, her mythological, historical past is ubiquitous. For example, the line in the center of the poem, ". . . clacking prayer wheels jolt the hissing spine to uncoil wailing tongues of Nahuatl converts. . ."[21] illustrates how the serpent sound made as the ceremony is being performed, recaptures the matriarchal history of the woman, and merges the woman's presence into the center of the ceremony. Furthermore, this image produces an androgenous imagery. For example, the ageless serpent "was also Kundalini, the inner female soul of man in serpent shape, coiled in the pelvis, induced through proper practice of yoga to uncoil and mount through the spinal chacras toward the head, bringing infinite wisdom."[22] The presence of the Nahuatl converts in the center of the poem also links the ceremony to the Aztec Goddess, Tlazolteotl, her symbol was the broom, and she was usually associated with the snake, moon, and the screech owl. In Mexico, missionary clergy diabolized the Mother-deities by teaching the legend that Tlazolteotl's sacred women wandered "through the air, descending when they wished to earth. . . They haunted cross-roads to practice their maleficient deeds. . ."[23] This legend is very similar to the legend of *La Llorona* in the Southwest. The image of the wheel suggests yet another goddess imagery, for the karmic wheel was a "primary Oriental symbol of the Goddess as ruler of Fate."[24] Furthermore, "Tantric tradition showed the wheel as a mandala centering on the three totems of the Triple Goddess, the dove (Virgin-Creatress), serpent (Mother-Perserver), and sow (Crone-Destroyer). This mandala established 'the six realms of the round of being,' the sacred Hexagram,"[25] also an androgynous symbol.[26]

Once the Goddess' presence has entered the center of the ceremony, the *alabado*, an authentic *alabado* sung by penitents, seeks its original messengers, the women. The gospel says that originally only women announced Jesus' resurrection and that only Mary Magdalene and her women attended Jesus' tomb, because men were barred from the mysteries of the Goddess.[27] Of course, now the legend of Mary Magdalene has undergone a lot of myth-making that has changed her role in the crucifixion of Jesus Christ,[28] but Zamora reclaims woman's history by use of feminine symbols and imagery. Consequently, the significance of the line, "From the mountains alabados are heard:"[29] becomes evident as mountains are viewed as representing the Great Mother. Mountains also have a sexual symbolism associated with them "for in every land the mountains were identified with breasts, belly or mons veneris of the Earth."[30] Bruce-Novoa's study also states that the woman's presence in the ceremony is exemplified by the "type O blood" used in the ceremony — O being the universal symbol for woman.[31] In addition to this symbolic meaning, the universal symbol, O, combined with the visual image of the cross that is alluded to in the *alabado*, produces the symbol that represents sexual harmony. The origin of this symbolic representation dates to pre-Christian times when the cross, a male symbol of the phallic Tree of Life, often appeared in conjunction with the female genital circle or oval to signify the sacred marriage.[32] In Egypt "the male cross and female orb composed the amulet of blessedness, charm of sexual harmony."[33]

Finally, in the final stanza of the poem, the ceremony, having been violated and desecrated as "crater lakes and desecrated groves" allures "irresistibly" its original performers, the women. The reader's consciousness is thus raised and, like the woman in the poem, "wished to swim arroyos and know their estuaries where, for one week, all is sacred in the valley."[34] Zamora has skillfully and successfully created a matriarchal milieu within the poem that recaptures woman's mythological past by encircling the poem within feminine symbols and images — the poem starts with the letter "O", the symbol for woman, and the first letter of the goddess, Ostara, and ends the poem, as Bruce-Novoa indicates, with a fertile feminine symbol, the valley.

Bernice Zamora, like Rosario Sansores and Maria Enriqueta, confronts the destructiveness of a society that is male-oriented, but unlike Sansores and Maria Enriqueta who are very closely tied to the Romantic literary tradition, Zamora's aggressive, blunt, angry poetry seeks to humanize the inhuman by reclaiming her matriarchal history to create a harmonious, androgynous existence.

Notes

[1] In my study concerning Victorian attitudes the following are some of the sources that I have used: Walter E. Houghton, *The Victorian Frame of Mind* 1830–1870 (New Haven: Yale Univ. Press, 1957); Lytton Strachey, *Queen Victoria* (London: Chatto & Windus, 1969); Lytton Strachey, *Eminent Victorians* (London: Collins, 1967), and Anne Goodwyn Jones, *Tomorrow is Another Day: The Woman Writer in the South, 1859–1936* (Baton Rouge: Louis. State Univ. Press, 1981).

[2] In my study concerning the Feminist Movement the following are some of the sources that I have used: Sheila Rowbotham, *Women, Resistance and Revolution* (New York: Pantheon Books, 1972); Sheila Rowbotham, *Hidden from History* (New York: Pantheon, 1974); Ellen Carol DuBois, *Feminism and Suffrage: The Emergence of an Independent Women's Movement in America 1848–1869* (Ithaca: Cornell Univ. Press, 1978); Sarah Eisenstein, *Give Us Bread But Give Us Roses* (Boston: Routledge & Kegan Paul, 1983); and Barbara Mayer Wertheimer, *We Were There: The Story of Working Women in America* (New York: Pantheon Books, 1977).

[3] Sandra M. Gilbert and Susan Gubar, *The Madwoman in the Attic* (New Haven: Yale University Press, 1979), p. 17.

4   "La Leyenda de la Virgen India," *La Prensa*, 19 December 1919, p. 13.
5   James W. Wilkie, *The Mexican Revolution: Federal Expenditure and Social Change Since 1910* (Berkeley: University of California Press, 1970), pp. 64–65.
6   "La Soldadera Mexicana," *La Prensa*, 14 February 1916, p. 4.
7   E. V. Neimeyer. Jr., *Revolution at Queretaro: The Mexican Constitution Convention of 1916–1917* (Austin: The University of Texas Press, 1974) pp. 206–10.
8   Neimeyer, p. 240.
9   Wilkies, p. 65.
10 "Lo que pierde la mujer a cambio de su libertad," *La Prensa*, Suplemento Ilustrado, 23 June 1929, p. 6.
11 Rosario Sansores. "El Compañero," *La Prensa*, 27 October 1919.
12 Maria Enriqueta. "Carta de Mujer," *La Prensa*, 21 November 1914, p. 5.
13 Maria Enriqueta. "Para Tus Manos," *La Prensa*, 27 November 1914.
14 Ruth Horowitz, *Honor and the American Dream* (New Brunswick, New Jersey: Rutgers University Press, 1983).
15 [Juan] Bruce-Novoa, *Chicano Authors: Inquiry by Interview* (Austin: University of Texas Press, 1980).
16 Bernice Zamora, *Restless Serpents* (Menlo Park, Calif.: Disensos Literarios, 1976), p. 8.
17 Barbara G. Walker, "Easter," in *The Woman's Encyclopedia of Myths and Secrets* (San Francisco: Harper and Row Publishers, 1983), p. 267.
18 Walker, pp. 267–69.
19 Donaldo Urioste, a short conversation during the First International Symposium on Chicano Culture, July 5–7, 1984, Universität Mainz at Germersheim, West Germany.
20 Bruce-Novoa, Seminar Lecture at San Antonio College, Summer 1980.
21 Zamora, p. 8.
22 Walker, p. 903.
23 Walker, p. 1001.
24 Walker, p. 1072.
25 Walker, p. 1072.
26 Walker, p. 402.
27 Walker, pp. 613–16.
28 Walker, p. 616.
29 Zamora, p. 8.
30 Walker, p. 695.
31 Bruce-Novoa, Summer Seminar at San Antonio College, Summer 1980.
32 Walker, p. 188.
33 Walker, p. 188.
34 Zamora, p. 8.

III CHICANO THEATER

From Stereotypes to Archetypes: Chicano Theaters' Reflection of the Mexicano in the United States

Jorge A. Huerta

Much has been written about the Chicanos' view of themselves in Chicano theater, both by the playwrights and the observers of this theatrical movement, since 1965. The majority of Chicano dramas have centered around the Chicano as a disenfranchised member of the North American society, a sort of marginal participant in and non-beneficiary of the "American Dream." Within the broader context of the Chicano experience is the Mexicano experience in this country: what it is like to be a recent immigrant or even a long-standing transplant from the mother country.

Throughout the canon of Chicano drama there is a link with Mexico, foremost through the language, and secondly through the characters' references as immigrants or as the children of Mexican parents. The focus is usually on the Chicano, but the presence of the Mexicano is seldom ignored. It is the purpose of this paper to investigate this presence in the drama and to come to a conclusion about how the Chicanos view their Mexican counterparts in the United States.

Luis Valdez, founder of the Teatro Campesino, first created the actos using commedia dell'arte techniques. The teatro satirized the villains in their daily struggles, using stereotypical characters to get their points across. According to Valdez in 1971, "The reality reflected in an acto is thus a social reality, whether it pertains to campesinos or to vatos locos, not psychologically deranged self-projections but rather, group archetypes."[1] However, an archetype is representative of universals such as God, The Mother, the first-of-its-kind. The characters in the early actos were more often stereotypes, especially the villains, for the audiences of farmworkers loved to see their enemies ridiculed. However, Valdez and other playwrights and teatros have been reticent to portray Mexicans in a disrespectful manner, especially if those Mexicans were parent figures. Usually the parents were born in Mexico, while their children were born in the U.S. and identified themselves as Chicanos or Mexican-Americans. Valdez attempted to portray his Mexican characters with cautious respect, yet he also underscored their human foibles.

Valdez' first full-length play, *The Shrunken Head of Pancho Villa*, dramatizes the plight of a Mexicano/Chicano family struggling to survive in rural California.

Like all of Valdez' later plays, the family is foremost in *The Shrunken Head of Pancho Villa*, and like most of his other works, this play exposes the dissolution of that nuclear unit. It is a Chicano play because its focus is on the Mexican in this country, but its roots are firmly planted in the Mexican heritage of the parents, Cruz and Pedro.

From the beginning, it is apparent that Pedro is an alcoholic, ineffectual as parent, husband or worker. In contrast, Cruz is stronger, although she is also unable to improve their lot in life. Thus we see the parents in constant conflict with their Chicano children, each of whom suffers his or her cultural identity crisis. The children represent types: the pachuco, the sellout, and the Chicana who does not know what she is. The play cannot be classified realistic because of its surreal elements: the oldest son is only a head, he and his sister eat the cockroaches that keep getting larger as the play progresses. Yet the characters of Cruz and Pedro are as true to nature as possible, while the others are close to stereotypes or even caricatures. The Mexicans are real, the Chicanos and Anglos are not.

From the inception of the contemporary Chicano theater movement in 1965, with Valdez always at the lead, we see Mexicans as parents, keeping that link with the mother country through their customs and language. Pedro and Cruz speak broken English, often confusing words, creating a comic effect, but Valdez does not do this in order to ridicule them. They are ultimately very real to the Mexican/Chicano audience who can relate to these people, and their laughter is based on loving recognition rather than scorn.

In the second act Pedro is awakened by Cruz when she catches their daughter Lupe in the arms of her boyfriend. "He was after Lupe, hombre," Cruz tells Pedro, to which he replies: "Where's he at?" as he heads for the kitchen. Pulling him back, she points him towards the front door shouting "He went that way! Go, hombre, serve for something." Still not leaving, Pedro shouts "Where's my rifle! WHERE'S MY GUN?" Lupe throws herself on him crying "No, Papa!" Pedro shouts "You chattap! WHERE'S MY GUN WOMEN!" After a brief pause Cruz replies "You don' got a gun Pedro." Silence. When Lupe tries to explain the situation Pedro interrupts her with "CHATTAP! Dios mio, how lousy." He grabs his wine bottle and says "You see? This is what I get for coming to the land of the gringos. No respect! I should have stay in Zacatecas."[2]

Although the author is depicting a Mexican father who is certainly not a role model, he is lovingly portrayed. His human foibles are forgiven by a barrio audience because Chicanos and Mexicans understand his defeat. Certainly, Pedro and Cruz could be portrayed as caricatures, but this would lessen the effect of their plight: we must be able to discover their common humanity even as we understand their familiar foibles. Cruz and Pedro represent all Chicanos' parents in a way, and if not their parents, then certainly their grandparents.

They are Valdez' first archetypical parents, reminders of the need for family unity.

In his early mito, *Bernabé*, Valdez explored a neo-Aztec mythic realm, combining contemporary characters with allegorical and historical archetypes. Bernabé is *el loquito del pueblo*, the village idiot who is in love with La Tierra, The Earth. Bernabé is a Chicano, but his mother is Mexican, referred to in the cast of characters simply as La Madre. In her analysis of this mito Betty Diamond asserts that ". . . this mother is someone we would all flee and disrespect — a hypochondriacal, selfish, possessive, shrewish woman who thinks sex is dirty and yet sees herself as a 'good Catholic. . .'"[3] Yes, La Madre is a good Catholic, and yes, she's got aches and pains, and yes, she is possessive of Bernabé, for he is all she has in the world. "Shrewish?" I do not think so; but definitely a woman who stands up against her alcoholic brother, and who finds Bernabé's habit of masturbating in a hole in the ground disgusting. Bernabé's mother is as close to archetypical as Valdez has gotten, for she represents a force opposite that of the father, El Sol, the Supreme Giver of Life. In fact, La Madre loses Bernabé to El Sol when he symbolically marries La Tierra, daughter of the sun in a re-creation of an Aztec sacrifice recognizing that "la vida es muerte, y la muerte es vida."[4] In the "real world" Bernabé is buried in his hole; on the spiritual plane he joins La Tierra to become a New Man. Bernabé finds ultimate fulfillment, but his mother is left behind to suffer in loneliness.

Perhaps because La Madre expresses her suffering to those around her, Ms. Diamond finds her excessively self-centered and hypochondriacal, but these characteristics are common in the barrio among older women, and the mother's suffering, her crosses, add to the pathos of her station. La Madre is a terrestrial, contemporary symbol of a Mexican mother, but El Sol is a celestial representation of an indigenous father-figure, indeed pre-Mexican although he speaks Spanish rather than Nahuatl. In his power and stature, he goes beyond an earthly father to the archetypical Creator.

Thus far we have dealt with Valdezian Mexican parents in only two plays, for they are representative of others such as the mother and father in *Soldado Razo*[5], or the mother in *Dark Root of a Scream*[6], the first an acto and the second its contrasting mito about the death of a Chicano in the Vietnam War. Those parents are typical; loving and warm towards their sons. And like the mother in *Bernabé* or the parents in *The Shrunken Head of Pancho Villa*, these Mexican parents are not at the center of the story. Instead, the parents frame the event, giving the Chicano characters their Mexican identity, contrasting with their Chicano characteristics. The parents reveal the differences between the Mexican and the Chicano in all of Valdez' plays, in fact, demonstrating the "culture gap" between Mexican customs and Chicano attitudes.

Whereas Valdez includes Mexicans in all of his plays, Carlos Morton writes almost exclusively about Chicanos and Chicanas, as well as allegorical figures.

Mr. Morton creates his own vision of the Chicano in history, and the Mexican does not play a major role in his dramaturgy. The only Mexican characters that do appear in Morton's published plays are Adan Pelado and Eva Martini in *El Cuento de Pancho Diablo*. This play is a "cosmo-comic" tale of what would happen, if the Devil resigned his post in Hell and ascended to earth, with the result that Dios descended to investigate the situation. The play takes place in Heaven, Hell, and on earth in Manhattan and a town in Texas where Eva runs "El Dry Martini" bar. Although Eva and Adan tell us they are from Mexico, their characters are very Chicano. They speak the bilingual jargon of Chicanos, as do all of the other characters, and although they originated in Penjamo, Jalisco, it is evident that they have become "Chicano-ized" over the years. Eva calls herself "Martini" when her actual surname is Martinez, because she does not want to be considered either Mexican or Chicana, but eventually she realizes her cultural roots.

When Pancho Diablo quits his post in Hell he soon becomes disgusted with a life of menial labor on earth and uses his skills to establish "Pancho's Palacio," the world's largest funeral parlor, in the middle of Manhattan. Adan Pelado has been denied entrance to Heaven because, in his words, "Es que I never went to church and I passed most of the time pistiando y chasing viejas."[7] Forced to wander the earth, a lost spirit, Adan finally finds refuge in one of Pancho's coffins. But instead of resting peacefully, Adan joins forces with Pancho to establish the Diablo Liberation Army. This is Morton's allegorical portrayal of a Mexican, based on pure imagination, but important because Adan is a revolutionary, in battle against economic and political forces while in league with the Devil himself. The juxtaposition is pure Morton, comic in its technique, but ultimately symbolic of the fact that indeed, many Mexicans have led the struggle in the United States.

El Cuento de Pancho Diablo is Morton's modern morality play, recalling elements of Biblical lore with a distinctly Chicano flavor. He describes Pancho as "un vato loco. A pachuco type with bigotes who wears shades, huarachis, and a poncho."[8] Thus the Devil is clearly a Chicano. Dios, however, is described in general terms, with no particular ethnicity, although he is "a very hip and unfathomable vato with a Zapata mustache who smokes Cuban cigars."[9] The use of the colloquial term, "vato," indicates Morton's linguistic predilection in the entire script, for most of the characters use pachuco caló such as "ese," "vato," and the like, again heightening the Chicano flavor of the play.

Adan is representative of the Mexican as political activist. Because he is an Everyman, not really a recognizable Mexican type, Adan cannot be analyzed in the same manner as the Mexican activists in Teatro de la Esperanza's docu-drama *Guadalupe*. In this play about a group of Mexicans and Chicanos who take action against the town fathers in the town of Guadalupe, the major figures are the Mexican parents. But unlike the Valdezian parents who seem unable to change their fate, the parents in *Guadalupe* take action.

In a series of thirteen scenes held together by musical narration, we see the parents as central figures, mobilizing against the racist schools and other oppressive elements in their small rural community. The people in this piece are based on actual persons whose lives were investigated by members of the Teatro and then dramatized. True to life, the Mexicans speak only Spanish while the Anglos and Chicanos communicate in either English or Spanglish. The villains are Anglo or Mexican-American in *Guadalupe* and their characters are not as developed as those of the Mexican heroes and heroines.[10]

Another Teatro de la Esperanza collective creation is *La Víctima*. This play is based on a fictitious situation framed by documentation of the factual mass deportations of Mexicans during the current century. The plot follows Amparo Villa as a young child leaving Mexico during the tumult of the Revolution, growing up in the flapper era in the U.S., marrying, returning to Mexico and eventually being smuggled back into the States when her husband dies in the homeland. Crucial to the plot line is the loss of her first-born, Samuel, who is inadvertently separated from Amparo at the train station when the Mexicans are being deported in trains like cattle. Thus in this play we see a Mexican central figure as child, young woman, parent, and old woman. And although Amparo has been raised in the U.S., she is definitely Mexican in her language, customs, and character.

Amparo is an archetypical mother figure whose entire life is spread before us; whose struggles and tragedies become larger-than-life. Her separation from her son, the death of her husband, and the ultimate pain of being denied by her first-born who is now an officer for the Immigration and Naturalization Service and deports her to Mexico — these are events and coincidences that the great tragedies are based upon. When her son is interrogating her, Amparo knows who he is and even lets him know that she is aware of his identity, but he refuses to acknowledge her as his mother shouting " ¡Sáquenla!" in one of the great dramatic moments in Chicano theater.[11]

Amparo represents all Mexican mothers who have suffered the pain of denial by their children. Yet she is not portrayed as another helpless victim, for the real *víctima* is Sam. In fact, Amparo is another activist, urging her children to stand up against the factory owners and join the strike. It is her presence in the picket line that causes her arrest and eventual deportation/rejection by Sam. In this play the archetypical mother is contrasted with the Mexican-American son, doing his job, who is in turn contrasted with his Chicana daughter. None of these characters are shallow "types," but full-blown characters. Sam's daughter is discovering her Chicanismo in college while Sam is struggling with his identity; a man in conflict with himself. Amparo knows who she is.

In contrast to the fully-developed Amparo, one of the earliest stereotypical Mexicans to appear in Chicano drama is the Revolucionario in the Teatro Campesino's *Los Vendidos*, written in 1968. The action of this acto takes place in Honest Sancho's Used Mexican Lot in which Sancho is attempting to sell a Mexican to a Miss JIM-enez from the governor's office. Sancho is demonstrating different "models," or types to her and when he comes to the Revolucionario the audience is prepared for the stereotype. The stereotyping is intended, for the Teatro was exposing the negative images of the Mexican that the media have projected over the years. Miss Jimenez asks "What does he do?" to which Sancho replies:

> You name it, he does it. He rides horses, stays in the mountains, crosses deserts, plains, rivers, leads revolutions, follows revolutions, kills, can be killed, serves as a martyr, hero, movie star – did I say movie star? Did you ever see Viva Zapata? Viva Villa, Villa Rides, Pancho Villa Returns, Pancho Villa Goes Back, Pancho Villa Meets Abbott and Costello –"[12]

Although Ms. Jimenez has not seen the revolutionary in any of these movies, she does recall seeing him on television when he asks: "Is there a Frito Bandito in your house?" taken from a popular commercial of the time.[13] This is not the Teatro Campesino's image of the Mexican revolutionary, but the distorted portrayals the Teatro is attempting to expose. It is the Chicano's image of the media's caricatures replayed for the audience's edification.

In sharp contrast to the stereotyped revolutionary in *Los Vendidos*, Valdez later protrayed La Tierra in *Bernabé* as a *soldadera* of the Mexican Revolution. The Earth is therefore characterized as one of the masses, in battle with oppressive forces. When Bernabé tells La Tierra that she is his, she asks: "¿Y como soy tuya, Bernabé? ¿Como y cuando has luchado por mi? Toda tu vida has trabajado en mis files como un perro ¿y para qué? Para que otros se hagan ricos con tu sudor, para que otros hombres sean mis dueños."[14] She exhorts Bernabé to kill for her and die for her in exemplary revolutionary fervor, but instead he simply dies for her in his symbolic marriage. Still, it is important to note that La Tierra is a Mexican, a woman, and a revolutionary archetype. Further, we are reminded of Cruz in *The Shrunken Head of Pancho Villa* who finally reveals the fact that she was a soldadera with Villa herself.[15]

In the Teatro Campesino's *La Gran Carpa de los Rasquachis*, we again see a Mexican as immigrant, one Jesus Pelado Rasquachi who crosses into the U.S. in search of a better life. His fortunes are few, and after the dissolution of his family he dies, a broken man. However, in a later version of the piece Yvonne Yarbro-Bejarano points to the fact that Jesus is resurrected and joins forces with the Farmworkers' union, and is thus another revolutionary Mexican.[16]

Beyond the Mexican as revolutionary or political activist, Chicano playwrights have explored the image of the Mexican as dreamer as well. Perhaps the best example of this kind of portrayal is seen in *Puente Negro*, by Estela Portillo Trambley. Portillo Trambley is the most important Chicana playwright to date, a writer whose vision is firmly rooted in her native El Paso. Her border play, *Puente Negro,* is important because it presents the Mexican as dreamer, artist, and visionary. Most importantly, Portillo Trambley leaves her audience with a sense of hope rather than despair. Hers is a vision of poetic grace, of people who are talented; who know what they want and may be able to achieve their goals despite the odds. Although the play takes place in an abandoned shack on the U.S. side of the border, its characters evoke images of the life back home and especially of the life ahead of them.

Unlike the majority of Chicano dramas to date, *Puente Negro* deals only with Mexicans. Also unlike many of the other plays, the language is almost all in English. Thus it is not through the language that we know these people are Mexican, but by what they say and do. These people are on their way to becoming undocumented workers, but their dreams are not ordinary. Contrasted with the dreamers is their smuggler, La Chaparra, whose realistic vision of life gives her a contrasting cynicism necessary for the fuller development of the other characters.

The major dreamers in this play are a brother and sister dance team, Narciso and Amalia, who are intent upon seeing their names on a marquee in Chicago. Amalia tells Inocencia, who is in love with her brother that their dreams are inherited from their mother, a free spirit: "I loved what she was – brave, free. She danced like that. If we worked hard and loved what we were, she said, her dream for us would come true. But we had to make it come true."[17] For Amalia, Narciso tells the others, "Dancing is all."[18] There are no other undocumented workers in Chicano drama who are dancers or artists of any kind.

El Topo, another of the immigrants who crosses illegally with frequency, has dreams, but of a different, non-aesthetic nature. He tells the others of a place in California that people flock to to worship a mouse called Mickey. He understands what it takes to survive and conquer in the States and tells them: "I like gringos. They taught me something very important. It doesn't pay to work with your hands. It pays to work with your – cunning. It's part of their magic."[19] Perhaps because of its realistic style, *Puente Negro* is unique in its portrayal of undocumented immigrants in teatro Chicano. These Mexicans reveal their hopes above their frustrations, and expose the audience to their common humanity. El Topo tells the others: "Dreams! That's what the United States is made of. Gringos are not happy about mojados, but they have dreams – fairy tales."[20] In Portillo Trambley's vision these Mexicans just might get a piece of that dream.

In *Blacklight,* Portillo Trambley presents us with a Mexican father, Nacho, as dreamer, but his life has been shattered by too many tragic events and we are reminded of Pedro in *The Shrunken Head of Pancho Villa.* However, Portillo Trambley's portrayal of this father is more complete, more psychologically developed in this realistic/mythical play than is Valdez' Pedro. Nacho has a past that goes beyond familial relationships to his indigenous roots. He is perhaps too much in touch with his past, for in the present he is another alcoholic with little to show for his life. He calls upon the Maya gods and goddesses, and knows their myths; but he does not know his own family. His dreams are of the past, of returning to the old ways, but he cannot even grow a few stalks of corn in his dusty yard. He is contrasted with his dead brother, Polo, who was another kind of dream-seeker. Nacho's wife, Amalia, had been involved in an affair with Polo and refused to run off with him when she discovered she was carrying his child. Referring to Polo's special magic she tells her children: "The miracle was there, the discovery of something beyond the physical pleasure. My body was nourished, my spirit. A return to innocence, you could say, in spite of the scars and fears. . . ."[21]

Like the old gods, Polo is an invisible character, the Mexican as wonder-maker, a teller of tales and a man who could create beauty out of misery. Although we never see Polo, we get to know him through what the others say about him and realize that he is the other half of his brother; duality in indigenous terms. Polo is the invisible Mexican in a Chicano play about shattered dreams and broken lives; he is not the central figure, of course, but complements and completes the character of his brother by demonstrating what Nacho might have been. However, unlike *Puente Negro*, with its hope for the future, *Blacklight* leaves its audience with a sense of calamity, for Nacho's son, Mundo, is killed while Nacho is helplessly tied to a wooden carving of his Maya deities. The son is sacrificed, but the father lives on, another Chicano attempt to recall the ways of the past.

Finally, it is necessary to note the Mexican as comic figure, although the examples are few. Two plays that ridicule the Mexican in the U.S. are from El Paso: *Sun Images*, by Portillo Trambley, and *La Chamaca Brava*, by Lino and Ricardo Lopez Landy. Again, Portillo Trambley's script is mostly in English, although the major characters are Mexican. *Sun Images* employs a dual plot to demonstrate the amorous adventures of an old Mexicano contrasted with the exploits of his youthful Chicano counterparts. Don Estevan brings young Mexican women across the border to be his resident paramours. In this light-hearted tale, the ladies retain their virtue by putting him to sleep each night with brandy in his coffee and telling him ribald tales the next morning to satisfy his male ego. They call him "Don Estufas" because, as one of the women says: "He thinks he's one big furnace."[22] This is a definite caricature of a lecherous old man, in the tradition of commedia dell'arte and Moliere. Combined with the author's songs and music, this play pokes fun at the universal foibles of the old and the young, concluding with the obligatory "boy gets girl" and "woman gets man."

La Chamaca Brava ridicules upper-middle class Mexicans living in El Paso in a theatrical style that has its roots in farce. Written in a border dialect of Spanish, English and colloquialisms only the initiated can comprehend, the play satirizes the language, mores, morals, and masters in a typical Mexican bourgeois family aspiring to the American ideal. In this case the ideal is based on the liberation of the men rather than the women and the play can be criticized for its sexist message. Nonetheless, by satirizing a certain class of Mexicans the play could find great appeal in barrio theaters.

The opening lines of the play say it all:

LA ESPOSA: Ya, tu, buey! deja tu miquimaus mediteision y vete a lavar los platos. Miren, nomas que queique mas a todo dar me avente.
EL MARIDO: (Deja de leer y obedece sin disimular el panico) Si, si, como tu mandes, jany, como tu digas.
LA ESPOSA: Pronto, que no me gustan los maridos egones.
EL MARIDO: Si, si, ya voy, mujer . . .
LA ESPOSA: Y no me digas mujer, que soy la presidenta del Uimens Libereision.
EL MARIDO: Si, mi presidente, mi reina . . . (Sale)
LA ESPOSA: Y nada de reina, que somos republicanas.[23]

These are pure stereotypes, and we laugh at the language and the mannerisms. As the plot evolves the situation becomes central, rather than the characterizations, and the authors intend the humor to come from the eventual taming of the wife and daughter. In classical fashion, the young man who tames his shrew tells the audience the moral at the end of the play: "Si no te pones chango el primer dia, tendras que ser buey toda la vida."[24]

In conclusion, it becomes clear that in the Chicano's view of the Mexican there is a sense of brotherhood and empathy. There are few Mexican villains in Chicano drama; in fact they are often the most oppressed. Sometimes the Mexicans lead the struggle, while in other instances they soon become willing participants. Sometimes the Mexicano characters are archetypical representatives of a given force or theme; yet they might just as easily be presented as a stereotype, but only in order to draw attention to the media's usual practice.

The Mexican is representative of all ages, from kindergarten student, unable to speak English, to young migrant worker, to older, traditional parents and grand-parents. In most cases the Mexicano is not alone, but has a family to support him or her. Indeed, the Mexicans in Chicano theater seem to constantly assert the image and importance of La Familia to the Chicanos, whose struggle for survival sometimes makes them deny their heritage and/or their families. By examining the foregoing plays it becomes clear that the Chicanos view the Mexican as a sort of cultural connection, grounding their existence in United States society in a deeper heritage of myth, fantasy, and dreams. The Mexicans represent an indigenous past and a political present, expressed through pathos, comedy, melodrama, farce, ritual, and the surreal. By defining the Mexican, the Chicanos reinterpret their own identity — touching upon the collective uncon-scious to plumb the depths of their daily lives.

84

Notes

1   Luis Valdez, *Actos* (San Juan Bautista: Cucaracha Publications, 1971), p. 6.
2   Luis Valdez, *The Shrunken Head of Pancho Villa*, in *West Coast Plays*, 11/12 (Winter, Spring, 1982), p. 20.
3   Betty Ann Diamond, *"Brown Eyed Children of the Sun": The Cultural Politics of El Teatro Campesino* (Ann Arbor: University Microfilms, 1977), 149.
4   Roberto Garza, *Contemporary Chicano Theatre* (Notre Dame: University of Notre Dame Press, 1976), p. 55.
5   *Soldado Razo* is in Valdez, *Actos*, pp. 131–45.
6   *Dark Root of a Scream* is in Lilian Faderman and Omar Salinas, *From the Barrio* (San Francisco: Canfield Press, 1973), pp. 79–98.
7   Carlos Morton, *El Cuento de Pancho Diablo*, *Grito del Sol* I (July–September 1976), p. 58.
8   Morton, p. 39.
9   Morton, p. 39.
10 From the unpublished ms. in the author's collection.
11 From the unpublished ms. in the author's collection.
12 Valdez, *Actos*, p. 43.
13 Valdez, *Actos*, p. 43.
14 Garza, p. 52.
15 Valdez, *West Coast Plays*, p. 48.
16 Yvonne Yarbo-Bejarano, "From *acto* to *mito*: A Critical Appraisal of the Teatro Campesino," in *Modern Chicano Writers*, ed. Joseph Sommers and Tomás Ybarra-Frausto (Englewood Cliffs, N.J.: Prentice-Hall, 1979), p. 183.
17 Estela Portillo, *Sor Juana and Other Plays* (Ypsilanti: Bilingual Press, 1983), p. 18.
18 Portillo, p. 15.
19 Portillo, p. 24.
20 Portillo, p. 23.
21 Portillo, p. 130.
22 Estela Portillo, *Sun Images*, *Revista Chicano-Riqueña*, 7 (Winter 1979), 22.
23 Lino and Ricardo Lopez Landy, *La Chamaca Brava*, *Grito del Sol*, 1 (April–June 1976), p. 39.
24 Lino and Ricardo L. Landy, p. 54.

The Mexican Stage in the Southwestern United States as a Sounding Board for Cultural Conflict

Nicolás Kanellos

As I have shown elsewhere, the Mexican/Hispanic professional theatre in the Southwest dates back to the mid-nineteenth century.[1] It is my thesis that from its origins up to the present day, the Mexican/Hispanic theatre, besides serving esthetic and entertainment needs, also served the social and political purpose of the community, which conceived of itself at different times as a conquered people whose culture was threatened, later as a colony in exile ("México de afuera"), and today as a minority oppressed by a larger, monolithic culture.

One writer, Brokaw, has questioned the reality of political motivation for the theatre of the past. Writing in 1977, he categorized as "mythology" the belief that today's teatros, like El Teatro Campesino, which "cleaves to certain social and political issues which date back at least to the Anglo occupation,"[2] are more or less continuing the tradition of a resident theatre. According to Brokaw, "controversial subjects, therefore, had no place in such enterprises," i.e., Mexican theatre in the Southwest. "When Mexican affairs were mentioned in the plays, it was invariably in terms of political celebration." (Brokaw, p. 538). It was Chicanos, according to Brokaw, who began to use theatre for a political purpose. In the late 1920s, "The teatros ceased and theatrical production in the Spanish language was left in the hands of the Church and its annual productions of *Los pastoreles* [sic]. There it remained until the Chicanos of the 1960s decided that drama had a function to fulfill in their scheme of things." (Brokaw, p. 540).

Brokaw does not take into account the nature of the audiences that attended the shows in question, nor the social, political, and cultural environment of the Mexican colonies during the period which he studies, i.e., the 1880s through the 1920s. On the other hand, judging from documentary evidence in newspapers, I have observed that the special social and political relations of the stage to the Mexican community begin to take shape very early. Of the ten or so resident theatrical companies that were performing in California during the 1860s, the company directed by the great Mexican actor, Gerardo López del Castillo (Compañía Dramática Española) may serve as an early example of the special relationship that Mexican and Hispanic theatres would always maintain with their communities in the United States.

First of all, the Company's director, Gerardo López del Castillo, was an intensely patriotic individual who fought against Maximilian and, after returning to Mexico following his residence in California, became known as a tireless promoter of a Mexican national theatre. In San Francisco, López del Castillo served as the very active president of the Sociedades Patrióticas Mexicanas. At all times, his patriotic activities, his acting and his speeches — the latter were published in the San Francisco newspaper, *El Eco del Pacífico*[3] — were considered as the finest example of the Spanish language and as furthering the preservation of Mexican and Hispanic culture in an alien environment.

At all times the Compañía Dramática Española was available to the community for benefits and fundraisers. In fact, one of the most important causes that was supported by its performances was the raising of funds for Juárez' army; after the war, funds were also raised for the widows and orphans produced by the war.

Finally it is important to note that companies like the Compañía Dramática Española served the Hispanic community at large, not just the elite, but the grass roots as well. This fact is illustrated by the defense of the grass roots audience made by a *La Voz de Méjico* critic writing in 1862 when a writer for the French-language newspaper, *Le Phare*, penned "injurias e insultos a todo un público. . . Si algunos vaqueros descubrió el Sr. del Phare en la reunión y si tal oficio le parece bajo, el trabajo es en América el mejor título que se puede tener al respeto general. . . ."[4]

Along those lines, as far as the theatre appealing to broad sectors of the society and its producers having political and social motivation, there is an earlier example. The theatre house in Monterey, California, was the billiard hall in José Abrego's Inn, and there is ample evidence that the performances of Spanish-language melodrama by subscription were attended by both Spanish and English-speakers.[5] In an 1847 fire at the inn, four hundred volunteers of the Stevenson Regiment came to the rescue and stole everything from Abrego. During the process, they discovered barrels of lead for bullets.[6] It is very possible that Abrego was an insurgent!

By the turn of the century, companies were touring throughout the Southwest. But the rapid expansion and boom of the Spanish-language stage really began with the massive immigration that took place during the Mexican Revolution. Theatres became the primary cultural and entertainment institutions for Mexican and Mexican American families alike. Following the initiative of elites who came as religious and political refugees of the Revolution, the theatres became an integral part of the concept of "colonias mexicanas en el exilio" or "el México de afuera." As such, theatrical performances in the Spanish language were seen as preserving the language, customs, and mores of transplanted Mexicans and culturally oppressed Mexican Americans. The theatre further offered clean and healthy entertainment for the whole family in contrast to what was considered as the looser morality of Anglo-American diversions.

In the April 26, 1916, edition of San Antonio's *La Prensa*, a critic commented on the importance of the theatre in this regard. For the community, the Spanish-language stage was ". . . un espectáculo verdaderamente artístico, culto moralizador. Por otra parte puede considerarse como una obra patriótica y de solidaridad de raza, el concurrir a las veladas artísticas del Teatro Juárez donde un modesto grupo de actores mexicanos luchan por la vida en suelo extraño, haciéndonos conocer las más preciadas joyas del teatro contemporáneo en nuestra lengua materna o sea el dulcísimo y sonoro idioma de Cervantes."

On February 23, 1918, *La Prensa de Los Angeles* justified the construction of the Teatro Hidalgo as follows: "En esta ciudad se hacía sentir ya la imperiosa necesidad de tener espectáculo de alta cultura y moralidad en nuestro idioma."

The June 1, 1919 issue of San Antonio's *La Prensa* gave the following reason for the Sociedad de la Unión's construction of a theatre: "levantar el concepto que nuestra raza tiene en el extranjero." And, indeed, the sale of bonds for the construction of the theatre was highly promoted as patriotic. What is evident from the three quotes, is the patriotism and "solidaridad de la raza," as well as the reinforcement of Cervantes' sweet and sonorous language, and that the community felt that its culture was threatened and that the theatre had a definite role to play in its protection and survival.

Even attendance at the more modest Mexican circuses and tent shows was a motive for nationalism. In the December 16, 1917 edition of Los Angeles' *El Heraldo de México*, the public was exhorted to attend the Escalante Circus in this manner: "Si usted no ha ido al circo, dispóngase a hacerlo hoy mismo, no olvidando que se trata de un espectáculo mexicano que en muchos sentidos, como en arroyo y limpieza de sus actos, es superior a los grandes circos americanos." Once again the looser morality of Anglo-American entertainments, besides language and nationality, was in question.

And as the stage declined during the Depression and the great repatriations which devastated theatre audiences, theatre critics made last-ditch appeals to the nationalism of Mexicans and the need to protect the culture.

"Necesitamos teatro . . . siquiera sea para contrarrestar la influencia de letras, costumbres y tendencias sajonas que nos envuelven por momentos," decried Los Angeles' *La Opinión*.[7] The same newspaper also appealed for the community to support struggling companies of actors: ". . . todos son nacidos y educados en México, entusiastas de la conservación de la cultura hispana que ellos adquirieron, y unidos ahora por la necesidad artística de contrarrestar la influencia del teatro

88

extraño a nuestras tendencias, nuestra tradición y nuestras costumbres."[8] In 1931 another *Opinión* writer promoted theatrical attendance "por amor a nuestra cultura agonizante."[9]

But during the heyday of the Mexican/Hispanic stage in California, the culture was far from agonizing. Eight major theatre houses kept their stages busy during the 1920s offering everything from Spanish melodrama and *zarzuela* to vaudeville. The professional stage did not only prosper from the standard works from the stages of Mexico and Madrid, but dramatic and comedic material relating directly to the culture of Mexicans in the Southwest was developed. In fact, the greatest box-office successes were those involving the production of plays and *revistas* that reflected Mexican history and society in California and the Southwest.[10] In Los Angeles, a healthy cadre of playwrights developed to supply the stages with original scripts and librettos that dealt with the epic of California history, such as Adalberto Elías González' *Ramona* and *La Conquista de California*; discrimination and the clash of cultures, as in Brígido Caro's *Joaquín Murieta* and Eduardo Carrillo's *El proceso y muerte de Aurelio Pompa,* and of course, the great Repatriation, as in Antonio Helú's *Los mexicanos se van.* Caro's *Joaquín Murieta* was taken from the professional stage and produced by amateurs as a fundraiser for the Alianza Hispano Americana.[11] And Carrillo's politically sensitive play about the condemned Pompa was produced so many times that one critic finally appealed to the producers to let poor Pompa rest in peace.[12] The Pompa play was also used quite extensively to raise funds for the accused's defense (then entitled *El proceso de Aurelio Pompa*), as well as to raise funds for his widow after his execution.[13] Another work by Brígido Caro, *México y los Estados Unidos*, was a dramatic response to Calvin Coolidge's insulting statements about Mexico in 1927. A play about the Repatriation, Gabriel Navarro's *Los emigrados*, written in 1930, was promoted as a drama "fundado en una base del absoluto realismo."[14] Antonio Helú's *Los Mexicanos se van*, tauted by the June 13 and 20, 1932 editions of *La Opinión*, as an important play by a local author, openly criticizes the repatriation of Mexicans from California "en que algunos de ellos eran obligados a abandonar este país." The Mexican side of the Repatriation was depicted in Juan Bustillos Oro's 1933 drama, *Los que vuelven*, whose theme was described by the February 27, 1927 edition of *La Opinión* as "el doloroso tema de la Repatriación. En sus cuadros desfilan los desventajados, los que habiéndose adaptado a un medio de comodidades en el suelo extranjero, se ven ahora viviendo una vida precaria en su propia patria, luchando por readaptarse al nuevo medio."

So popular were these plays based on California Hispanic history, and the real life drama that the communities were experiencing, that in 1930 theatre impresarios banded together to try to change the royalty arrangements accorded the playwrights, as the latter were perceived by the impresarios as getting too much of the profits from the full houses that they brought in.

Whereas the full-length plays concentrated on the serious and epic dimensions of Hispanic life in California, the world of the *revista* and musical comedy treated the same topics with satire and low humor and provided an escape valve for working-class frustration. Such comics and *peladitos* as Don Chema, Guz Aguila and Roberto Soto el Panzón had been associated with the *revista* as a forum for piquant political commentary. In fact, before emigrating to the Los Angeles stage, Roberto Soto had been persecuted and censored repeatedly in Mexico for his biting commentary on the corrupt labor leader Morones.[15]

With such talented and well known comedians as Soto, Guz Aguila and the beloved Romualdo Tirado, Los Angeles' playwrights created such librettos about immigration and culture shock as Gabriel Navarro's *Los Angeles en Pijama*, Romualdo Tirado's *La Pocha y el Charro* and Ernesto González Jimenez' *De México a Los Angeles o Aventuras de un Sastre*. The latter is a typical tale of comedy and pathos in which a humble tailor emigrates to the big city in search of fortune, but the foreign customs and that impossible language, English, only bring him to confrontations with the police. Of course, included among the broad array of *revista* topics was the Repatriation. Ironically, the topic which was potentially controversial and sad for the community, was made light of in Don Catarino's *Los repatriados*: "En esta comedia podrá usted saborear las graciosas tribulaciones de los repatriados."[16]

It was on the vaudeville stage where that underdog, the forerunner of Cantinflas, appeared: the *pelado*. And there was no more fertile material for his biting satire, his picaresque adventures and his verbal gymnastics than the conflict of Mexican and Anglo-American culture, and the appearance of his Americanized or "agringado" compatriots. Such was the song composed by Romualdo Tirado and incorporated into his *pelado* routines in Los Angeles in 1927:

> Andas por hay luciendo
> Gran automóvil
> Me llamas desgraciado
> Y muerto de hambre
> Y es que no te acuerdas
> cuando en mi rancho
> Andabas casi en cueros
> Y sin huaraches.
> Así pasa a muchos
> Cuando aprenden un poco
> de americano
> Y se visten catrines
> Y van al baile
> Y el que niega a su raza
> Ni madre tiene,
> Pues no hay nada en el mundo
> Tan asqueroso
> Como la ruin figura del renegado.

Y aunque lejos de ti,
Patria querida,
Me han echado
Continuas revoluciones,
No reniega jamás
Un buen mexicano
de la patria querida
de sus amores.[17]

But the *pelado*, who began to use *caló* and Spanglish humoristically and later evolved into the stage *pachuco*, while dearly beloved by the working class of the *colonias*, was censured by the bourgeoisie, ever mindful of impressing upon Anglos the high quality of Mexican and Hispanic culture. One offended San Antonio critic wrote of the comic hobo, ". . . 'peladito' descamisado y calamburero, que de nuevo torna a presentarse en el escenario del Nacional como avanzada de la tan decantada 'producción artística nacional' que no se entiende si no viene el 'mecapelero,' el 'corredor de loterías,' el tenorio del barrio de largos bigotes y mechón rebelde que hace de su léxico una letanía de insulseces y de su presentación un descrédito para el que no conozca a México."[18] In the delicate balance of protecting the culture and language of the Mexican immigrants while maintaining wholesome entertainment for the families, especially middle class families, the theatre house itself joined the mutualist society and the church as a refuge, a community center, a place for social and political organization. The theatres served as one of the primary institutions for raising funds for all types of community projects, for flood victims, the construction of schools and hospitals, for defense committees for Mexicans confronting the American judicial system, and for labor organizing.

Besides providing the community with a good dose of psychosocial therapy through the unbridled satires at the hands of the *peladitos*, the theatres also provided some real instances of activism. Although theatre owners, impresarios, and playwrights may have been elites in the community, they often identified with the plights of their working class brethren, many of whom supported the shows quite handsomely.

In 1933, at the height of the Depression, the professional theatres in Los Angeles dedicated a percentage of their box office to support striking Mexican farmworkers.[19] The plays that were presented often dramatized the plight of the workers, such as did *La pizca de la uva*, produced at Los Angeles' Teatro Hidalgo.[20] An El Paso benefit performance for the Unión Internacional Obrera in 1935 was typical of the events for union fundraising, with the production of the very appropriate play, *El sacrificio del jornalero*, followed by organizing speeches, 21 songs, and dances.

With the demise of the professional stage brought on by the Depression and the Repatriation, many of the artists that did not return to Mexico continued to exercise their profession on behalf of the community. Daniel Ferreiro Rea in Los Angeles, and Manuel Cotera and Bernardo Fougá in San Antonio performed with their companies, now made up of amateurs as well as professionals, in the Catholic churches in their communities and contributed the proceeds from their performances to the church and other worthy causes. For the most part they continued to stage the most popular plays from their secular repertoire. They, along with the churches supporting and supported by the Mexican community, continued to be a refuge for their language and their culture while offering wholesome entertainment in the face of the evergrowing threat of cultural obliteration.

Could this be what Brokaw has referred to as the theatre falling exclusively into the hands of the Church and its yearly performance of the *pastorelas*?

In conclusion, from the above we have seen that the stage indeed had a multifaceted role to play in the Mexican community and, indeed, it was at times a sounding board for cultural conflict, a forum for direct and indirect criticism of both Mexican and U.S. society and politics, as well as a meeting place, a place for political and social organizing. More importantly, the stage reflected a society coming to terms with an alien environment while bemoaning the loss of a Mexico that would never be the same. The stage offered reflection, communal therapy through the opportunity for the audiences to laugh at themselves; it was a protected sanctum in which to voice frustrations freely. If politics was not addressed as openly as in today's Chicano theatre, we must remember that the audiences were for the most part made up of aliens who were liable to deportation. What is noteworthy, however, is that despite the precariousness of their status, they did allow for controversy and sociopolitical commentary.

Notes

[1] See my article, "Nineteenth-Century Origins of Hispanic Theatre in the Southwest," *Critica*, 1, No. 1 (1984), 79–90.

[2] John W. Brokaw, "Teatro Chicano: Some Reflections," *Educational Theatre Journal*, 29, No. 4 (December, 1977), 535.

[3] See the intensely patriotic letter from Gerardo López del Castillo, Presidente de la Junta Central de las Sociedades Mexicanas, to C. José Marcos Mugarrieta, the Mexican Consul, dated February 23, 1863, and published on the front page of the March 10, 1863 issue of *El Eco del Pacífico*. Also see "Oración Cívica Pronunciada por el C. Gerardo López del Castillo en el Puerto de San Francisco el día 16 de Septiembre de 1862" in the September 18 and 20, 1862, issues of *La Voz de Méjico*. For further information on the patriotic motivation of López del Castillo in his theatrical work, see Armando María y Campos, *La dramática mexicana durante el gobierno del Presidente Lerdo de Tejada* (México: Ediciones Populares, 1946) p. 22.; and Manuel Mañón, *Historia del Teatro Principal* (México: Ed. Cultura, 1932), pp. 241–243.

[4] *La Voz de Méjico*, April 3, 1862.

[5] See *The Californian*'s October 6, 1847 review of a Spanish play presented at Abrego's inn.

6   See the José Abrego (1813–1878) archive, C–D 86 V.2, at the Bancroft Library, University of California-Berkeley.

7   *La Opinión*, September 2, 1932.

8   *La Opinión*, September 11, 1930.

9   *La Opinión*, July 14, 1931.

10 According to playwright and theatre critic, Gabriel Navarro, ". . . las mejores entradas de 1929, en el Teatro México se registraron con motivo de los estrenos de autores mexicanos radicados en Los Angeles," *La Opinión*, April 12, 1930.

11 *La Opinión*, April 11, 1932, The Alianza Hispano Americana's amateur theatrical company also produced Caro's intensely nationalistic *La gloria de la Raza*, under the direction of the author; see *El Heraldo de México*, January 30, 1928.

12 On March 17, 1924, the play was debuted at Los Angeles' Teatro Hidalgo, according to *La Opinión*, on March 14, 1924. This is not the only case of benefit performances to raise funds for the defense of incarcerated Mexicans. The Circo Escalante on March 29, 1927, for example raised funds for the accused Alfredo Grijalva in Phoenix, Arizona. See the "Folkloric materials" file of the Manuel Gamio Papers at the Bancroft Library of the University of California-Berkeley.

13 See *El Heraldo de México*, May 23, 1924.

14 *La Opinión*, December 12, 1930.

15 John B. Nomland, *Teatro Mexicano Contemporáneo (1900–1950)* (México: Instituto Nacional de Bellas Artes, 1967), p. 174. Nomland's chapter, "La revista política y humorística," pp. 145–169, is an interesting discussion of the importance of politics to the Mexican *revista*. Another great Mexican comic, active in *revistas* as a political satirist, was Leopoldo Beristáin, who also spent a few years on the Los Angeles stage; see Armando María y Campos, *Archivo de teatro y Crónicas* (México, 1947), pp. 59–61. Even the great actresses, Virginia Fábregas and María Teresa Montoya, who also were active performers in Los Angeles and the Southwest, were involved in political theatre in México; see "La Influencia de la Política en el Teatro Mexicano," in Armando María y Campos, *Presencias de Treatro. Crónicas 1934–1936* (México: Ediciones Botas, 1937), pp. 189–194. Pablo Prida Santacilla, the author of some of the most famous *revista* librettos, in his autobiography, . . . *y se levanta el telón* (México: Ediciones Botas, 1946), pp. 60–61, states that he came to New York as an exile from Mexico because of his burlesques of political figures.

16 *La Opinión*, July 23, 1934.

17 "Observations, Notes and an Itinerary of Diary of a Trip to Mexico" File in Manuel Gamio Notes, ZR-5, Bancroft Library, University of California-Berkeley.

18 *La Prensa*, September 4, 1922.

19 *La Opinión*, June 21, 1933. The Spanish-language newspapers of the Southwest mention many titles suggestive of the labor movement and politics, such as *El Túnel o Huelga de Obreros*, but we have not been able to locate scripts, authors or the social and political circumstances that they relate.

20 *La Opinión*, August 27, 1933. It was specifically noted here that the Friday, Saturday, and Sunday performances would appeal especially to "las clases populares . . . que concurren al Teatro Hidalgo."

21 *El Continental*, March 24, 1935.

Dialectics of the Masks in El Teatro Campesino:
From Images to Ritualized Events

Geneviève Fabre

From its first *actos* to its more sophisticated shows, El Teatro Campesino has made a more or less extensive use of masks. The early *actos*[1] present masks that are similar to those of the most radical theatres of the 1960s and reminiscent of the techniques of *commedia dell'arte*, masks that serve mainly as instruments of social and political satire. Like some of the masks of the San Francisco Mime Troupe or of the Bread and Puppet, they offer stereotypes and also group archetypes, caricatures of rulers, employers as well as of their too subservient farmworkers, of arrogant capitalists and of their servile underdogs. But masks have another function that is present in most ethnic theatres, in their exploration not only of the sociopolitical situation of the group in American society but of its history, its past, its roots in a different culture and environment. In the mask, important symbols are represented, ancient myths are recreated and come to life again, through which the group can reconstruct its history. Masks therefore are not mere theatrical objects and props, indicating the setting or the mood of a performance. They are signs that must be read and deciphered; they also become dramatic elements, fully integrated into the action, where the past is constantly confronted with the present, the sacred with the secular, where conflicting forces are at play. As such, masks become ritualized events in which the audience must participate. They invite the community to reflect upon and understand its destiny and to create a new future. Even though they are instruments of knowledge, identification, and clarification, they touch upon a world that remains mysterious. They bring us back to primal times, summoning the awesome presence of the dead, of gods, and ancestors as well as of our demons and fantasies. They embody the familiar and the weird, are both reassuring and disquieting. The recourse to masks becomes a significant trend in modern American performances and testifies to the desire to go back to the origin and to the very essence of the theatrical act.

In the first *actos*, masks are directly related to the political work undertaken by El Teatro; short, incisive skits are improvised to spur on the Campesinos in their revolt against the landowners and their allies in the Southwest. At this early stage when El Teatro aimed essentially at supporting the movement initiated by César Chávez, the masks were used as a twofold device: one was to offer to the actors (nonprofessionals recruited among farmworkers) the possibility of being more daring in their representation of characters who were seen as the embodiment of oppression; masks proved an efficient training technique. The other device was aimed more at the audience and its understanding of the message of the play. Masks should convey an immediate, evident meaning, bringing a sense of recognition of both situation and characters. They served the dual purpose of distantiation and identification in a theatre that wanted to follow the Brechtian principles.

In *Las dos caras del patroncito*,[2] the donning of the mask assumes the same significance for the actor and for the character he is playing: it is a magical act, a symbolic and spiritual victory. It enables the unexperienced farmworker-actor to control the situation in his sudden confrontation with his master. The *acto* shows the magic at work in the most simple elemental form. A patroncito (played by an actor who wears the mask of a pig) weary of his plight as employer and farmer offers a deal to his farmworker: they will exchange roles. The campesino takes on the mask of El Patron and is immediately able to imitate his master. What begins as a game, a performance initiated and controlled by the employer, soon gets out of hand. Having lost the emblem of his power, El Patron returns to his former condition and starts complaining about the fate of the farmworkers. When he becomes aware of the loss of his power he wants to stop the game and reclaim his mask. The masked campesino refuses and continues to indulge in his new role of oppressor, taking his master's goods and property. At the end of the *acto*, however, he gives his mask back to El Patroncito, surrenders the property and only keeps the cigar. The first *act* of the revolution is accomplished. The swapping of roles has served as a demonstration of both the strength and the frailty of those in power and of their victims. The farmworker has refrained from completing the process of identification with his employer. Total identification would have meant alienation from his true nature as campesino. Yet this act has given him a new awareness of his subordinate situation and of his potential power. He is reborn, a new and stronger man, and can confront the world with his true, naked face. The power of the mask is at the same time asserted and negated. In the *actos*, true human beings do not wear masks, only the wicked, the hypocrites or corrupt do; or those who are undergoing some kind of change. The campesino has been strong enough to resist the magic of the mask, yet the mask has enabled him to reach his truer self and a better understanding. This *acto*, through the interchangeability of roles, offers a statement on the dual nature of most Chicanos, in whom good and evil coexist and wage a constant battle. The Chicano has two faces: "born of an Indian mother and of a Spanish father," he is the son of the noble Indian and of the more aggressive Spanish conqueror; he is both patroncito and farmworker, oppressor and oppressed. The farmworker himself has two faces — he is a blind, submissive, naive campesino, and he is the revolutionary who cannot be fooled and can create a more equitable social order.

The situation of farmworkers is further explored in *La quinta temporada* where masks assume a more symbolic character and become allegorical figures. Each season represents the benevolent or malevolent forces — natural or social — that beset the lives of the campesinos who have become the toys of agribusiness speculators and of the institutions that support the growers. But the masks of this *acto* are also an investigation into a rich cultural past of former Meso-American agrarian societies where cultivation of the land and intellectual pursuit (mathematics, astronomy) were conceived of as complementary. The past is opposed to the bleak present in which land has become an instrument of oppression and the campesino has lost his sense of place in the cosmic order. The number five, as indicated in the title, refers to a complex symbolic system related to Mayan cosmogony and to the myth of the fifth sun, a sun created to fulfill the functions the four suns failed to accomplish. It also evokes the Quincrux, the cross in whose center the four cardinal points meet and from which all light radiates, a cross whose significance was to be enriched by that of the Christian cross introduced by the Spanish.

In *La conquista de Mexico*, another *acto*, "la piedra del sol" which frames the face of the narrator is an implicit reference to the Aztec calendar. The mask here again has an ambivalent character: it evokes at the same time the height of a civilization that radiated through the world and its dramatic fall, since it fell victim to its own cult of the sun. The sun is a symbol of both power and doom, life and death.

Whether they look at the past or at the present, the Chicanos seem to be caught constantly between two antagonistic worlds and reminded of their *mestizo* nature, heirs as they are to a past which has two faces and offers contradictory images of splendor and of destruction, living in a present that is still beset by such antagonisms.

Thus, instead of using slogans, El Teatro offers images that, from one *acto* to the next, from the *actos* to the *mitos*,[4] build up a complex symbolic structure where all the great myths of the past are told again, enriching the drama of modern times. Ancient stories are woven into the simple story of the plight of the Chicano worker. Under the threefold influence of popular Mexican tradition, and particularly of the *corridos*,[5] of religious Spanish theater and its mystery plays, and of pre-Columbian ritual ceremonies, the mask is more diversified and becomes the repository of several cultures, composing a syncretic combination between Maya and Aztec civilizations, a religious culture transplanted from Spain into Mexico, and the popular beliefs and indigenous traditions of the Indians. In the mask, history and myth converge, evoking stories of greatness and downfall, of conquests and subordination, of loyalty and deceit. Ancient myths thus become relevant to the history of the Chicano, and the symbolism developed through the *actos* and *mitos* is organized again around the complementary forces of light and darkness, embodied in two images that are at the same time emblematic figures and dramatic characters: Death and the Sun. La Calavera is escorted by envy, cupidity, vengeance, and often assisted by the mischievous Diabolo. The Sun is embodied in Quetzalcoatl, life bringer, herald of eternity, who offers his life so that the world can be reborn and saved from destruction, and also in Huitzilopochtli, his counterpart, the sacrificer that thrives on the blood of its victims.

In *Soldado Razo*, the story of Johnny, a young "razo" killed in the Vietnam war, Death is the invisible narrator and the *acto* is punctuated with Johnny's encounters with la Calavera. In the final scene, he wears the mask of death and before being killed he performs his role as a soldier and kills an enemy. He is thus both instrument and victim of American imperialism. In *The Dark Root of a Scream*,[6] one finds in the coffin of a young soldier a heart and feathers, the attributes of Quetzalcoatl. The major motif of the play evolves around the image of the feathered serpent (where the earthly: the serpent, and the heavenly: the quetzal bird, come together) blending the stories of the God Quetzalcoatl, of the Toltec leader named after him (ce Acatl Toplitzin Quetzalcoatl) and of the contemporary Chicano leader who is an embodiment of both. The parallel with the legendary figure, who was betrayed by Tezcatlipoca and forced to flee on a raft of serpents, introduces a fit metaphor on the theme of deceit; the contemporary hero and the indigenous Quetzalcoatl wage the same struggle against war, destruction, and the perpetuation of human sacrifice. In this new *mito* of Chicano life the sacrificed will not totally die. A pyramid serves as a structural image of the play: at the basis, the barrio and its *vatos*, the young defiant *pachucos*, the *malcriados*; at the top, the religious and mythical universe. References to the social and political realities of the barrio are blended with allusions to the Aztec and Christian mythologies.

In the *mitos* — an attempt to combine the traditions of political theatre and of religious ritual — a new mythology emerges. The mask often serves to operate a synthesis between two great principles underlying Maya and Aztec philosophies, between the dualism postulated by the Aztec — life is in death and death in life — and that of universal harmony to be found in Maya cosmogony. In *Bernabé*,[7] the fundamental relation of man to the cosmos, of the Chicano to the land is explored. Bernabé, a village idiot ("un loquito del pueblo") must be sacrificed to atone for the errors of his brothers and oppressors who have done wrong to the "Tierra." This dramatization of rites of ancient mythologies reaffirms the basic claims of the Chicano movement: the land rights, the claim to territorial sovereignty that are common to all Indian peoples. It also reasserts the enduring love of the Chicanos for the land, their devotion to the Earth, la Tierra. Bernabé dies to be born again; his sacrifice will stop the multilation and destruction inflicted upon the earth. It is an act of defiance to those who want to negate the union of men to the land. To the Chicano, la tierra still is a divinity, for which he is ready to die; it is a token of the permanence of the sacred in a culture whose values will not be jeopardized.

Valdez deals with all the different levels at which death can be apprehended by the Chicano people. At the cosmic level, it is apocalyptic and brings with it destruction and disintegration. Yet it is never final since death ultimately generates life again. In daily life, it perpetuates violence and crime, but it is also a revealer of the self and an indispensable malicious companion — who can tease, question, and from whom nothing can be kept secret — an embodiment of the wit, humor and of a spiritual force that have helped the Chicanos in their struggle for survival. *La gran carpa de los rasquachis* is one of Valdez' most ambitious yet none too successful attempts at presenting these various conceptions and roles. The play is at the same time a masque, a pageant and a fable. This *carpa cantinflesca* (such was the first title of the play) was inspired by a form of popular theatre, the *carpas*, shows performed under tents which developed after the Mexican revolution; it tries to emulate the broad sense of humor developed by the comedian Cantinflas. Yet this ballad, or *corrido*, of the underdog Jesus Pelado Rasquachi fails to create what we could call "rasquachi" masks, from a term Valdez himself used in order to describe his theatre, a theatre emerging out of the sweat and blood of the campesinos, of the *pelados*, a fit expression to evoke the predicament of the destitute Third World who bleeds, sweats, and farts.

El fin del mundo, which Valdez described as a half-improvised calavera show, blends more successfully all the elements — the religious and the secular, the spiritual and the earthly, the serious and the *cantinflesco*, the modern and the traditional — that Valdez wishes to integrate into his masks. Death masks and costumes, skulls and white skeletons, are worn by all characters present on bodies and faces alike. Mime and pantomime dramatize the various acts of death, acts of violence and destruction perpetrated by the military, the police, la "Migra," by men and women, by parents and children. This allegorical fable of the modern world conveys all the messages of radical theatre, revealing the mechanisms of exploitation and oppression, preaching the necessity of the struggle for peace, for the respect of the land, of the earth, of man, but expressing these ideas through a systematic exploration of the collective imagination of the Chicanos. The medium and the idiom are distinctly Hispanic and very much influenced by the work of a contemporary Mexican group, Los Macarones.[8]

In the complex cultural heritage that inspired the visual and dramatic images of El Teatro, some Christian elements predominate in certain shows, a sort of *pastorelas* or pastoral plays, presented around Christmas time and celebrating San Juan and the Virgin. These elements reappear, reshaped and modified into a new mythology where ancient gods merge with Christian deities and saints — Quetzalcoatl with Christ, Tonantzin (the mother of the Aztec gods) with the Virgin Mary — and where indigenous and Catholic rituals combine.

More convincingly integrated in the dramaturgy — both scenography and drama — than Jesu Cristo Quetzalcoatl, the Virgin of Guadalupe, Brown Virgin Mary Tonantzin, becomes a fit symbol both of the syncretism which Chicano culture operated between its pre-Columbian and its Christian heritages, and of the national reunification under the various struggles led for "la Causa Chicana." Valdez has dedicated to the Virgin several shows which are presented each year in December. *La Virgen del Tepeyac, Las cuatro apariciones del Virgen de Guadalupe* recall the legend of a young Indian, Cuauhtlatoctizu (Eagle that speaks) renamed Juan Diego who, in 1531, saw the Virgin on a hill once sacred to Tonantzin. The Virgin spoke to him in Nahuatl and announced that she would save "los Indios" from annihilation, if they would believe in her son. Valdez' version of the legend tries to set history straight: in contrast to traditional dramatizations of the miracle which present the humble Indian as a mere messenger, it shows Juan Diego forcing the Catholic church to accede to his Indian vision. Juan challenges the power of the Church, indicting it for conquering the Indian and forcing him to adopt an alien, European religion. Juan, "el Indio," symbolizes the resistance of the Indians against all forms of violence and oppression and the permanence of a spirit that will not die. An image of love and justice, the Brown Virgin provides the Chicano people with a token of their own divinity and grants them protection through trials and revolutions. Chosen as a sort of emblem, next to the Aztec eagle, it accompanies them in all their struggles and spurs them on in times of political effervescence.

The Virgin finds her place in this modern pantheon next to the Plumed Serpent, her ally in the constant battle waged against corruption, violence, and death. The serpent, however, is a more complex and enigmatic mask, an embodiment of the principles at work in the metaphysical system which inspires the political philosophy of Valdez.[9] Undergoing continual metamorphoses, Quetzalcoatl is both bird and snake, creature of the air and of the earth, of the spirit and of matter – a god and the son of a god. The mythical struggle that confronts him with his twin brother ("coatl" means both serpent and twin) Tetzatlipoca, associated with nocturnal and chtonian forces, and with his other brother Huracan, the Maya god who represents disorder and unbridled energy, becomes an archetypal struggle. The image of the feathered serpent offers a pervasive metaphor of the dual nature of the Chicano, torn between conflicting impulses, forced to lead an endless battle. It also represents the process of change, of permanent evolution.

Emerging from the Chicano's deepest cultural experience, the masks become instructive fables in which a people is invited to read its fate, to become aware of its own rhythms of change. All the masks are brought together into a kind of unifying myth presenting the epos of a people who had to negotiate many transitions: from the world of Meso-American grandeur and decadence to that of the fields of the Southwest and the barrios of big American cities; from Spanish conquest to American domination; from the sacrifices exacted by the Aztec gods to those requested by the Conquistadores and the more recent hawks of American imperialism. Inhabited by all the gods and legendary figures and the cultural heroes of modern times, each holding a mirror to the other, the theatre *is* the world, the stage of a great pantomime, a gigantic improvisation, a farce and a tragedy performed by gods and men, by masters and by slaves. The Serpent becomes the central symbol in this theatre in which the essential rites of death and rebirth are reenacted. It is through him that the creative principle is manifested, it is he who communicates this energy to the other. The actor is the mask, an embodiment of the other, his "double" who must be recognized and dealt with — an idea which is expressed in another principle dear to Valdez: "tu eres mi otro yo," "in lak'ech." In the mask are thus dramatized the various rites of passage, stages of evolution and revolution through which political and cultural awareness can be achieved.

Notes

1 *Actos* (San Juan Bautista, Calif.: Cucaracha Press, 1971).
2 In *Actos*, pp. 7–19.
3 In *Actos*, pp. 20–34.
4 This new form of drama developed by Valdez after 1970 was defined by Valdez as "a teatro of ritual. . . of spiritual sensitivity, a teatro of legends and myths" that presented the internal struggle in the *corazón* of the Chicano people.
5 These are stylized dramatizations of Mexican ballads.
6 In *From the Barrio*, ed. L. Faderman and O. Salinas (San Francisco, Calif.: Canfield Press, 1973) pp. 79–98. Some of the shows described here have never been published. In most *mitos* the performance depends mostly upon the staging, on visual images, etc.
7 In *Contemporary Chicano Theatre*, ed. R. J. Garza (Notre Dame, Ind.: University of Notre Dame Press, 1976), pp. 30–58.
8 The work of the Macarones was presented in Europe at the same festivals as that of El Teatro Campesino in the early 1970s.
9 This philosophy is expressed in a long poem, *Pensamiento Serpentino* (San Juan Bautista, Calif.: Cucaracha Press, 1971).
10 M. Leon-Portilla, *Aztec Thought and Culture* (Norman, Okla.: University of Oklahoma Press, 1963).

Corridos Modernos y Elaboración de una Crónica del Pueblo Chicano: Parentescos con el Teatro Chicano

Annick Tréguer

Las reflexiones y observaciones que siguen fueron inspiradas, básicamente, por los trabajos recientes de Dan William Dickey, en Tejas,[1] y los de Luis Leal y Armando Vallejo,[2] en California, cuyas referencias se citan en la bibliografía adjunta.

No puedo dejar, de paso, de expresar mucha admiración por la labor inapreciable a la que se han dedicado, individualmente y con sus equipos, en localizar, recopilar, estudiar o grabar unos corridos contemporáneos (desde el año 1963, fecha del asesinato del Presidente John F. Kennedy, hasta 1980). Dichos estudios constituyen, de por sí, una aportación valiosa a la preservación de la tradición oral y de la cultura popular de los méjico-americanos de los Estados Unidos de América.

En las páginas que siguen, se describirá, aunque modesta y brevemente, cómo el corrido y el acto, en cierta medida a pesar de sus diferencias, han desempeñado funciones complementarias en la elaboración de una crónica del pueblo chicano en años recientes. Al mismo tiempo, se señalará el interés de otra problemática socio-política: la permanencia, por medio de una tradición oral y teatral profundamente arraigada, de una cultura popular auténtica al lado de la cultura oficial y "legítima" de la sociedad norteamericana.

A modo de paréntesis, y antes de entrar en el tema de nuestras reflexiones, cabe insistir en la importancia que puede cobrar, para el observador europeo, el uso exclusivo del idioma español en el corrido: prueba, por lo tanto, de que sigue siendo un vehículo lingüístico muy adecuado para expresar las emociones, la sensibilidad y la cultura de un grupo numéricamente minoritario, que no se deja absorber ni siquiera por un grupo tan mayoritario como el anglo-americano de Estados Unidos.

No se trata de estudiar aquí el corrido, desde el punto de vista formal de las convenciones que rigen el género de manera más o menos flexible, o de su historia; ya lo hicieron con maestría unos especialistas tan famosos como Américo Paredes,[3] Arthur Campa, la familia Espinosa, Merle Simmons[4] y Vicente Mendoza[5]. Tampoco se trata de analizar y teorizar sobre el teatro chicano y el acto, ya que esto es cosa de destacados especialistas como Jorge Huerta y Nicolás Kanellos. Lo que sí haremos, en cambio, después de observar unos parentescos patentes entre ambos, será enfocar el corrido como el aspecto dinámico de una historia vista y relatada, día tras día, (de ahí el uso de la palabra crónica) por "los de abajo," la gente del pueblo, sean éstos trabajadores de zonas rurales o urbanas, legales o no. El acto, por su parte, sería, más bien, el aspecto más activo de una historia vivida y actuada por "los de abajo" mismos, al menos en los albores del teatro chicano y hasta 1976.

Desde tiempos remotos, el corrido y el teatro figuran entre los modos más auténticos de expresión de los primeros méjico-americanos; encarnan lo más hondo de su cultura, desde la conquista por los españoles, pasando por su evangelización, hasta la ocupación efectiva de los territorios del suroeste por los norteamericanos, tras el Tratado de Guadalupe Hidalgo.

Desgraciadamente, habían caído en el olvido debido al odio anglosajón, consecuencia de la guerra mantenida por años entre Estados Unidos y Méjico, y que había originado desinterés y desprecio por todo lo que no fuera anglo.

Afortunadamente, a principios del siglo XX, el interés por el folklore los salvó de la sepultura, y sigue salvándolos ahora el impulso del movimiento cultural chicano.

Hablemos primero del corrido: herederos modernos de los juglares de la Edad Media, los guitarreros y poetas mejicanos nunca habían dejado de ir de pueblo en pueblo, animando fiestas y cantinas. Así fue cómo el corrido vino a sustituir al romance de origen español, a fines del siglo XIX, en el norte de Méjico. Como lo indica su nombre, un corrido cuenta con rapidez una anécdota o un acontecimiento, que se canta; a veces, tiene rasgos de reportajes, en los que ocasionalmente apunta la sátira o el humor. Se presenta como una sucesión de coplas octosilábicas de cuatro versos, que se añaden una tras otra, según se le antoje al corridista; éste se dedica también a celebrar hombres poco comunes, convirtiéndolos en héroes, cuyas proezas estimulan la imaginación popular. El corrido no es claramente didáctico, aunque sirva este propósito, al relatar hechos y acontecimientos actuales o históricos. A través del corrido, se vislumbra la experiencia del mejicano en tierra estadounidense, sus manifestaciones hacia el ocupante odiado, en las luchas fronterizas; las labores del vaquero, las andanzas patéticas de los emigrantes, de su explotación y de su discriminación; y por fin, sus reacciones conflictuales con relación a otra civilización.

El corrido también cobra cierto carácter épico, que contribuyen a darle las convenciones formales, que citaremos rápidamente, a continuación: llamamiento al auditorio; indicación de la fecha, del lugar y del personaje o del asunto; argumento del poema o canción; mensaje; despedida, que suele recordar el título o contenido. Dicha estructura será evidente en las corridos citados más adelante.

El teatro chicano, si nos referimos a sus raíces más profundas, sean éstas indias (es decir, el teatro maya o azteca), o españolas (es decir, teatro litúrgico, religioso, misionero), estuvo presente en todas las etapas de la experiencia méjico-americana, exactamente como el corrido. Sus metas eran paralelas a las del teatro chicano contemporáneo: instruir políticamente y religiosamente, educar y evangelizar. Tales eran, en cierto modo, las intenciones de Luis Valdez y del Teatro Campesino, en sus primeras manifestaciones: politizar y convertir a la gente a la acción, a la resistencia, a la protesta, a la unión.

Otra meta didáctica común al teatro y al corrido es informar y servir de órgano informativo. Obviamente, el teatro chicano y el movimiento teatral al cual dio luz, han sido un medio de vulgarización de la Causa chicana entre numerosas comunidades y agrupaciones de trabajadores. Hasta llegó a crear un nuevo estilo de folklore, y forma ahora parte de la cultura popular chicana, sin la menor duda.

Otra semejanza entre el corrido y el teatro radica en el público a quien se dirigen. Debido a la relativa poca importancia de las clases medias y altas entre los chicanos, es verdad que el concepto de chicano suele asociarse con el de la clase pobre, eje central de ambos géneros.

El teatro chicano ha sabido reflejar con autenticidad, y con humor, la historia cotidiana de los campesinos y vendimiadores, y su toma de conciencia progresiva, a lo largo de la Huelga de Delano, de la necesidad de su sindicalización. Incansablemente, desde 1965 hasta 1976, el teatro chicano fue sirviendo de medio educativo para las masas pobres y abarcó cuestiones de alcance político e histórico para los chicanos de los barrios de las grandes ciudades. Cumplió con una tarea imprescindible para las generaciones venideras: preservar y presentar la otra cara de la historia oficial.

Volvamos ahora a otro aspecto propio del corrido. Por cierto, a través de los corridos nacidos de la pobreza, se fue elaborando la imagen de un pueblo en lucha por la libertad, por la igualdad. Sin embargo, el corrido no es esencialmente político, es ante todo, una respuesta puramente emocional, una expresión sencilla y espontánea de un dolor sincero, de una pena profunda. Por eso, se le ha atribuido a menudo el papel de "válvula de escape." Gracias al corrido, el méjico-americano ha logrado aguantar sus infortunios, sus penas, al mismo tiempo que transmitía a la posteridad un documento, un archivo de su historia invisible.

Nos ha parecido particularmente fascinante el estudio de Dan William Dickey, centrado sobre los corridos que surgieron espontáneamente tras la muerte trágica de John F. Kennedy. Casi todos los corridos que recogió en su investigación se compusieron la misma tarde del asesinato. A continuación, se citan dos de los corridos más característicos publicados por Dickey.

El primero reproduce perfectamente la estructura propia del corrido mejicano:[6]

EN HONOR A KENNEDY

by Gastón Ponce
Castellanos
recorded by the Trío
Internacional

Voy a cantarles señores,
sólo así puedo expresar
el dolor de mis dolores
mi gran pena y mi pesar.

Año del sesenta y tres
del veintidós de noviembre,
entre la ciudad de Dallas
mataron al Presidente.

Tres balazos bien certeros
el asesino tiró,
dos dieron al Presidente,
el otro al Gobernador.

Y era casi el medio día
cuando este caso pasó,
donde a este gran Presidente
la vida se le quitó.

Que Dios lo tenga en su gloria
como ejemplo de razón,
y a su familia aconseja
mucha fe y resignación.

Aquí termino señores
la tragedia que escribí,
con dolor de mis dolores
en honor a Kennedy.

El segundo, fiel a las convenciones del género, empieza por una larga citación, en español, de parte del discurso inaugural de Kennedy en 1961.

CORRIDO DE JOHN F. KENNEDY

by Ray Pérez y Soto
recorded by Lupita y Ray

[Spoken]

Y Kennedy dijo:
El clarín nos llama de nuevo, no a las armas aunque
armas necesitemos, no al combate aunque estemos
en plena lucha, sino a llevar el peso de una larga
pelea crepuscular, luchando contra los enemigos comunes del hombre. Yo no retrocedo ante esta respon-
sabilidad; yo la deseo.

[sung]
Escuchen señores lo que ha sucedido,
aquí les voy a cantar,
que por mala suerte el mundo ha perdido
a un gran hombre de verdad.

El mes de noviembre, veintidós por cierto,
el año sesenta y tres,
John Kennedy en Dallas fue asesinado,
¡y quién lo pueda creer!

[Spoken]
¡y llore esa arpa, compañero!
[sung]
John Kennedy quiso así como Lincoln
para todos la igualdad,
el gran estadista que llevó por lema,
"Democracia y libertad."

Todo el mundo llora a aquel hombre bueno
y México mucho más,
murió un gran amigo de López Mateos
que devolvió el Chamizal.

Estados Unidos tendrá presidentes
que a su patria sepan guiar,
pero como Kennedy no habrá ninguno
se los puedo asegurar.

Así como Cristo él quiso a los negros
con todo su corazon,
San Martín de Porres, el santo mulato
y Kennedy están con Dios.

Si adoptáramos la denominación de Julio Rodríguez Puértolas,[7] dichos corridos se verían calificados de "colaboracionistas," ya que convierten a John Kennedy en un héroe méjico-americano. Muy fácilmente se puede rechazar la etiqueta de colaboracionismo; en efecto, queda bien claro que en tan trágica ocasión, los corridistas de Tejas y del Suroeste de Estados Unidos se hicieron naturalmente portavoces de sus compañeros, expresando la emoción profunda que engendró el asesinato del Presidente, en aquellos lugares como en el mundo entero; tal es el tema del "Lamento a Kennedy" recogido por Gilberto López y su equipo.[8]

Año de mil novecientos
sesenta y tres al presente,
en el estado de Texas
mataron al Presidente.

El veintidós de noviembre
fue un día de mucho dolor,
toda la gente gritaba
" ¡castiguen al malhechor!"

Kennedy, fuiste valiente
no se te puede negar,
toda la gente sabemos
no se nos ha de olvidar.

Toda la gente sabía
que tu ibas a ser reelecto,
porque para presidente
tu eras el nombre perfecto.

Todo el mundo está de luto
con sentimiento lloramos,
Kennedy fuiste tan bueno
con todos los mexicanos.

El corrido, en esta circunstancia peculiar, fue el molde en el cual se manifestó el afecto de todo un pueblo. Kennedy había llegado a simbolizar las aspiraciones de los méjico-americanos en conseguir los plenos derechos civiles y su reconocimiento efectivo como ciudadanos; estatutos que siempre se les había negado, debido a los prejuicios raciales y sociales, y a la explotación económica. Los méjico-americanos también se habían ido identificando con los orígenes y la lucha de Kennedy, miembro de una minoría étnica, y católica además. El vínculo étnico, el lazo religioso, la muerte trágica de John F. Kennedy, en cierto modo cristalizaron los sentimientos que experimentaban hacia él los méjico-americanos . . . y se manifestaron en corridos escritos, cantados, grabados. Dickey, al juntar diecisiete entre ellos, nos da la prueba de que el corrido, aunque quede en un estado estancado por años, sigue siendo parte inherente del alma mejicana y chicana, parte asimismo del inconsciente colectivo. Refleja a la vez las transformaciones que vive el hombre del pueblo, al pasar de un ambiente rural a un ambiente urbano. Y ésta es una de las etapas capitales en la crónica del pueblo chicano, etapa que también transparece en la evolución de los actos del teatro chicano.

Los nuevos héroes nacidos con el movimiento chicano inspiraron a la Raza, nuevos corridos, nuevos temas de canciones. En los Corridos de César Chávez, de Reies Lopes Tijerina, en los del famoso corridista Rumel Fuentes,[9] queda manifiesta una crónica más militante de los acontecimientos, de los sentimientos.

Sería interesante detenerse en algunos de los corridos recogidos por el equipo de Armando Vallejo y de Luis Leal, a modo de ejemplo de la evolución que ha venido marcando los corridos modernos, tanto en cuanto al tono como al contenido.[10]

Numerosos son los que al evocar los sueños y las ilusiones del chicano, al mismo tiempo contribuyen a darle una mejor imagen de sí mismo. Hemos aquí dos ejemplos:

Corrido del Chicano Mexicano

Voy a cantar un corrido
del chicano mexicano
porque este apodo pusieron
en este país hermano

Fue el veintinueve de agosto
mil novecientos setenta
cuando mataron a un grande
que hacía por el mexicano

Como un héroe en la historia
su nombre ha sido grabado
nunca será olvidado
como el apodo mojado

El mexicano señores
es raza muy poderosa
porque se parten el alma
por conseguir cualquier cosa

Siempre abandonan su tierra
para venirse al norte
a conseguir el sustento
aun sin tener pasaporte

Yo también soy mexicano
y he recorrido fronteras
pero me gusta esta tierra
sobre todo este condado

Les contaré que el condado
lleva por nombre Ventura
su gente es noble y pura
su orgullo es la agricultura

El mexicano señores
es raza muy poderosa
porque se parten el alma
por conseguir cualquier cosa

Letra y Música
Ramón Fajardo
Fillmore, Ca

Yo Soy Mexicano, Señores
Corrido

Yo soy mexicano señores
nacido en Michoacán
en Cotija para ser exactos
soy purepecha por Gracia de Dios

Cuando yo tenía catorce años
mis padres se separaron
cuanto duele no quiero ni acordarme
cuanto sufres si no tienes hogar

Por ahí contaban las gentes
que en el norte
el dinero se barría con escoba
Y nosotros creyéndonos el cuento
decidimos venirnos para acá

¡Ay senores no quiero ni acordarme!
los trabajos que pasamos en Tijuana
Cuando ya veníamos excusando
la migra que nos echa pa'tras

Un coyote tienen que conseguirse
nos decía la voz de la experiencia
Un coyote que con su buena lana
por fin nos ayudó a cruzar

Y aquí estoy todavía mis paisanos
trabajando pa'ser rico al patrón
Y aquí estoy todavía mis paisanos
rogando los surcos con sudor

Con estas coplas termino mi corrido
que perdonen si los he ofendido
se despide su amigo el michoacano
que aún vive aquí en Saticoy

Letra Juan Manuel Valdonvinos Ochoa
Saticoy California
Música Jose Cruz Carrera
Santa Paula, Ca

Otro corrido demuestra la modernidad y la adaptabilidad del género, se titula:

Liberación Femenil
Canción Corrido

Voy a cantar el corrido
Liberación Femenil
con el permiso de todas
no se vayan a sentir

Fíjense bien las mujeres
para que lleguen al fin
a realizar sus anhelos
y no las hagan sufrir

Para que sean liberadas
y no las quieran tener
en su casa como esclavas
todo lo bueno y lo malo
primero en su proceder

Dicen que todos los hombres
somos el tal por el cual
dicen que somos muy machos
hombres a carta cabal.

Cuando tomamos la copa
y estamos en el jacal
le gritamos a la vieja
como si fuera animal

Yo estoy de acuerdo ante todo
porque los dos son igual
porque los mismos derechos
tenemos en el hogar
porque lo mismo sentimos
Cuando alguno queda mal.

Letra y Música Ramón Fajardo
Fillmore, California

El valor sociológico del "Corrido de Rancho Sespe" es obvio. Tras una referencia a la sindicalización de los campesinos de un rancho, una alusión al triunfo de César Chávez, se denuncia objetivamente la explotación del trabajador. Aquí existe un parentesco indudable entre el tono irónico del corrido y el acto "Las dos caras del patroncito". Hasta se mencionan unos émulos de los "Vendidos" (otro acto del Teatro campesino), que aquí se ven calificados de comprados. También se recogen los temas del la Huelga y se expresa el desprecio por los grotescos agentes del rancho que "se hicieron en los calzones," frente a los valerosos chicanos. Termina el corrido, incitando a la acción, a la participación, con los gritos de "Viva Chávez y también la Unión," bajo la protección y bendición de la Virgen de Guadalupe.

El Corrido de Rancho Sespe
El día 9 de Mayo

oiga bien lo que decimos
fue ganado El Rancho Sespe
Pa' la unión de campesinos

Es que vino César Chávez
a invitarnos a su unión
pa'acabar malos tratos
y también la explotación

nos decía Mr Lombardo
vénganse mis muchachitos
no ven que esos de la unión
no más son puros malditos

y nosotros nos reímos
de verlo tan campujido
pues le apretaba la soga
que el mismo se había tejido

Andaban muy apurados
mandando cartas de amor
y también unos comprados
decían no quiero unión

nos mandaron sus agentes
para dar explicaciones
cuando oyeron VIVA CHAVEZ
se hicieron en sus calzones

Ahora que ya les ganamos
con honor las votaciones
lucharemos por contratos
que nos den más protecciones

Compañeros campesinos
que votaron por la unión
La Virgen de Guadalupe
les dará su bendición

Ahora sí mis compañeros,
ya les cante mi canción
ahora griten VIVA CHAVEZ!
y también VIVA LA UNION!

Letra Jaime Zepeda
Santa Paula, California
Música Manuel Unzueta
Santa Bárbara, California

Al citar tan sólo esos ejemplos, se ha intentado señalar cómo dos acontecimientos, que tuvieron repercusiones descomunales para el pueblo chicano, imprimieron nuevos impulsos tanto al corrido como al teatro, formas tradicionales de expresión popular de las comunidades chicanas.

A modo de conclusión, se impone la constatación de que el corrido sigue vivo en Estados Unidos (y también el idioma español), y es probable que siga siéndolo, mientras el pueblo tenga necesidad de héroes, de ideales. Entretanto, seguirá elaborando una clase de "autobiografía" de los chicanos, contando

"aquello que la historia
no quire recordar."[11]

Notas

[1] Dan William Dickey, *The Kennedy Corridos: A Study of the Ballads of a Mexican-American Hero* (Austin: University of Texas, Monograph no 4., Center for Mexican American Studies, 1978).
[2] Armando Vallejo y Luis Leal, "Corridos y canciones de Aztlán," *Xalman*, 3 (Fall 1980).
[3] Americo Paredes, *With His Pistol in His Hand, A Border Ballad and Its Hero* (Austin: University of Texas Press, 1958).
[4] Merle E. Simmons, *The Mexican Corrido as a Source for Interpretative Study of Modern Mexico (1870–1950)* (Reimpreso en Nueva York, 1969).
[5] Mendoza, Vicente T., *El Corrido Mexicano* (México: Fondo de Cultura Económica, 1954).
[6] Dan William Dickey, pp. 88, 92.

111

7 Rodríguez Puértolas, Julio, "La problemática socio-política chicana en corridos y canciones, *Aztlán*, Vol 6, Spring 1975.
8 Dan William Dickey, p. 98.
9 Rumel Fuentes, "Corridos de Rumel," *El Grito*, Vol. V1, n° 3, 1973.
10 Armando Vallejo, pp. 91, 77, 97, 79.
11 Cantata de Santa María de Iquique (Prólogo), interpretada por el grupo chileno "Los Quilapayun."

Discos:

Philip Sonnichsen, Texas-Mexican Border Music, Vol. 2 y 3, Folklore Records, Records 9004, 9005.

Ideology and El Teatro Campesino

Dieter Herms

I

"El Teatro continues to die and be reborn, crawl out of the skin of the serpent."[1] Luis Valdez uses ancient imagery to describe the periods of transition and change, the Teatro's and his own struggle for new orientation and survival in the modern context of the U.S. Of the changes, there have been many, and drastic ones: After an intensive founding phase of performing actos in the context of the campesinos' fierce struggle for recognition as the first American farmworkers' union, Valdez, and the Teatro severed their close ties with the César Chávez movement and turned into El Centro Campesino Cultural.

The major ideological orientation alongside this development was prompted by the advent of cultural nationalism in the movement of Chicanismo. The labor struggles of the San Joaquín Valley broadened into the national movement of Aztlán. Again, Valdez was one of the foremost thinkers and theatre practitioners. He added to the social philosophy of oppression in the Southwest, the historical depth of Aztec and Mayan philosophy. To the *acto* was added the *mito* as new dramatic form.[2]

Meanwhile El Teatro's work had sparked the rise of many active Chicano theatre groups. A national association was formed (TENAZ) which held its annual festivals. In 1974, when the festival took place in Mexico City, El Teatro Campesino severed its ties from this organization also, rejecting any political and artistic dictate from outside. *La Carpa de los Rasquachis* emerged from this period, the Teatro's most ambitious effort to date, achieving, in its final version, a complex integration of *acto, mito,* and *corrido.*

After the solidification of its base in San Juan Bautista, with the annual presentation of the ritual historical cycle (*El Día de los Muertos, La Pastorela, La Virgen del Tepeyac*) a new development occurred in 1978/79. The Los Angeles success of *Zoot Suit* led to its staging on Broadway in New York and, subsequently, its adaptation into a movie. Valdez states:

> ... I see us growing to a point where we can, in fact, function as an organization that serves the nation, that serves Chicanos from all over. We'll have to give up a certain amount of our romantic notion of "rasquachiness." But it's there in our history. It's part of us. And I never want to lose the ability to be able to perform in a labor camp.

I never want to lose the opportunity to perform in a barrio. At the same time I don't want us to shy away from the ability of staging a play on Broadway with the Teatro Campesino, if we want to, because that's part of the national expression right now.[3]

Finally, and not without some historical irony, the opening of the first permanent theatre house (a new version of the Teatro's adaptation of Belasco's and Tully's *Rose of the Rancho* in 1981) meant closing the Teatro Campesino as a permanent company. Professional actors are now hired for each new production. Some continuity is achieved through a core group of basically administrative staff, a musical director, and one or two actresses.

II

The discussion of ideology and ideological changes within minority cultures inevitably has to take into account the situation of the mainstream, the interrelation of ruling power, ideology, and culture, on the one hand, with the struggles of the ethnic, or in case of a specific political consciousness, of the third world groups and nations in the U.S., on the other. Chicano historians and sociologists, in fact, have never shied away from viewing the evolution of Chicano history and culture in the Southwest in class-oriented, i.e. Marxist terms.[4] Moreover, around 1975, it was also seen as apt and pertinent to analyze the politics of the Chicano movement from a Marxist perspective.[5] In recent years, that readiness has subsided. And it is particularly in the area of Chicano cultural theory and literary criticism, that attempts of this kind have been at best scattered and incomplete.

Juan Gómez-Quiñones[6] comes to the conclusion that among North Americans of Mexican descent, three cultures and identities can be distinguished, that of the dominant U.S. orientation, the Mexicano culture and identity, and a "fluid" transitional culture, hovering between the two. This is a descriptive notion of culture and ideology in the Southwest which does not particularly dwell on values or positive emotional/ideological content. Joseph Sommers, in his historical materialist approach,[7] which — after its theoretical derivation — he applies to a reading of Tomás Rivera's ... *y no se lo tragó la tierra*, combines textual insights with a class-oriented historical perspective, thus coming close to traditional European Marxist approaches toward the literary work. His advantage over them is a good balance of theory and practical application. Armando Gutiérrez, from a rather rigid Marxist position criticizes Rudolfo Anaya's *Heart of Aztlán* for its lack of political perspective, and its failure of presenting a model revolutionary figure.[8] Gutiérrez falls prey to a schematic reflection theory, whereby the social reality should be directly translated into the literary text, not mediated through a set of symbols, and a fictional ambience that creates its own "literary" reality.

José Saldívar, in his paper in this volume, applies the post-modernist Marxist approach provided by Frederic Jameson to an analysis of two leading Chicano novelists. He points to a new dialectic of aesthetics and politics by uncovering in Arias and Rivera "narrative paradigms of an ideological and utopian liberation."

My 1984 NACS paper[9] argues that the generally descriptive notion of cultural clash in the Southwest, namely the collision of dominant Anglo and subordinate Chicano culture and ideology be modified by a content-oriented "vertical" dialectic of first and second cultures, examining the emotional and ideological perspective "from below" which largely informs Chicano literature in the sixties and seventies.

It is, at this point, probably too early to decide whether the ongoing debate in the West German periodical *Das Argument* on the relationships between literature, philosophy, and ideological power,[10] can be made productive for explaining the specific contradictions experienced by Chicano cultural producers within the complex, multinational, neocolonial, postindustrial, mass-media-oriented reality of the U.S. in the early 1980s. Suffice it to say, at this point, that Frieder O. Wolf's plea "for a subversive praxis of philosophy" forms a fitting link with Luis Valdez' attempt of applying the energies gained from Mayan thought to the struggle for cultural survival in Aztlán.

Wolf argues in this context that it is not sufficient to take up the battle at specific collision points ("Sollbruchstellen") determined by Marxist theoreticians, i.e. in many isolated spots only, where the struggle is particularly obvious; he rather propagates the generalization of all isolated opposition into a comprehensive unifying concept of opposition. "A materialist subversion of this dominant praxis of philosophy must (and is able to) set out from the unification of oppositions, to be found both within theory and within ideological everyday life, and must not only freeze its topical peculiarity, but analytically uncover the efforts and achievements of generalizations contained within these opposition movements."[11]

III

There are basically two ways in which national cultural traditions of the Southwest are introduced into the ideological subject matter of Valdez' scripts and Teatro productions. Aztec mythology and increasingly Mayan philosophy are shaping their reference patterns and determining their principal modes of expression. Characteristically, traditional concepts "from above" are integrated with the "rasquachi" experience "from below."

Bernabé, the village idiot, is placed between *la tierra* and *la luna*. Jesús Rasquachi is inspired by Quetzalocoatl to correct his decision, against the growers, and for the union. Mata is heightened into Reymundo, the King of the world. The pachuco is stripped down to his indigenous loin-cloth as a sign of utter humiliation. Juan Diego, the simple peasant, forces the mighty bishops to accept *his* vision of the Virgen del Tepeyac. The examples could be continued. Color symbolism, mysticism of numbers, the mathematical conception of the universe, the recapturing of god as zero, "the great No-Thing from which every other thing springs ... una tremenda matriz cósmica" — all these serve as a reservoir of aesthetic energy and as wealth of ideological reference.

Corridos, the Teatro's latest achievement,[12] has been criticized for its lack of political focus, and its insistence on trivial love and violence patterns. True, the first four corridos, performed in San Juan Bautista, were "Delgadina," "Rosita Alvarez," "Tierra Sin Nombre," and "Cornelio Vega." They are about lust, incest, love triangles, violence, and death. Even "La Rielera," added in the San Francisco production, centered around three women in the Mexican Revolution, using John Reed's perspective, did not live up to the expectation of politically-oriented Chicanos and Chicanas: "Through a flurry of ragtime music and Charleston dance, la Viuda is portrayed manipulating the judicial system by using her sexuality through the ranks of the judicial system."[13]

Corridos, the review summarizes, perpetuate "la vida del rancho," the struggle for turf, the ownership of women, machismo, and the fight to the death.

Valdez has announced that more political corridos are to follow. One could criticize these particular choices as the opening ones. However, on the other hand, it has to be taken into consideration, that, in the Teatro's view, the corrido as such is already highly political. The corrido is created by *el pelado*, the Mestizo, the colonized man of Mexico, the "stripped one":

> The pelado is the creator of the corrido and the eternal patron of mariachi. His music, in turn, inspires him to express all his joy and sorrow in a single cry. So he lets out a grito that tells you he feels life and death in the same breath. "Viva la Raza, hijos de la chingada!"[14]

Taking into consideration that the Teatro's work evolves in cycles (*La Carpa, Fin del Mundo*, the historical cycle of San Juan Bautista), we have to allow for cyclical growth in *Corridos*, too. The fact that the individual first few corridos dramatized and performed, are not overtly political, does not exclude the entire venture from being an integrated political and aesthetic act. Thus *Corridos* will not contribute towards an isolated social question, but the entire concept is rooted in a social historical ideology.

Thus, the other important dimension of historical ideology is the merging of contemporary Chicano experience with the elaboration of Mexican history in the region of Aztlán. And it is in this context of contributing to a reinterpretation of California history, that both *Rose of the Rancho* (1981) and *Bandido* (1982) could be viewed. The plot of the 1904 Belasco/Tully Broadway melodrama is set in San Juan Bautista in the 1850s, when the land-grabbers invaded California, closely following the Treaty of Guadalupe Hidalgo and the gold rush. Simply by virtue of watching El Teatro perform this play in San Juan Bautista the audience becomes aware "that the American invaders could not displace

Spanish culture in California any more than it could be comfortably assimilated."[15]

Redefining California history: yet another plan issued in 1978 came to fruition with *Bandido*, and again it is the immediate region around San Juan Bautista, where the action is set. Tiburcio Vasquez was from Monterey, and it is with the raid on Tres Pinos, south of Hollister, only a few miles from San Juan Bautista, that the play begins. Felipe's restaurant in San Juan Bautista, where the reception after the premiere took place, was apparently built on the very spot of a tamale shop once operated by Tiburcio Vasquez' mother. Considering that Teatro plays usually evolve through several versions, the *Bandido* first version is comparatively clear in its message, and impressive in its melodramatic art. Both plays, *Rose* and *Bandido*, introduce a subtle Chicano perspective into what is otherwise the collision of Spanish colonialism and expansionist Yankee capitalism. The ground trodden is shaky with class and race lines constantly overlapping and intermingling. The form of the musical melodrama serves as a distancing device just at the point when a Chicano audience might be ready to identify too heartily with a noble Spanish *rico*. Vasquez — complexity and contradictions of his life retained — however, comes out as a politically conscious guerrillero, whose struggle is a rightful one to counter Anglo domination of the state.

IV

The President of the United States of America recognizes Luis Valdez for his extraordinary achievements and continuing creativity in the field of theatre.

The White House, May 17, 1983

Ronald Reagan

The document displayed in a not very prominent place of the lobby of the San Juan Bautista spinach warehouse turned theatre, epitomizes very well a process called "mainstreaming" by some, termed "selling out" by others. For Valdez it is the step of "taking power," the second important step — aside from presenting Aztec mythology, Mayan philosophy, and Mexican regional history as subject matter of drama.

Mayan philosophy prompts an aggressive thrust into the professional world of movies, TV, Broadway.[16] Thus the professionalization of the Teatro, the hiring of new actors on equity base for individual production rather than keeping the continuity of an atmospherically and politically unified group, emerges as a purposeful concept. In fact, this drive towards professionalism is viewed as a major achievement.[17]

Luis Valdez — apart from functioning as artistic director for the Teatro, in this respect — is also using professionalism as a base for his own personal career. The movie *Zoot Suit*, although more popular in Mexico than in the U.S., may serve as a sign of this trend. More so: his recent script-writing for Jane Fonda Productions (adapting Carlos Fuentes' unpublished novel about the Mexican Revolution, *Gringo Viejo* into the movie *Gringo Bravo*, of which he is also going to be the director) and the use of Carl Orff's *Carmina burana* as the musical base for a video rock opera, his latest version, so to speak of *Fin del Mundo*.[18] Obviously, projects of this kind have to be realized through a capitalistically organized structure of cultural production. The strategy is to keep control of the process, not to allow restrictions of content and message or censorship. By and large, it worked with *Zoot Suit*. Certain contradictions which occurred, can be viewed as contradictions of the cultural producers themselves, who are, in turn, products of a contradictory societal system.[19]

The attempt, then, of traditionally culturally deprived groups or individuals – in the case of Valdez and the Teatro, prompted by the reappropriation of the comprehensive and cosmic philosophy of the Mayas – to assume control over a cultural process by instrumentalizing the dominant economic structures, is in its tendency a departure from the old left thesis that alternative culture has to realize itself through alternative channels, thus bypassing the central points of the dominant marketplace. The balancing act that this involves is the price to be paid for the courageous step toward what could be, to a modest extent, the cultural hegemony of a subordinate culture.

The possible advantages of such a venture are twofold: By professionalizing its own base, the Teatro will give work to actors, directors, musicians, etc. and contribute to a professionalization of Chicano theatrical artists. By using film and television, secondly, Valdez may be successful in carrying a "Chicano message," even if somewhat diluted, to a much larger Chicano public than could have been reached through San Juan Bautista performance runs, and even the occasional Teatro tour, or guest performance runs in San Francisco or Los Angeles. It is important, however, that *all* these endeavors are carried on at the same time.

It is also important that in evaluating these proceedings, we do not focus exclusively on the Teatro Campesino, but become aware that there is a gamut of activities in Teatro Chicano. El Teatro de la Esperanza, as the only full-time company at present, fulfils a significant role in touring Chicano communities all over the Southwest. Many a smaller community amateur company, such as the Teatro Aguacero of Albuquerque, with its wonderful production of *The Teachings of Doña Juana*, performs an important function in educational theatre, reinterpreting and reappropriating for itself and its audience the essence of the Chicano movement in the 1960s and early 1970s.

We also have to partly depart from yet another old left concept, namely the abolition of the division of labor in political theatre and Teatro Chicano. The collective production of *actos* all the way from script-writing to the actual performance, or the writing of a "house-playwright" exclusively for one group is still taking place, but it is no longer the only form. The recent publications of first collections of plays by Chicano/Chicana dramatists[20] indicate a process that has become increasing practice: playwrights who do not work with a group, produce for a general Chicano theatre market.

Only, if we view *Zoot Suit*, and *Sun Images, Gringo Bravo*, and *Doña Juana, Corridos*, and *Octopus* as different aspects of one unified cultural process and reality in Teatro Chicano, will we be able to grasp this complex phenomenon of theatre within the two cultures, which is not primarily Anglo vs. Chicano, but has to do with the ideological and emotional perspective "from below" within its content and its message.

Notes

[1] Statement by Luis Valdez in several interviews; most recently in a conversation with me, conducted at San Juan Bautista, March 19, 1984.

[2] These changes have been dealt with in a number of publications, see among others: Yvonne Yarbro-Bejarano, "From *acto* to *mito*. A Critical Appraisal of the Teatro Campesino," in *Modern Chicano Writers*, ed. Joseph Sommers and Tomás Ybarra-Frausto (Englewood Cliffs: Prentice-Hall, 1979), pp. 176–85.

[3] Dieter Herms, "Luis Valdez – Chicano Dramatist. An Introduction and an Interview," in *Essays on Contemporary American Drama*, ed. H. Bock and A. Wertheim (Munich: Hueber Verlag, 1981), p. 277.

[4] See, in particular, the work of Mario Barrera. Also some of the case studies in *Perspectivas en Chicano Studies*, ed. Reynaldo F. Macías (Los Angeles: National Association of Chicano Social Science, 1977).

[5] Cf., among others, Tatcho Mindiola, "Marxism and the Chicano Movement. Preliminary Remarks," in *Perspectivas*, pp. 179–86; Richard A. Garcia, "The Chicano Movement and the Mexican-American Community, 1972–1978. An Interpretative Essay," *Socialist Review* 40/41 (1978), 117–36.

[6] Juan Gómez-Quiñones, "Toward a Concept of Culture," in *Modern Chicano Writers*, (Note 2), pp. 54–66, especially pp. 61–62.

[7] First published as "From the Critical Premise to the Product: Critical Modes and their Applications to a Chicano Literary Text," *The New Scholar*, 5, No. 2 (1977), and then variously reprinted. Enlarged and split into two articles in *Modern Chicano Writers*, (Note 2), pp. 41–40 and 94–107.

[8] Armando Gutiérrez, "Politics in the Chicano Novel. A Critique," in *Understanding the Chicano Experience Through Literature*, Mexican American Studies Monograph Series, No. 2 (April 1981), pp. 7–14.

[9] Dieter Herms, "Chicano Literature – A European Perspective," currently in print, *Revista Chicano-Riqueña*.

[10] See for instance Joachim Bischoff, "Projekt Ideologie – Theorie" and Stuart Hall in *Das Argument*, 122 (1980), 479–517; or Klaus R. Scherpe, Lauri Mehtonen, Thomas Metscher, Frieder O. Wolf in *Das Argument*, 137 (1983), 10–53.

[11] Frieder O. Wolf, "Für eine subversive Praxis der Philosophie," *Das Argument* 137 (1983), 52; (my translation of quote). Obviously, there is no "streamlining" application of cultural theory to ideological praxis. But Wolf's approach may throw some additional light on Valdez' attitude towards U.S. reality.

[12] Two successful runs in 1983, both in the theatre house of San Juan Bautista and in a major theatre of San Francisco; further showings are planned for San Diego and Los Angeles.

120

[13] Margarita R. Segura, "Corridos by Luis Valdez and El Teatro Campesino – Perpetuating El Rancho," *Tecolote Literary Magazine* (July 1983), 8.

[14] Luis Valdez, Introd. *Aztlán. An Anthology of Mexican American Literature*, ed. Luis Valdez and Stan Steiner (New York: Vintage, 1972), p. XXIX.

[15] Terry C. Fox, "Home on the Rancho," *The Village Voice* (September 2–8, 1981), Theater section.

[16] Cf. Valdez' statement in T. Benitel, "Facing the Issues Beyond 'Zoot Suit'. An Interview with Playwright Luis Valdez," *New World*, 3 (1978), 37.

[17] See Jorge Huerta, in an interview with Dieter Herms, currently in print for *Gulliver*, 17 (1985).

[18] Both projects were still in the state of preparation, when I visited in San Juan Bautista, and talked to Luis Valdez (March 1984).

[19] Contradictions can hardly be avoided in the marketing process of the product; I refer to the Coca Cola advertizing gig both in my paper (note 9) and my earlier piece "Zwischen Mythos, Anpassung und Rebellion – El Teatro Campesino 1978"; first published in *Iberoamericana*, 3, No. 2 (7; 1979), 14–32; reprinted in Dieter Herms/Arno Paul, *Politisches Volkstheater der Gegenwart* (Berlin-West: Argument-Verlag, 1981), p. 97.

[20] See for instance: Carlos Morton, *The Many Deaths of Danny Rosales, And Other Plays* (Houston: Arte Público Press, 1983).

IV CHICANO POETRY

Alurista's Flight to Aztlán: A Study of Poetic Effectiveness

Yves-Charles Grandjeat

Alurista's Work has been acknowledged both by critics and readers of Chicano poetry as an outstanding landmark. "A seminal figure," according to Tomás Ybarra,[1] he is considered by many as "the poet laureate of Aztlán."[2] But fame never comes alone: he has also been one of the most controversial Chicano writers. Indeed, while everybody has hailed the breakthrough he has achieved from a linguistic point of view, his ideology has stirred up much heated debate; especially among political activists. I think such a debate is often irrelevant, if understandable, and I would like to offer a reading which does not stress the link between his poetry and the ideology of cultural nationalism, but instead focuses on his use of poetic imagery and symbolism. My contention is that a work of poetry cannot and should not be analyzed according to political standards, even when the poet is also an activist. A poem is not a political platform and the poet moves his reader with symbols that often reach beyond his own grasp, more than with ideas with which the intellect can agree or disagree.

However, it is the political reading of Alurista's work which has prevailed for long. Juan Gómez-Quiñones' preface to *Floricanto en Aztlán* thus suggests that we should assess the poet's work as a realistic and therefore enlightening description of the Chicanos' condition.[3] Along that same line, Gary Keller's long introduction to the volume *Return* strives hard to show that, although not realistic, Alurista's poetry is ideologically correct, and, all in all, constructively "in service of el movimiento."[4] Of course we know that the poet has been deeply involved both as a person and as a writer in the movement, and that, for instance, he contributed a resolution to the *Plan de Aztlán* adopted by the Chicano Youth Conference in Denver in 1969. Besides, apart from pamphlets such as *The American Nightmare*, even his poetry is loaded with political undertones and interspersed with such catchwords as "liberation," "exploitation," "revolution," "economic independence," "genocide," "dictatorships," etc. "It Is" and "Mar de Sangres," in *Nationchild Plumaroja* both illustrate this kind of political rhetoric. However, the poet himself has warned us against approaching his work from a purely political perspective. And indeed, in the light of a careful reading we find that the revolution he advocates is first and foremost a spiritual one, one that must be achieved through a mental process rather than a political program. The poem "Who are We? Somos Aztlán" is a case in point:

We shall walk the path of courage
and disciplined
defeat the people's enemy, fear, with non-violently
rooted power, our weapon justicia
to: establish peace
restore the earth
and respect the sun   (R. p. 81).[5]

Alurista's revolution must arise from a struggle between fear and peace, ignorance and knowledge, a struggle of attitudes and values. The symbols he wields are intended to alter our perception of ourselves and of the world, thereby opening up to us new areas of action. This is not achieved through realism, but through what we might call "poetic effectiveness," after Levi-Strauss's definition of "symbolic effectiveness." The anthropologist used the expression in his analysis of the healing effectiveness of language and representations in the shamanistic cure. He compares it to other therapies such as psychoanalysis and shows that in both cases, the healer provides the patient with symbols that allow him to regain some control over physiological and emotional trouble, by offering a mental structure which enables the patient to understand and organize his feelings. "That the mythology of the shaman does not correspond to an objective reality does not matter. (. . .) The shaman provides the sick woman with a language by means of which otherwise unexpressed and inexpressible psychic states can be readily expressed."[6] This description strikingly echoes what Alurista himself is trying to achieve: "I think that part of what literature can do, or at least what I'm trying to do, is make it a healing art, not only a reflective art. It is also a surgical tool." This therapeutic effectiveness comes from the power of representations to alter reality: "I realized early how metaphors and images and words shape the way I see the world, shape the way I behave in the world. By now I'm convinced that, given the power to describe reality, we can construct a more human reality beginning with a more human description."[7] I will try to show how both in *Floricanto en Aztlán* and *Nationchild Plumaroja*, considered to be his most heavily political volumes, written in the heat of the Chicano Movement, Alurista's poetry is geared towards this kind of symbolic effectiveness. Moreover, they both evidence obvious similarities between the structure of the poet's imagery and that of the shaman's symbolic journey.

Just like the shaman who comes to embody the group as a whole and its cohesion in front of a threatening disorder, Alurista's poetry is collective insofar as it is directed towards a communal audience, involves an identification between the "I" of the poet and the "we" of the group, and attempts to build up collective identity through positive symbols. The poet constantly reminds Chicanos of their collective heritage, their common oppression and their common fate. Words referring to a collective unit, such as "gente," "people," and "raza" keep on recurring. "Raza" for instance is used at least 112 times in *Floricanto*, by my count. In a poem such as "We can work it out. Raza," the word echoes like an incantation designed to summon up unity. Together with "Raza," Alurista harps on the feeling which ties the group together, i.e. "carnalismo," which recurs at least 45 times in the same volume.

The poet calls forth symbols likely to reinforce group solidarity as they stir up love pulsions to channel them towards the group. Strikingly, Alurista never mentions sexual love in these two volumes. But the mother figure hovers above them as an outstanding symbol, meant to direct energy in a subliminal way towards the group which it embodies. In "Bendita Suerte" (*F.* 70) group solidarity is endowed with the strength and sacredness of matrimony:

> today I marry la Raza
> — hasta que la muerte nos separe

When the woman is present in a sensual way, as in "La Carne de tus Labios" (*F.* 41), she becomes a symbol of collective pride, an allegory of positive identity:

> el plumaje guerrero
> in her arrogant walk
> to pace
> and have
> to run behind no more

Moreover, in the end of this poem, the woman turns into the collective mother, the Indian goddess Tonantzin, through the evocation of the Virgen de Guadalupe. Throughout both volumes, the mother figure is overbearing, mostly associated with the earth, the universal mother — 26 times in *Floricanto*, and sometimes with the Virgen, as in "Bendito sea tu Vientre" (*F.* 26), where she is paradoxically the symbol of both fertility and virginity, both suggesting and denying sexuality. Sexuality *is* mentioned but in a negative way, as is the case in "Bronze Rape" (*R.* p.67), and "Mar de Sangres" (*R.* p.88) where the poet evokes the rape of Indian mothers and sisters by colonial invaders, another image intended to bolster collective cohesion, this time in a negative way. Without venturing into a psychoanalytical reading, although poems such as "Levántate y Rie" seem to demand this kind of approach (*R.* p.94), we can see that the poet attempts to merge the individual with the group, symbolically identified as a family, through figures such as the threatened or the loving, providing mother. In doing this, Alurista not only evidences a typically male attitude, he also appeals to a psychic structure described by Octavio Paz as characteristic of the Mexican collective psyche, torn between the image of the virgin and that of the "chingada."

Mexican symbols of collective identity are also drawn from folklore and history. Through their repeated use, the poet tries to come across as a medium between all members of the group, as the voice of collective consciousness: *"I am not the author of my words, my images or metaphors.* I am the weaver of these things. The people are the authors of the language; the people are the authors of the imagery, of the symbols."[8] However, the symbols through which collectiveness is achieved are also meant to perform some major functions in a context of violent opposition.

Like the shaman, the poet is caught in a struggle against the deadly forces of evil, a fight in which the survival of the group is at stake. The oppositional, binary structure which sets the Indio or the Chicano against the white man is at the core of most of his poems. Indigenous, natural food is equated with cosmic life – the tortilla is round as the earth, the beans have its color, the salsa is hot as the sun and as red as rushing blood, whereas chemical U.S. food epitomizes a decadent inorganic lifeless civilization. Opposition takes all possible shapes: perfume is contrasted with stench, heat with frigidity, music with howling, organic life with mechanism, action with abstract intellectualism, passion and feeling with barren rationalism, love with money, slavery with freedom, growth and movement with paralysis, life with death, etc. . . . Alurista's poetry stems from this clash between the East and the West, between two visions of the world. There, the Indian world becomes a fantastic version of the promised land, while the industrialized Western world represents a gate to the apocalypse. In fact, far from trying to give a realistic rendering of historical conflicts, the poet uses reality to provide him with symbols setting the stage for the essential struggle between life and death.

In this struggle, like the shaman, the poet can use the power of the words conveying the sacred wisdom, the superior knowledge he has acquired through dreams and visions. But the power of the word is reinforced in Alurista's poetry by words of power, dynamic, thrusting images designed to induce an attitude of self-confidence and rebellion in the face of the enemy. Figures drawn from Mexican history, from Cuauhtemoc to Zapata symbolize a spirit of rebellion and resistance. The precolumbian imagery offers a large variety of such symbols. The pyramid, the epitome of the power and the glory is the most common one. Recurring references to the "caballeros tigres, montañas de voluntad" (*R*. p.8) crowned with their "proud guerrero plumaje" (*F*. 5), to the Aztec warriors and aristocracy, "our royal lineaje con plumas de quetzal" (*R*. 37), fulfill the same function. In the same group of symbols we find weapons such as the axe or the arrow, the machete, as in the poem "Me retiro con mis Sueños":

> me retiro con mis sueños
> con las plumas de guerrero
> con el hacha de tizoc (*R*. p. 26),

which are meant to evoke and bolster determination, will, and passion. Indeed, "will," "voluntad," and "passion" are three other key words, and can be found in at least every other poem in the beginning of *Floricanto*, several times in "I Can't," "Libertad," "La Cucaracha," "Chicano Heart," etc. They represent life energy brought to a climax.

But this aggressive, outward symbolism is balanced by a more intimate one hinging on images of sharing and dissolving, aimed at reconnecting life with death. Thus, after confronting hostile forces with a warlike attitude, the poet, like the shaman, withdraws to the center of the earth where he learns how to join opposites. The earth and food imagery are at the core of Alurista's symbolism. The earth is both the universal womb and the inevitable tomb, equally connected with life and death. It is associated with fertility and birth in a poem such as "Danza Leonina":

> Proviniente de fecundo vientre
> man stands and walks again on earth
> to listen with plantas descalzas
> to the murmuring caress of
> motherearth's latidos
> she gave us birth in blood (*R*. p. 92).

But the earth is linked up with death in the poem that immediately follows, "Aqui Nomas":

> Motherearth devours her children (...)
> our motherearth
> will welcome the return of her children
> to her womb and our flesh
> and her flesh shall be our dormant life ...

Death, the mother figure, and the earth are thus closely associated in a number of poems such as "Madre Tumba Soledad," or "Corazon Lapida," or, again, in the poem "It is," where the author calls up "the spirit / that binds us to this earth and to the death" (*R*. p. 52).

Death is another key motive in Alurista's poems; it appears at least 78 times in *Floricanto* alone. As for *Nationchild*, it opens on a meditation upon death with the poem "We Would Have Been Relieved with Death," which develops in "I Have Found my Flesh" and "Construyendo una Balsa." What might seem paradoxical in a symbolism designed to stir up energy is actually in keeping with this goal. Like the shaman who surrenders to death, the poet shows that encountering death and coming to terms with it is a step towards a life without fear, and the violence it begets. The dialectical relationship between life and death is clearly stated in poems such as "I Have Found my Flesh": "I suffer y estoy vivo en el acto de mi afecto por la muerte" and the following one where we are faced with "a calavera romantica que cena con la muerte tortilla en mano and entirely committed to the act of being" (*R*. pp. 4—5). On the opposite, fear of death implies rejecting life, as the Yankees did:

> they refused to accept death
> and/froze/their/bodies/cold/mechanic flesh
> of efficient immortality/in ice (*R*. p. 88)

The motive of the cave in the earth, which shares the ambivalence of being connected with both life and death helps the poet to make his point. The cave is both a "caverna de miedo," a place of terror and darkness, but this passage of trial opens up to a life purified of the ugliness of fear, as it is clear in "Marrana Placa":

> Razared be born to the cavern
> to the obscurity, to the blackdark stench
> Razared be born
> after your suicide mutation birth to quench
> to the caverns bring a river crystal bath (R. p. 47).

Images connected with the earth and motherhood thus evidence another attitude regarding fear and death. Rather than confronting it with a flurry of aggressive symbols, we are induced to make friends with death, to welcome it, thus getting rid of fear, as it becomes connected with protective, positive images. The poet, through a symbolic transfer, subverts traditional meanings, and death far from being a threat to growth, is turned into a dynamic image of life itself:

> The lapida of our flesh
> shall caress the stolen land
> and kiss the rocas, a mother
> indiamuerte en plumas
> y en cananas
> junto a la tumba, la madre!
> our sangre, la resurrection morena! (R. p. 40).

In this poem for instance, the linking up of images brought out by words such as "land," "mother," "tumba," "caress," "kiss," "sangre," "muerte," "resurrection" clearly achieves this aim.

Fear does not only arise from the thought of death, it also stems from the fear of separation in general, fear of being divorced from the other and from the world. The poet will therefore, like the shaman who understands how each element of the universe communicates with the other, carry on his purpose of linking opposites through ambivalent or even polyvalent symbols, such as those related to eating and food. For if communion can be reached through death, when nature incorporates man, it also happens through the reverse process of eating in which man absorbs nature. The tortilla and the taco, two other recurrent symbols must be understood as related to this sacred communion between man and cosmos.

But linking takes place within each major symbol itself; as it branches out towards a wide range of meanings. The motive of blood for instance is connected with war, death, and wounds on the one hand, but also with birth and passion on the other. The sun is linked with both the heat of oppressive work, and the fertility of the earth, with violence and love. Moreover, the poet repeatedly uses what we could call "linking symbols," symbols which are related to an in-between state, and provide intermediate links between separate and distinct

elements. The *sarape*, which weaves various colors together may be the archetype of such symbols. The poet also lays the stress on such elements as blood,
sweat, tears, elements through which abstract feelings take a material shape, in
between matter and emotion, elements through which man pours his inner self
into the outside world. Other basic symbols seem to fulfill the same function.
The hair and the feathers are both in between the body and the air, they fly but
they are attached. Alurista's animal imagery strikingly fits into this pattern. The
symbol of the eagle and the serpent has often been referred to, but the cockroach, creeping and flying, connected with both the air and the earth has the
same implications. The crickets evoke the hierogamy of the sun and the earth
through their singing, and so do the rattlesnakes which are also linked with
music and dancing through the symbol of the *cascabel*, evoking the jingling bells
of the Aztec ritual dances as in "Before the Flesh in Bones" and "Clamped
Almas." Sound and movement thus meet, as the sun fuses with the earth. On
the other hand, the *ranas* and the *sapo* (the frogs and the toad) are connected
with night and water. Moreover, while animals connected with the sun evoke
heat, passion, and action, those connected with the moon are meant to suggest
remembering and meditating. Thus mental attitudes are associated with cosmic
elements.

Once the linking up is achieved, the poet, like the shaman has the whole world
to draw power from: each element fans out towards the totality of which it
is part, and one can move forward with a new strength, derived through a
transcendent kind of awarenesss. Walking and flying, and all the images gravitat-
ing around forward and upward movements are pervasive in this regard. References to 'walking' — "yo no se correr, se caminar" (*F.* 64) — keep on recurring and are reflected in the image of the alley, or the path. The journey
to Aztlán, the land of origin, is a journey "down age carved alleys" (*R.* p. 36),
towards "the marcha que mis padres engendraron." The tradition of migration
and walking, is summoned up in "We Walk on Pebbled Streets," where it is
directly linked with growth and fertility to images of fruits:

> we like to walk
> mi gente ha caminado mucho
> -desde el Asia
> through North America
> to the land of pulque and tunas
> where the bean grows (*F.* 20).

Walking is therefore connected, through the notion of growth, to vertical symbols. Horizontal and vertical symbols are also brought together through the
motive of fertility and make up a complex network in a poem such as "Insane
Buildings" (*F.* 76):

> my anger crawls
> to rise and spit the laughter
> of my cry (...)
> in tears I water meadowed paths
> bushy ahuehuetes escalan y me rodean; ...

Numerous symbols related to birth, dawn, growth, — the 'tuna' is one of the most frequent ones — finally associate walking, the movement which ties man to the physical earth, with the vertical surge which sends him towards the transcendent wisdom and spirituality epitomized by the sun:

> flying to
> the cloudy pillow of a dream
> of winds that wind
> around and upwards
> to the sun (*R*. p. 57).

These remarks could and should be backed by many more examples but there may be just enough here to suggest that Alurista, as a poet, does not respond to conflict with a political ideology, but with an imagery which combines four basic attitudes, and which can be structurally organized in a pattern that follows the various stages of the shamanistic cure. First, we find an attitude of proud armed opposition:

> rhythmic arrows bathed in war paint
> fog festival of rising red struggle (sink never) (*R*. p. 8).

Second, an attitude of quiet withdrawal to the intimacy of the earth and to the place of origin:

> back, back to the flowing
> water causeways
> of Tenochtitlan
> back to the tears of Tlaloc's agony ... (*R*. p. 86).

Third, and in my opinion, this is where poetic effectiveness is the strongest, drawing multiple connections between once separate elements and weaving them into a complex network, gathering the chaotic multiplicity of experience into a coherent whole:

> in the trepidous flight of a bird
> Quetzalcoatl gave birth to its death (*R*. p. 42),

and finally a passage from quiet acceptance to the movement of a fearless life endowed with superior knowledge:

> in the mud
> butterflies found birth
> flying to the sun
> from the stillness of time calaveras (*R*. p. 94).

We might end these remarks wondering whether we should say that Alurista's poetry has well served the Chicano movement, or whether the Chicano movement, through Alurista's writings has well served poetry. Maybe both.

Notes

[1] Tomás Ybarra-Frausto, "Alurista's Poetics: the Oral, the Bilingual, the Precolumbian," in *Modern Chicano Writers*, ed. Joseph Sommers and Tomás Ybarra-Frausto (Englewood Cliffs: Prentice-Hall, 1979), p. 117.

[2] [Juan] Bruce-Novoa, *Chicano Authors, Inquiry by Interview* (Austin: Univ. of Texas Press, 1980), p. 267.

[3] Juan Gómez-Quiñones, Pref., *Floricanto en Aztlán* (Los Angeles: UCLA Chicano Studies Center Publications, 1971).

[4] Gary D. Keller, Introd., "Alurista, Poeta-Antropólogo, and the Recuperation of Chicano Identity," *Return, Poems Collected & New* (Binghamton, N.Y.: Bilingual Press, 1982), p. 20.

[5] The poems quoted are all taken from *Floricanto en Aztlán* and *Nationchild Plumaroja*. The notes should be read as follows:
F. 70 = *Floricanto en Aztlán*, poem no. 70.
R. p. 67 = *Nationchild Plumaroja*, in *Return, Poems Collected and New*, p. 67.

[6] Claude Levi-Strauss, *Anthropologie Structurale* (Paris: Plon, 1958 and 1974), pp. 217–18.

[7] Bruce-Novoa, pp. 279–80.

[8] Bruce-Novoa, p. 273.

Mothers and Grandmothers: Acts of Mythification and Remembrance in Chicano Poetry

Wolfgang Binder

> Mi abuelita ya está muriendo lentamente.
> Cierra los ojos. Cierra la boca. [...] And
> what goes with her? My claim to an internal
> dialogue where el gringo does not penetrate?
> Su memoria a de noventa y seis años going back
> to a time where 'nuestra cultura' was not the
> subject of debate.[1]

There exists hardly any male Chicano poet[2] (or prose writer, for that matter) who has not produced a piece on a mother or a grandmother. The persistent literary presence of the two female exponents of cultural and familial stability comes not as a surprise to any critic who is familiar with Chicano existence in and Chicano resistance to a society that is dominated by Anglo values. While the individual, privatistic motivation of the respective author behind the mother or grandmother poem may not be of prime interest, the use made of both figures certainly is.

I.

In the early phase of Chicano cultural nationalism, from the late sixties to the mid-seventies, the mother appears in the mythified shape of the Mexican Virgin of Guadalupe and as the mother of the brown Chicano *Raza.*[3] It is relevant to note that this mythification does not involve a nebulous and/or complete removal of the figure into distant times, since her function as the mother of a race which is very much alive in Aztlán links her with an embattled presence and a postulated affirmation of *mestizaje.* The apparition of Guadalupe/Tonantzin in 1531, which through the creole apologists has become an indelible emblem of national Mexican pride[4] both in "México de adentro" and "México de afuera,"[5] also carries vast political Pan-American and Pan-Indian connotations that should not be ignored.

In 1969 the activist Abelardo Delgado ("Lalo") had his poem "Mamá Lupe" not by chance printed opposite his poem "La Revolución," on the same double page. Delgado, who is a naive and often enough didactic poet, portrays the Virgin as one who gave "soul birth to a race of strong will," and defines her as "root [...] of mestizos." A rediscovery and propositioned acceptance of the Chicanos as a mestizo nation[6] can be found in the last stanza of "Mamá Lupe," where the speaker turns to self-accusation and a plea for forgiveness: "morena dulce, don't do what I do / and forget me like I've forgotten you."[7]

Two years later, Alurista refers in his first published volume of poetry[8] in a quasi-religious incantation to Guadalupe as "virgin of love," names her "madre," and in a circular movement connects the initial blessing of her "vientre" with that of the whole Chicano people: "bendita seas / Raza." The birth of a nation is celebrated in "fruto de bronce," and again a circular movement derived from Aztec philosophy and art is used. Guadalupe as the Virgin is holding the newly born infant in her arms in a posture known from classic Christian iconography:

> su madre guadalupe
> con el infante
> en sus brazos
> i've seen her bronze skin [...] .

A seemingly individualized act assumes gradually emphatic, ritual, collective racial dimensions, as the process (not just the result), the growth of a consciousness is rendered:

> el nacimiento de mi pueblo
> bronze child
> bronze skin
> bronze virgin
> i've seen the bronze birth
> [...]
> i have seen la Raza
> i have seen la Raza be born.[9]

Sergio Elizondo mixes intense religious feelings with rather carnal ones that are directed towards a girl by the name of Lupe (from Guadalupe) in his "Domingo Bright Morning." Yet even there we have an affirmation of cultural nationalism in connection with the symbol of a national Mexican/Chicano epiphany:

> [...] el pueblo canta.
> 'O María, madre mía
> o consuelo del mortal'
> María ojos azules se alegra;
> le cantan las mañanitas
> Lupe ni encela.
> El pueblo, los batos, las chavalas
> a la güera cantan [...]
> pero en los corazones Chicanos
> la Santísima Virgen Guadalupe
> manda.
> Per omnia secula seculorum —.[10]

José Montoya established in 1969 what becomes a pattern in many later poems by male Chicano poets: the speaker recalls his mother in highly selective activities which, in addition, place her in the context of a thus recorded family history. The act of remembrance goes hand in hand with an act of idealization, of bestowing honors *post festum*. In the dramatizing technique characteristic of this great master of intralingual Chicano poetry,[11] dialogues and monologues in "La Jefita" alternate with description, observation, and reflection. The never tiring "jefita" is painted as a life force within the modest household. Cooking, feeding, caring are her essential activities — a life of devotion to others, a life of sacrifice. Her son muses: "(¡Me la rayo, ese! My jefita never slept!)," and her husband is reported as saying: "That woman — she only complains / in her sleep."[12]

The topical image as the cook, the feeder, and the devoted servant reappears in Alberto Ríos' "Nani":

> Sitting at her table she serves
> the sopa de arroz to me
> instinctively, and I watch her,
> the absolute *mamá*, and eat words
> I might have had to say more
> out of embarrassment.[13]

Extreme idealization of the mother occurs, understandably, in prison *(pinto)* poetry. Frank Galindo, Jr., is a case in point. His "Brown Beautiful — Brown Mother" contains unadulterated macho attitudes:

> For she yearns for her 'Macho'-till with
> morn comes
> the light —
> Her love knows no limits —, for those that
> she's born.

The same author does put her into a racial context with: "She carries the scars —, of a beautiful brown race —," and sounds an echo of the Guadalupe motif with: "Brown Beautiful, — Brown Mother —, glowing/ with faith- / God knows you — 'Lady' —, it shows in your / face —."[14]

Alberto Ríos' "Rodriguez Street," a reckoning of his childhood, contains the double image of a mother. It is an image split along cultural, affective, and linguistic lines. The hated Anglo "mother" is contrasted with a warm, permissive Chicano "mamá," whom he remembers fondly. While it looks at one point as if the two women were actually a composite of one and the same person, it is ascertained early on that they are two separate beings:

> I must have been just over three,
> when mother sent me to Maestro's for milk
> and I knew mamá would give me
> a big box of Jell-o to eat
> on her porch, all mine [...] .

The Anglo version was "the one yelling,/ that smelled like a busy dry-cleaners,/ and lived with me." The Chicano mamá had the "smell of wood stoves at dusk and spit/ from new children" and "was always laughing/ like she'd never stop [...]."[15]

A very different mother image surfaces in Luis Omar Salinas' poetry. Salinas lost his mother at an early age;[16] the traumatic experience made him people a series of his surreal, haunting poems with a mother who is clearly physically absent. In "This Is What I Said," a childhood recollection, he "saw ghosts in the garden/ and my mother consoled me."[17] But she is in the same poem brought into the realms of a more sombre nature:

> There was a time when I chased
> butterflies in Mexico, and the
> mad nearby grinned with huge
> faces which seemed to be made
> of my mother's apron.

At other instances her absence is painfully present. The speaker is yearning for "a fistful/ of tenderness/ from my absent mother" in "Autumn."[18] Or she becomes his *confidante*, as in "What Is This Something?": "Mother, tomorrow I'm leaving for/ San Francisco and I'm sadder/ than the seagulls circling your forehead."[19] In "After Your Absence" he conjures up her presence, and she becomes charged with the function of an interlocutor whom he fills in on developments in the family and to whom he accounts for his achievements:

> In your absence your son
> has turned handsome /.../
> Your sisters are alive
> and getting old.
> [...] Father
> remarried, and is still
> the same,
> with a gusto
> and love for the restless.
> Oh, I write poetry
> now, mother.
> You won't have to worry
> I've got good friends
> in addition to God.[20]

"To an Old Woman," by Rafael Jesús González, carries a note of reproachful didacticism, as differences in acculturation between two generations are mentioned in the anecdote of an elderly seamstress of modest means, who is used as an addressee to whom questions are directed that remain unanswered in the text. Of course, the reader is invited to answer them him- or herself: "Where are the sons you bore?/ Do they speak only English now/ And say they're Spanish?" Despite the distance that emanates from the speaker's approach, it is clear that he treasures the visits of the old lady to his store: "One day [...] I know I'll wait in vain / For your toothless benediction." The old client represents cultural traditions that the writer sees menaced and worthwhile to defend: "I'll look into the dusty street/ [...] Until a dirty child will nudge me and say:/ 'Señor, how much ees thees?' "[21]

II.

Written from the perspective of a speaker who remembers a grandmother who has passed away, Leonard Adamé's "my grandmother would rock quietly and hum," confirms the nostalgic trend of many poems that take up this topic. In addition to a portrait of a dedicated woman who fed her family and lived a hard life — he mentions "her swelled hands" — she forms part of collective history by being a storyteller. In one sense, she is removed from present day life:

> now,
> at the old house,
> there are
> worn spots by the stove
> where she shuffled; and Mexico
> hangs in her
> fading calendar pictures [...] .

Yet with the account of her life she gave (presumably) to her grandson, she becomes a repository of collective Chicano history, of death in the Mexican Revolution, of the northbound migration, of thwarted hopes in the American Dream:

> she sat and talked
> of girlhood
> — of things strange to me:
> Mexico
> epidemics
> relatives shot
> her father's hopes
> of this country,
> and how they sank
> with cement dust
> to his insides.[22]

A poem by Gary Soto entitled "History" gives an unequivocal initial clue to what follows and how the author wants his reader to interpret it. Again a grandmother is observed at early morning kitchen chores. Her Mexicanness is indi-

138

cated by her being "wrapped in a shawl," by "pound[ing] chiles/ With a stone/ Brought from Guadalajara." A delightful roguish trait — and a glimpse of survival techniques — is revealed in the old lady's ability to make victuals dissappear "under a paisley bandana" and bring them home from the market for free. Once more the reader witnesses aspects of hardship, illness, and death:[23]

> I remember her insides
> Were washed of tapeworm,
> Her arms swelled into knobs
> Of small growths —
> Her second son
> Dropped from a ladder
> and was dust.

The function of the grandmother as a symbol of and a repository for oral, largely migrant history that transcends individual family history becomes established at the end of the text:

> [...] the stories
> That pulled her
> From Taxco to San Joaquín,
> Delado to Westside,
> The places
> In which we all begin.[24]

Soto's poem contains one aspect that we have so far not touched upon, but which was mentioned above in L. Adamé's poem. The speaker admits to his ignorance as far as the inner life of the spent old woman is concerned. He is honest enough not to gloss over the distance that life had put between the two persons:

> And yet I do not know
> The sorrows
> That sent her praying
> In the dark of a closet,
> The tear that fell
> At night
> When she touched
> Loose skin
> Of belly and breasts.
> I do not know why
> Her face shines
> Or what goes on beyond this shine.

He remembers, however, what he saw and, above all, what he heard.

A rather cruel facet of cultural and emotional estrangement between grandchildren and grandmother in a culture of poverty is dealt with in one of the sections of Soto's "The Street." Here the grandmother is viewed as ugly, despicable, as a subhuman old Indian squaw.

> The grandmother
> shuffles
> From one fruit tree
> To the next, her hands
> Skinned with dirt,
> Her breathing
> A hive of gnats.
> She is Indian,
> My brother believes,
> And lassoes her to a fence
> With the rope
> That pulled a cow
> To its death,
> A sow to the market [...]

Even though the ending of the episode moves the stark realism into imaginary psychological and cultural grounds with the "Americanized," tragically ignorant youth, who is evidently influenced by a confused cowboy and Indian syndrome, it remains incisive enough. Soto's remarkably cool verbal economy renders the message all the more effective:

> Poverty is a pair
> Of boots, rain,
> Twin holters, slapping
> His side, and a hand
> Cocked into a pistol.
> When he points
> And he points
> And the smoke lifts,
> She is gone
> In the notch
> He scratches into his wrist.[25]

The grandmother, or any elder, as a storyteller, as a person of respect and authority, who gives meaning and coherence to a fragmented collective existence, reminds any student of American Literature of a vital element in Native American Literature, for instance in the poetry of Simon Ortiz and Leslie Marmon Silko. In the context of an ongoing *rapprochement* between Chicano and Native American cultural elites this parallel gains a momentum that can hardly be overestimated.[26]

Leroy V. Quintana centers his book *Sangre* on a matriarch,[27] on "Grandma," the bloodgiver of the whole "family tree," and just about everyone else in the extended family is defined according to his or her relation to her. Above all, she is a cultural force by remembering and transmitting stories, anecdotes, history. The verbs in "Sangre 2" reveal what Quintana sensed as relevant in the speaker's relation with the grandmother: She would "tell me," "show me," "explain." She was also one who "survived" and represents a personified lesson of endurance.[28]

Along with G. Soto's "History" the most moving and artistically most successful tribute to a grandmother coming from a male Chicano poet was written by
Tino Villanueva. "Now, Suns Later" is preceded by an unveiled dedication to
his grandmother as a historically secure figure — her full name, dates and places
of birth and death are given. The author thus pushes his resonant poetic text
towards a chronicle, an impression we find confirmed in his chronological procedure, his mentioning of dates, places, seasons. What happens on the page is a
merging of chronological and very personal time frames, a highly emotional
re-calling, the claiming of a past and a person hitherto not fully acknowledged.

History in this story begins as the lady takes a husband and becomes a ninefold
mother, facts which will determine the rest of her life.[29] Once again, an individualized context sees itself widened and assumes collective racial significance
in one of the figure's most salient functions, that of cooking and feeding: "She
[...] was up before the sun struck dawn,/ kneading *tortillas*/ to keep a race
going." Clara Solana Ríos is celebrated as a hard working, a crafty heroine within
a culture of subsistence: "From ready remnants, she patterned light glowing
quilts;/ from remnants of remnants, she braided a rug." Despite a move from
rural life to a town in Texas in the thirties, the "family" kept "following the
sun," was dependent on stoop labor. In the tradition of the pious, civilization-
spreading pioneer woman, she "assembled" her family "at her feet in Bible-
black nights." Villanueva's poem would not be complete without a passage
about the grandmother as oral historian:

> When asked about torn history,
> she'd squint past you through wrinkles
> into that imaginary distance of indefinite
> cottonfields,
> recalling her favorite dawns,
> the drought of '25,
> the Christmas of '48 when her three quick sons
> marched out of the distant seas.

Her life-giving faculty is associated in another stanza with a peaceful pastoral
setting, her garden, where

> she goes trimming the twilight of leaves;
> caressing the buds afire;
> making a Spring bloom year-round from flowerpots:
> her cupped hands kindling a wilting flower
> back into light.

With a chronological distance of ten years to her death and a geographical
distance to Texas — the poem was written in Boston, Massachusetts, "with a
promise of sure snow" — the poet reflects not without bitterness on the hard-
ships that this woman had to face, when no political or feminist movement
existed to cushion the blow, "to slow down/ the strides of the sun for her,
that woman,/ moving always in rhythms of labor in Texas sprawling days."

Yet, the painful act of remembrance "warms the day for me." Her life serves as a lesson of endurance, patience and survival. Villanueva may be a romantic poet, but he is not a naive one, nor does he simplify complex matters. He will not spare his readers what he perceives as an ennobling if distressing ordeal of self-effacing sacrifice and duty:

> And I endure,
> for patience must have been her only strength,
> her only movement, truly private.
> Lonely.[30]

III.

The interest that many Chicano poets showed in producing texts on mothers and grandmothers cannot simply be attributed to expressions of familism. It corresponds to the therapeutic mechanisms of a people who, by claiming a complex past and the persons who shaped it (and thus shaped the present) bring a certain amount of order into immanent chaos.

It remains noteworthy to state that the vast majority of these works have a first person singular speaker and that these acts of recalling include not only mothers and grandmothers, but whole families and a (more or less veiled) personal childhood experience. This gives many poems an urgency that the reader, especially the Chicano reader, can easily identify with.

That mothers are, if they are not totally idealized as quoted in the examples from the *pinto* poetry, portrayed in limiting, subservient, self-effacing, yet noble activities, does not imply that the writers approve whole-heartedly of what was, up to recent scholarship, frequently seen as the traditional role model for women in Mexican and Chicano societies. All of the poems amount to tributes and eulogies; some carry avowed expressions of regret or bitterness. L.V. Quintana's and J. Sagel's works on matriarchs contain elements of *hembrismo*.

All of the male poets share a distinctly asexual view of the women in these poems, if we exclude what appears in this context as far-fetched interpretations of cooking, serving, feeding as sublimated sexual metaphors. Chicana poets like Barbara Brinson-Piñeda, Lorna Dee Cervantes, Carmen Tafolla or Alma Villanueva[31] show less inhibitions in that taboo area. But then they may have different axes to grind.

Structuring and interpreting the past, be it via myth (Alurista), realistic (Montoya) or more metaphorical (Villanueva, Salinas) renderings implies a conscious verbal gesture of preservation, a lesson, an effort of holding one's ground in the face of potential and not so unreal cultural dilution. Gary Soto's "History" and "The Street," and Leonard Adamé's "the grandmother [...]" thus function also as warning poems.

142

The grandmother figure as a respected link with Mexico, as a repository of orally transmitted collective history, rises from the poems with a catching aura of misery, frailty, strength, and grandeur.

Notes

1 Cherríe Moraga, *Loving in the War Years* (Boston, Mass.: South End Press, 1983), III.
2 Since with Tey Diana Rebolledo, "Abuelitas, Mythology and Integration in Chicana Literature," *Revista Chicano-Riqueña*, 11, No. 3 and 4 (1983), 148–58, exists an informative contribution to a similar topic dealt with by female Chicano poets, it was felt appropriate to limit this study to poems by male authors. Given the limited space, hardly any critical works that refer to individual writers could be considered. The subject as such has, to my knowledge, not been entered into so far.
3 See, for instance, "The Spiritual Plan of Aztlán" of March 31, 1969, part of which is reprinted in Armando B. Rendón, *Chicano Manifesto* (New York-London: Collier Macmillan Publ., 1971), pp. 336–37.
4 See Jacques Lafaye, *Quetzalcóatl et Guadalupe. La formation de la conscience nationale au Méxique* (Paris: Gallimard, 1974).
5 Américo Paredes, "The Folk Base of Chicano Literature," in *Modern Chicano Writers. A Collection of Critical Essays. Twentieth Century Views,* ed. Joseph Sommers and Tomás Ybarra-Frausto (Englewood Cliffs, N.J.: Prentice-Hall, 1979), pp. 4–17.
6 See the statements by Alurista and Juan Felipe Herrera in *Partial Autobiographies: Interviews with Twenty Chicano Poets,* ed. Wolfgang Binder, Erlanger Studien, Vol. 65 I (Erlangen: Palme und Enke, 1985), pp. 3–15; 95–108.
7 Abelardo [Delgado], *Chicano. 25 Pieces of a Chicano Mind* (N.p.: n.p., [1969]), p. 27. For a brief summary of Chicano history and the Chicano Movement see Wolfgang Binder, ed., *"Anglos Are Weird People for Me." Interviews with Chicanos and Puerto Ricans. With a Preface and Introductions.* Materialien Vol. 12 (Berlin: J.F. Kennedy-Institut für Nordamerikastudien, 1979), pp. 11–34.
8 Alurista, *Floricanto en Aztlán* (Los Angeles, Cal.: University of California: Chicano Studies Center, 1971).
9 Alurista, "bendito sea tu vientre," p. 17; and "fruto de bronce," p. 53.
10 *Libro Para Batos y Chavalas Chicanas* (Berkeley, Cal.: Justa Publ., 1977), p. 46.
11 For interpretations of J. Montoya's "El Louie" see [Juan] Bruce-Novoa, *Chicano Poetry. A Response to Chaos* (Austin, Texas: University of Texas, 1982), pp. 14ff., and Wolfgang Binder, "Die Lyrik der Chicanos seit den sechziger Jahren. Sprache als soziokulturelle Bestandsaufnahme und emanzipatorisches Verfahren," in *Alltagssprache in der modernen Lyrik,* Erlanger Forschungen, Vol. 35, ed. Harald Wentzlaff-Eggebert (Erlangen: Universitätsbund Erlangen-Nürnberg,1984), pp. 85–112.
12 "La Jefita," in *El Espejo. The Mirror. Selected Chicano Literature,* ed. Octavio I. Romano-V. and Herminio Ríos C. (Berkeley, Cal.: Quinto Sol Publ., 1969), pp. 232–33.
13 *Whispering to Fool the Wind* (New York: Sheep Meadow Press, 1982), p. 59.
14 Another example of extreme idealization by a *pinto*, and proof of a touching emotional closeness between son and mother is Gilberto Ambriz' "Madre": "Tu eres la mujer mas preciosa/ En el mundo no hay joya mas valiosa./ [...] Tu a mi lado nunca has dejado,/ Siempre conmigo en todo lo que hago./ Bueno Madre te dejo por ahorita,/ Pero en mi mente simpre [sic] te traigo a ti." The lack of accentuation corresponds to the original. Both poems in *Alma Abierta. Pinto Poetry, MAYO de CRP,* Monograph No. 1, ed. Alfredo Mirandé (Riverside, Cal.: University of California; Chicano Studies Publications, 1980), n.p.
15 *Elk Head on the Wall.* Chicano Chap Book No. 4 (Berkeley, Cal.: University of California; Chicano Studies Program, 1979), pp. 7–8.

[16] For an autobiographical statement by L.O. Salinas see *Partial Autobiographies*, pp. 147–49.

[17] L.O. Salinas, *Darkness Under the Trees/Walking Behind the Spanish* (Berkeley, Cal.: University of California; Chicano Studies Library, 1982), p. 49.

[18] L.O. Salinas, p. 19.

[19] L.O. Salinas, p. 51.

[20] L.O. Salinas, p. 94.

[21] In *We Are Chicanos. An Anthology of Mexican-American Literature*, ed. Philip D. Ortego (New York: Washington Square Press, 1973), p. 170.

[22] In *Entrance: 4 Chicano Poets*. Leonard Adamé, Luis Omar Salinas, Gary Soto, Ernesto Trejo (Greenfield Center, N.Y.: Greenfield Review, 1975), pp. 22–23.

[23] For a poem on approaching death and fear which unite grandmother and grandchildren, see Alberto Ríos, "Belita," in his *Whispering to Fool the Wind*, pp. 9–10.

[24] Gary Soto, *The Elements of San Joaquín*. Pitt Poetry Series Vol. 121 (Pittsburgh, Pa.: Pittsburgh Univ. Press, 1977), pp. 40–41.

[25] *Where Sparrows Work Hard*. Pitt Poetry Series Vol. 176 (Pittsburgh, Pa.: Pittsburgh Univ. Press, 1981), pp. 5–6.

[26] A faculty of a more archaic nature, the grandmother's sensitivity to folk religion, witchcraft and superstition is used in Leroy V. Quintana's anecdotal "Sangre 5" poem and in Gary Soto's dramatic "Spirit." In the latter the apparition of the speaker's deceased father is taken very seriously. The grandmother is the one who sensed the presence first and responded with powerful intensity: "When Grandma cried/ Hugging the shirt/ You stood in the room again/ You saw her drop/ To her knees/ Kiss the rosary/ And repeat prayers/ Until a white paste/ Gathered in the corners/ Of her mouth [...] . *The Elements of San Joaquín*, pp. 50–51; L.V. Quintana, *Sangre* (Las Cruces, N.M.: Poema Agua Press, 1981), n.p. See also Alma Villanueva, *Mother, May I?* (Pittsburgh, Pa.: Motheroot Press, 1978), p. 10, p. 18, and Pat Mora's likening of her "Abuelita Magic" to the wisdom of a "grey-haired shaman" in *Chants* (Houston, Texas: Arte Público Press, 1984), p. 33. The technique of storytelling surfaces in L.V. Quintana's first lines of "Sangre 7" and "Sangre 8," respectively: "Grandma would tell a tale about an uncle," and "Grandma liked to tell a story about a dog." *Sangre*, n.p.

[27] Jim Sagel views the everlasting, unwielding, manipulating Mrs. Tafoya in "matriarch" with a mixture of irony and admiration: "Mrs. Tafoya runs the pueblo/ her way – / like a venerable block of cement –/ she decides who will run for governor/ she decides who will win/ and she wears her bleached-crow hair/ in a bun [...] and though winters upon winters must eventually claim their toll,/ my money's still on the old lady/ to keep right on baptizing half the pueblo,/ outlasting everyone." *Small Bones, Little Eyes* (Fallon, Nevada, 1981), n.p.

[28] *Sangre*, n.p.

[29] For an autobiographical account and Villanueva's motivation in writing this poem, see his interview in *Partial Autobiographies*, pp. 203–20; a shorter version appeared in *Imágenes de la Raza, Selbstzeugnisse mexikanisch-amerikanischer Kultur. Selfportrayals of Mexican-American Culture*, ed. Amerika Haus Berlin (Berlin: Amerika Haus, 1982), as " 'Hay Otra Voz'. Die Stimme eines Chicano Dichters. The Voice of a Chicano Poet," pp. 40–50. Villanueva is also one of the writers represented in *Chicano Authors. Inquiry by Interview*, ed. [Juan] Bruce-Novoa (Austin-London: University of Texas, 1980), pp. 253–64.

[30] "Now, Suns Later," *Latin American Literary Review*, 5, No. 10 (1977), 170–72.

[31] See B. Brinson-Piñeda, "María la O," in *A Decade of Hispanic Literature: An Anniversary Anthology*, ed. Revista Chicano-Riqueña (Houston, Texas: Arte Público Press, 1982), pp. 38–41; L.D. Cervantes, "Beneath the Shadows of the Freeway," in her *Emplumada*. Pitt Poetry Series Vol. 171 (Pittsburgh, Pa.: Pittsburgh University Press, 1981), pp. 11–14; C. Tafolla, "Mother Mother," in *Revista Chicano-Riqueña* 11, No. 3 and 4 (1983), 26; A. Villanueva, *Mother, May I?*, passim.

Song for Maya: A Discussion of the Poem by the Poet

Melba Joyce Boyd

> Maya resembles
> an ancient Aztec,
> as pretty as
> an autumn garden,
> eyes as warm
> as amber.
>
> she is
> the great, great
> granddaughter
> of the Blue
> Circles.
> a red-brown
> fusion
> of three and
> a half races:
> an Anglo, African
> Jewish Cherokee —
> a farsighted,
> diametrical thinker
> reading the wind.

Song for Maya is an epic poem that attempts to construct an American mythology that engages the historical and cultural experiences of three races converging in the poet, Maya, who leaves the modern world after four unfortunate relationships. When she crosses the Trail of Tears, she awakens in another cosmic order that originated in the ancient Mayan civilization. Her vision is stimulated by the spirit of Tsali, the Cherokee chief who sacrificed his life in order to stop the total removal of his people to the Oklahoma reservations in 1838. She also encounters Sequoyah, the scholar, who developed the Muskogean syllabary in the 1820s.

When Maya returns to America, she is a Meridian, a citizen of the future. She draws her strength from the complexity of her heritage and a new concept of God and the universe. She encounters and mourns the violations of the modern society against the human spirit and the desecration of the Land, the Sky and the Rivers. She expresses her impressions in the pulse and rhythms of jazz. She lives only with her son because American men are hypnotized by the illusions of power, and most women are manipulated by the impulses of those men.

146

The first section of the poem presents the difficulties she encounters as a person with a multiracial background. Her physical presence attracts men who desire her, but do not understand her. The women are jealous of the attention she receives from these men, and they reject her, by cursing and labeling her a witch. When, in fact, she searches "for fresh rivers and empty images to close."

> At first
> it was difficult
> to distinguish
> the variety
> of energy
> and the complexity
> of egos.
>
> even though
> she came to know
> that the spy,
> the scholar,
> the musician
> and the chinaman
> were different
> angles
> of the same
> plane.

The various American male pursuits for identity and recognition reveal the egotism that typifies modern confusion, which leads to the same dead end. The spy has mobility and financial security. He speaks six languages and has 27 credit cards. The scholar has mastered intellectual masturbation, and the jazz musician loses himself in indecipherable, musical illusions. But the chinaman is different, until he learns English. Then, he is corrupted by the American cultural context.

All of the relationships come to their predictable ends. The spy has a dramatic, but unimpressive death — shot on a ghetto street corner by an enraged, unemployed alcoholic.

> The scholar
> married
> a secretary.
> and the jazzman
> went wild
> in the urban
> cosmos.
>
> The chinaman
> absorbed the language
> by osmosis,
> and like the others
> slowly

> went mad,
> thinking
> he owned her.

Nine months later, Maya leaves the modern world when she crosses the Trail of Tears into the cosmic dimension where she has contact with her Native American ancestors and the true source of human fulfillment. She is removed from a materialistic reality of a corrupt society that was built on the backs of Africans and fertilized with the blood of Indians. Maya communes with the spirits of the past and the future, and she conceives and composes "The Last Poem," which is the conclusion for *Song for Maya.*

The section, "Tuskaseegee," explains the holistic balance of Cherokee culture before European contact. This trip into the past expands the universal concept of America before Columbus — B.C. The history of disintegration is described:

> Before the English
> America
> was an
>   egg
> on the
>   edge
> of birth
> and Death.

The greed of the developing capitalist culture brought slavery, private property laws, and its byproducts — racism and classism. In order to survive genocide or the reservation, many Indians intermarried with Blacks and Europeans and a new people evolved — the Meridians.

> they began
> to intermarry
> and to expand.
> to plant seeds
> in veins
> that explain
> the combinations
> of colors,
> lines,
> and the angles
> of distance
> and time.
>
> Their grandchildren (like Maya)
> speak multi-spatial
> rhythms
> untangle tongues
> and diffuse
> confusion.
>
> but the lies
> are thick.

> other tongues
> sound like one.

The present imbalance has disrupted the universal order and harmony, as the values and actions of the technological society threaten nuclear disaster and human extinction.

> Hostility
> breeds disruption
> that imbalances
> the planet,
> splits sunrays,
> warping time,
> slanting the axis,
> reflecting irregular
> angles
> into the face
> of God.

Maya gives birth to her son, Joaquín, in the moonrise of the Smoky Mountains at the moment John Lennon is assassinated in New York City. When five bullets catch John's throat, like the five nails in the body of Christ, another transcendent spirit is sacrificed and betrayed by his followers.

The forth section is entitled "The Meridians." They are the melting of world cultures and the coming together of Africans, Europeans, Asians and Americans, embracing the spirit of freedom and respect for nature. But this is a dream, a future struggle for the Meridians, who must build another America while dealing with the destructive forces of the present one.

> The Meridians
> don't think
> out loud
> anymore.
> their neighbors
> have become
> gray
> and absent.
> only the quiet
> Christians
> to the left
> hear the
> children's laughter.

> It's not
> a question
> of taste.
> it's simply
> too late
> to worry
> about the
> likes and dislikes

of ragdolls
with stuffed tongues
of traditions
of contradictions
or the disturbances
of distortions
at the galleries
of misnomers.

There is nowhere
to go.
the next line
crosses the
same tracks
into the
television zone,
where psychotics
lead the race
with tangent intellect,
best sellers,
and prime time
admiration
for insult,
distilling
the discoloration
of mediocrity
as California Negroes
impersonate Africans
in Chicago
as savages
in the mouths
of alligators,
waiting for
indigestion

"America" details the neurotic, societal elements of the United States. As people crowd the freeways a "dotted line drags caffeine tongues back and forth on radios in deaf traffic," while "price tags and paranoia dilate in foreheads like blowfish." Pollution, illiteracy and deception plague the day to day existence of the population; all of which leads to confusion and insanity.

The old folks
tell her
it's in the
water.
that's why
disenfranchised
revolutionaries
wander,
wear earrings
and shell

150

Georgia peanuts
for wide-eyed women
with mildew voices
rappin' to paperbags
and exaggerated statues
of embassaries
calling
from the grave

Evidence of increased paranoia can be witnessed with the visibility of the Ku Klux Klan on television programs broadcasted from Canada, where they have extended their membership. The power structure moves swiftly, as "the western winds crisscrossing the next street, sealing old cracks and slots in the dark." The illusions of grandeur continue to mystify hopeful immigrants, "under stars and televisions." But the truth cannot be heard, because it is too painful for western ears.

Leroy Jones, your typical, hard-working-American, flips out at the moment he realizes his life has no meaning. In a violent explosion he attacks and curses his family, shoots two policemen, and sends his declaration of war to the newspaper:

,,give me a
Cadillac
and a chocolate
blues suite,
pointed-toe shoes
in a xmas stocking
for 1953.
Pour my blood
in red clay.
plant my fingers
in a cottonfield.
throw my eyes
in the Atlantic Ocean,
but send my teeth
to Washington, D.C."

The six o'clock news provides a montage of international repression and violence. The fighting in El Salvador symbolizes C.I.A. subversive activity, and the shooting of Leroy's son by a storekeeper because the boy stole an ice cream cone, demonstrates the extremes of insanity. Unemployment in Detroit, the repression of workers in Poland, or the looming threat of cancer for people living and working around nuclear power plants, interrelate the complexity of modern tragedy.

Race is culture. Class is culture. The cross-fertilization of internationalism leads to a complex framework for the future, which few people understand. The majority still clings to false perceptions, stereotypes, and oversimplifications.

```
reduced to
a plastic cross
and Easter bunnies
served in supermarkets
with frozen french fries
to subterranean housewives
spliced between
commercials
and N.F.L. (National Football League)
quarterbacks
```

The disparity of young Blacks, Chicanos, Puerto Ricans, or Native Americans, as well as the working class in general, is based on the lack of opportunities in a declining industrial age, that is undermined by popular culture.

```
Maya believes
it is a
counterproduction
for unemployment
and the food shortage
for the fraternity
of warped-backed crows
spitting
acid rain
in our faces
bringing blood
home.
```

"2001" takes Maya into the future. "It is science fiction." The people, with their caffeine tongues, have become even more neurotic. Continuing to function out of habit and fear, we find "their signatures cringing there, confused and ordinary." The neurosis has developed into psychosis, as the cultural structure begins to crumble at a more rapid rate; "the accumulation of pain and the ambiguity of guilt can no longer be forgotten in withered weekends."

The problem of illiteracy leaves many of them sightless, unable to find fundamental truths.

```
Some try to
hide
in the church
and unscramble
the scriptures.

but,
they cannot
read.
```

Pollution has poisoned the environment beyond repair. People try to protect themselves with vitamin E lotion, "but, their skin is shrinking." And in a state of complete psychosis, many lash out blindly and violently at the unseen and the unknown.

Others try to fool it.
by sliding out
the side door,
afraid of
prefabricated food
on the table
that may be
dead babies
taken from
suburban shopping carts
rolling around
the equator
where Idi Amin's Army
raped eleven year old
girls,
and the imperialists
drove Cadillacs
from Hamtramck.

Meanwhile, the technocratic neurotics of the international ruling class continue their pursuit to colonize the universe, "trying to rope the moon before twilight."

On Independence Day, July 4th, Joaquín is startled into his true identity as a Meridian when he tries to stop a fight between two men arguing under the influence of alcohol about crucial questions on racism and religion in the Third World. Joaquín, who has until this moment followed the pattern of repression, aspiring to be a boxer in order to fight his way out of the barrio, becomes a peacemaker.

Joaquín
turns
in time
to catch
5 bullets
in his hand.

he falls
into the
sand.

his blood
is blue.

a constipated Earth
shakes.
the oceans heave.
the concrete separates.

"God Almighty!"
Maya shouts.

"Wait! "

"The Last Poem" is Maya's plea to the planet to transcend the trappings of nationalism and materialistic decadence. She calls for movement into an egalitarian and spiritual world where the interconnectedness of human history and culture must be accepted and understood. And only when this perspective has been adopted will the human race be capable of reversing the destructive direction of the planet. Balancing on the axis of contemporary chaos in America, the Meridians must struggle against extinction and refocus vision.

"The Last Poem"

If the Earth explodes
the Sun will swallow
his daughter.
and the Moon
will burn
in Hell.

so, tell
your sons
that steps
bring death
when you carry
hate under
your armpit
like a fat cow
gnawing
at your
knees.

Wear a
"many-colored coat."

it will take
three centuries
and nine planets
of thought
to restore balance
to a dismantled village
disturbed
about the shortage
of blond wigs
and the high cost
of cocaine
at xmas time.

Yes,
they are insane.

you don't belong
to the city
or the state
or the church
or the bank
or the proclivities

of those
who believe
in kings.

Blue Spirit
emanates
across rooms,
leaps buildings
and infinite
insanity.

oblivious to gravity
and the lunar
fanatics,
full-blooded Americans
are working
and dying
in an "angle
of ascent."

Believe what
we feel.

too much death
is buried
between
our eyes
to listen
to the limits
of the living.

We are the unknown,
invisible Indians
planting corn.
Meridians
who walk
in sidewalk seams,
spinning the spiral
in between,
blending clouds
above
midnight trees.

waiting ...
for fresh breath
of Mayans
spreading tears
on the dawn.

The Land gives
and receives.

Rain cleans.

Winter in reflection.
Spring is resurrection.
touch me.
         i
do   not
      burn.

V CHICANO FICTION

Regionalist Motifs in Rudolfo A. Anaya's Fiction (1972–82)

Alfred Jung

Rudolfo Anaya's three novels *Bless Me, Ultima* (1972), *Heart of Aztlán* (1976) and *Tortuga* (1979), and eight of the ten short stories that were published under the title of *The Silence of the Llano* (1982)[1] are set in the author's native New Mexico. In these works, themes, characterization, and imagery are often dependent on motifs which reflect the setting of each of these works, motifs which grow out of regional traditions, beliefs and patterns of interaction. These motifs penetrate the individual work, appearing and reappearing like leitmotifs. Yet they are no leitmotifs in the original sense of the term as it was used in German literary scholarship because they do not repeat a "significant phrase,"[2] but a "set description, or complex of images, in a single work."[3] Hence I call these repetitions *motifs*.

Antonio, the protagonist of Anaya's first novel *Bless Me, Ultima,* finds himself in the middle of two conflicting family traditions: the farmers of his mother's family, the Lunas, and the cowboys of his father's family, the Márezes. Antonio's father, Gabriel Márez, has grown up in the New Mexican Llano Estacado and loves his freedom and a restless and rootless life. Before Antonio's birth, Gabriel had been working as a *vaquero*, a cowboy, like all men of his family. After Antonio's birth Gabriel gave up his *vaquero* job and became a highway construction worker. He had to give away his horse, stop his restless life and settle down in a small town with his wife and children. Times had changed: not horses but automobiles had become the contemporary means of transportation, and Gabriel's jobs and life symbolize this development: he had to give up a life with horses and start building roads for automobiles. The novel's first-person narrator makes it clear from the beginning that Gabriel's life as a *vaquero* had been typical of the region, but had become an anachronism: "My father had been a vaquero all his life, a calling as ancient as the coming of the Spaniard to Nuevo Méjico. Even after the big rancheros and the tejanos came and fenced the beautiful llano, he and those like him continued to work there" (2). But things could no longer go on like this, and Gabriel dreams of his past nostalgically: "those were beautiful years, ... then the tejano came and built his fences, the railroad came, the roads — it was like a bad wave of the ocean covering all that was good" (51).

Antonio's mother María, a born Luna, is clearly contrasted to the restless Gabriel

160

Márez by the narrator: "My mother was not a woman of the llano, she was the daughter of a farmer. She could not see beauty in the llano and she could not understand the coarse men who lived half their lifetimes on horseback" (2). The Luna family loves the fertile river valley, not the arid llano, and feels rooted to the land. In contrast to the peripatetic *vaqueros* of the Márez family the Lunas have always been settled farmers and are still living on the same land which they had received during the Spanish colonization of the Mexican North centuries ago. The founding father of the Luna family had not been a farmer however, but a Roman Catholic priest. He had been the leader of the erstwhile colonizers. Although the devout Catholic María regards his sexual prowess as an embarrassment, she is nonetheless proud of the progenitor of her family and wants Antonio to become a priest as well. She teaches Antonio to be a pious Catholic. She had made her husband Gabriel move the family to the town of Guadalupe so that her children could have a good education.

The above quotations from *Bless Me, Ultima* make it clear that in the fictional world of the novel the cowboy and the farmer are considered callings typical of the region. In an interview in 1979 Anaya was asked by David Johnson if this had also been the case in the actual world outside of literature: "We hear about the dichotomy between the people – the Lunas of the valley and the people of the llano. Was that in that area then? A conflict of lifestyles? People who farmed as opposed to the people who ranched?"[4] And Anaya replied: "There's a definite difference in lifestyle. In *Bless Me, Ultima* I happened to attribute the lifestyle of the jinete, the vaqueros, to the llanero, which are the Márezes who are tied to the restless sea, the ocean. And the lifestyle of the more passive, more settled Luna to the lifestyle that goes on along the river valley. The dichotomy of a nomadic versus a civilized, settled people."[5] Something typical of the region became a regionalist motif in literature.

In the interview Anaya said that the Márezes "are tied to the restless sea, the ocean." This symbolic attachment to the restless element is achieved by Anaya through his creation of a telling name: *Márez* is derived from Spanish *mar*, ocean. The same device is employed in the name of the farmer family because *Luna* means *moon* in Spanish. Anaya wanted to make sure that his readers notice the symbolic connection of the families, their ways of life, the ocean and the moon. He makes Antonio ponder, "My name means sea, ... My father says our blood is restless, like the sea" (110), and also: "it is the Márez blood in us that touches us with the urge to wander. Like the restless, seeking sea" (61).

The blood of the Lunas seems to have other qualities. The old and wise healer Ultima, who has come to live with Antonio's family in her old age and who becomes a mentor for Antonio's spiritual development, says, "It is the blood of the Lunas to be quiet ... They are quiet like the moon" (38). But what has the moon got to do with a farming family? Anthropologist George M. Foster has noted that "the moon is felt to play an important part in agricultural practices"[6] of those Hispanic Americans who believe in their cultural folklore. This would hold true for persons like Ultima and the members of the Luna family. In particular, the narrator talks about a habit of Ultima's to go out into the llano at night to gather herbs that "can be harvested only in the light of the full moon" (2). According to literary critic Oscar Somoza, astrologists approve of this procedure.[7] The novel also says that the Lunas and Narciso, a character who has an Eden-like garden, only plant by moonlight (cf. p. 101). Anaya has turned a regional folkloristic belief into a literary motif.

From the very beginning of the novel, each of the two families is trying to dominate the young protagonist's life. The sensitive Antonio has noticed this and dreams about this interfamiliar conflict various times. In the first of these dreams he is watching his own birth. When he, the newborn baby, is lying at his mother's side, members of the Luna family enter the room, rub earth on his forehead, surround the bed with fruits of their harvest and say, "This one will be a Luna, ... he will be a farmer and keep our customs and traditions. Perhaps God will bless our family and make the baby a priest" (5). But then members of the Márez family storm into the room, smash the fruits and vegetables surrounding the bed and replace them with a saddle, horse blankets, bridles and other utensils of their way of life and rub the earth from the baby's forehead because they think that "man was not to be tied to the earth but free upon it" (5). "He will make a fine vaquero!" (5) they shout. Then each of the two families wants to have the afterbirth because due to an old belief this ensured that the baby followed in their footsteps. At this point, a brawl between the two families is imminent. But the old midwife stops the clash by saying, "I pulled this baby into the light of life, so I will bury the afterbirth ... Only I will know his destiny" (6). The old midwife is Ultima. The outcome of the dream symbolizes that Antonio will develop into neither a Márez nor a Luna, but will, under the tutelage of Ultima, develop an identity of his own and not just copy his forefathers. This is made plain in a conversation between father and son at the end of the novel, when Gabriel says, "Perhaps it is time we gave up the old differences," to which Antonio replies, "Then maybe I do not have to be just Márez, or Luna, perhaps I can be both ... Take the llano and the river valley, the moon and the sea ... and make something new" (235–36).

It should actually be considered a surprise that in Antonio's dream the angry men, traditionally-minded members of a patriarchal society, should so easily be pacified by a woman. But Ultima is not an ordinary woman. She is a *curandera*, a healer with mysterious, often supernatural powers, and because of these powers she wields tremendous authority over people, who regard her with a mixture of awe, love, and fear; some call her a saint, others a witch. Ultima's *curanderismo* is another regionalist motif. Novelist and literary critic Alejandro Dennis Morales wrote in his doctoral dissertation: "en cada barrio del suroeste hay un hombre o una mujer que sabe 'hechizar' y 'remediar hechizados.' "[8]

162

The fact that *curanderismo* is still alive and well in the barrio in the age of high-tech medicine and specialized physicians is corroborated by Armando Rendón, who in his famous *Chicano Manifesto* also mentions a *curandera's* powerful charisma: "there are still curanderas, old women with a unique and mysterious aura about them who prescribe cures for everything from a boil to impotence."[9] According to George Foster, this "vigorous body of folk medicine ... plays a functional part in the everyday lives of the people and ... will resist the inroads of modern medical science for many generations."[10]

But what is the literary purpose of the Márez-Luna conflict, Ultima's *curanderismo* and the young protagonist Antonio in the middle of it all? Literary critics Roberto Cantú and Faye Nell Vowell have come to the conclusion that Anaya portrayed two cultural archetypes in the Márez and Luna families. Cantú interprets the Márezes and Lunas as "personajes simbólicos de dos coordenadas históricas del chicano: el agricultor y el jinete."[11]

Vowell regards the two families from an ethnic point of view: "The Márez and the Lunas are symbolic of the two racial strains, the Spanish father and the Indian mother, which mingled to form the Mexican people."[12] Unfortunately, Cantú and Vowell both fail to mention the priest, who also plays an important part in the Luna family tradition, the development of Antonio's personality, and the novel's religious themes and motifs. In addition, I would like to raise the objection that farmer and horseman are not only "coordenadas históricas" of the Chicano, but of many rural people of the Southwest, including Indians and Anglos. But indeed, the Márez and Luna families have a certain typicality, and by that token Antonio becomes a typical, a representative Chicano. He is aware of his Mexican cultural roots without falling prey to them by simply imitating them, but through the help of Ultima he makes use of the best elements of his Mexican culture to achieve an identity of his own.

Remembering Mexican cultural roots has been an important concern for the Chicano Movement from the late 1960s on because before that time many Chicanos had tried to assimilate into an Anglo-American mainstream. José Antonio Villarreal's novel *Pocho* (1959)[13] is a literary document of this former assimilationist tendency, *Bless Me, Ultima* is a literary document of the contemporary emancipatory tendency. Anaya employs the New Mexican regionalist motifs of farming, horsemanship, and *curanderismo* to get across his view of a modern Chicano who knows and loves his Mexican cultural heritage, yet does not simply look back nostalgically but wants to, as Antonio says, "make something new" (236).

Another element of regional folklore which Anaya turned into a literary motif in *Bless Me, Ultima* is the story of *la llorona*, the weeping woman. Her story can be traced back to the year 1550, when a woman in a white, shroud-like garment allegedly roamed the streets of Mexico City, crying plaintively for her lost lover and children she herself had killed. Because of these cries she was called *la llorona* and has become a popular figure in Mexican and Chicano folklore ever since.[14] Her story is still told nowadays to scare little children and keep them at home after dark.[15] Antonio is no exception. At the beginning of the novel he is afraid of *la llorona* but loses this fright after some time: he sheds a negative aspect of his Chicano heritage.

In *Heart of Aztlán* (1976), Anaya also uses the *la llorona* motif, but this time he adapts it to the urban setting: "They thought they heard the cry of la Llorona as she ran along the dark river valley, crying for her demon-lover, mourning the death of her sons. But no, this was a new llorona! It was the siren of a police car crying through the streets of the barrio, searching out the young men who possessed the magic plant of summer, marijuana" (18). *La llorona* is no longer a make-believe scare for little children, but a very real danger for the drug-trafficking young Chicanos on Albuquerque's streets. Those of their fathers who have a job are threatened in their health and lives by the unnecessarily dangerous and hard work in the railroad factories. And again, the *la llorona* motif becomes functional here as the men and women of the barrio call the factory whistle *la llorona*. The characters in the novel and the reader know that this appellation signifies real dangers of factory work. The *la llorona* motif creates an atmosphere of oppression and menace.

The issue of the lost home land becomes another literary motif inspired by the author's close relation to the region. Through no fault of his own, the novel's protagonist Clemente has to sell his ranch in rural New Mexico[16] and move his family to the big city of Albuquerque. Shortly before signing the contract, his attachment to the land becomes obvious: "When I sell my land I will be cast adrift, there will be no place left to return to, no home to come back to" (3), he says. The third-person narrator adds: "the roots of his soul pulled away and severed themselves from the earth which had nurtured his life" (3). The image of the "roots of his soul" reveals the intense contact with the land and Clemente's dependence on it: it had nurtured his life not only in a literal sense because he had grown his crops and bred his cattle on it, but also in a figurative sense, because it had been his family's home for many generations. "Roots" symbolizes nourishment and contact, "soul" refers to the inner person, the psyche. To alleviate Clemente's anguish, his wife Adelita fills an old coffee-pot with earth and says, "We will take it with us, ... we will journey across the earth, but we will never leave our land" (7). Yet Clemente does not only mourn his individual case of losing his land, but he also thinks of the collective land loss of the Chicanos in the history of the Southwest: "Somehow we began to lose the land a long time ago. The tejano came, the barbed wire came, the new laws came" (5). The individual's fate ties in with the group's fate. Here the land motif becomes relevant for the novel's overall political theme of Chicano social emancipation.

In Anaya's third novel, *Tortuga* (1979), we come across the *la llorona* motif again. This motif, the Spanish names of some characters and some small talk about Mexican food are the only reminders of Chicano culture in this book. Whereas themes, motifs, setting, figures, and subject matter of *Bless Me, Ultima* and *Heart of Aztlán* were closely connected to Chicano life, this does not apply to *Tortuga*. This novel deals, roughly speaking, with life as a physically handicapped patient in and out of a hospital and the problem of euthanasia. This development away from an exclusively Chicano cultural ambience is reflected by an explanation which the narrator, a teenager nicknamed Tortuga, who suffers from paralysis and looks like a turtle in his plaster cast, gives to the reader when he mentions *la llorona* for the first time: "la Llorona, the old and demented woman of childhood stories who searches the river for her drowned sons ... sons she herself has cut into pieces and fed to the fish" (66). The narrators of *Bless Me, Ultima* and *Heart of Aztlán* had mentioned *la llorona* as a matter of course, without any explanation. But this time Anaya reckons with addressing a reading audience which is not restricted to Chicanos versed in their own culture. And this larger group needs some additional information when it comes to Mexican and Chicano folklore.

Most of the time when Tortuga thinks of *la llorona* he remembers a group of young girls dancing near a river on their and his first communion day. Common features in content between *la llorona* and the girls are that they are all women dressed in white, calling the male protagonist. But why does he associate the serene and idyllic image of the dancing girls with the ominous idea of *la llorona*? This association in the protagonist's mind gives the reader a clue to the reason of Tortuga's paralysis about which no information is given explicitly except that it was the result of an accident. When the *la llorona* motif in connection with thoughts of the girls appears for the first time, Tortuga is dreaming the following: "I step off the narrow path, totter at its edge, see the bright green of the river below, then I ... leap off the cliff and fall and tumble into the air ... fall until I can fall no more" (66). This happened on the day of his first communion, and later in the novel Tortuga remembers this day as "that same Sunday I had met la Llorona along the river, on the path beneath [sic] the cliff" (131) and he remembers the place as "the winding path where I had met la Llorona" (141). On that day the young protagonist suddenly felt the girls' erotic attraction on him: "where was my innocence, which of these girls of the windfall light had stolen it away with her quick glance, with a toss of her head, with a whisper ... my girls ... the soft, pink flesh of their eager tongues" (140). The protagonist considers his first feelings of sexual arousal as a loss of his innocence which bewilders him even more because he thinks that the girls still possess this kind of innocence: "They had remained innocent" (141).[17] In his confusion he runs to the river where he meets with some accident, possibly falling down a steep cliff. In his memory he regards the girls as the cause of his accident, since they were the cause of his bewilderment, but substitutes them with *la llorona* because he likes the girls and his subconscious is conditioned by education to consider *la llorona* as the evil demon plotting men's and boys' destruction.

Another regionalist motif is the mountain motif. A big mountain, also called Tortuga because of its shape, can be seen from the hospital. According to regional Chicano folklore, the mountain is indeed a huge turtle which has fallen asleep and will wake up and move again some day. So, at the beginning of the novel, which sets off in a cold and dreary winter rain, old Filomón tells the protagonist Tortuga: "Just wait till spring and you'll be better ... in the spring ... even the mountain moves" (5). Here already common features of protagonist and mountain are prepared by the author: protagonist and mountain are unable to move now, but there is a promise that they might be able to move in the spring. Soon the protagonist gets the same name as the mountain and because of the same reason: they both look like a turtle. Shortly after, it seems to the protagonist as if the mountain was indeed moving:

> Through the window I could see the top of the mountain ... Tortuga seemed to lift his head into the setting sun ... he turned to look at me, another crippled turtle come to live at his feet. The rheumy eyes draped with wrinkled flaps of skin bore into my soul and touched me with their kindness. For a moment the mountain was alive. It called to me, and I lay quietly in my dark room, hypnotized by the sight. Now I knew what Filomón had meant. There was a secret in the mountain, and it was calling me, unfolding with movement and power as the dying rays of the sun infused the earth with light (21).

The protagonist falls asleep and wakes up a few hours later because he himself has moved: "I reached out in the dark ... My arms and legs shook uncontrollably. Searing jolts of electricity surged through my body ... I jerked spasmodically on the wet bed ... Something had happened in the magic of my dream to help me tear loose from the paralysis ... A strength had returned, ... thanks to the grace of the mountain" (25–27). After the mountain has moved, the protagonist has also moved. When he tries to repeat his movement, the protagonist shouts passionately at the mountain, but in reality at himself: "Move, Tortuga! Get your fat ass off the ground and move! Trample everything! Show us you can move. Move ... please move..." (28). He identifies himself with the mountain and later, when he is able to move and people speak of a moving Tortuga, patients think that the mountain is talked about (cf. pp. 30, 113, 163). In the spring, Filomón's prophecy seems to come true. "We looked at old Tortuga ... 'The ground is thawing up there,' [Ismelda] said. 'The thaw always creates a movement in the earth. Old Tortuga acts like he's coming out of a long winter sleep' " (164). And the protagonist's convalescence has made so much progress that he can walk again and leave the hospital. Both Tortugas are indeed moving; man and nature are closely related to each other.

The Silence of the Llano (1982) contains seven short stories, and one excerpt, respectively, from each of the three novels. This book hardly reveals any regionalist motifs except for the title story, in which the atmosphere of the New Mexican llano is portrayed vividly. This story is set in and near a detached ranch in the llano. The third paragraph begins like this: "The people of this country knew the loneliness of the llano: they realized that sometimes the silence of the endless plain grew so heavy and oppressive it became unbearable. When a man heard voices in the wind of the llano, he knew it was time to ride to the village just to listen to the voices of other men. They knew that after many days of riding alone under the burning sun and listening only to the moaning wind, a man could begin to talk to himself" (10). Man is in close contact with nature, and nature has an important impact on his psychological well-being. This condition of man in general also holds true for the protagonist Rafael: "Only the weather and the seasons marked time for Rafael as he watched over his land and his herd. Summer nights he slept outside, and the galaxies swirling overhead reminded him he was alone. Out there, in that strange darkness, the soul of his wife rested. In the day, when the wind shifted direction, he sometimes thought he heard the whisper of her voice. Other times he thought he saw the outline of her face in the huge clouds which billowed up in the summer" (20). Not only is Rafael in close contact with nature, but he even envisions his dead wife as a part of nature. At the end of the story, Rafael overcomes the desperation he feels because of the death of his wife, and this change is symbolized by llano imagery, blending descriptions of nature and images of a woman:

> without warning a dark whirlwind rose before him, and in the midst of a storm he saw a woman. She did not smile, she did not call his name, her horse was the dark clouds which towered over him, the cracking of her whip a fire which filled the sky. Her laughter rumbled across the sky and shook the earth, her shadow swirled around him, blocking out the sun, filling the air with choking dust, driving fear into both man and animal until they turned in a wide circle back towards the ranch house. And when he found himself once again on the small rise by his home, the whirlwind lifted and the woman disappeared. The thunder rumbled in the distance, then was gone, the air grew quiet around him. He could hear himself breathe, he could hear the pounding of his heart. Around him the sun was bright and warm (29–30).

In the course of Anaya's literary career so far, regionalist motifs have gradually lost importance. Not surprisingly for a young author, he had started out writing about aspects he knew best: his native region, its people and customs. This helped him to find and develop subject matter, plots, themes and style. But after he had become more assured of his stature as a writer, he began to look for material outside of his native rural New Mexico.

Notes

[1] Rudolfo A. Anaya, *Bless Me, Ultima: A Novel* (Berkeley: Quinto Sol, 1972); *Heart of Aztlán* (Berkeley: Justa, 1976); *Tortuga* (Berkeley: Justa, 1979); *The Silence of the Llano: Short Stories* (Berkeley: Tonatiuh-Quinto Sol, 1982). All page references to these works will be given in the text of this article.

[2] M.H. Abrams, *A Glossary of Literary Terms: Fourth Edition* (New York: Holt, Rinehart and Winston, 1981), p. 111. Examples are the frequent repetitions of the phrases "I'll never desert Mr Micawber" in Charles Dickens' *David Copperfield* (1849–50) or "Das ist ein weites Feld" in Theodor Fontane's *Effi Briest* (1894–95).

[3] Abrams, p. 111.

[4] David Johnson and David Apodaca, "Myth and the Writer: A Conversation With Rudolfo Anaya," *New America*, 3, No. 3 (1979), 76.

[5] Johnson and Apodaca, 76.

[6] George M. Foster, "Relationships Between Spanish and Spanish-American Folk Medicine," *Journal of American Folklore*, 66, No. 261 (1953), 210.

[7] Cf. Oscar Urquídez Somoza, "Visión axiológica en la narrativa chicana," Diss. Univ. of Arizona 1977, pp. 20–21.

[8] Alejandro Dennis Morales, "Visión panorámica de la literatura méxicoamericana hasta el boom de 1966," Diss. Rutgers/State Univ. of New Jersey 1975, p. 177.

[9] Armando B. Rendón, *Chicano Manifesto* (New York: Macmillan, 1971), p. 172.

[10] Foster, p. 217.

[11] Roberto Cantú, "Degradación y regeneración en *Bless Me, Ultima:* el chicano y la vida nueva," in *The Identification and Analysis of Chicano Literature,* ed. Francisco Jiménez (New York: Bilingual, 1979), p. 383.

[12] Faye Nell Vowell, "The Chicano Novel: A Study in Self-Definition," Diss. Univ. of Cincinnati 1979, p. 181.

[13] José Antonio Villarreal, *Pocho* (Garden City, NY: Doubleday, 1959).

[14] see Bacil F. Kirtley, " 'La Llorona' and Related Themes," *Western Folklore*, 19, No. 3 (1960), 156–61, and Raymund A. Paredes, "The Evolution of Chicano Literature," *MELUS*, 5, No. 2 (1978), 106.

[15] see Guillermo Lux and Maurilio E. Vigil, "Return to Aztlán: The Chicano Rediscovers His Indian Past" in *The Chicanos: As We See Ourselves*, ed. Arnulfo D. Trejo (Tucson: Univ. of Arizona Press, 1979), pp. 10–11, and Rendón, p. 174.

[16] In the small town of Guadalupe which was the setting of *Bless Me, Ultima.*

[17] Later, however, Anaya commits the error of making Tortuga contradict himself by thinking of "the day we all made our first communion, the day *we* lost *our* innocence" (p. 145, my emphasis).

Costumbrismo in Sabine R. Ulibarrí's
Tierra Amarilla: Cuentos de Nuevo México

Donaldo W. Urioste

Among the oldest literary traditions in the Chicano Southwest is the short story. As with poetry and drama, this genre was initially introduced into the region in the form of folktales by the Spanish colonists of the sixteenth century, and was passed on orally from one generation to another. The vast majority of these folktales are of Old World origin and still represent the lore and cultural heritage that Hispanic settlers brought with them, when they first settled the area.[1] Moreover, during the colonial period the American Southwest also experienced great influxes of Mexican immigration which brought with them folk narratives originated in Mexico. Introduced by these settlers was lore dealing with such subjects and motifs as *la llorona, la malinche, las ánimas, la muerte, la Virgen de Guadalupe* and the lives and miracles of other Mexican saints. As with the earlier Spanish folktales, the Mexican *cuentos* were interwoven with local culture and geography to forge a new literary reality.

Following in the molds established by these traditions of folk literature, much of the early fiction written by Chicanos also drew heavily from elements of a folk existence.[2] With its multifaceted history of story and lore, rich in so many ways so as to function as a muse for literary inspiration, the Southwest first produced writers whose fiction was deeply rooted in the traditions, beliefs and customs of its people. Folklore, in this sense, forms an integral part of the writings of Nina Otero, Jovita Gonzales, Fray Angélico Chávez, Josefina Escajeda, and Arthur L. Campa,[3] and to this day continues to be a major source of inspiration for many writers of fiction and poetry.[4] However, whereas the primary intention of the earlier writers was generally limited to recapturing, recording and romantically depicting memories, forms, and images of a bygone time, the objective of the contemporary writers is more literary and social. That is, the latter group is not only inspired by the urge to recapture and salvage forms and meanings from the past, but also by the desire to create works of art and to record and critically reflect upon the present.

Among the short story writers notable for this trait is the New Mexican, Sabine Reyes Ulibarrí. To date, Ulibarrí stands out as one of the most versatile and prolific of Chicano writers. In addition to his highly acclaimed *Tierra Amarilla: cuentos de Nuevo México* (1964), he also has to his credit two other collections of short fiction, two books of poetry and a major work of literary criticism.[5] As the title of *Tierra Amarilla: cuentos de Nuevo México* suggests, these tales, as well as those in the other two collections, focus on the life and people of Tierra Amarilla, the northern New Mexican village of Ulibarrí's birth and childhood. They are, in essence, memories of a bygone day in which the author-narrator nostalgically recalls particular events, mysteries, and inhabitants of his native *pueblo*. Like the traditional *cuadros de costumbres* of Spanish and Spanish American letters, Ulibarrí skillfully and poetically describes that provincial milieu's most intimate life patterns: its customs, traditions, manners, beliefs, language, types, dress, etc. Notwithstanding this marked concern for the culturally quaint and picturesque, however, Ulibarrí's skillful use of language, irony, caricature, and humor add an ever present vitality to the stories.

Tierra Amarilla: cuentos de Nuevo México consists of five short stories and a novelette. Varying in theme and structure, all narrations are in the first person and with the exception of "El hombre sin nombre," the novelette, all reflect recollections of childhood experiences and/or acquaintances. In this presentation we will limit our comments to three of the stories: "Mi caballo mago," "Juan P.," and "La fragua sin fuego."

"Mi caballo mago," the first selection of the work, is a poetic rendition of a child's *rite de passage* into manhood. In a lyrical style and fairy tale-like quality reminiscent of Juan Ramón Jiménez' *Platero y yo*, an adult narrator recalls the circumstances leading to his capturing, as a youth, of a legendary white stallion that roamed the wilderness around Tierra Amarilla, an event that symbolically takes him to the threshold of manhood. The story begins with a metaphorical description of the white steed, establishing it as a symbol of masculine virility and the dream horse of all the local ranchmen:

> Era blanco. Blanco como el olvido. Era libre. Libre como la alegría. Era la ilusión, la libertad y la emoción. Poblaba y dominaba las serranías y las llanuras de las cercanías. Era un caballo blanco que llenó mi juventud de fantasía poesía. Alrededor de las fogatas del campo y las resolanas del pueblo los vaqueros de esas tierras hablaban de él con entusiasmo y admiración. Y la mirada se volvía turbia y borrosa de ensueño. La animada charla se apagaba. Todos atentos a la visión evocada. Mito del reino animal. Poema del mundo viril.[6]

The poetic imagery created by Ulibarri's compact, telegraphic-like style evokes the impression that the stallion is indeed an illusion, a phantom horse that has eluded all attempts of capture and has left its pursuers, its would-be masters with only words of awe and admiration with which to describe their encounter.

As the story unfolds, the image of the stallion becomes more majestic and legendary. Through a series of metaphors and similes, he becomes lord of the animal kingdom, comparable to an Oriental monarch, proudly parading his harem throughout his bucolic kingdom. The more the horse is seen and avoids the lasso, the more he becomes the talk of the village *vaqueros*. In fact, such is his evasive presence that he has become more legend than reality, a distinction giving him the notoriety of "el caballo brujo" (p. 5). To capture and possess such a wonder horse would certainly raise one's stature within the community, gracing the captor with such qualities as valor, masculine strength, and sex appeal.

Like the village *vaqueros*, our narrator-protagonist is also entranced with the possibility, the illusion of possessing the phantom horse, and thereby entering the realm of manhood. Though he has never seen the animal, the tales of its feats have filled his young mind with ambition and imagination:

> Escuchaba embobado a mi padre y a sus vaqueros hablar del caballo fantasma que al atraparlo se volvía espuma y aire y nada. Participaba de la obsesión de todos, ambición de lotería, de algún día ponerle yo mi lazo, de hacerlo mío, y lucirlo los domingos por la tarde cuando las muchachas salen a paseo por la calle (p. 5).

The boy's first sight of the stallion is one of everlasting durability. One summer evening, as he is lethargically herding cattle in the forest, he accidentally comes upon the animal. Like in a still-life picture, everything around seems to fall silent and come to a complete standstill, as he spots the horse in a nearby opening:

> ¡Allí está! ¡ El caballo mago! Al extremo del abra, en un promontorio, rodeado de verde. Hecho estatua, hecho estampa. Línea y forma y mancha blanca en fondo verde. Orgullo, fama y arte en carne animal. Cuadro de belleza encendida y libertad varonil (p. 7).

And just as quickly as this beautiful still-life image is formulated in the child's mind, it is shattered by the stallion who, also aware of the boy's presence, defiantly challenges his intrusion and escapes into the forest.

Subsequent to this brief encounter, the child becomes even more obsessed with the possibility of capturing the wonder horse. He dreams of the steed day and night, and is constantly investigating its whereabouts. Then on one wintery Sunday afternoon he again comes across the phantom steed. As with the first experience, this one is equally dramatic and poetic. This time however, our protagonist is determined to pursue and capture the animal, and he follows it for hours through the snow-covered hillside. Little by little the malnutritioned beast gives way to exhaustion and the boy apprehends and captures it, a feat no other individual, boy or man alike, had been able to accomplish. As the narrator recalls the dramatic incident, he utilizes the present tense to make the experience more immediate and vivid:

Me siento seguro. Desato el cabestro. Abro el lazo. Las riendas tirantes. Cada nervio, cada músculo alerta y el alma en la boca. Espuelas tensas en ijares temblorosos. Arranca el caballo. Remolineo el cabestro y lanzo el lazo obediente.

Vértigo de furia y rabia. Remolinos de luz y abanicos de transparente nieve. Cabestro que silba y quema en la teja de la silla. Guantes violentos que humean.

Ojos ardientes en sus pozos. Boca seca. Frente caliente. Y el mundo se sacude y se estremece. Y se acaba la larga zanja blanca en un ancho charco blanco.
Sosiego jadeante y denso. El caballo mago es mío (p. 11)).

Having captured the stallion, the boy's rite of passage into manhood is completed. He has, in essence, successfully met his initiatory trial of strength — his test of manhood — and is ready to be received by his father as a man. Sensing this coming-of-age, he triumphantly parades the steed through the village, leading it homeward where his father proudly acknowledges his feat with a handshake "un poco más fuerte que de ordinario" — and a very gratifying " 'Esos son hombres' " (p. 15).

The child's victory over the wonder horse leaves him with mixed emotions. He is indeed overcome with joy that he has succeeded in capturing the majestic steed, that local symbol of masculinity and virility, and thereby entered into the world of manhood. Nevertheless, at the same time he is deeply saddened by the fact that in depriving the once indomitable stallion of its freedom to roam the wilderness, he has also deprived future generations of children and *vaqueros* of a dream or an ideal to pursue. Consequently, the following morning, when he discovers that *el Mago* has escaped from the pasture, his eyes fill with "lágrimas infantiles." The tears, however, are not out of sadness, but out of happiness. As the protagonist himself informs us:

Lloraba de alegría. Estaba celebrando, por mucho que me dolía, la fuga y la libertad del Mago, la transcendencia de ese espíritu indomable. Ahora seguirá siendo el ideal, la ilusión y la emoción (p. 17).

In other words, he is overjoyed that the phantom stallion was once again free to roam the wilderness and thus continue being "el brujo" and "el mago," or as so appropriately stated by Erlinda Gonzales Berry, "to fill the fantasies of both child and man with the transcending power of idealism and illusion."[7] In this light, "Mi caballo mago" stands out not only as a story in which the young protagonist comes of age physically and sexually, but also intellectually, for his final understanding and appreciation of the values of hope, freedom and the ideal certainly bear resemblance to those of a mature and sagacious humanist.

In "Juan P." and "La fragua sin fuego," Ullibarrí takes a much more critical view of his native Tierra Amarilla and its inhabitants. Like in the previous story, both of these narrations are rendered from the perspective of an adult narrator recalling images of his childhood past in Tierra Amarilla; the focus here being on local personalities. However, whereas the outlook of the previous story is nostalgically happy and warm, the underlying tone of these two stories is melancholic and somewhat adverse.

"Juan P." is the tragic story of Juan Perrodo, the town drunk, and his spinster sisters who, once very promising and charming members of the community, were compelled into living a life of humiliation and seclusion due to the thoughtlessness and cruelty of their neighbors. In keeping with the *costumbrista* mode, the story begins with a detailed discussion of the origins of the rounded hummocks beside each of the village homes on which firewood was stacked during the winter months. These mounds, formed from the splinters, chips, and sawdust of cutting wood, not only provided the stacked firewood with the proper ventilation in times of rain and/or snow, but were also a means of determining the age and social status of the family living in the household: the higher and wider the heap, the older and more influential the family on the property. Moreover, the formation of these mounds entailed hard work in the chopping and sawing of the wood, and thereby provided a worthwhile activity to develop the young males into robust and strong men.

After introducing this age-old custom of Tierra Amarilla, the narrator informs us that, though unwillingly, as a young boy he, too, was involved in the molding of his family's wood pile. Annoyed by his son's preference for books and poetry, and obsessed with the idea of making a man out of the boy, the narrator's father set up a schedule of household chores that would assure his virile development. Of course, among the many tasks the boy had to perform was the cutting of the family firewood. On one occasion, while carrying out this duty, he is approached by Juan P. riding on a magnificent sorrel horse, the envy of all the local *vaqueros*, and the rider's only remaining symbol of his once prominent position in the community — a life that had been, a life that might have been. As the rider passes in his usual drunken state, he is singing a self-composed ballad:

> A mí me llaman Juan P.
> Soy el borracho del pueblo.
> Tengo dos hermanas escondidas:
> Son las perrodas del pueblo (p. 41).

Though he senses something humiliating in the words of Juan P., until this time the child had been totally ignorant as to the tragic plight of Juan and his sisters. Since in Hispanic cultures it is a customary practice to give nicknames based on the physical and/or character handicaps of an individual, he assumed that the "P" of Juan's epithet was an abbreviated form of *pedo*, a term referring to the man's reputation as a drunk, and that the name of the sisters, *las perrodas*, was merely an extension of their brother's nickname. Now, upon noting the tragic words and tone of Juan's song, the child wants to learn more about the origin of the insulting epithet, of Juan's drunkenness and of the seclusion of the sisters;

and at his insistence he is given an account of the situation by Brígido, one of his father's hired hands.

From Brígido's account (presented in the form of a *racconto*), we learn that Juan and his sisters came from one of the oldest and most prominent families in Tierra Amarilla, and that the people of the village were responsible for their tragic demise. This "riches to ruin" transition is explained to have begun, ironically, when Juan and the sisters, along with the entire community, were respectfully praying at the wake of a deceased neighbor. During one of the occasional pauses in the rosary, when all is absolutely silent in the church, one of the sisters shattered the silence with a burst of human explosion — "uno de esos ruidos que ... Aun en privado, cuando nos ocurren, nos dejan un poco rebajados, un poco envilecidos" (p. 47). Of course, such an untimely outburst caught the immediate attention of all the villagers present, but it was not until later that they react. In the days following the incident, as gossip of the shocking incident spreads throughout the community, Juan and his sisters — until then, highly respected neighbors — begin to be known by their new and humiliating nickname: *Los Perrodos*.

In response to the humiliating gossip and the insulting epithet, the trio withdraws, in shame, into the solitude of their home and seclude themselves from the rest of the community, emerging from the household only on occasions: the women to attend mass, and Juan to patronize the local saloon. As Juan takes to drinking more and more, he neglects the homestead and crops, until finally the place appears to be totally deserted:

> Se secaron los rosales, antes tan cuidadosamente atendidos. Los campos, trigales y alfalfares, se veían cada día más tristes, más abandonados. ... La tristeza, la soledad y el abandono invadieron la heredad y tomaron posesión de ella (pp. 47—49).

And as time takes its toll he peddles off the family possessions until all that remains are the house in which the sisters live in seclusion, and the beautiful sorrel horse on which Juan scornfully and dejectedly parades through the community singing his tragic ballad:

> A mí me llaman Juan P.
> Soy el borracho del pueblo.
> Tengo dos hermanas escondidas:
> Son las perrodas del pueblo.

By the time Brígido concludes the tragic story of Juan P. and his two spinster sisters, the young protagonist is overcome with indignation and anger directed toward that community that had senselessly and unjustly condemned those three human beings to an existence of shame and despair. And as he continues his initial chore of cutting the firewood he hacks furiously and vengefully, imagining each log to be the face of one of the ugly villagers who had poisoned the honorable family with their filthy gossip. In recalling his desire for vengeance the narrator informs us:

> Partí leña como loco. El montón, el promontorio de mi casa creció aquella tarde con la inmundicia de la mente y la lengua de los hombres. Y si ustedes pasan hoy por Tierra Amarilla fíjense en el montón de mi casa. Si escarban poco hallarán allí ojos y lenguas y sesos humanos. Son los de los que bautizaron a "los Perrodos" (p. 51).

As such, like the story previously discussed, Ulibarrí concludes "Juan P." with a profoundly humane and compassionate note. And as is typical of most narratives in the *costumbrista* mode, also evident in this story is its nostalgic depiction of the customs and traditions of a bygone day. However, what differs in "Juan P." is its critical perspective. While the other narrative alludes to village customs and/or traditions in a positive, somewhat romantic light, this story is critical and even disapproving of them; especially when they can lead to the senseless harm and demise of another human being, as they did in the case of Juan P. and his two beautiful sisters.

A similar note of criticism is found in "La fragua sin fuego," a sketch in which Ulibarrí passionately censures narrow-minded social rejections. Like in "Juan P.", the focus of this story is on one of the many personalities who played an important role in the narrator's strides toward maturity while still a child growing up in Tierra Amarilla. Here he recalls Edumenio, the village blacksmith. Edumenio, who lives alone in a small white house at the village's edge, is portrayed as a quiet, hardworking, Atlas of a man, also living at the margins of the town's social structure. Nevertheless, he is quite taken in by the village children (our narrator included), who would spend many an afternoon in his blacksmith shop curiously observing him at work and joyfully playing with scrap metals and the tools of his trade. Moreover, because he treated the children as adults, their attraction toward him is enhanced. Our narrator recalls:

> Era muy bueno. Nos componía los juguetes rotos. Nos hacía trompos con unas puntas como espadas. Hacía maravillas con hoja de lata. Nos daba aros, tejas, y mil piezas de desperdicio que a los niños les gustan tanto. Nos dejaba hacer. ... Otra cosa. Nunca nos trató con esa condescendencia que tienen los mayores para los niños. Nos hablaba de hombre a hombre. Cuando podíamos ayudarle en algo, traerle una herramienta, animar el brasero con el fuelle, ir a comprarle unos cigarros, eso nos llenaba de importancia (p. 71).

A true companion to the children he was indeed. However, as the story unfolds, we also learn that he was a lonely man nonetheless, and, in order to fulfill his needs for adult companionship, he would occasionally close down his shop and go into the city where, as we are informed, "se ponía una borrachera imperial y se entregaba por completo al mal andar" (p. 75). On one such occasion Edumenio returned to the village accompanied by a beautiful young woman

176

who immediately catches the attention of the community and our child narrator. In a poetic fashion reminiscent of Eduardo Barrios' child protagonist in *El niño que enloqueció de amor,*[8] he describes his infatuation for her:

> Se llamaba Henriqueta. Desde que la vi la primera vez quedé convencido que era la criatura más hermosa que Dios había puesto en la tierra. ... Yo la miraba con ojos de becerro en cara de cordero, y la seguía como un perro. Era un amor que no pide nada y lo da todo: la inteligencia, la voluntad y la fuerza. ... Amor limpio, puro, nuevo; sin manos, ni palabras, ni labios. Mudo y secreto, no va ni viene, ni siquiera está — sólo es (pp. 75–77).

Undoubtedly, with the companionship of his newly acquired spouse things were due to change for Edumenio in the community; and change they did. The once unloquacious, introspective blacksmith became a talkative, jovial individual; backslapping and joking with all who came near him. No longer alone, he was indeed a happy man. The happiness, however, was short-lived. Soon after their arrival to the community, rumors began to spread that Henriqueta, who wore makeup, flashy jewelry, tight dresses and short skirts — that is, who dressed and carried herself in city fashion — was a loose woman. And when Edumenio began making courtesy calls, wishing to introduce his bride to all the good families of the community, they are coldly and snobbishly rejected. As a result of the snobbery Henriqueta eventually abandons the community and Edumenio, humiliated and emotionally distraught, soon follows suit; thus leaving forevermore, *la fragua sin fuego.*

Having witnessed this haughtiness even in his own home, our nine-year-old protagonist witness is overcome with indignation and anger, and later in life, as he narrates his account, he candidly directs himself to the victims of his village's social snobbery and fervently apologizes for its shameful behavior:

> Ya no tengo nueve años. Ya soy hombre. Pero recuerdo y lloro. Y me avergüenzo de la condición humana que les negó, a ti, Edumenio, a ti, Henriqueta, el don de la felicidad que Dios les dio. Dios manda y el hombre dispone.
>
> Edumenio, en dondequiera que estés, espero que tengas otra fragua, y que sigas haciéndole la guerra al hierro indócil. Espero que hayas encontrado a tu Henriqueta. Espero que tengas una casita blanca y limpia con macetas de geranios y claveles en el jardín. Henriqueta ... espero que hayas conseguido la honradez que buscabas. Espero que en otro sitio, entre otras gentes más generosas, tú y Edumenio hayan fraguado una vida llena de dulzura, de amor propio y de dignidad que los dos se merecen (pp. 81–83).

Consequently, in a manner similar to that found in "Juan P.," Ulibarrí closes "La fragua sin fuego" with a note of profound human compassion, and what had begun as a simple nostalgic sketch about one of the many villagers who once resided in Tierra Amarilla, ends up being a condemnation of this village's —

and that of all small isolated communities' – narrow-minded social codes and suspicious nature.

That Sabine Reyes Ulibarrí's stories are *costumbrista*, there is no denying for, as we have seen, they do indeed focus on a facet of New Mexican life that is rapidly disappearing or is already bygone, and nostalgically depict regional customs, manners, language, types, and all the quaint local-colorist motifs that characterize this genre. But simple and local as these tales manifest themselves, they transcend the superficially picturesque and quaint intent of *costumbrismo* to present larger, more universal lessons about life and human conduct, be it man's eternal search for the ideal, the pursuit and/or negation of freedom, happiness and justice; or even more simply, the manifestation of innocent curiosity. Key to this subtle transition is the author's skillful manipulation of the adult/child points of view. By combining these two perspectives, Ulibarrí is able, not only to nostalgically recall images of a bygone day, but to restore a state of innocence and compassion lost collectively in the process of individual and/or social maturation. While the adult narrator functions primarily as the agent of recalling that golden age, the child protagonist-witness, innocent and uncorrupted by social constraints, focuses on and denounces the foibles and sometimes unwarranted behavior of the adults in his village; and thereby imbues these short sketches with a note of human compassion seldom found in the pages of traditional *costumbrista* literature.

Notes

[1] As in Spain and other Mediterranean countries, many of these tales deal with such motifs as kings, castles, princesses, courtships, magic enchantments, animal lore, and the picaresque. Some tales are adapted to local customs while others introduce regional characteristics and types such as *brujerías* and indigenous themes; hence making the stories seem more realistic and dramatic to the reader. It is from this oral tradition that Chicanos have inherited the likes of "Los tres principes," "La niña perseguida," "El príncipe encantado," "La princesa encantada," "Juan el oso," "Juan el tonto," "Juan sin miedo," "Pedro Ordimales," "Los dos compadres," and "El tonto y la princesa." For these and additional folktales of Old World origin, see Juan B. Rael, *Cuentos españoles de Colorado y de Nuevo México* (Stanford: Stanford University Press, 1957); José M. Espinoza, *Spanish Folktales from New Mexico* (New York: American Folklore Society, 1937); and Aurora Lucero White, *Literary Folklore of the Hispanic Southwest* (San Antonio: The Naylor Company, 1953).

[2] Phillip D. Ortego, ed., *We Are Chicanos: An Anthology of Mexican American Literature* (New York: Washington Square Press, 1975), p. 272.

[3] See for example, Otero, "Count La Cerda's Treasure," Gonzales, "Don Tomás," Fray Angélico Cháves, "Hunchback Madonna," Escajeda, "Tales from San Elizario," and Campa, "The Cell of Heavenly Justice," all of which have been reprinted in Philip D. Ortego, ed., *We Are Chicanos: An Anthology of Mexican American Literature*.

[4] See for example, Sabine R. Ulibarrí, *Tierra Amarilla: Cuentos de Nuevo México* (Albuquerque: University of New Mexico Press, 1974); Alurista, *Floricanto en Aztlán* (Los Angeles: UCLA Press, 1971); Rudolfo Anaya, *Bless Me, Ultima* (Berkeley: Quinto Sol, 1972); Rolando Hinojosa, *Estampas de Valle y otras obras* (Berkeley: Quinto Sol, 1973);

178

and Orlando Romero, *Nambé-Year One* (Berkeley: Tonatiuh International, 1976), all of which develop around or expound upon folk beliefs and lore of the Chicano Southwest.

5 *Mi abuela fumaba puros y otros cuentos de Tierra Amarilla* (Berkeley: Quinto Sol, 1977), *Primeros encuentros* (Ypsilanti, Michigan: Editorial Bilingue, 1982), *Al cielo se sube a pie* (Madrid: Ediciones Alfaguara, 1966), *Amor y Ecuador* (Madrid: Ediciones Jose Porrua Turranzas, 1966), and *El mundo poético de Juan Ramón Jiménez* (Madrid: Artes y Grafical Clavileno, 1962).

6 Sabine R. Ulibarrí, *Tierra Amarilla: Stories of New Mexico/ Cuentos de Nuevo México,* trans. Thelma C. Nason (Albuquerque: The University of New Mexico Press, 1974), p. 3. Quotations cited in this paper are from the Spanish text, and all subsequent references to this work will appear with page numbers in parentheses in the body of the text.

7 Erlinda Gonzales Berry, "Chicano Literature in Spanish: Roots and Content," Diss. The University of New Mexico 1978, p. 53.

8 Eduardo Barrios, *El niño que enloqueció de amor,* 1915.

Fragmentarismo en *Klail City y sus alrededores* de Rolando Hinojosa

László Scholz

La novela *Klail City y sus alrededores* de Hinojosa, siendo una verdadera obra maestra de los años setenta, ofrece múltiples posibilidades de análisis. Convencido de que todos los caminos nos llevan a Roma, voy a proceder, esta vez, de manera inversa a la que consideraría la más oportuna para tratar el mundo espacio-temporal de una novela como *Klail City*. Es decir, mi punto de partida no va a ser el medio socio-geográfico que tiene una presencia muy marcada desde el propio título hasta las frases en inglés del final; partiré más bien de algunos parámetros intrínsecos de la obra y sólo en base a los resultados obtenidos tocaré el fundamento referencial de la novela.

Comencemos tal vez con el espacio novelesco. En lo que al escenario se refiere, se trata de un mundo muy amplio que abarca no sólo calles, barrios, ciudades, sino que a través de los viajes al norte, incluye también lejanos estados. Estos elementos constituyen un marco general en el cual todavía tendremos que buscar el espacio central, es decir, cierta zona sagrada que, como un imán, atrae a los demás círculos; o valiéndonos de la terminología de Gaston Bachelard, debemos encontrar el espacio feliz, el espacio vivido que concentra ser.[1] Sin hacer una lista exhaustiva, se podría mencionar recintos como una que otra cantina — por ejemplo, la del Oasis o la de Lucas Barrón —, algún rancho o casa de los personajes, o el parque de Klail city donde se elige Big Foot, o cierto cementario, iglesia y puente que son testigos de acontecimientos trascendentales en la novela; o ahí está el río como línea divisoria, y el famoso garaje del señor Villalpando o la barbería donde se desarrolla la chismografía de siempre, o la propia escuela o, perdón, High School, donde se prepara un cronicón del condado de Belkén. El registro completo es impresionante; gracias a la invención de Hinojosa sobran los elementos que pudieran servir para crear la mencionada zona sagrada; sin embargo, y es fácil de comprobar, ninguno de ellos responde a los requisitos de Bachelard: en esta novela no existe el espacio feliz, de posesión que defendiera a los protagonistas contra las fuerzas adversas, espacio dominante que sea vivido y, por consiguiente, ensalzado de alguna manera por sus habitantes; o, poniéndolo más exactamente, hay varios elementos que se acercan a tal objetivo, pero siempre quedan irrealizados. Pongamos un ejemplo: en el primer capítulo de la primera parte nos salta a la vista la casa de los Tamez, no sólo por ser ella un antiquísimo arquetipo artístico, sino también por estar aprove-

chada magistralmente para llevar al lector a una zona delimitada: los jóvenes –
Jovita y Joaquín – han de casarse en un cuarto; dicha habitación había sido de
la difunta esposa de Don Salvador; unos pocos pueden entrar, otros – como
Emilio y los de Anda – quedan afuera; sin embargo, este acertado germen novelesco no se desarrolla después, al contrario, Hinojosa da una vuelta a la tortilla
y en el capítulo A de la tercera parte nos comunica con una ironía sutil que
Don Marcial, quien antaño no pudo pisar dicha casa, está "meciéndose en el
corredor," y tiene "su cuartito, su chocolate con canela ..."[2] Y este procedi-
miento del autor es válido también para los demás elementos espaciales, por
consiguiente, nos trazan ellos un mapa de puntos discontinuos, puntos que son
de perfil agudo, pero que no llegan a producir ningún centro, puntos que constituyen sendos núcleos de futuras ramificaciones, pero tan pronto como comien-
cen a llenarse de vida, a cargarse de símbolos, de ser, se esfuman, se abstraen,
se nos deslizan. El espacio de Hinojosa, a pesar de su fina elaboración, tiene un
carácter latente, es más potencial que virtual.

El tiempo representado en la novela es igualmente muy variado. Se encuentran
referencias, al menos, a unos sesenta años de historia; entre otras, se hace
mención de la época de la fundación de Klail City, es decir, los años diez, después hay fechas como 1973, 1918, así como indicios de Obregón en poder, de
la Segunda Guerra Mundial, de los años cuarenta, de la guerra de Corea, etc.
Tal horizonte temporal no se demarca, naturalmente, con una sola línea crono-
lógica, sino al contrario, sigue un plan caprichoso de saltos, flash-backs, ana-
cronismos, ampliaciones y condensaciones. Si uno se propone ubicar el punto
clave que podría servir de eje temporal para toda la obra, hay dos posibilidades:
o se acepta alguna de las fechas significativas del pasado novelesco, o todo debe
entenderse desde el momento de ahora de la escritura. Veamos una tentativa
para la primera opción; en el segundo capítulo de la primera parte aparecen unos
momentos concretos y objetivos – el asesinato de Julián Buenrostro, la venganza
del hermano, el viaje *across the river*, la aparición de la primera esposa de don
Julián, etc., pero el autor los intercala en un ambiente que nos despista inmedia-
tamente: se hace mención a 1914, 1915, 1917, 1918, a la guerra de Corea, lo
que se amplía de una manera muy sutil con lo del capítulo 'B' de la tercera
parte y con varias intercalaciones del presente. La segunda posibilidad se realiza
por medio de repetidas referencias al momento de la escritura. A manera de
ilustración recordemos la frase siguiente del cuarto capítulo de la primera parte:
"Al hermano le conté bastante poco de mi vida, pero ahora, años después ...,"[3]
etc.; sin embargo, hay otros 'presentes', no sólo los que se dan como auto-
rreflejo, como una especie de metaliteratura, sino los que son momentos evidentemente pretéritos que llegan a actualizarse debido al tratamiento que Hinojosa
les da, a saber: los interpola en diálogos o a veces monólogos sin indicación
temporal, convirtiendo el pretérito en un prolongado momento del presente.
Por consiguiente, igual que el espacio, el tiempo representa un mundo muy heterogéneo, discontinuo que se compone de momentos aparentemente fáciles

de identificar, sin embargo, como totalidad escapa a los criterios unificadores, produciendo una noción bastante abstracta del tiempo.

Veamos entonces un enfoque que enlace los dos parámetros arriba detallados y que con criterios post-einsteinianos analice tiempo y espacio a la vez. El fundamento teórico se lo debemos a M. M. Bajtin quien elaboró todo un sistema de requisitos espacio-temporales para la clasificación de las obras narrativas.[4] Sus famosos 'cronotopos', entre otras, definen las obras de aventuras, de pruebas, de viajes verticales, así como las de caballería, de idilio, del salón, del castillo, de los pueblos pequeños, etc. ¿ A cual de sus dos categorías principales pertenecería *Klail City*? En principio se podría agrupar con la primera que se caracteriza por tener un espacio extensísimo que por ello no deja de ser mera abstracción, un tiempo amplio, que por ello no deja de ser estático, y por tener únicamente lazos eventuales, casuales entre los dos. Tampoco el segundo grupo parecería ajeno a la novela de Hinojosa, dado que reúne obras que se basan en presentar alguna historia valiéndose de unos cuantos momentos destacados y el resto no es sino un gran número de variantes o sus metamorfosis; su parte correlativa, a la vez, se define como un mundo cotidiano poblado por unas pocas figuras aisladas. Un análisis más detenido mostraría, sin embargo, que *Klail City* nunca llega a una abstracción tal que carezca, del todo, del factor de la causalidad y de la dependencia temporal; y sus formas tampoco se convierten en meros títeres cuyo destino se forje más por el Destino que por el autor o por sí mismos. Por otra parte, a pesar de la afinidad con el segundo grupo, la obra de Hinojosa conlleva un gran número de episodios que de ninguna manera se consideran variaciones de otras. El cronotopos de *Klail City* nos parece más bien un elemento estructurador cuyo rasgo definitivo se da en su carácter autodestructor, a saber: el mundo espacio-temporal de la novela se edifica paso a paso y cuando está a punto de cuajar en un todo, se autodestruye, se esfuma como si nada. En otras palabras, se basa en un vaivén que vacila entre lo amorfo y una forma definida, entre lo heterogéneo y lo homogéneo. Me parece que *Klail City* necesita de una categoría nueva en la lista de Bajtin, y sería tal vez el término de 'cronotopos como si' que indicara adecuadamente su vertiente espacio-temporal.

Por razones de brevedad prescindiré de detallar los demás parámetros significativos de la novela — entre los cuales merecerían atención especial las funciones del yo narrador y de las referencias entrelazadas de la trama; puedo afirmar, sin embargo, que todos ellos, igual a lo visto más arriba, apuntan en último término a una sola característica decisiva: al fragmentarismo; éste penetra en cada uno de los niveles artísticos de la obra y — aunque suene paradójico — constituye el elemento unificador de una mar de medios heterogéneos. Si llegamos a captar la naturaleza de ese fragmentarismo particular que elaboró y montó con tanta destreza el autor de *Klail City*, a lo mejor, demos con la médula de su obra.

Unos vistazos comparativos van a ayudarnos en su definición. El fragmentarismo más simple se da en la narrativa post-vanguardista como una forma de romper con las categorías tradicionales; autores como Borges, Onetti, Asturias, Cela, insistieron en su uso — entre otros fines — para rebelarse contra la narración unilineal, de estirpe decimonónica. El resultado de sus esfuerzos se ve en que gran parte de las obras constituyen sendos rompecabezas; mas ellas son fragmentarias sólo en su presentación, el mundo subyacente sigue intacto de la explosión estética. Otra forma del fragmentarismo se observa en las construcciones elípticas que se basan en general en el juego dialéctico con lo conocido y lo ignorado o callado. Las carencias, las faltas, pueden ser diseñadas y estratégicamente colocadas a fin de que cobren un énfasis mucho más fuerte que cualquier elemento explícito. Tras el curso de las llamadas líneas negativas se nos dibuja un mundo cuya importancia supera la de las figuras de carne y hueso. En *La hojarasca* de G. G. Márquez, por ejemplo, la intensidad de las descripciones se debe más a las cosas y acontecimientos callados que a lo narrado. El fragmentarismo en una forma más elaborada y acentuada puede ser la rotunda negación de la continuidad y, además, de la causalidad del mundo. En tales casos, todos los elementos aparecen intencionadamente aislados, son autosuficientes, ninguno de ellos se relaciona con otro para evitar nexos de contigüidad o de causa y efecto. El resultado se manifiesta en un panorama desierto, inhumano, estático, exento de cualquier noción de evolución; es, en general, como la nueva novela francesa lo testimonia, la imagen del mundo cosificado. — De otra posibilidad aprovechan los autores quienes quieren contar con un co-partícipe en la creación. A los llamados 'lectores cómplices', 'lectores machos', 'lectores iniciados', los escritores les dejan cierto margen de participación, huecos por llenar con su propia fantasía, o algunos hilos sueltos que los 'compañeros del viaje' estético podrían retomar. Sobran los ejemplos: los cuentos de Borges, Rulfo, las novelas de Vargas Llosa y Cortázar. — El fragmentarismo, a la vez, puede servir de elemento clave para la representación del insalvable mundo caótico. Su rol consiste entonces, como en *Rayuela* de Cortázar, en crear carencias existenciales, agujeros del ser, huecos metafísicos: o como lo define Johnny de *El perseguidor,* todo es 'como una jalea', 'todo lleno de agujeros, todo esponja, todo como un colador, colándose a sí mismo, ...[5] Un mundo fragmentario también puede servir de marco para los conocidos viajes épicos de hoy; viajes que — como *The End of the Road*, de John Barth — pueden ser la negación de estar en alguna parte definida, representando el 'movimiento por el movimiento', la locomoción como salvación; o viajes centrífugas (ver la brillante clasificación de Fernando Ainsa en su libro *Los buscadores de la utopía*[6]) que son traumaticos tanto en el inicio como en su final dado que constituyen huidas condenadas necesariamente al fracaso.

¿ A cuál de estas variantes pertenecería *Klail City* de Hinojosa? A primera vista, contiene bastantes elementos comunes con los ejemplos arriba mencionados: sí que hay en ella cierta rebelión contra las formas redondas, tradicionales; sí que hay elipsis en la obra que contribuye a producir un énfasis acumulativo; sí que hay eslabones que se dejan pendientes en espera de lectores ágiles para integrarlos en la cadena histórica de la obra. Lo que no se perfila es evidentemente el mencionado mundo caótico, cosificado, humanamente desierto. Pero tampoco se esboza el otro extremo de dicha visión, no se especifica ningún centro que significara un puerto seguro para los estudiantes de Klail High. Ahí está la cosa: el fragmentarismo de Hinojosa realiza justamente esa modalidad que consiste en presentar elementos constituyentes que en principio pudieran desembocar en la creación de un sistema unitario, pero nunca lo hacen; es un fragmentarismo que no es la negación del sentido de cierta vida, pero tampoco es su convincente confirmación; es un estar difuso que se depura en ser, pero ese ser — a pesar de las múltiples proyecciones — no llega a cobrar una forma auténtica. Valiéndonos de las propias palabras del autor, se trata de unos viajes que "son como la reconstrucción de una casa que se quiere salvar";[7] o parafraseando la introducción de *Klail City*, su mundo se define como un vaivén entre 'un ir y venir' y su resultado que se da en la frase de que "aquí no ha pasado nada, señores."[8] Este proceder, a mi modo de ver, es un acierto pocas veces visto en la literatura chicana porque el fragmentarismo se maneja de tal manera que la forma no sólo da cabida al contenido sino que lo simboliza a la vez. Esta unidad forjada por medios tan elaborados, sin duda alguna, constituye un valor estético de alto nivel que va ganando contra los hallazgos anteriores. El fragmentarismo de *Klail City* encarna en términos artísticos el fenómeno que arriba llamamos 'situación como si' que también tiene un nombre explícito: se llama marginación; y este término — que es la terminal de este breve recorrido estético — nos devuelve ineludiblemente al inicio, dado que coincide, ha de coincidir, con el punto de partida para un itinerario en sentido contrario.

Notas

[1] Gaston Bachelard, *La poética del espacio* (México: FCE, 1975), pp. 27–28.
[2] Rolando Hinojosa, *Klail City y sus alrededores* (La Habana: Casa de las Américas, 1976), p. 117.
[3] Hinojosa, p. 41.
[4] M.M. Bahtyn, *A szó esztétikája / La estética de la palabra, ensayos* (Budapest: Gondolat, 1976).
[5] Julio Cortázar, *Cuentos* (La Habana: Instituto del Libro, 1969), p. 228.
[6] Fernando Ainsa, *Los buscadores de la utopía* (Caracas: Monte Avila, 1977).
[7] Ainsa, p. 97.
[8] Ainsa, p. 11.

State of Siege in Alejandro Morales'
Old Faces and New Wine

Francisco Lomelí

"Get up, Henry, and escape through the barrio streets of your mind."
> Pachuco to Henry Reyna in
> *Zoot Suit*

... everything can be taken from a man but one thing: the last of human freedoms — to choose one's own attitude in any given set of circumstances, to choose one's own way.
> Viktor Frankl's account in
> Auschwitz

Shortly after the Quinto Sol Generation of 1970[1] grounded the Chicano novel in culturalist literary terms, another wave of experimental writers, which we will call the Isolated Generation of 1975,[2] tapped new dimensions of the urban experience within the mode of a nouvelle vision. The Quinto Sol Generation enjoyed a high degree of promotional success because of the way they depicted cultural values as well as social types, often highlighting positive aspects of Mexican culture. In their approach to their subject, they had two principal objects in mind: first, they aimed to destereotype Chicanos in an American social context and, second, they attempted to dispute the second-class categorization. They demonstrated through literature what Chicano scholars in other fields of inquiry also proved: that the ahistorical label placed on Chicanos was not only inaccurate but damaging. Though more sophisticated than earlier works such as José Antonio Villarreal's *Pocho* (1959), the central theme of the Quinto Sol Generation still concentrates on a cycle involving an identity search. The relative dynamism of the people portrayed, however, remains somewhat restricted by elements that endure as cultural fixtures. Some critics have accused this generation of writing from a rosy prism in order to provide an uplifting effect at the expense of realism. For example, the absence of the direct mention of the Anglo, done perhaps to shun obvious heavy-handedness, can be seen as self-censorship aimed at focusing the novels on intrahistorical issues which pertain to the Chicano experience. They did not engage in identifying the sources of causes of a people's plight, offering instead an existential sense of belonging in their respective locus. Their ultimate objective encompassed two concerns: to put Mexicans/Chicanos on a literary map within American and world literatures and to place a human experience within a cosmic scope. A conscious ideology of culture was therefore propagated to represent Chicano characters as real persons with strengths and frailties, thus underscoring their full humanity even in contradictory terms.

Whereas the Quinto Sol Generation resorted to the story as a pretext to characterize a regional aspect (e.g., the mysticism of New Mexico, the border culture between the United States and Mexico, or the immigrant/migrant experience in the farm fields), the Isolated Generation of 1975 with writers such as Alejandro Morales, Isabella Ríos and Ron Arias use location as the primary medium to examine a particular milieu. This contrasts sharply with the first group of writers who offer a picturesque portrayal with philosophical overtones. By comparison, the Quinto Sol Generation still seemed couched in promoting folkloric abstractions without addressing historical questions to unearth an evolutionary process for the Chicano in modern times. If the Quinto Sol Generation presents a horizontal view of experience, the Isolated Generation of 1975 advances a vertical conceptualization of marginalized social sectors. The former sought to legitimize what Chicano meant and the latter proceeds to probe into the meaning of Chicanismo with a magnifying glass in order to unfold the internal life of the Chicano experience, a life rich in contradictions and conflicts, but one that certainly goes beyond an illusory optimism.

The writers of the Isolated Generation show a capability toward molding reality while depending less on already established Chicano novelists. In a sense, they "return home" through the novel after having learned from other literary models, such as the ones provided by James Joyce, American science-fiction, the Mexican Literature of the Onda, and other contemporary Latin American authors (Jorge Luis Borges, Gabriel García Márquez, Carlos Fuentes and others). This break signaled self-affirmation that they *can be* Chicano writers without limiting themselves to predictable situations through prescribed paradigms. Although rarely explicit, a quiet rebellion against the previous generation is evident; the language itself, wrought with ambiguity, is made to seem more than what it is. Idealizations of characters or place are less desirable because the writers choose to delve behind the obvious. They expose an anguish which is truer and richer than a simple cultural catharsis. Part of their main objective is to set out to take the pulse of a microcosm of lifestyles and supersede a sociological casebook approach, thus involving themselves further in paradoxes of the imagination. As one example of this new trend, Alejandro Morales intuits a complex network of circumstances that have been internalized by a certain type of Chicano character who begins to ponder on how and why social behavior has its origins beyond the person.

Perhaps the most shocking novel from the Isolated Generation, *Old Faces and New Wine*,[3] originally published in Spanish in 1975, attests to a radical departure from other novels in its depiction of a hard-core barrio[4] replete with unadulterated language. Conceived within a neorealist mode, although seemingly neonaturalist, the work suggests more than what it actually tells, while depending a great deal on sensorial qualities to express much of the non-language effects. What results from minimum description is a personification of the barrio as something that can be heard, felt, smelled and touched. Bare objects and semantic codes of non-euphemistic language aim to test the senses, especially the imagination of the beholder. The novel does not claim to be comprehensive, nor is it determined to unveil everything. The intent, rather, is to captivate by enticing the reader into the shadows of a nameless urban setting, a ghettoized underside of an inner city. Although absorption is the method, ambiguity becomes the way to provoke meaning between the lines. The barrio, alluded to as "this side," is consequently contrasted with another area called the "other side," and together they comprise an ambivalent comparison of two separate areas that acknowledge each other's boundaries and differences. An apparent division exists without any specific landmarks, implying that the borders are more mental than physical. The significance lies in the fact that the barrio inhabitants of "this side," who describe themselves as those who "suffer from a stigma" (p. 14), do in fact perceive demarcations and feel confined in a dead-end world. The "other side" to them simply remains an abstraction of the outside, the beyond or part of the unknown. The barrio assumes a metaphoric configuration of an insular fortress whose principal function does not protect from outer forces; instead, it operates as a magnet to keep the characters in. They realize that they act out and are an integral part of a state of siege from within as controlled by a well rehearsed script.

The thematic exposition of *Old Faces and New Wine* is designed to illustrate a vicious circle of the characters' lives as they feel trapped and manipulated under an "enslaved sun" (p. 69) in which "The sky is not close" (p. 37). Their sense of place reflects an awareness of stagnation which reminds them they are participating in a regressive process. To accentuate this notion, most of the novel occurs at night. To further emphasize a sense of going nowhere, the action appears structurally framed by the deaths of the two main characters, Julián at the beginning and Mateo at the end, who act as opposites, although they are intimate friends. Totally different in terms of motivation and outlook, they both succumb to death, victims of the barrio's inevitable influence. Julián's death is a result of violence as a way of life, but Mateo's death seems to result from a deterministic futility to instill change. Both stand as pillars which pay homage to the many others who died, confirming what Malraux stated: "The terrible thing about Death is that it transforms life into Destiny."[5] A prophecy of failure prevails in the barrio, one which is seen as the generator and nurturer of its own world view and one which diminishes the difference between life and death. In other words, this permits death to define life. As Octavio Paz wrote: "Our deaths illuminate our lives. If our deaths lack meaning, our lives also lacked it. (...) Tell me how you die and I will tell you who you are."[6]

If the infernal ambience, where degeneration and decadence reign, what consequently unfolds is an aesthetic of violence, brutality, and ugliness in which reality is perceived and captured under the influence of drugs, alcohol, sexual ecstasies, and instinctive drives. Objectivity seems foreign to describe the surroundings because the characters opt to obfuscate what they see or experience. Their harsh interactions compel them to find other means to be able to deal with the barrio; they often opt for drugs. In order to escape the daily reality they confront, they decide to distort their perception of it. The underlying motive here is that society to them seems deformed. Through drugs they find one way of replacing one illusion for another. The result is a phantasmagoric representation of chaos and tension in an environment that is falling apart at the seams.

Described as a maze in which one is destined to be lost, this hermetic world emerges with its respective trappings of inner isolation and misguided goals. If the internal structure is expectedly confounded by the mental divagations of the characters, the 33 narrative fragments (including the epilog) of the external structure support the notion of an almost plotless novel, one in which visceral impulses override action. No one is particularly going anywhere with the exception of Mateo who seeks a solution to the vicious circle of barrio existence. Both the novel's internal and external structures serve to confuse and absorb the reader, thus providing the reader with an experience which parallels the characters themselves. The novel, by and large organized in reverse order, conveys the idea of complete and total confusion. The first and last fragments attest to this reverse order, since they function as frame chapters, and the remaining narrative fragments are shuffled almost at random with evidence of certain blocks. However, the clue to the theme of a state of siege emerges in the last third of the novel when a hint is provided to its historical context. Fragmentation, then, functions on two levels: on the level at which lifestyle is perceived and in the language used to describe it. The work's overt intent to experiment with narration and language, as if they were objects of hallucination, can be traced to the influence of the New Novel from Latin America, particularly as it relates to fragmentation of time and space, the fluctuating focus, the multiple points of view, the vague references, the deconstructed language, the ambiguous narrators, the simultaneity of action and suggested discourse, the haphazardly associated imagery and syntactical dislocation.[7] All contribute to create a disjointed environment of social upheaval that is in gestation waiting to explode.

Marred by elements of explosiveness, the novel resembles a ticking bomb. As tension mounts in a highly charged atmosphere, we are given the sensation of placing the fragmented action in the eye of the storm. A condition of unchained violence pervades, as we sense the uncertainty of curtailing it, and a feeling of exasperation increases, as if various forms of death are the norm. Hostility hangs as an invisible force to denote a place under attack. The invading forces, however, do not necessarily come from without. Much seems self-inflicted. This is precisely the central point to resolve in order to unravel what meaning is camouflaged amidst the graphic chaos of the novel.

Old Faces and New Wine offers much more than first meets the eye. On the surface it presents a provocative x-ray vision of the cannibalistic qualities of violence and hate, implying that the barrio characters repeat prescribed roles. Fatalism seems to overtake religion as sacred, and resignation becomes the means with which to achieve the final state of union with nothingness. True, the "old faces" do refer to sameness or a lack of visible change, but the term "veteranos" brings to mind that there is a sense of having participated in battle. Therefore, "old faces" is associated with the ageless process of being beaten down or defeated; also, by extension barrio life is viewed as a battleground of constant skirmishes. In this locale under siege, it is not coincidental that numerous sketchy metaphorical reverberations hint at a police or military state with echoes of an oppressive condition: "machine-gun gurgle" (p. 9), "The machine-gun sound filled the sky" (p. 24), and "The face of terror could not move the lips" (p. 41). The vertical location of the barrio is emphasized to give the sensation of an abyss below a blood-stained sky: "The afternoon freed the wind and the sky was immense, far away, decorated with red clouds scratched across the soft blue" (p. 116).

In addition, a satanic omniscient presence haunts the inhabitants with a "diabolical laugh": these are the Buenasuerte brothers whose ironic name embodies the temptation of death. As agents of decadence, they play an instrumental role in others' self-destruction, providing Julián, for example, first the paraphernalia of addiction and finally the vehicle to his death. Serving as efficient instigators, they roam the streets and frequent gatherings to promote vice. The Buenasuerte brothers act as male counterparts to the *llorona* figure (the wailing woman), except they lure people toward death instead of warning them against it. They provide one of the multiple forms of certain sirens in the novel that fill the air with frightful shrills which consequently helps establish a continuous state of alert. Other sirens amplify the sense of terror: they signal violence, danger or death. They also function as voices from the underworld: "The cold wind drifted in space. The grim siren made its mournful journey, caressing the trees. One could hear the sorrowful sound in all one could see in the barrio. The tips of the fingers dried the eyes, but the Siren [sic] continued crying" (p. 86). Personified through surrealistic images, the sirens at times appear as objects with a mind of their own, thus figuring as characters with hidden motives:

> ... upon coming home from school, he saw several sirens and an ambu-
> lance siren across the street... he noticed that the sirens and the people
> were not in front of his house... From where he stood, he could see
> the white-attired attendants take someone out on a stretcher to be
> eaten up by the siren. (...) His open hands were stuck to the siren's
> eyes, his nose was pressed against the glass (p. 58).

The sirens augment tension and their constant presence denotes a state of social paralysis, which recalls a number of ambivalent associations. For example, they echo the mythological mermaids whose enchanting songs attracted sailors to their deaths. The inevitable relationship with the Mexican *llorona* figure emerges because legend has it that she sought the children she killed. This parallels Julián's guilt for having contributed to his mother's death. This sense of loss — physical, existential or moral — serves as the central motif of the novel and Mateo's quest is to respond to that loss by collectivizing it. Therefore, the sirens symbolize these two characters' enticement toward base ends or the burning desire to overcome the torment of their self-destruction.[8]

In conjunction with all the ambiguous elements, the barrio finds itself at a critical juncture struggling with itself in order to achieve something positive out of its putrid conditions. Here Mateo becomes instrumental in a process of awareness because he intends to break away from the institutionalized denigrating traditions. Even when resignation seems on the brink of change in order to consider new behavioral patterns, the characters find that the hallucinogenic elements of their reality tend to undermine any efforts for adopting new ways. Having reached the ultimate degree of denial, the barrio stands out as its own worst enemy. It is Mateo who displays signs of coming to grips with the causal relationships of his surroundings. He intimates a return to self-actualization because otherwise death will be the only alternative. In accordance with Mateo's revelations, an omniscient narrator describes the intolerable condition of an inner state of siege: "The vein is about to burst and the ancient passion of all men will come again to proclaim that it is not what they say, but the timeless anger of the stirp [the people] which becomes stronger and stronger" (p. 114). The rampant inversion of the traditional values of family respect, religion and love make Mateo seek a radical change to break the circle of alienation and behavioral warfare. Swollen with an accumulated rage, the people, or stirp, seek to find an outlet for their anxiety which appears in various forms. The enclosed sense of their environment is symbolically alluded to as cages, darkness in the form of a cave, boxed-in homes and fragile glass boxes. Glass boxes are repeated in numerous ways and Mateo reaches a significant conclusion about people's plight in his meditations: "How many little glass boxes are there in this world. Millions and millions. How can one be to find the right instrument to shatter his own box" (p. 100). As the visionary who loves his barrio, Mateo feels a calling to save his barrio and its inhabitants. The leitmotif he enunciates three times, his pledge to come back dead or alive, defines his commitment to return in an Ulysses fashion at the same time that it foreshadows his own death.

The focal point of the novel is centered in a paradoxical vortex between a struggle of old and new, as initially insinuated by the title. The decoding of this vortex becomes a key obstacle to fully understand how the novel is composed and how narrative components deliberately obscure the meaning. An ageless sameness implies that new forms of existence are in order, as is exemplified when a friend tells his compadre: "don't fear the darkness because the light of the new sun will soon shine on your face" (p. 119). In this way language shades clarity through its truncated bluntness, but it also serves to define the ambience without having to describe it. Language can be regarded as both the outer shell of what the barrio contains as well as the only thing it offers. Its abrasive nature of raw and unadorned crudeness reflects violence nakedly and it manifests a bottled-up rage of the infrahuman conditions. A double-edged aberration, language is the weapon used to survive in this harsh environment and it also indicates the degree of degeneration found in the hard-core barrio. As one critic observes: "The language is hazy, even unintelligible to the reader. But this does not imply an idiolectical mutation of Spanish which the author has created; it is, rather, a language whose code the narrator has reserved for himself."[9] The violent realism introduces the reader — often through shock images akin to *tremendismo* — into the realm of social determinism as a system of life in which these external manifestations have become internalized. A victim of this internalization, Julián, who can no longer envision a future, feels destined to fail, live by violence and ultimately die. Ironically, this same language also marks the clear signal of liberation in its incessant pursuit to see beyond the auras of taboos, euphemisms, and mystifications.

As one of the novel's main narrators, Mateo reflects his concept of a besieged place via his gained self-awareness. From this we can extract a sense of a moral indictment. Instrumental in giving meaning and proper perspective to the tempest of free associations, Mateo becomes the narrative conscience for his barrio. He strives to regain and salvage whatever positive qualities his barrio might hold. Consequently, the ironic and sacrilegious use of the term "místicos" for drug addicts and alcoholics acquires a sense of perversion as well as a parody of the uselessness of institutionalized religion. The characters' mystical experience, rather than seeking a higher order, is indicative of a descent into nothingness. María González points out: "They neither seek divine communication, nor perfection of the spirit; better yet, this type of inverted mysticism serves them as a way of escape from the immediate world that surrounds and asphyxiates them. Nevertheless, they believe to have found themselves under a spiritual ecstasy without realizing that in fact their ecstasy is only a manifestation of mental alienation."[10]

Once Mateo judges the values of the barrio as inverted, he wishes to return them to a proper humanistic function. At this point, the novel assumes greater meaning. For instance, the significance of Christmas, the peak in Christian religiosity, is that it is shown as an empty series of rituals celebrating a divine being who has no real relevance to the barrio and its people. We are invited to assume that perhaps other forms of salvation ought to be sought. This symbolic back-drop reinforces the presence of Mateo in a stage of gaining awareness, thus bringing to mind one of the main apostles and evangelists responsible for writing key portions of the Bible. He, in effect, takes on the role of a Christ figure filled with messianic motives and who begins to challenge social conventions, be they inverted or otherwise. His death, occurring in the 33rd fragment, parallels Christ's, except that the cause of his death, leukemia, attests to the fact that decadence had overtaken even him. Through a consistent repetition of themes the novel illustrates an effort to symbolically represent an ambivalence: it strengthens the notion of Mateo's spiritual synthesis in order to reverse the current trends in his environment; also, it denotes the configuration of his own sacrifice in order to instill that synthesis. Some of the numerological examples include the following: a youth is kicked three times; it rains for three days; dogs bark three times; three pills are ingested. What slowly emerges is a new type of siege to counteract the presently existing one. Trumpets sound. Fires and kilns burn as a result of the heated urban atmosphere of an angry and restless people. The implication is that fire will be fought with fire: "The crackling violence of the wood sent hot needles into space" (p. 118). A purging effect becomes inevitable in order to start anew: "Human fires flare in the streets of the country, burning the past, protesting the present, and fornicating the future" (p. 128).

The key to this incoming onslaught of renewed vigor and purpose is consequently placed in an historical context during the civil rights decade of the 1960s, specifically when Julián, who most needs the help, enters a bathroom. After witnessing the stench and seeing himself reflected in the black water of the toilet bowl, he notices a 1965 calendar behind the door. This reference is crucial within the obscure scene in that it places the action at the height of the beginnings of the Chicano Movement when César Chávez' farmworkers' movement in the California farm fields would soon produce effects in the cities. Therefore, the novel presents a Chicano urban community — since it is nameless, it can be any one of them — that is on the verge of catching the fever in involvement in a social cause to improve a people's lot. The novel in this way serves to provide the retrospective view of the barrio which helps us better appreciate the reasons why it came to the point of exploding.[11] At the same time, it establishes a point of reference for the barrio before it became affected by the fervor of the Movement. If we unravel the novel from this crowded bathroom and the landmark date mentioned, this work acquires a sense of order by proceeding to join the fragments as extensions of this narrative nucleus. From this point, we can tie the various fragments into respective categories and thus develop the idea of a social novel. The bathroom scene, as the pit of decadence and ultimate lack of dignity, becomes a reminder — especially for Julián — to stop his self-denial and flagellation so that he may retrace his steps to a more productive life.

The muted symbols and rampant violence in *Old Faces and New Wine* by Alejandro Morales offer a devastating view of barrio life, its predicaments and dilemmas. The fact that Mateo dies confirms a pessimistic outlook about what can be effectively done, but the author has achieved a naked exposition of a place and its disturbing elements without offering facile moralistic attitudes. Dichotomies such as victim-victimizer, oppressed-oppressor here become academic categorizations in that they paradoxically coexist. Simplifications which aim to find causes for these conditions are beyond the realm of consideration in the novel. The work, instead, depicts effects as they manifest themselves as institutionalized behavior and values within a deconstructed world of perverted alienation. The main focus is in terms of unfolding the internalization processes that have their reason for being, but they are too complex to be defined adequately, since the novel does not represent a sociological treatise about a barrio. It metaphorically represents an internal colony that becomes isolated and insulated through its stigmas and prejudice, and these consequently influence the persons' behavior through self-victimization. By probing into the internalization of a state of siege, the author allows for a vicarious recreation of a truncated social reality that urgently requires attention to break the vicious circles of violence and death. Although the novel is affectionately dedicated to the barrio in the epigraph, the gesture seems bittersweet given that there is an acknowledgement of the barrio's inherent qualities of its own destruction. In other words, this love is also painful. But, if change is to be instituted, the individual must begin from within, as is well exemplified with Mateo. By altering the foci, a new chain of events might occur as long as the imaginary guards are eliminated or the walls are destroyed. To begin, the individual might consider decolonizing himself from the effects of victimization and from there overcome the inner walls of an even more entrenched Auschwitz that besieges the barrio inhabitants.

Notes

[1] The designation is reserved only for novelists such as Tomás Rivera, Rolando Hinojosa-Smith, Rudolfo A. Anaya and Miguel Méndez, who definitely exhibit a Berkeley, California connection. Instrumental in promoting a whole series of writers, not only novelists, Quinto Sol as the publishing house was the key organism responsible for instituting literary tastes in the 1960s and early 1970s among Chicanos. Through extensive publicity, Quinto Sol created a market for the Chicano novel and it also instilled the notion that the novel marked the epitome of a people's creative sophistication in literature.

[2] The proposed classification seems appropriate for various reasons: although this new group of writers had no prior knowledge of each others' writings, their isolation did in fact enhance narrative experimentation by producing very distinct works in subject matter but similar in scope. They emerged on their own onto the Chicano literary scene and their personal circumstances give credence to the isolation factor. For example, Berta Ornelas published *Come Down From the Mound* (1975) out of a small printing

press in Arizona, emphasizing that a power structure can be influenced by the power of love. Unable to find a publisher, Chicano or otherwise, Isabella Ríos was compelled to produce *Victuum* (copyrighted in 1975; published in 1976) on her own, literally as a garage enterprise. Alejandro Morales was confronted with other obstacles; his harsh portrayal of the barrio and the violent language did not appeal to the positive image-makers. Discouraged from having his first work, *Caras viejas y vino nuevo*, accepted in the United States, his next recourse was to try Mexican publishers in Mexico City. From this emerged the contract with the prestigious publisher Joaquín Mortiz in 1975. Ron Arias, with *The Road to Tamazunchale* (1975), sensed limited publishing outlets for and by Chicanos, but managed to receive favorable reviews from *West Coast Poetry Review* from Nevada that later published his novel. Clearly, each author holds a unique relationship with the already established Chicano circles, as it pertains to content, style and an uninhibited desire to be themselves as writers. Their overt independence becomes a conscious way to associate themselves with other literatures while maintaining a Chicano character.

[3] For the purpose of limiting possible confusions with respect to the first edition of *Caras viejas y vino nuevo* (Mexico City: Editorial Joaquín Mortiz, 1975), and its subsequent translation, *Old Faces and New Wine*, trans. Max Martínez (San Diego: Maize Press, 1981), we have limited most of our discussion to the latter edition. Many discrepancies exist between the two editions, especially important differences that pertain to structure, but the central focus of this study is meaning and not specific points where possible contradictions might be in evidence. The translator's poetic license as well as the publisher's alteration of the structure can well serve as the basis for another study. All quotations from the text are attributed to the translator's edition.

[4] The barrio refers to a neighborhood in an urban setting, although it does not have all the connotations of *ghetto* with its decrepid conditions. However, barrio in the context of this novel does in fact resemble ghetto, because in other occasions it serves also to indicate simply a place to live as characterized by a Mexican or Chicano presence.

[5] André Malraux, *Man's Hope* (New York: Random House, 1938), p. 261.

[6] Octavio Paz, *The Labyrinth of Solitude: Life and Thought in Mexico*, trans. Lysander Kemp (New York: Grove Press, 1961), p. 54.

[7] For further discussion on some of the points mentioned, see Nuria Bustamante's unpublished study, "Permanencia y cambio en *Caras viejas y vino nuevo*," forthcoming in *Bibliotheca Americana*.

[8] J.E. Cirlot, A *Dictionary of Symbols*, trans. Jack Sage (New York: Philosophical Library, 1981), pp. 297–98. The concept of siren is amply discussed here, although no distinction is made with *llorona* in Spanish which manifests itself as a unique variation. See also Joseph Campbell's *The Masks of God: Primitive Mythology* (New York: Viking Press, 1959), pp. 61–62, in which he associates sirens as "life-threatening" or "life-furthering." Both serve our purpose to demonstrate their respective ambivalence as an integral component of symbolism and style in *Old Faces and New Wine*.

[9] Ricardo Benavídez, "Review of *Caras viejas y vino nuevo*," *Books Abroad*, 50, No. 4 (Autumn, 1978), 837–838.

[10] María González, "*Caras viejas y vino nuevo*: Análisis temático y estructural," *Tinta* (Department of Spanish & Portuguese, University of California, Santa Barbara), 1, No. 1 (May 1981), 15–18. Translation is mine.

[11] It can be argued that Alejandro Morales' novel accomplished for the Chicano novel and the Chicano Movement what Agustín Yáñez achieved for the novel of the Mexican Revolution through a retrospective view of a social situation before exploding. Both novels poignantly recreate conditions as they were before a social movement and why the latter was an inevitable result.

Fiction and Politics in Acosta's
The Revolt of the Cockroach People

Horst Tonn

Oscar Zeta Acosta's second book *The Revolt of the Cockroach People*, first published in the fall of 1973, has to be seen within the context of a body of works which continues to be obscured by a number of designations. From a variety of labels this literary corpus has become most widely known as the "New Journalism."[1]

Hunter S. Thompson, one of the more prominent practitioners of "New Journalism," was a personal friend of Acosta's. Allusions to their friendship can be found in several of Thompson's writings. Acosta appears as Doctor Gonzo, "the 300-pound Samoan attorney," in Thompson's drug-crazed farewell sermon to the American Dream entitled *Fear and Loathing in Las Vegas.*[2] By the same token, Thompson drifts through Acosta's novels, first introduced as "the tall, baldheaded hillbilly from Tennessee," and although the name is changed from King to Stonewall in *The Revolt of the Cockroach People*, the references to Thompson still remain obvious.[3]

Since definitions of literary categories tend to be either arbitrarily exclusive or superficially broad, I will merely note here that in their writings the representatives of "New Journalism" focus attention on authentic events and at the same time freely draw on fictional techniques, thus creating inextricable clusters of fiction and reality. Their concern is clearly more an existential than an aesthetic one. Most of the writers would probably agree with Hunter Thompson who considers the distinction between "fiction" and "journalism" to be a mere academic quibble: " ... both 'fiction' and 'journalism' are artificial categories; ... both forms, at their best, are only two different means to the same end.'"[4] While all practitioners of "New Journalism" display varying degrees of adherence to fact, Acosta certainly belongs to those who show little hesitation to blur the line between fact and fiction.

From the point of view of literary genre Acosta's book is clearly a "hybrid" form – a combination of the elements of journalistic reporting, autobiography and the novel.[6] The central conflict of the novel – the political activism of Chicanos challenging the dominant society on various fronts – is clearly identifiable as a phenomenon of recent history. Many of the characters appear as authentic personae, with their proper names, public functions, and their respective roles in the confrontation. This is true for movement leaders César Chávez and Corky Gonzales as well as for Los Angeles mayor Sam Yorti, Cardinal McIntyre and the author-protagonist Oscar Zeta Acosta himself.

Time and place of Acosta's novel coincide with a major moment in Chicano history. The setting Los Angeles, which is the home of the largest Chicano community in the United States, was in the 1960s and early 70s the major site for much of the political activism culminating in the "Chicano Moratorium" of 1970.[7] The narrated time of the novel covers that historical period which saw some of the most powerful manifestations of protest and resistance initiated and carried out by Chicanos in the United States. Not only are the major events and characters in *The Revolt of the Cockroach People* historically verifiable, but also the author's role as active participant is confirmed by Hunter Thompsons's article "Strange Rumblings in Aztlán" from 1971 and other sources.[8]

Acosta distances himself slightly from the protagonist of his novel by introducing the latter under the name of Buffalo Zeta Brown. Brown arrives in Los Angeles in January of 1968, thus directly linking the beginning of *The Revolt of the Cockroach People* with the ending of Acosta's first novel *The Autobiography of a Brown Buffalo* where his desperate and obsessive wanderings across the United States had finally left him off in a shabby hotel in El Paso, without a sense of direction and, more severely, without the necessary money to continue his erratic trip. As a last resort, he calls his brother who, instead of granting the hoped for money, tells him that Chicanos in East Los Angeles are about to stage a "revolution." This notice serves as the spark which sets Acosta on his way to Los Angeles where he finally hopes to get in touch with his Chicano soul and perhaps find the story which will bring him fame as a writer.

Brown arrives in Los Angeles just in time to witness the massive school-walkouts which in actuality did take place in March of 1968. While trying to maintain his stance of the detached observer who only intends to write about the events, Brown gets caught in the whirl of political turmoil from which, for various reasons, he fails to disentangle himself. He goes to meet with farmworkers' union-leader César Chávez in the spring of that same year when Chávez, as a fact of recent history, did undertake a major fast to help bring an end to the violence committed against members of his union. The novel focuses on authentic events of national scope such as the assassination of Robert Kennedy, the Vietnam War and the killings at Kent State University in 1970, but it also touches on local issues such as police brutality in the barrios and the construction of a pompous church in Los Angeles which evokes public indignation and is then chosen by Chicano militants as the site for one of their demonstrations. Finally, the killing of journalist Ruben Salazar and its surrounding events move to center stage in the narration. Ruben Salazar, who appears under the name of

Roland Zanzibar in the novel, has since become a martyr figure of the Chicano movement and in relating his case it seems to be Acosta's prime concern to present a counter-version of the killing which unhinges and sometimes ridicules the official version, according to which the case was dismissed as an unfortunate accident.[9]

Faced with the intricacies of authentic events presented in a fictional text, a further discussion of *The Revolt of the Cockroach People* requires some consideration of the question how fiction and reality can be said to relate to one another. Instead of positing fiction and reality as two separate spheres and setting them even further apart from each other by assigning the value of the "real" to the latter while blemishing the former as "imagined," recent efforts in literary criticism have attempted to collapse this dichotomy of separate spheres. These efforts are based on the notion that what we much too readily refer to as "reality" is more accurately a product of our cognitive efforts. "Reality" as such can at best be described as a "virtual chaos of events."[10] It is defined by the absence of order and meaning: reality manifests itself in the flow of events, it has none of the attributes which we usually assign to well-written stories as there are "... central subjects, proper beginnings, middles, and ends, and a coherence that permits us to see 'the end' in every beginning."[11] In order to be able to function in the world and to communicate our world to others, we are forced to impose some kind of order or meaning on a chaotic and incoherent universe. Thus, our perception of reality is always and inescapably the result of interpretation, abstraction, and selection and this applies to fictional as well as so-called non-fictional texts. Rather than being distinct from each other in their orientation towards reality, they have this in common that they are both human constructs of order and meaning imposed upon an otherwise incoherent universe. The notion that nonfictional texts present the reader with a slice of reality whereas fiction roams in the vague sphere of the imagination ceases to be valid:

> ... all hierarchic separation of the "real" from
> the "imagined," of life from art, of politics
> and history from fiction ceases to be valid.
> "Reality" can no longer be conceived of as
> mirrored, or reproduced by the imagination but
> as co-produced by it — as always already staged,
> narrated, performed; as a chained analogy of
> dramatized events that leads back, eventually,
> to the eye of the observer (or the actor) who,
> in the very act of observation (or of action),
> creates his own order of events. (12)

If we are willing to discard the concept of fiction and reality as two separate domains, new possibilities of talking about fictional texts emerge. The text then can be taken as a mediating ground for competing and potentially contradictory constructs of reality.[13] Victor Turner reminds us that this is always a two-way street, that stories always make important statements about our social life, but that also much of our social behavior is influenced and guided by our knowledge of stories which are the source of significant cultural paradigms in every society.[14]

Finally, the whole world of culture appears in a different light, if we accept what has been said so far. Culture then never exists as a finished product, instead its elements are constantly being rearranged and renegotiated by individuals and social groups. Culture is never a "given," it has to be seen as something that is "gropingly discovered."[15] To emphasize the dynamics of culture is to subscribe to a view that attempts to come to terms with culture "not as a more or less static realm, but as a living, constantly changing field of interaction in which the relations between received constructs of reality and subjective experience are continually reassessed and symbolically rearranged."[16]

To return this discussion to the text, an ongoing juxtaposition of adversary and sometimes contradictory outlooks on the events portrayed stands as the central narrative paradigm of Acosta's novel. The central concern of *The Revolt of the Cockroach People* is to weigh the gains and losses of Chicano political activism. Acosta's version of the confrontations between Chicanos and the dominant society in Los Angeles from 1968 to 1972 is couched in terms of conflict without resolution. While the author as participant-observer in this case readily identifies with the fervor and revolutionary euphoria of the Chicano movement, his narration also reveals a second element which is the anticipation of defeat. The blatantly obvious rhetoric of victory and salvation is effectively counterbalanced by another perspective in which the prospects of movement politics are more modestly assessed in terms of physical, cultural and psychological survival. Rather than envisioning a version of the post-revolutionary society the objectives of the day-to-day political struggle are to avert destruction or loss: to fight means to avoid having to go to Vietnam, to manage to stay out of prison, to salvage one's own identity from assimilation, and to rescue one's sense of self-esteem by retribution against insults and injuries suffered.

Acosta's entanglement in Chicano politics falls into a time when some of the most powerful manifestations of resistance are followed in close sequence by other events which point to a decline in hope and anticipation. Historian Rodolfo Acuña's assessment of the transition from the 1960s to the 70s accurately expresses this sentiment of ambivalence which can be traced throughout Acosta's novel:

> The decade began optimistically. Some
> Chicanos referred to themselves as
> the "sleeping giant." ... By the 1970's
> it was clear that even the small gains
> made by the Chicano community were
> checked by those in power to keep

Chicanos in their place and were
therefore illusory. (17)

Here the novel and the account by the historian affirm each other. Both capture that brief period of recent history when high expectations and a wave of political activism almost coincide with the decline and steady disintegration of political momentum which has its impetus firmly rooted in the 60s, but fails to sustain itself into the 70s.

In the novel, the anticipation of defeat sets in with the assassination of Robert Kennedy. Significantly, his tragic death occurs almost immediately after the protagonist's involvement in movement politics has reached a point which he himself compares to having "stepped off a cliff" (p. 53), thus indicating that he is without control in a potentially suicidal situation. According to the lawyer-activist's own interpretation of events as related in the novel, Kennedy's death paved the way for Nixon to become elected President, and it also effectively undercut the momentum of liberal politics in general without which all prospects for the Chicanos seem to have vanished as well. Both events, Kennedy's death and Brown's full-blown immersion into politics, form a strange pair where the former incident reduces the efforts of the protagonist to futility, if not absurdity. Brown devotes all of his energies to the cause while he clearly realizes that the odds are high, and it is precisely this unresolved contradiction originating in the author-protagonist himself which then becomes the central narrative paradigm for the novel. Having its origins in a contradictory setup, the narration never arrives at any state of resolution, but remains in tension oscillating between hopeful anticipation and apparent desperation, between promise and doom, between renewal and self-destruction.

The court scenes are set in a similarly ambiguous light. For one, the courts are the site of triumphant victory for Brown and his friends. Frequently he turns the courtroom into the stage for a performance in which he himself stands out as the only acting character. Skillfully and with the necessary disrespect for trial procedures he manages to transform court hearings into political demonstrations. However, perhaps more importantly, the courts are the home ground of Brown's enemies. They are a crucial factor in the strategy of the dominant society to maintain the status quo, and it comes as no surprise that most of Brown's victories in court are won on the defensive. At best he can expose dubious practices or reveal racial prejudice in the grand jury system, beyond that he fights to keep his movement friends out of prison. The high point in his career as attorney for the Chicano movement is reached when he can unveil the lies, contradictions, and obvious cover-ups surrounding the death of Ruben Salazar. As has been pointed out by Ramón Saldívar, the depiction of the court hearings investigating allegations in conjunction with the Chicano Moratorium clearly marks a climax in the novel.[18] Here testimonies of participants and so-called eyewitnesses are effectively brought to bear upon each other and are ultimately revealed as being informed by self-interest and self-deception rather than a sincere desire for the truth:

> *All of them... every single witness, both*
> *prosecution and defense... is lying.* Or not
> telling the whole truth. The bastards know
> exactly what we have done and what we have
> not done. They *know* for a fact that Corky
> was not involved in any conspiracy, in any
> arson, in anything. And they know how and
> why Zanzibar was killed. But they have all
> told their own version of things as they
> would like them to be. (p. 272)

The victory in this trial is as ambiguous as Brown's personal attitude when he talks about himself as being a lawyer "who actually hates the *law*" (p. 231). While the defendants are ruled to be innocent of all charges, there is clearly another edge to all of this. The verdict is nothing else but official confirmation of what Brown and his friends had known all along and considering the enormous amount of time, strength and manpower absorbed by the trial, this was clearly another battle won on the defensive. The following quotation illustrates the less than enthusiastic reaction to the verdict:

> We've waited for fifteen days. Or is it
> fifteen years? We've come to this court-
> house for nearly a year on this case. A
> year ago they killed Zanzibar and only now
> have we come to the end of this trial. Only
> after we spent our last dime, wore ourselves
> to the bone and marched a thousand miles on
> the sidewalks of LA, only after I have really
> broken down with paranoia and suspicion, only
> now has the jury come back and told us what
> we knew all along: the Tooner Flats Seven are
> innocent of all the felonies. (p. 275)

The ending of *The Revolt of the Cockroach People* is as much a foreshadowing of the decline of radical politics in the 1970s as it is one more example for the ambiguous and contradictory narrative strategy of the novel. Self-destruction prevails when a young man "of presumably Latin descent" (p. 279) is killed by a bomb which Brown and his friends had installed in the courthouse as retribution against a sell-out Chicano judge, who remains unharmed. The re- volutionary fervor from the beginning is weakly carried on when the author announces that the Chicanos "only temporarily lay down their arms" (p. 280), and that the rest of that story will shortly be told in another book. However, this proclaimed optimism does not seem to be based on any real progress. Rather, the early anticipation of defeat first expressed after the assassination of Robert Kennedy is confirmed by the ending of the novel. The bombing of the courthouse symbolizes the continuity of this narrative thread. An innocent by-stander is killed while Judge Alacran, the actual target of the operation, remains unhurt.

Thus, at the end of his stay in Los Angeles, which also marks the end of the novel, Acosta-Brown acknowledges that the fictional account of his career as lawyer-politician will be a "swan song" (p. 281). Or, to use another image here, Hunter Thompson's prophecy that "there is no light at the end of this tunnel" serves well to characterize the prevailing sense of accomplishment.[19] Whereas the title of the novel may suggest the all-too-familiar theme of underdog throwing off its oppressor, the novel itself cannot be read as a linear progression from a state of oppression to some desired realm of freedom. Acosta's novel will frustrate any reader's attempt to align the text with a given political stance. The novel brings into focus some of the accomplishments, promises and prospects of Chicano politics as well as its casualties, dead ends and insurmountable barriers. Rather than setting up a case for the "right" ideology, the author's narrative strategy rests on the notions of unresolved conflict and openly displayed contradictoriness.

Notes

[1] See Ronald Weber, *The Literature of Fact* (Athens, Ohio: Ohio U. Press, 1980), pp. 1–4.
[2] Hunter S. Thompson, *Fear and Loathing in Las Vegas* (New York: Random House, 1971). See also his article "The Banshee Screams For Buffalo Meat," *Rolling Stone*, No. 254 (December 15, 1977), 54.
[3] Oscar Zeta Acosta, *The Autobiography of a Brown Buffalo* (San Francisco: Straight Arrow Books, 1972), p. 137.
Oscar Zeta Acosta, *The Revolt of the Cockroach People* (New York: Bantam Books, 1974²), p. 12. All further references to this work appear in the text.
[4] Hunter S. Thompson, *The Great Shark Hunt* (New York: Summit Books, 1982), p. 120.
[5] For a full discussion of the impact of "New Journalism" and Gonzo writing on Acosta see Juan Bruce-Novoa, "Fear and Loathing on the Buffalo Trail," *MELUS* 6, No. 4, (1979), 39–50.
[6] Bruce-Novoa, p. 44.
[7] The Chicano Moratorium marks the peak of protest against the Vietnam War organized by Chicanos. On August 29, 1970 a mass demonstration drawing Chicanos from all over the United States was staged in Los Angeles. In the ensuing confrontations between demonstrators and police the well-known and widely respected Chicano journalist Ruben Salazar was killed. See also Rodolfo Acuña, *Occupied America* (New York: Harper and Row, 1981²), pp. 366–71.
[8] Hunter S. Thompson, "Strange Rumblings in Aztlán," *Rolling Stone*, No. 81 (April 29, 1971), 30–37. See also Albert Herrera, "The National Chicano Moratorium and the Death of Ruben Salazar," in *The Chicanos*, eds. Ed Ludwig and James Santibañez (Baltimore: Penguin Books, 1971), pp. 235–41.
[9] For an extensive discussion of the Salazar killing see Thompson, "Strange Rumblings in Aztlán" and Acuña, pp. 369–71.
[10] Hayden White, "The Narrativization of Real Events," *Critical Inquiry*, 7, No. 4 (1981), 795.

[11] Hayden White, "The Value of Narrativity in the Representation of Reality," *Critical Inquiry*, 7, No. 1 (1980), 27.

[12] Heinz Ickstadt, "History, Fiction and the Designs of Robert Coover," *Amerikastudien*, 28, No. 3 (1983), 352.

[13] See Winfried Fluck, "Literature as Symbolic Action," *Amerikastudien*, 28, No. 3 (1983), esp. pp. 364–66.

[14] See Victor Turner, "Social Dramas and Stories about Them," *Critical Inquiry*, 7, No. 1 (1980), 153.

[15] Edward Sapir, "The Emergence of the Concept of Personality in a Study of Cultures," quoted in Turner, "Social Dramas and Stories about Them," p. 144.

[16] Fluck, p. 364.

[17] Acuña, p. 379.

[18] Ramón Saldívar, "A Dialectic of Difference: Towards a Theory of the Chicano Novel," *MELUS*, 6, No. 3 (1979), 83 f.

[19] Thompson, *Fear and Loathing in Las Vegas*, p. 179.

The Ideological and the Utopian in Tomás Rivera's … *y no se lo tragó la tierra* and Ron Arias' *The Road to Tamazunchale*

José David Saldívar

The conception of the ideological and the utopian which informs this study of Rivera's and Arias' narratives may be seen as an exploration of Fredric Jameson's definition of dialectical thinking in *The Political Unconscious* as "the anticipation of the logic of the collectivity which has not yet come into being."[1] For well over a decade now, Jameson has pursued his inquiry into the ideological and the utopian in advanced capitalism: the goal of humankind's striving to realize its dreams of a better life. From *Marxism and Form* (1971), through *The Prisonhouse of Language* (1972) and *Fables of Aggression* (1979), to his most recent book, *The Political Unconscious* (1981),[2] Jameson's work, like Herbert Marcuse's and Ernst Bloch's Frankfurt school critical interpretations before him, provides us with a blueprint for analyzing the crucial contradictions in the society surrounding the work of art and the desire to transcend these contradictions through an affirmative vision of cultural unity. Which is to say: an ideological analysis, for Jameson brings to light the gaps in the illusory coherence of the textual surface and a utopian analysis reconstructs the totality of the literary text.

Jameson's radical, new hermeneutic, I believe, makes *The Political Unconscious* especially useful and suggestive for the reading of contemporary Chicano narratives. Rather than proposing one-dimensional readings of texts, Jameson argues that all texts possess fossilized remnants of several genres, each of which carries its own ideological master code as a "sedimented content." Thus, instead of containing a single formal impulse, the literary text is actually a "symbolic act that must rewrite or harmonize heterogeneous narrative paradigms;" and so the literary text is best apprehended as a field of forces in which "the dynamics of sign systems of several distinct modes of production can be registered and apprehended" (Jameson, pp. 144 and 98). What I want to argue in my essay is that an ideological and utopian analysis of Rivera's and Arias' narratives is necessary because each of these Chicano texts can be seen as objectifying ideological critiques of religious idealism, racism, solitude, death, dying and senility, while, at the same time, proposing utopian possibilities within their narrative form and content for the real world. Further, I suggest that a dialectical reading of the ideological and utopian thrusts in Rivera's … *y no se lo tragó la tierra* and Arias' *The Road to Tamazunchale* will illuminate the political as well as the aesthetic dimensions of these Chicano texts.

I.

Tomás Rivera's *...y no se lo tragó la tierra* — misread in its early years[3] — is one of the Southwest's richest dialectical novels. It is the story of the subjective and collective experiences of Texas Chicano migrant farmworkers. Rivera's novel delves deeply into the life of a young anonymous migrant by analyzing his growth and maturity within the cyclical frame of reference of a year. *Tierra*, however, not only studies the protagonist's rites of passage, but it also shows how his solitary chaotic life fits together within a collective class pattern of solidarity among other migrant farmworkers. This class pattern, in turn, has its own utopian pattern, because it is not a picture of an American social and economic world in an uncritical perspective, but a reality apprehended in terms of a Texas Chicano political struggle during the 1940s and 1950s in South Texas. The aesthetic quality of the work, moreover, is achieved by means of dialectical folkloric and (post)modernist techniques, a process similarly rendered in Juan Rulfo's *El llano en llamas.*

Among existing dialectically-mediated fields of semiotic forces, the most significant in Rivera's *tierra* are a negation of a fixed, coherent narrative sequence and the structural breakdown of conventional cause and effect sequence. Rivera's narrative offers a disordered and fragmented story line, but it succeeds in creating a view of the Chicano migrant world from the protagonist's consciousness.

Rivera's world is an extremely condensed rural world and a profoundly accurate rendering of the migrant farmworker's stark social and economic conditions. The atmosphere of *tierra* is full of shocks, tragedies, and political and social repressions. Unfulfilled passions and desires, fear and chaos stand out as tangible phenomena in Rivera's work of art.

The migrant farmworkers who live and die on the agricultural fields of South Texas and on the long, lonely roads of the Midwest are treated by Rivera as nameless individuals whose lives are full of suffering, misery, and anguish. Collectively, however, these migrant workers, like their honorable and dignified ancestors celebrated in the *corridos* of the Southwest borderlands, struggle against injustice, hardship, and physical as well as psychological abuse. Beyond our anonymous protagonist's inner world of fragmentation often lurks an unspeakable world of violence and suffering: murder, child abuse, labor exploitation, guilt, and grief. Nevertheless, the protagonist, like his fellow migrant workers, lives on and struggles. Indeed, a covert utopian impulse, though it scarcely appears explicitly in the novel as a whole, plays implicitly an important part in Rivera's *tierra*, for those farmworkers who must work and produce *surplus value* for others necessarily grasp their own solidarity — initially, in the unarticulated form of rage, helplessness, victimization, oppression by a common enemy — before the dominant or ruling class has any incentive to do so.[4] *Tierra,* I want to suggest, is about this dawning sense of solidarity of migrant farmworkers with other members of their class and race. Class consciousness, as such, in *tierra,* is utopian insofar as it expresses the unity of a collectivity; yet it must be stressed that this proposition is an allegorical one.[5]

To understand Rivera's novel, to understand his striking folkloric and postmodernist fictional representation of the Texas Chicano farmworkers character, one must first comprehend, I think, Rivera's dual purpose in *tierra* as a social documentation of the 1940s and 1950s in America, and as a heterogeneous, multidimensional Chicano novel. And the novel in its entirety is — as Rivera tells us — a metaexpressive commentary on the Texas Chicano farmworker struggle, and *tierra* is Rivera's attempt to express that struggle.

Here I am primarily interested in suggesting that *tierra* registers and apprehends a new political consciousness which came into being during the late 1960s and early 1970s in the United States. As Joseph Sommers said in "Interpreting Tomás Rivera,"[6] we need to identify the issues and conflicts to which the author responded in *tierra.* Foremost among these issues is the literary influence of Américo Paredes' *With His Pistol in His Hand.*[7] In an interview with Bruce-Novoa, Rivera spelled out clearly this influence:

> I was hungry to find something by a Chicano or Mexican American. [Paredes' *With His Pistol in His Hand*] fascinated me because, one, it proved it was possible for a Chicano to publish; two, it was about a Chicano, Gregorio Cortez, and his deeds. And the ballads, the corridos too. I grew up with the corridos de Texas. That book indicated to me that it was possible to talk about a Chicano as a complete figure .... More importantly, *With a Pistol in His Hand* [sic] indicated to me a whole imaginative possibility for us to explore.[8]

Thematically and ideologically, then, Rivera benefitted tremendously from Paredes' descriptive and analytical study of the folklore and history of Gregorio Cortez, a border vaquero of the early 1900s who resisted legal injustice, fought the Texas Rangers, and became a legendary folk hero of Chicanos. On an intertextual level, it can be said that Rivera's migrant farmworkers, like Paredes' Texas Chicano characters, are simple, honorable men and women who will defend their families, homes, and honor with courage. On a metahistorical level, moreover, after reading Paredes, Rivera clearly came to see himself as a potential documentor of Chicano social history. As Rivera says, "I felt that I had to document the migrant worker para siempre [forever], para que no se olvidara ese espíritu tan fuerte de resistir y continuar under the worst of conditions [so that their very strong spirit of endurance and will to go on under the worst of conditions should not be forgotten], because they were worse than slaves."[9] Américo Paredes' book, *With His Pistol in His Hand,* thus opened a new window into the Southwest borderlands and established, for Rivera, a new philosophical-social hermeneutic for analyzing and studying the past.

Other windows opened for Rivera's development as an artist as well. During 1968–1969 – when *tierra* was written – Chicano political activity was at its peak. According to Ricardo Romo, a Chicano historian, as a result of protest movements among students, antiwar demonstrations, and the development of La Raza Unida Party, the Chicano Movement was born.[10] With considerable success, Romo stresses, the Chicano Movement attempted to instill ethnic pride, point out inequities in the judicial system, and these developments gave rise to a new political consciousness. Perhaps the next greatest contribution to Rivera's literary coming of age was a political movement in Crystal City, Texas, where Texas Chicanos began to appropriate political power from what until then had been a politically dominant Anglo minority.[11] Many members of this majority in Crystal City were migrant farmworkers. Indeed, as Rivera himself notes in his interview with Bruce-Novoa, his family had been workers in this migratory cycle.[12] For this reason, the reader needs to consider these events when interpreting *tierra*. On an ideological level, *tierra* might be said to fight for the memory of the social struggle of these forgotten and undocumented migrant workers in American history.

Tierra is also ideologically important, because it vividly reveals the progressive shocks and fragmentation of the self in advanced consumer capitalism.[13] Our anonymous protagonist is initially unable to decide, whether he wakes or dreams, whether his own voice is present or absent. And like Arias' Don Fausto Tejada, the migrant child is unable to distinguish clearly between the different realms of consciousness and unconsciousness: "... oía que alguien le llamaba por su nombre pero cuando volteaba la cabeza a ver quien era el que le llamaba, daba una vuelta entera y así quedaba donde mismo." ("He would hear someone call him by name. He would turn around to see who was calling, always making a complete turn, always ending in the same position and facing the same way.")[14] Figuratively, the protagonist in the first chapter, "El año perdido," is caught in a vicious cycle of subjectivity from which he desperately wishes to escape. In this early part of *tierra*, there is little or no contact with the outside world, or with other migrant workers, for the protagonist is trapped figuratively in the prisonhouse of the self. Not until he enters the fresh air of the outside world in the last section of the novel, "Debajo De La Casa," does he emerge into the collective utopian world of the human community, for he now desires to see "a toda esa gente junta. Y luego si tuviera unos brazos bien grandes los podría abrazar a todos." ("all those people together. And if I had long enough arms, I could hug them all at the same time." Rivera, p. 125). Rivera's *tierra* thus moves from an inside, alienated subjectivity in "El año perdido" to an outside reconstructed world in "Debajo De La Casa."

From the first section of the novel, the events in the narrative draw psychological urgency, since we sense that the protagonist does not have a clear sense of his identity and does not perceive himself free to create his own identity.[15]

Further, the protagonist is always thinking or attempting to think dialectically: "Se dio cuenta de que siempre pensaba que pensaba y de allí no podía salir" ("He discovered that he was always thinking that he was thinking, and that he was trapped in this cycle." Rivera, p. 1). That is, dialectical thinking is, as Jameson said in *Marxism and Form*, "thought about thought, thought to the second power, which at the same time remains aware of its own intellectual operations in the very act of thinking."[16] Such self-consciousness, then, is the very subject dramatized in the sentences of Rivera's *tierra*. Indeed, "El año perdido" dramatizes the beginning of consciousness and the inability to so articulate the fact; it also shows why dialectical thinking is at one and the same time both indispensable and impossible. In broad terms we should regard this book, then, as a novel about the development of political and dialectical thinking, where the reader reconstructs, analyzes critically, and reorganizes the past. In "La noche estaba plateaba," "... y no se lo tragó la tierra," and "Cuando lleguemos," Rivera's ideological and utopian trajectories are most discernible, for these chapters of the novel are structural breakdowns and reconstructions of transcendental, economic, and utopian views. In "La noche estaba plateaba," our protagonist begins structurally to break down his mother's passive Catholicism, with its well-known binary operations of good and evil, God and the Devil. At midnight, the boy walks into the woods, to summon the devil. He searches for the devil, because he has been immersed in Mexican and Chicano folkloric tales about the devil: "Lo del diablo le había fascinado desde cuando no se acordaba" ("The thought of the devil had fascinated him ever since he could remember," Rivera, p. 40). Like many young people with Catholic backgrounds, the boy simply desires to know whether the devil, and, by extension, God exists, for "si no hay diablo tampoco hay ... No, más vale no decirlo" ("But if there is no devil, then there is no ... No, I'd better not say it," Rivera, p. 42). The boy calls out to the devil, but the devil never appears. If there is no devil, then it follows for the boy that there is no God. Through this logic, then, the boy destroys Catholicism. In other words, Rivera's ideological critique in *tierra* begins not at the sociological level of culture, but instead at the tropological level of discourse.[17]

This tropological deconstruction, more logical than political, in *tierra* is then followed by another deconstruction in " ... *y no se lo tragó la tierra.*" The story begins in the midst of a hot South Texas day, in an agricultural field. The hot, suffocating Texas humidity hangs in the air, ready to undo a small group of migrant workers who are weeding a crop. Working under these horrible dehumanizing conditions, the boy's father had suffered, the day before, a heatstroke. Rivera now turns his critique to the exploitative agribusiness in South Texas. Beginning with an account of the father's heatstroke, the boy proceeds to recall the events that will eventually lead him to curse God. Next, he tells us how he yelled at his mother, for all his brothers and sisters to hear:

208

¿Qué se gana, mamá, con andar ... [clamando por la misericordia de
Dios?] ... si Dios no se acuerda de uno ... N'ombre a Dios le importa
poco de uno ... ¿Dígame usted por qué? ¿Por qué nosotros nomás
enterrados en la tierra como animales sin ningunas esperanzas de nada?
("What does Mother gain by doing that [clamoring for the mercy of
God]? ... God doesn't even remember us ... So you see, God doesn't
give a damn about us ... Can you tell me why? Why should we always
be tied to the dirt, half buried in the earth like animals without any
hope of any kind?" Rivera, pp. 48—50).

From this picture of the reality of conditions in the fields, the boy also has to
face the tragic reality of his younger brother's heatstroke: " ¿Por qué a papa y
luego a mi hermanito? ... ¿Por qué?" ("Why my father, and now my little
brother? ... Why?" Rivera, p. 54)

Instructed by his parents never to curse God, for he will be swallowed up by
the earth if he does, the protagonist violates a Catholic taboo: "Entonces le
entró el coraje de nuevo y se desahogó maldiciendo a Dios" ("Anger swelled
up in him again and he released' it by cursing God," Rivera, p. 54). Although
the boy imagines that the earth is opening to "devour" him, by this act, once
and for all, the boy breaks free from his mother's Catholic ideology. And just
as he had experienced a joyous serenity in "La noche estaba plateaba," here
in this section of *tierra*, he feels "una paz que nunca había sentido antes" (Rivera, p. 54). In short, by liberating himself from the cloudy transcendental
idealism of Catholicism, the protagonist is now able to continue on his lonely
road of reconstructing a holistic sense of self and group idenity.[18] As such, *tierra*
dramatizes the symptoms of the experience of our protagonist in consumer
capitalism: an experience which is able to accommodate a sense of psychic dis-
persal, fragmentation, fantasy, and insane-like sensations. From a poststructura-
list-marxist point of view, Rivera's *tierra* thus maps out the signs of dissolation
of an essentially bourgeois ideology of the subject and of psychic unity or
identity. For Rivera's protagonist, and for Marxists, indeed, only the emergence
of a postindividualistic social world, only the reconstruction of the collective
and the utopian, can concretely achieve a new consciousness; only a new and
original form of collective social life in the human community can overcome the
isolation in such a way that an individual consciousness can be lived.

Although there are many moments of hopelessness in Rivera's *tierra*, and Rivera
often dramatizes the anguish, fear, and chaos of the existential Chicano subject
in his narrative, the overriding history he tells is less tragic than hopeful. This
happens because Rivera sees a future out of the stark working conditions of
the past, an ideological order of solidarity and liberation reasserted in brief
sections of the novel as in "Cuando lleguemos..." In "Cuando lleguemos ...,"
for instance, Rivera focuses on the everyday routine events in the life of migrant
farmworkers, that is, on the scene of all social struggle in our lives. "Cuando

lleguemos..." dramatizes the journey of over forty workers traveling on the back of a truck on their seemingly endless journey from Texas to Minnesota. Often traveling over twenty-four hours at a time without rest, the migrant workers survive with what one critic has called "an indomitable will to endure."[19] One night, somewhere near Des Moines, the truck breaks down. The migrant workers must wait until the truck can be repaired. As in most of the sections of the novel, Rivera gives us a series of stream-of-consciousness monologs which contain the private thoughts of about ten migrant workers. Each nameless individual gives voice to a variety of thoughts, especially frustration and suffering. Although one worker thinks about the profound beauty and stillness of the dawning stars ("De aquí se ven a toda madre las estrellas," Rivera, p. 112), the majority of the workers express the futility of their lives: "Cuando lleguemos, cuando lleguemos, ya, la mera verdad estoy cansado de llegar" ("When we arrive, when we arrive. At this point, quite frankly, I'm tired of always arriving someplace," Rivera, p. 114). In the end, however, what keeps these workers struggling is the faint hope implied in the repeated phrase "cuando lleguemos" ("when we arrive"). "Cuando lleguemos...," I believe, can be said to represent the utopian surplus of the migrant workers' unfulfilled dreams and desires. The story and the phrase, "Cuando lleguemos" is the process motif in Rivera's narrative, which, if it is realized in the utopian sense of liberation, will be the solution to these workers' world problem: to the problem objectively present in the world itself as an unfinished and unresolved world. As such, Rivera's utopian perspective in *tierra* is not an abstract static concept. Rather, Rivera's hope is a concrete utopia, grounded in immanently developing tendencies working out of the present in the direction of something better. In *tierra,* I am suggesting, there is always an underlying concrete hope that the migrant workers will someday arrive in the full light of stability, justice, and freedom. As one migrant worker says, for instance, "Yo creo que siempre lo mejor es tener esperanzas" ("I guess it's always best to have hope," Rivera, p. 94).

It is thus important to bear in mind that, while the majority of episodes in *tierra* deal with fear, chaos, absence, exploitation, and alienation, the novel has a hopeful thrust as well. The migrant workers − as Rivera tells us − contain within themselves and as part of a collective class and ethnic consciousness a revolutionary spirit which enables them to survive and struggle. In this way, Rivera seems to agree with Louis Marin that "Utopia is an ideological critique of ideology."[20]

II.

The primary consciousness of Ron Arias' *The Road to Tamazunchale* is Don Fausto Tejada. Like Rivera's unnamed protagonist in *tierra*, Don Fausto stands beyond the other characters, comprehending in his deathbed in a small room in East Los Angeles, his past and future totality from a utopian perspective. And like García Márquez' Melquíades, Don Fausto Tejada seems to remove himself from history's successiveness, at least for a fleeting moment, escaping a passive Western cultural death in order to create a more active and meaningful utopian world — Tamazunchale — for himself, his friends in the barrio, and for an army of undocumented workers from Mexico. His narrative is an enunciation, at once magical and utopian, of all that he has been and read, and all that he might be in past, present, and future, filling in the spaces, bridging the sixteenth and twentieth centuries in the Americas, redressing his past mistakes as an exploiter of undocumented workers in El Paso, Texas. Don Fausto knows clearly that East Los Angeles is no place to die: "I wont stay here, Marcelino. This is the worst place in the world to die. Anyplace but here."[21] The magical real narrative begins at once with Don Fausto's dream of bodily decay:

> Fausto lifted his left arm and examined the purple splotches. Liver. Liver caused them. He tugged at the larger one, near the wrist. His fingertips raised the pouch of skin as if it were a small, wrinkled tent. The skin drew tight at the elbow. Slowly it began to rip like slipping off nylon hose (Arias, p. 16).

We are thus introduced to Don Fausto, Arias' dying protagonist, ripping off his skin, much like the Aztec God Xipe Totec, who each spring sheds his skin in order to renew himself.[22] Fausto's shedding of his skin, itself a magical moment in his last living hours, quickly gives way to numerous fantastic border crossings between the real and the imagined, between the United States, Peru, and Mexico, and finally between life and death. His continued shifts through time and space weigh the present with a utopian anticipation of Tamazunchale.

The importance of Don Fausto's record of Tamazunchale is suggested by Arias' epigram to the novel, a section of a Nahuatl poem by King Nezahualcoyotl:

> Must I go like the flowers that die?
> Won't nothing be left of my name,
> At least flowers ...
> At least songs ...[23]

A coherent indigenous set of values permeates Don Fausto's utopian vision in *The Road to Tamazunchale*. Further, Arias' epigram to Fausto's narrative intimates a will to triumph over death, a will to survive what Ernst Bloch, a Marxist-Utopian philisopher of the Frankfurt School, said are among the ultimate symbols of hope.[24] In this world of death and dying, Don Fausto begins the most unlikely utopian quest Southwestern man has undertaken. Pursued by death, Don Fausto decides to find in present real terms, a life within the borders of death.

Although Don Fausto seems to go off quite dementedly, he, in fact, has a definite plan in mind. In the course of his (mis)adventures no police harrassment, border patrol imprisonment, or community mockery can deter him from his plan to help an army of undocumented workers from Mexico cross the geopolitical border between Juárez and El Paso, Texas, and lead them up into Los Angeles and beyond to Tamazunchale. He also plans to extend his life beyond and toward "the song of life," a utopian leitmotif in the novel of the triumph of life over death. Is Fausto's narrative truth or falsehood, blindness or insight? For the sake of his supreme Chicano odyssey, Fausto renounces the political imprisonment of the aged and prepares to explode and deconstruct the West's view of death and dying. He is committed to his people in the barrio and on the other side of the border, and to his Faustian enterprise of immortality.

Throughout the novel, dreams and Fausto's hallucinations are important to Arias' dialectics at every level of the narrative. These narratival dialectics serve the special purpose of Don Fausto's border crossing by establishing the criss-cross association between the real and the imaginary, between his dying life in East Los Angeles and his dreaming rebirth in the symbolic utopian site of Tamazunchale.

Once Don Fausto begins his trip we cannot be sure when fantastic and imagined events end and real ones begin. In fact, in scenes of Fausto's slapstick escape from the L.A. police by hiding and later emerging from a cramped coffin (chapter three), of the appearance of a "curiosidad," a snowcloud over the Los Angeles area (chapter five), of Marcelino's folkloric Peruvian restoring of life to a drowned undocumented worker (chapter seven), the conventional borders between the real and imaginary have disappeared.

Throughout the rest of the narrative, the border themes of undocumented workers ("mojados") are quite prevalent. The "mojado" incident is one of the more famous chapters in the novel. David, a handsome Mexican worker, drowns in an East Los Angeles dry riverbed. He is cared for by the people in Fausto's barrio: Carmela, Mario, a lowrider *vato*, Smaldino, the fishman, Marcelino, a Peruvian herder of alpacas, and Mrs. Rentería, the barrio spinster, who uses David's cadaver for her unrepressed libidinal desires.[25]

As I have suggested, in the past Don Fausto actively engaged in the illegal smuggling of Mexican workers for profit; that is, he probably once lived as a *coyote*. However, in his present utopian frame of mind, Fausto explodes the geopolitical border between the United States and Mexico by seeking to bring an army of undocumented workers across the border and giving them dignity.

Fausto's impossibly grand plan to bring these undocumented workers across in ships is not realized in actual life. Nevertheless, in his symbolic and imaginary world of magical realism, Don Fausto leads them across the border, up through southern California, and into Los Angeles. Eventually, the undocumented workers and East Los Angeles barrio residents act out scenes from a play entitled "The Road to Tamazunchale." Fausto's play-within-the-novel, as Ramón Saldívar emphasized in "The Dialectics of Difference," sums up the fact that what persists in the novel is a metaphor of the Real.[26]

Tamazunchale is a real Mexican village, but more significantly, it becomes a metaphor for the utopian in Chicano fiction. Tamazunchale is a space where there are no problems or worries. This place, as such, utopian in atmosphere, is what Don Fausto envisions for himself, his neighbors, and the undocumented workers.

For Don Fausto Tejada, Tamazunchale is the philosophical and materialist ideal at a time when such ideas have collapsed in the face of advanced capitalism. For example, when a child asks the Tío in the play "What's Tamazunchale like?," he responds by saying:

> Like any other place. Oh a few things are different...
> if you want them to be... If you see a bird, you can talk
> to it, and it'll talk back... If you want to be an apple,
> think about it and you might be hanging from a tree...
> No one dies in Tamazunchale... Because Tamazunchale is our
> home. Once we're there we're free, we can be everything
> and everyone (Arias, pp. 105–106).

The Tío in the play clearly makes Tamazunchale utopian. Tamazunchale, as such, is a place and metaphor whose function in the novel is to help humankind shape the world in a concrete liberating direction.

Don Fausto's imagination thus emphasizes the fecundity of Tamazunchale as utopia: its cognitive function as a mode of constructive reason, its educative function as a new Chicano mythography which instructs us to treat the aging better, and its political possibility, as a futurology which may later become actual.

Rightly understood, Arias' *The Road to Tamazunchale* is a revolutionary book, for the site of Tamazunchale is fundamental to the ontology of a world open to new development, to a world which is not pre-given. Tamazunchale, I believe, is a process in which the new content of the world emerges as a result of human intervention and labor. Before Don Fausto vanishes "between the horizons and the stars," he manages to break through the mystified and petrified social reality of East Los Angeles, opening up a horizon of liberation in the world, for his family, his neighbors in the barrio, and a group of undocumented workers.

Thus, in two of the most celebrated Chicano novels, we find the most ideological and utopian representations of Chicano life. The narrators of these novels share a political as well as aesthetic world view in analyzing and transcending the crucial contradictions in society. The narrative paradigms of an ideological and utopian liberation provide for Rivera and Arias a means of reclaiming in art their particular reconstruction of a new Chicano consciousness in the Americas.

Notes

[1] See Fredric Jameson, "The Dialectic of Utopia and Ideology," in *The Political Unconscious: Narrative As a Socially Symbolic Act* (Ithaca: Cornell Univ. Press, 1981), p. 286.

[2] Fredric Jameson, *Marxism and Form* (Princeton: Princeton University Press, 1971), *The Prisonhouse of Language* (Princeton: Princeton University Press, 1971), *Fables of Aggression* (Berkeley: University of California Press, 1979).

[3] See Juan Rodriguez' excellent article "The Problematic in Tomás Rivera's ... *And the Earth Did Not Part,"* *Revista Chicano-Riqueña,* Año 6, No. 3 (1978), pp. 42–50, for a summary of the most blatant misreadings of *tierra.*

[4] According to Marx, the extraction of surplus value is the specific way exploitation takes place under capitalism, in which the surplus takes the form of profit, and exploitation results from the working class producing a net profit which can be sold for more than they receive as wages. See Karl Marx, *Capital,* Vol. 1, Part Three, "The Production of Absolute Surplus Value" in Robert Tucker's anthology, *The Marx-Engels Reader,* 2nd ed. (New York: Norton, 1978), pp. 344–88.

[5] Fredric Jameson argues in "The Dialectic of Utopia and Ideology" that "all class consciousness... all ideology in the strongest sense, including the most exclusive forms of ruling-class consciousness is in its very nature Utopian," p. 289. Such collectivities are allegorical insofar as they are "figures for the ultimate concrete collective life," p. 289.

[6] Joseph Sommers, "Interpreting Tomás Rivera," *Modern Chicano Writers,* ed. Joseph Sommers and Tomás Ybarra-Frausto (Englewood Cliffs: Prentice-Hall, 1979), pp. 94–107.

[7] Américo Paredes, *"With His Pistol in His Hand": A Border Ballad and Its Hero* (Austin: Univ. of Texas Press, 1958).

[8] See [Juan] Bruce-Novoa, *Chicano Authors: Inquiry By Interview* (Austin: Univ. of Texas Press, 1980), p. 150.

[9] Bruce-Novoa, pp. 150–51.

[10] See Ricardo Romo, "Afterward – East Los Angeles Since 1930," in *East Los Angeles: History of a Barrio* (Austin: Univ. of Texas Press, 1983), pp. 164–73.

[11] Rodolfo Acuña, *Occupied America: The Chicano's Struggle for Liberation* (New York: Harper & Row, 1972), pp. 233–37, details this ascendancy.

[12] Bruce-Novoa, pp. 139–41.

[13] See Gilles Deleuze and Felix Guattari, *Anti-Oedipus: Capitalism and Schizophrenia,* trans. Robert Hurly, Mark Seem, and Helen R. Lane (Minneapolis: Univ. of Minnesota Press, 1983). The authors reassert the specificity of the political content of everyday life and of individual fantasy experience in advanced capitalism.

[14] Tomás Rivera, ... *y no se lo tragó la tierra* (Berkeley: Editorial Justa Publications, 1977; originally published by Quinto Sol Publications, 1971), p. 1. All citations are from the Editorial Justa bilingual edition of Rivera's novel.

[15] Rivera's concept of identity in *tierra,* I believe, is essentially an existentialist concept. Rivera sees identity as the sum of his characters'choices, of their projections of themselves into the world. Identity, then, is a process of becoming. For an interesting view of this subject, see Juan Rodriguez, "La Busqueda De Identidad Y Sus Motivos En La Literatura Chicana" in *The Identification and Analysis of Chicano Literature,* ed. Francisco Jimenez (New York: Bilingual Press, 1979), pp. 170–78.

[16] See Fredric Jameson, *Marxism and Form: Twentieth-Century Dialectical Theories of Literature* (Princeton Univ. Press, 1971), p. 53.

[17] For a complete tropological and dialectical reading of Rivera's *tierra,* see Ramón Saldívar, "The Dialectic of Difference: Towards a Theory of the Chicano Novel," in *MELUS,* 6, No. 3, (1979), 73–92. In formulating my reading of Rivera's and Arias' narratives, I have also been influenced by Héctor Calderón, "To Read Chicano Narratives: Commentary and Metacommentary," *MESTER,* 11, No. 2 (1983), 3–14.

[18] See Juan Rodriguez, "La Busqueda De Identidad."

214

[19] Ramón Saldívar, "The Dialectics of Difference," p. 80.

[20] See Louis Marin, "Theses on Ideology and Utopia," trans. Fredric Jameson, *The Minnesota Review* (Spring 1976), 71–75.

[21] Ron Arias, *The Road to Tamazunchale* (Albuquerque: Pajarito Publications, 1978; originally published by West Coast Poetry Review, 1975), p. 58. All subsequent citations are from the Pajarito edition.

[22] For a further analysis of the Aztec god, Xipe Totec, see Michael C. Meyer and William L. Sherman, "Aztec Society and Culture," in *The Course of Mexican History* (New York: Oxford Univ. Press, 1979), pp. 67–92.

[23] King Nezahualcoyotl (literally, "Fasting Coyote") is known for his cultural refinement and for his philosophical verse. See Meyer and Sherman, *The Course of Mexican History*, pp. 53–66.

[24] See Ernst Bloch, *Das Prinzip Hoffnung* (Frankfurt, 1959).

[25] Mrs. Rentería takes David home, bathes and shaves him, and honeymoons with his cadaver. See Arias, *The Road to Tamazunchale*, pp. 72–75.

[26] Ramón Saldívar, "The Dialectic of Difference," p. 86.

John Nichols' *The Milagro Beanfield War* (1974).
The View from Within and/or the View from Without?

Heiner Bus

In their introduction to the bibliography *Chicano Perspectives in Literature*,[1] the critics Francisco A. Lomelí and Donaldo W. Urioste distinguish Chicano literature from *literatura chicanesca:*

> ... the uniqueness of Chicano reality is such that
> non-Chicanos rarely capture it like it is. For this
> reason, we propose the latter's efforts to be termed
> *literatura chicanesca* because it only appears to be
> Chicano. Therefore, it must be kept in mind that the
> perspective is from the outside looking in. This per-
> spective loses the spontaneity of a natural outpouring
> of a people's subsconscious through the writer's
> creativity; instead, it becomes a calculated object
> of study which is valued from a relative distance,
> that is, not lived.[2]

This definition combines the boldness of the explorer of an unknown territory with the caution of the experienced scholar who reserves the niche of the exceptional for the potential text defying the newly established categories. Lomelí's and Urioste's only seemingly unambiguous declaration that "Chicano literature is written by Chicanos. Any limitations put on these literatures should be recognized as impositions"[3] and the unnecessary opposition between the spontaneous and the calculated provoke the testing of these classifications with the help of John Nichols' *The Milagro Beanfield War* (1974). This novel irritated some of its readers because it possesses Chicano qualities in spite of the fact that the author is a non-Chicano. The opening and closing remarks of Lomelí's and Urioste's summary demonstrate this uneasiness:

> Perhaps the most convincing chicanesca novel. Written
> after Nichols studied his subject matter extensively,
> thus capturing local color, customs, legends, beliefs
> and geographical particularities with the insight of
> a keen eye... Makes entertaining reading and proposes
> a good example for non-Chicanos to follow.[4]

In his chapter on "Literatura Chicanesca" in *A Decade of Chicano Literature (1970–1979)*[5] Antonio Márquez derives his basic term in contrast to Lomelí and Urioste from Cecil Robinson's *Mexico and the Hispanic Southwest in American Literature*[6] but runs into the same difficulties with John Nichols:

> ... reveals a remarkable knowledge of the Chicano ex-
> perience in northern New Mexico, and offers an acute-
> ness and sensitivity that are extraordinary when com-
> pared to the general product of literatura chicanesca
> ... Nichols lives and works with the Chicano people that
> he represents in his fiction; he knows and shares their
> needs, fears, aspirations and dreams. One can even
> quibble that Nichols' work in one important aspect
> circumvents the category of literatura chicanesca;
> his point of view is not from without but from within
> the Chicano experience. The quibble aside, Nichols'
> point of vantage informs his fiction with authenticity
> and a compelling rendering of the Chicano.[7]

I want to concentrate on some of John Nichols' memorable characters which have inspired gross misunderstandings among prejudiced readers.[8] To see the novel in the context of the Chicano experience I shall also study its particular and universal messages. The results of this investigation will hopefully suggest new critical reflection on the nature of Chicano literature.

The Milagro Beanfield War is set in a North New Mexican small town whose socioeconomic situation is determined by the pressure from the Ladd-Devine Company and its local development project which involves the appropriation of land and water rights. This divides the community into winners and losers. Besides Ladd Devine the Third and his Anglo tools we are introduced to a group of profiteers, both Chicanos and Anglos, such as the real estate agent Bud Gleason, the town mayor Sammy Cantú, "the town's only rich Chicano rancher" (36)[9] Eusebio Lavadie, and the sheriff Bernabé Montoya. The realization of the Devine Project also depends on the state authorities whose reactions are do-minated by political opportunism.

John Nichols attaches great importance to the fact that most of his Chicano characters are caught in a double net of control mechanisms, thus indicating the actual political background and the representative quality of his novel. Local events are also described as another battle in the general war against the ideology of growth which Ladd Devine the Third defines as "to keep growing, building, expanding and absorbing and accumulating things and power and making money, and making more money on top of that" (434). The ruling class is well aware of the historical and cultural dimensions of the Beanfield War as statements like "The war never ended in 1848, you know." (68) or "Those damn old-fashioned people are a real thorn... They have strong roots." (613) prove.

From the Chicano majority the author selected a group of rather burlesque fig-ures. Joe Mondragón is the person to start the war when he decides to irrigate the little field in front of his dead parents' decaying west side home... and grow himself some beans. It was that simple. And yet irrigating that field was an act as irrevocable as Hitler's invasion of Poland, Castro's voyage on the *Grandma,* or the assassination of Archduke Ferdinand, because it was certain to catalyze tensions which had been building for years, certain to precipitate a war. And like any war, this one also had roots that traveled deeply into the past (28).

These comments of the third-person omniscient narrator suggest that Joe is not fully aware of the implications of his act, though his emotions and attitudes cannot be separated from the local resistance against the manifold manifestations of colonialism:

He was tired, like most of his neighbors were tired, from trying to earn a living off the land in a country where the government systematically gathered up the souls of little ranchers and used them to light its cigars... tired of spending twenty-eight hours a day like a chicken-thieving mongrel backed up against the barn wall, neck hairs bristling, teeth bared, knowing that in the end he was probably going to get his head blown off anyway. He was tired of meeting each spring with the prospect of having to become a migrant and head north... where a man groveled under the blazing sun ten hours a day for one fucking dollar an hour... And he was damn fed up with having to buy a license to hunt deer on land that had belonged to Grandfather Mondragón and his cronies, but which now resided in the hip pockets of either Smokey the Bear, the state, or the local malevolent despot, Ladd Devine the Third (26).

Joe's sentiments are part of a collective weariness originating from Milagro's historical experience since 1848, specifically the seizure of the Spanish-Mexican land grants by "those democratic and manifestly destined sleights of Horatio Alger's hand (involving a genteel and self-righteous sort of grand larceny, bribery, nepotism, murder, mayhem, and general all-around and all-American nefarious skulduggery)..." (29).

At the outset Joe refuses to become a leader, he is one of the last to sign the petition against the Devine Project, to fully integrate his individual act into the collective history. Later he will feel the rightfulness of his revolt and attempt a vague classification:

He felt truly tough and arrogant, indestructible and happy. His bean-field, purely and simply, was beautiful. And for a few seconds he experienced an almost embarassing and awkward sensation of well-being and importance. Like he was the King of the Castle. *Number One — El Número Uno* (162).

The switch to Spanish signifies his newly acquired sense of belonging:

... suddenly he held a profound tenderness for his people ... His people. His gente. His bunch of inbred, toothless, tubercular, flea-bitten, illiterate vecinos, sobrinos, primos, cuates, cabrones, rancheros, and general all-around fregado'd jodidos. Suddenly he loved the people he lived with, he cared about their lives. And this feeling, this *tenderness* oozing throughout his body, made him almost weak (163).

These feelings blend into nostalgic childhood memories when Joe was herding sheep with his father moving self-sufficiently through the country. Much later in the book he will be able to relate his father's story to the context of local history without sentimentalities. Joe will sketch his father's economic and psychological collapse caused by the Devine Company and the Milagro prairie dog war, an effort to prevent nature from reclaiming the arable land. The war served as an example for the Smokey the Bear Santo Riots about ten years ago, and the present Beanfield War trying to restore the old land and water rights.

Joe's initially fairly undirected protest stirs up the spirit of rebellion inherent in the Chicano community, though an actual war will never break out. His fight for a decent survival for himself and his people is later on evaluated in a night scene, when Joe and his wife are listening to the Mesa coyotes

> singing, calling each other or challenging the moon... No matter how much you poisoned them, shot them, scared them, trapped them, hated them, caged them, or generally raked over their habitat, you could not entirely kill all the coyotes, Joe thought. And the cottonwood leaves were so still... They could even hear the jukebox music at the Frontier Bar in town, the music remote like a fiesta memory from the old days (617–18).

The preservation of Joe's integrity depends on his acceptance of the productive tension between his own insignificance and significance, between the individual and the group experience.[10]

Part One of the novel introduces 94-year-old Amarante Córdova who "all his life... had lived in the shadow of his own death" (15–16). This miracle of survival is the first villager to join forces with Joe Mondragón. After having made reusable his 1914 sheriff's Colt Peacemaker and purchasing a box of shells on food stamps, Amarante takes his post at Joe's beanfield where he has a vision:

> ... he realized that, even though no rain had fallen at all for the past few days, the arching vision, shining faintly but unmistakably over Milagro, was a rainbow... that queer rainbow appeared in his dream ... and a few minutes later an angel showed up to complicate the miracle... a half-toothless, one-eyed bum sort of coyote dressed in tattered blue jeans and sandals, and sporting a pair of drab moth-eaten wings that looked as if they had come off the remainder shelves of a disreputable cut-rate discount store during a fire-damage sale, appeared (78–79).

When Amarante asks him to explain the rainbow sign, he mumbles: "Who knows, cousin...Maybe it's because for once in your lives you people are trying to do something right" (79). Notwithstanding this unglorious angel and its rather reluctant, cynical recognition of the Chicano efforts, Amarante succeeds in envisioning himself as a proud rider in the high open country around the Little Baldy Bear Lakes.

The imagination has still the lifting power to elevate the reality of such run-down but tough people like Amarante, though they can only conjure up a sad, shabby figure as their angelic messenger. The coyote very well compares with the name given by the Chicanos to Ladd Devine the Third, "the zopilote." When Amarante encounters "his second angelic apparition" (415), the link between the Anglo despot and the angel becomes even more evident as the feathers of his wings "rattled obscenely like those of a zopilote" (415–16). Amarante again inquires about the rainbow and this time the "disgruntled coy-ote figure" (416) retreats into sarcasm: "Jesus Christ... Three hundred years, and just about all you old farts got to show for it is seventenths of an acre of frijoles... You people don't deserve a gold star, let alone a rainbow" (416).[11]

In spite of the denial of the spiritual authority to provide the grand historical perspective, Amarante does not feel discouraged. He will have his finest hour actively defending the beanfield against one of the Devine Empire's agents. Immediately afterwards he meets Snuffy Ledoux, the local santero, who has returned to Milagro after a 10-years' absence following the Smokey the Bear Santo Riots. Ledoux carries the exhausted old man across the mesa:

> Amarante began to sing in a high hoarse voice, a song with no notes, really, it was more of an Indian-style chant, high and sing-song wonder-ful, with no words anyone could understand, his radiant face tilted to the blue sky, shining like the face of a little boy or of an old old being as powerful as God, and his eyes were fixed on the permanent rainbow he could still see arching delicately over his hometown. And although blisters formed on Snuffy's feet, and although they began to bleed, he found himself marching farther between rests, the old man growing lighter with this triumphant outpouring of song; and by the time they reached the deserted west side beanfields the sun was hanging like a fiery orange in the west, and Snuffy Ledoux had also broken out into victorious song. (532)

Their common defiance of Anglo authority has created a deep feeling of brother-hood and native harmony with the universe which is extended to mythical di-mensions in this St. Christopher scene. Under the impression of these emotions the two rebels try to design a pastoral future contradicting the pessimism of the coyote angel: "... not a vision of the future as totally unknown, but rather a vision of the future as composed, in part at least, of what had been okay about the past ... And people would return from faraway places, and chilies and pump-kins would grow in the cornfields, and you would be able to smell bread baking ..." (581–82).[12] Snuffy wants to destroy this vision by rational argument but is interrupted by the howl of the coyote, the symbol of survival. Amarante's and Snuffy's reflections refer to the night scene with Joe and Nancy Mondragón listening to the mesa coyotes. Nichols carefully links the two separate moments of experience with the final victory celebration of Milagro, when the Chicanos are "happily firing bullets at the general cosmos, or aimed more carefully, trying to perforate the moon" (627). Amarante Córdova, the coyote angel and the coyote itself represent the deplorable part of the Chicano experience but, at the same time, its powers to dream up "the flight to the sun," to communicate with the past, and to maintain an identity against all odds.

The narrator frequently comes very close to the commenting function of the coyote angel when he creates an emotionally ambiguous atmosphere round his characters by his selection of the incongruous detail. Amarante, the pathetic figure, goes on the warpath, he accepts the duties set to him by his heritage, projects himself out of the daily routine, fights the windmills and exposes himself to the laughter of the townspeople and, of course, the readers. His story began right after two Milagro miracle tales which document the importance of the storytelling tradition and the single-mindedness of the residents, their will of survival and their sense of the past. The Beanfield War and Amarante's personal involvement are destined to add another episode to the considerable record of miracles which identifies the place.

Joe Mondragón and Amarante Córdova were quite unable to directly relate their mental growth. With the Massachusetts lawyer Charles Morgan Bloom, Nichols introduces the eloquent intellectual who honestly tries to immerse in the regional culture, but fails because of circumstances and his "puritan New England upbringing" (111). After his divorce "Bloom had come out West in order to begin a new life" (108). "He worked in Colorado for a while, in Alamosa, in the Legal Aid program up there" (65). Gradually he developed "honest attachments... for the poor people in general, whose rights he was defending, and eventually for one of them specifically, a gentle skittish woman named Linda Romero" (113). She serves as an embodiment of the intellectual's longing for untainted reality thus becoming a mere object: "He sincerely believed that by marrying this good woman, the product both of a tough lower-class upbringing and of a rich communal culture very unlike his own, he was breaking with an establishment past, a liberal-conservative tradition that had always hung him up. Already he felt almost self-righteous about his new life because it was going to be Down to Earth, Humble, Unpretentious, *Real*" (114).[13] Bloom starts to write articles for *The Voice of the People,* not only on legal problems but also on Chicano culture, e.g. on the "feeling of uninterrupted history" (223) in a "people who refuse to die" (223). Bloom's one-sided embrace of the immediate exotic does not provide a firm basis for his marriage and his quest for a new identity. He is shocked when he discovers that Linda "almost hysterically wanted out of her poverty-stifled past" (114) which to her means "Guns, hunting, death, car crashes, frustration... Always talking, shouting, laughing, crying, bitching" (579). She denies the Chicano heritage and strives for the Anglo values Bloom wanted to leave behind. This irritating experience keeps him on the fringe of the native community. When he addresses a protest meeting, he fails to relate to his audience: "Their faces seemed so old, so dark, calling forth overworked clichés about the earth and the sky and the wind. Old, wrinkled, simple, profound. Bloom was afraid of these neighbors, feeling simultaneously superior and less of a man" (206). He cannot communicate by conscious, self-directed effort, rather "He was simply caught, trapped, wishy-washy, doomed" (207). Recognition requires a mutual romanticizing, an act of image-making: "Looking at them, he translated their faces into a strength he had once hoped somehow to marry into" (207). Paradoxically enough Bloom commits himself to the cause by temporarily abandoning his analytical faculties, the very prerequisite of his profession, *and* by offering his professional services to his fellow citizens.

In Milagro strong, undefined forces miraculously guide the actions of people; forces they never fully understand but accept as part of their common reality. This humbleness causes their resignation but also the regular cycles of rebellion, both signifying a deep trust in the continuation of life in dignity. These same forces keep Linda from falling into a void: "The Chicano roots she had rejected had refused to shrivel and die; the culture she had hoped to adopt had refused to compensate. Her true language kept twirling into her head unannounced, replete with an arrogant dazzling laughter, boisterous, obscene, illiterate, tickling her mind on twinkletoes of murder" (449). Bloom's eastern roots cannot resist the strong pull of Chicano culture, because it promises to satisfy basic human needs. This is clearly demonstrated by the imagery of fertility and growth used in the Chicano context of Linda whereas her desire for Anglo values is described in death metaphors.[14] Bloom's position among the people remains rather unstable as he occasionally falls back into the pose of intellectual and cultural superiority. In many passages his detachment resembles the aesthetic distance the narrator or author has to keep up to fix and interpret reality.

Looking back on the four characters and keeping in mind all the others, we can conclude that the socioeconomic situation, the fight for land and water rights,[15] the defense of one's native place, triggers off an individual act of protest which becomes a collective effort within the historical framework of one hundred years of Anglo colonization in the Southwest. Joe's move makes the Chicanos aware of their handicaps and strengths. As a result they assert their heritage via memory, attitude, gesture, and ritual in various degrees of intensity. In the novel they succeed in their struggle against the Devine project though, in the end, merely political opportunism in the governor's office tips the scales. It is another bitter victory like in the Smokey the Bear Santo Riots which delayed progress slightly, but did not seriously threaten Anglo domination. These Milagro rebellions cyclically inspire the Chicano will of survival by stressing the uniqueness and integrity of the group. The most obvious unifying value of the community is distrust of worldly, visible authorities, including the Church. In his novel John

Nichols argues that the people of Milagro believe in natural wisdom, in "An aura of mystery and of knowledge" (89), in storytelling, "strange doings and bizarre myths, legends, and fairy tales" (10), in omens and signs, in miracles and visions, in dreams of the past which can be projected into the future as an ideal state to strive after, in a set of inherited attitudes and in native institutions like the santero, the suspicion of the intruder, the basic wholeness of the family, in celebrating the day of San Isidro, the patron saint of the farmers, in the natural order of the animal world, in the sanitary effects of places like the Rio Grande gorge and the high country of the Little Baldy Bear Lakes.

At first sight this list seems to consist of the stereotypes we are all familiar with from literatura chicanesca. But John Nichols proceeds to an affirmative reinterpretation.[16] *The Milagro Beanfield War* advocates that the Chicano way of life in this particular rural community is valuable in itself because there is always the potential of breaking up the tedious daily routine. Even the return to a more relaxed state after the acts of rebellion and cultural reassurance is presented as a basic human necessity.

The closeness to the stereotypes is, of course, also due to Nichols' choice of the comic as his literary medium which forces him into a balancing act between superficial caricature and profound tragicomedy. In many places the author applies the folk humor of the oral tradition, ridiculing and affirming at the same time. There is the idea of grotesqueness as a typical human condition. People need the pompous, the blowing up of minor incidents to mythic proportions, the dreams of the wholeness of life, the nostalgia of the idyllic past as strategies of survival. In this respect Milagro serves as a universal example.[17]

Nichols' novel is a plea for the small identifiable community with strong ties to the larger cultural unit. This links him with the notion of minority cultures as preservers of the best American traditions. The novel is also a defense of the grown culture against the artificiality and inhumanity of the Anglo apostles of growth, exploitation and progress. In this respect it relates to the American small-town literature, the statements of the conservationist Edward Abbey, and the convictions of the anthropologists, ethnologists and ecologists of the late 19th and early 20th centuries exploring the multicultural Southwest. *The Milagro Beanfield War* even shares the escapist tendencies of these writers.

John Nichols provides the reader with a cluster of perspectives. If we take the Chicano community for the center of the novel, the group round Ladd Devine the Third, the agents of the political authorities would provide the view from without, while Amarante Córdova or Joe Mondragón speak from within. We would have to distinguish another small group of intermediaries, e.g. the sheriff Bernabé Montoya, Linda and Charles Bloom, all of them articulating or acting out culture clashes. The narrator would figure as another outsider who has the necessary distance to evaluate and to transport reality into the sphere of art.

With this ensemble of various degrees of detachment and the claim of universal significance Nichols opens the Chicano experience up for the non-Chicano.[18]

The Milagro Beanfield War tells a story "in relation to its cultural ambience."[19] This "aggregate reflection of numerous people and places"[20] is nourished by a "distinct cultural and historical regionalism"[21] which Carlota Cárdenas de Dwyer identified in the work of Tomás Rivera and Rolando Hinojosa. Nichols surely defends the idea of 'chicanismo' as e.g. defined in Lomelí's and Urioste's "Glossary": "a concept of life style or a system of values which provide a platform of survival,"[22] though it does not predict an all-splendid future for the cultural revival, at least on the level of the rural New Mexican community. Nichols' characters search for "lugar, modales, relaciones personales, conversación"[23] to establish community, an aim Tomás Rivera considers a constant motif in the major texts of Chicano literature.

The Milagro Beanfield War even gives affirmative answers to most of the questions specified by José Armas in "The Role of Artist and Critic in the Literature of a Developing Pueblo."[24] By focusing on the themes of discontinuity and revitalization of the cultural heritage through image retrieval the novel helps to expand the space of Chicano literature which Juan Bruce-Novoa tried to locate in 1975.[25] He understands this literature as "A Response to Chaos,"[26] thus indirectly acknowledging the aesthetic distance between the artist and his material. Distinguishing the artist's detachment from the notion of being out of touch with the people, he contradicts the idea of "a natural outpouring" presented in my introductory remarks. Juan Gómez-Quiñones plainly states in his article "On Culture":[27]

> Culture is learned rather than "instinctive" or biological. Genetic inheritance may be separate from culture. Ethnic characteristics are meaningful culturally only when expressed in relation to other individuals of a person's own group and/or in relation to other groups. Identity involves a cultural framework. An individual consciously identifies with the culture and practices the sum of it.[28]

These lines present a theory of culture distinct from Nichols'. Many of his characters act through conscious effort only after feeling the necessity of emotional release. In a way, the story of Charles Bloom seems to support Lomelí's and Urioste's definition of literatura chicanesca though, as we have seen, Bloom's situation remains a paradoxical one, suspended between success and failure. In the case of John Nichols the detachment of the artist more likely ties the author to his Chicano fellow writers, than his non-Chicano identity separates him from them.

Once again, the biological argument proves its inferiority to the laborious task of deriving criteria from the textual corpus itself.[29] Such an approach would liberate *The Milagro Beanfield War* and its author from the undeserved position

224

of the reputable but distant relative and, at the same time, would not dispute
the substantial sociopolitical relevance of Chicano literature.

Notes

1 (Albuquerque, N.M.: Pajarito Publications, 1976).
2 Lomelí and Urioste, p. 12.
3 Lomelí and Urioste, p. 12.
4 Lomelí and Urioste, p. 110.
5 ed. Luis Leal, Fernando de Necochea, Francisco Lomelí and Roberto G. Trujillo (Santa
   Barbara: Editorial la Cara, 1982), pp. 73–81.
6 Cecil Robinson, *Mexico and the Hispanic Southwest in American Literature* (Tucson:
   Univ. of Arizona Pr., 1977).
7 *A Decade...,* pp. 76–77.
8 See e.g. "An Interview with John Nichols," *New America,* 3, No. 3 (1979), 28–33; 30.
9 John Nichols, *The Milagro Beanfield War* (New York: Ballantine Books, 1976), p. 36.
   Subsequent references to this edition will appear in the text.
10 An idea which Dylan Thomas applies to the structure of his *Under Milkwood* (1954),
   where he builds a community from many individual voices. See also Edgar Lee Masters'
   Spoon River Anthology (1915), or Sherwood Anderson's *Winesburg, Ohio* (1919).
11 Refers to Jesse Jackson's 'Operation Headstart'.
12 They are very close to the world which Amarante Córdova tries to save by assembling
   his family for his birthdays forcing them to come from two continents.
13 In "An Interview with John Nichols" (See Footnote 8) the author made a very similar
   personal statement: "... longtime local residents still have roots and a language and a
   unique history to draw from, and people like me, who arrive from outside, may be
   invigorated by this fact, suddenly, that there's space to move around in and not too
   much spiritual smog making it difficult to breathe" (33).
14 See p. 116, p. 118, p. 121, pp. 360–63, and pp. 482–88.
15 A very common theme of Western American literature.
16 In this way he repeats a process typical of the early phases of any minority literature.
17 In his article on "Chicano Literature: The Establishment of Community" (in *A Decade
   of Chicano Literature,* pp. 9–17) Tomás Rivera contends "that the more definite and
   national the person in a literary setting, the more universal the motivation and the more
   revealing of original elements of human perceptions and motivations he or she possesses.
   In this manner both place and person exist as primary units that hold basic original elements of humankind, that is, the total crystalization of passions – love, hate, joy,
   tristeza, etc." (13).
18 John Nichols' use of this traditional literary technique makes the Chicano experience
   more easily accessible for the outsider than e.g. Rolando Hinojosa's revelation of the
   Chicano heritage through the connotative meanings of words and phrases in *Estampas
   del valle y otras obras* (Berkeley, Calif.: Quinto Sol Publications, 1973).
19 Joseph Sommers, "From Critical Premise to the Product: Critical Modes and Their
   Application to a Chicano Literary Text," *The New Scholar,* 6 (1977), 51–80; 59.
20 Carlota Cárdenas de Dwyer, "Cultural Regionalism and Chicano Literature," *Western
   American Literature,* 15, No. 3 (1980), 187–94; 194.
21 de Dwyer, p. 187.
22 *Chicano Perspectives in Literature,* p. 112.
23 "Chicano Literature: The Establishment of Community," in *A Decade of Chicano Literature,* p. 12.
24 *De Colores,* 3, No. 4 (1977), 5–11; see p. 11.
25 "The Space of Chicano Literature," *De Colores,* 2, No. 4 (1975), 22–24. To pursue
   the idea of expansion: If, as some critics have argued, the production of a great comic
   novel is the measuring stick of the maturity of any literature, we could conclude that

John Nichols broke the path for the prospective Chicano writer who will combine the view from within with the view from without.

[26] The subtitle of his *Chicano Poetry* (Austin, Texas: U. of Texas Press, 1982).

[27] Juan Gómez-Quiñones, in *A Decade of Hispanic Literature. An Anniversary Anthology* (Houston: Revista Chicano-Riqueña, 1982), pp. 290–308.

[28] Gómez-Quiñones, pp. 292–293. In this context we would have to consider the careers and personal statements of John Rechy and José Antonio Villarreal. See also the fate of the Black writer Jean Toomer. With him the discussion about the role of the particular and the universal contributed to the destruction of his art. Cf. my article on "Jean Toomer and the Black Heritage," in *History and Tradition in Afro-American Culture,* ed. Günter H. Lenz (Frankfurt: Campus Verlag, 1984), pp. 56–83.

[29] In some critical commentaries I can see a contradiction between the urgent call for good literary critics and a tendency to define Chicano literature as rejecting traditional modes of classification and interpretation. We can find similar ideas in recent Afro-American writing and criticism. See e.g. James T. Stewart, "The Development of the Black Revolutionary Artist," in *Black Fire,* ed. Leroi Jones and Larry Neal (New York: William Morrow and Co., 1968), pp. 3–10, and my article on "Afro-amerikanische Autobiographien von Frederick Douglass bis Eldridge Cleaver," in *Black Literature,* ed. E. Breitinger (München: Wilhelm Fink Verlag, 1979), pp. 255–94.

VI LANGUAGE, EDUCATION, AND IMPACT

Spanish/English Code-Switching: Literary Reflections of Natural Discourse

Carol W. Pfaff and Laura Chávez

0. Introduction

One of the outcomes of the prolonged contact between English and Spanish speaking groups in North America is the development of a variety of language, commonly termed code-switching, in which bilingual speakers use elements·of both languages within a single conversation. This type of language mixing in natural discourse has been observed in communities in the Southwest and in midwestern cities as well as in Puerto Rican communities in New York. Sociolinguists, many of them themselves bilingual code-switchers, have in the last ten years analyzed such speech events, both from a structural linguistic point of view and in terms of the social function and connotation of switching.

Our concern in this paper is to compare the use of code-switching in natural discourse with its use as a literary device by Chicano writers. In doing so, we address the following questions:

— first, to what extent do literary works reflect actual usage? (This question is relevant for linguistics attempting to use literary sources as evidence for synchronic or diachronic linguistic research — the philological tradition),
— second, what do literary uses of language variation reveal about the sociolinguistic functions of switching?

Our paper is divided into two parts; the first part deals with the sociolinguistic analysis of switching in natural discourse, the second presents our analysis of the use of switching in literary works, principally drama, the genre which most closely approximates natural discourse.

1. Code-Switching in Natural Discourse

In this section, we briefly review the literature on Spanish/English code-switching in natural discourse, taking up a number of problems touching on the following linguistic and social aspects:

— the definition of code-switching and classification of code-switching types,
— structural and functional linguistic constraints on switching,
— the relationship of switching to proficiency in both languages,
— historical development and social function of code-switching,
— overt and covert attitudes toward switching.

1.1 Definition and Syntactic Classification of Code-Switching

The term *code-switching*, as used in the present paper, refers to Spanish/English bilingual speakers' alternate use of Spanish and English within a single conversation. The following examples are taken from conversations of bilinguals in California and in Texas. Two (numbers 1 and 2) were recorded in an office and the other two within family gatherings. The recordings were made by bilingual participant-observers in each case. For each of the examples in this paper, the code-switching text as actually recorded appears on the left and a translation into English on the right.

(1) M: *Oye, ¿qué está haciendo*   Listen, what is Jason
Jason? Is he walking   doing? Is he walking
around?   around?
(6 turns in English follow)

F1: *Sí*, but the thing is   Yes, but the thing is that
que empiezan bien recio   they start pretty fast and
and then they slack off.   then they slack off.

F2: Then they go slow.   Then they go slow.

F1: Randy started out *bien*   Randy started out very young.
chico. The first time he   The first time he stood up,
stood up, he was six months   he was six month old. By
old. By the time I really   the time I really figured
figured out he was walking,   out he was walking, well you
bueno ves, but they go   see, but they go slow and
slow and sometimes fast   sometimes fast and then
and then they slack off.   they slack off.

F2: I keep thinking that   I keep thinking that Jason
Jason probably will be   probably will be walking
walking *cuando cumpla el*   when he turns one.
año.

(Pfaff, 1979:315—16)

(2) F: Well, I'm glad that I met   Well, I'm glad that I met
you. O.K.?   you. O.K.?

M: *Ándale, pues*. And do come   O.K. swell. And do come again.
again. Mm?   Mm?

(Gumperz and Hernández-Chávez, 1975:157)

(3) M: *¿Será que quiero la tetera?*   It must be that I want the baby
         para pacify myself.   bottle to pacify myself.

(Gumperz and Hernández-Chávez, 1975:157)

(4) Sentences (62.8%)*

a) M: *Yo no voy a Juárez.* It's   I'm not going to Juarez. It's
        not worth it.   not worth it.

    G: *Tengo que ir a visitar a*   I have to visit Sunsu, I didn't
        Sunsu, ayer no fui ni la vi. go nor did I see her yester-
        I didn't go to the Andritsos   day. I didn't go to the An-
        yesterday.   dritsos yesterday.

Nouns (15.8%)

b) M: *El* pie *está en la hielera.*   The pie is in the refrigerator.

    M: *... y Leti se devolvía a la*   ... and Leti would go back home
        casa con la maid *y ...*   with the maid and ...

Phrases (10.6%)

c) L: *Lo corrieron,* the board or   They fired him, the board or
        somebody.   somebody.

    M: *Le dan* three weeks.   They give him three weeks.

Adjectives (3.2%)

d) M: *¿De esas* electric?   Those electric ones?

    M: *¿Los huevos* scrambled   The eggs scrambled with
        con chorizo?   sausage?

Gerunds (2.0%)

e) M: *¿Para qué lo lleva* shop-   Why do you take him shopping?
        ping?

    M: *Que trabajando y estudian-*   That she's working and
        do y housekeeping.   studying and housekeeping.

Verbs (1.1%)

f) M: *Yo me voy a la noche a* baby- I will go babysit tonight.
        sit.

    Mi: *Entonces nos quedamos a*   At that time we will stay and
         babysit.   babysit.

(Huerta-Macías, 1981:156—57)

---

* Percentages in examples in (4) represent the instances of each code-switch type in family conversation reported in Huerta-Macias, 1981.

232

There are two common beliefs about code-switching:
first, that it is a random mixture of Spanish and English elements;
second, that it occurs because speakers lack the ability to stick to one language or the other.
Empirical studies of natural discourse show, however, that both of these presumptions are false. As can be seen in the examples, code-switching can be observed to take place at a variety of surface syntactic levels: the most important distinction to be made is between *inter-sentential switching* and *intra-sentential switching*. Inter-sentential switching occurs between two sentences as in the first turn in (1) or in the items under (4a) above.

1.2 Structural and Functional Linguistic Constraints on Switching

In contrast to such inter-sentential code-switching, which can take place quite freely, we also find instances of various types of *intra-sentential switching* of words or phrases within the sentence boundary. One of the most frequent types is so-called *tags* or *introducers* outside of the main predication as in example number 1, Fl's use of *sí* in response to an English sentence and then continuing in English, or her use of *bueno ves* in the middle of her second turn in the same conversation, or the use of *ándale pues* in the context of an exchange primarily in English.

In many instances, however, intra-sentential code-switches are fully syntactically integrated into the main predication of the sentences. Syntactically, such switches may be entire *clauses,* as in Fl's first turn in (1) or in F2's turn.

Switching may also consist of phrases, as in the adverbial *bien chico* in (1) or in the items under (3) and (4c). Finally, a very frequent type of switch involves only a single lexical item: nouns, verbs, adjectives – also illustrated in the various examples under (4) above. These switch types do not occur with equal frequency in natural discourse. Whole sentence switches and single nouns are highly frequent, the other types less so. The examples given under (4) include the percentages with which each type was found in the family conversation under investigation (Huerta-Macías, 1981).

1.3 The Relationship of Switches to Proficiency

The frequency of various types of switching seems to be correlated with the degree of proficiency of the speakers in English and Spanish. Quantitative work has not yet been done for Chicano speech, but the qualitative evidence indicates that it parallels the findings for Puerto Ricans' code-switching.

In a study of Puerto Rican bilinguals in New York, Poplack found the striking relationship shown on the figures below.

Figure 1. Percentages of switch types for Spanish-dominant and bilingual speakers

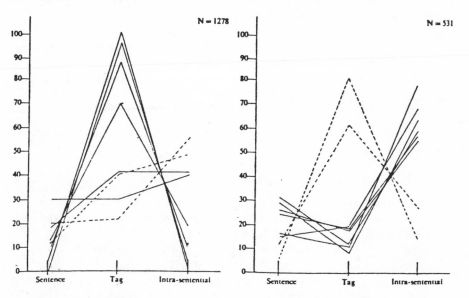

Figure 1a. Percentage of switch types for reported Spanish-dominant speakers

Figure 1b. Percentage of switch types for reported bilingual speakers

(Poplack 1982:15)

Spanish-dominant bilinguals, on the left figure, show high frequency of tag switches, while balanced bilinguals, proficient both in English and in Spanish, have very high frequencies of intra-sentential switching. This very interesting correlation can be partially explained by the degree of knowledge of the grammars of both languages that is necessary for a speaker to successfully integrate elements of both English and Spanish in a single sentence in such a way that the code-switching elements smoothly blend without violating the grammatical rules of either language.

Quantitative work on Chicano speech (Pfaff 1976), as well as that by Poplack on Puerto Rican speech (Poplack 1981, 1982) indicates that intrasentential switches are not random, but that they are constrained to conform to
the word order and morphology of both languages. For example, switches do
not take place between noun and adjective in Noun Phrases which would have
Adj + N in English but N + Adj in Spanish; or between verb and pronominal
object which are constrained to occur in the order: preposed enclitic object +
verb in Spanish, but verb + postposed object in English: *casa little, *lo trust,
*house chiquita, confío him. Poplack has formulated the following two general
syntactic constraints on code-switching:

(5) *The free morpheme constraint:* a switch may not occur between a bound
morpheme and a lexical form unless the latter has been phonologically
integrated into the language of the bound morpheme.

The equivalence constraint: the order of sentence constituents immediately adjacent to and on both sides of the switch point must be grammatical with respect to both languages involved simultaneously.

Note that these are descriptive, not prescriptive rules, that is, they are arrived
at inductively.

1.4 Historical Development and Social Function of Code-Switching

Having examined some examples of code-switching and briefly discussed the
syntactic description of this phenomenon, we want to turn now to a brief consideration of some aspects of the social function of code-switching, seen especially in light of its historical development as one of the outcomes of certain
patterns of bilingualism characteristic of immigration. Over the past 30 years,
a considerable body of linguistic work on bilingualism in the USA concerning
Spanish/English bilingualism has been published. If not numerically, the Spanish-
speaking minority in the USA is, politically and socially, one of the most important.

Among the most important general studies of bilingualism in the United States
are Weinreich's *Languages in Contact* (1953), Fishman's *Language Loyalty in
the United States* (1966), Haugen's reviews of *Bilingualism and Immigrant
Languages in the Americas* (1956 and 1973), Kloss's *The American Bilingual
Tradition* (1977) and, recently Grosjean's *Life With Two Languages* (1982).
Works specifically dealing with Spanish/English bilingualism include Fishman,
Cooper and Ma, et al, *Bilingualism in the Barrio* (1968), Peñalosa *Chicano
Sociolinguistics* (1980), Hernández-Chávez *El lenguaje de Los Chicanos* (1975),
and the two recent collections edited by Duran, *Latino Language* (1981) and
Amastae and Elías-Olivares *Spanish in the United States: Sociolinguistic As-
pects* (1982).

While none of these works treats the historical development of code-switching *per se,* all provide evidence on three socio-culturally determined aspects of usage in bilingual communities which provide the basis for code-switching in natural discourse:

a) the incorporation of loan words and fixed idiomatic phrases from the mother tongue into the ethnic variety of the second language;

b) the distribution of bilinguals' use of the two languages according to social setting, topic and participants; and

c) bilingual speakers' attitudes toward their two languages.

Loan word and phrase incorporation clearly comes about when speakers, speaking one of the community languages, have need to refer to persons, things, or institutions which are exclusively or primarily associated with the sociocultural context in which the other language is spoken. Thus mother-tongue words for kinship relations and other terms of address, food items and practices associated with holidays are regularly incorporated into the second language, while, on the other hand second language words which refer to places, food, work, or official institutions associated primarily with the second language community are incorporated into the mother tongue.

The distribution of bilinguals' two languages has been discussed by Fishman, who developed a well-established system of analysis in terms of what he calls "domains" — concepts such as "home," "school," "work," "religion," and so on (Fishman, 1971). The assumption underlying this system is that the choice of language in a bilingual community varies from domain to domain, and that domains are congruent combinations of a particular kind of speaker and addressee, in a particular kind of place, talking about a particular kind of topic. Fishman also extended the concept *diglossia* (a term previously defined by Charles Ferguson) as the use of "two or more varieties by the same speakers under different conditions." As defined by Ferguson, diglossia was intended to refer to the use of so-called "High" and "Low" varieties of the same language, such as Classical Arabic or Greek and the national spoken varieties (Ferguson, 1959). Fishman (1971:248) suggests that in many bilingual communities such domains as school, church, professional worksphere, and government are congruent with the use of the "High" variety, whereas domains like family, friendship, and neighborhood are congruent with the use of the "Low" variety. In the case of the United States, the "High" variety would correspond to English, the "Low" variety to Spanish.

Such complementary distribution of varieties in these domains, termed *"situational switching,"* contributes to the strengthening of associations of the two languages as the "they code" as opposed to the "we code." This, in turn, provides the basis for so-called *"metaphorical switching,"* where a bilingual speaker in conversation with another bilingual switches to the other language in the midst of a single speech event for emphatic or contrastive purposes. Metaphorical switching may be inter-sentential, as with parenthetical asides or repetitions for emphasis, or intra-sentential. Gumperz and Hernández-Chávez (1975) point out that many of the single-word introducers or tags in Spanish, such as *ándale, pues* in our example number 2, above, function metaphorically as "ethnic identity markers."

As we have seen in the other examples, however, many examples of switching within speech events in natural discourse do not appear to serve such an obvious metaphorical function. Indeed, it appears that a code-switching variety has developed as part of the verbal repertoire of Chicano and Puerto Rican speech communities in the United States. As Lucía Elías-Olivares found in her empirical study of the Chicano community in East Austin, Texas, alternating both languages constantly in a conversation "is the norm, rather than the exception in intra-group situations, especially those in which only young Chicanos are the participants" (1976:179). Further, her data indicate that "any topic could be discussed in code-switching, and perhaps the only necessary social category that needs to be present for code-switching to take place is that all participants be bilingual."

1.5 Overt and Covert Attidudes toward switching

When asked their opinion about this code-switching variety, Elías-Olivares reports, many especially older speakers overtly express negative views, maintaining that the "pure" languages should be used, that the two codes should be kept separate from each other. Younger speakers, on the other hand, responded more positively, stressing the convenience of using both languages together. Rosaura Sánchez (1976) attempts to make the covert attitudes explicit, suggesting that "code-switching reflects a life of alienation and at the same time integration that Chicanos have experienced in the dominant society, code-switching is a step toward complete acculturation and loss of the Spanish dialects." On the other hand, Elías-Olivares proposes that "the use of code-switching may indicate that these speakers are still willing to resist total submission in this society."

To summarize the discussion of code-switching in natural discourse, which we compare with its use in Chicano drama in the next sections, the following points should be stressed:

First, linguistically, code-switching is a rule-governed system rather than a random mixture of elements of English and Spanish.

Second, syntactically, intra-sentential switching is always a smooth blend which does not violate the rules of either language at switch points.

Third, intra-sentential switching is found with highest frequency in the speech of those who are proficient in both languages.

Fourth, code-switching has its roots in the use of loan words and domain-specific distribution of English and Spanish, but has developed from a simple situational alternation, to encompass metaphorical connotations and,

Finally, code-switching has developed into a variety in its own right, particularly characteristic of the relatively young, who may use it to identify themselves in their own particular social position within what they conceive of as a specifically Chicano culture.

2. Code-Switching in Chicano Drama

Bearing in mind the linguistic considerations discussed in part 1, we looked at some anthologies of Chicano literature: Antonia Castañeda Shular's *Literatura Chicana, Texto y Contexto* (1972), Luis Valdez' and Stan Steiner's *Aztlán, an Anthology of Mexican American Literature* (1972), Cárdenas de Dwyer's *Chicano Voices* (1975), Roberto J. Garza's *Contemporary Chicano Theatre* (1976), Dorothy E. Harth and L.M. Baldwin's *Voices of Aztlán, Chicano Literature Today* 1974), Rudolfo A. Anaya's *Cuentos Chicanos* (1980), and Toni Empringham's *Fiesta in Aztlán* (1982).

Our original intention was to make a comparison of the use of code-switching in various genres including essays, short stories, drama and poetry. We found that essays and short stories either contain very little code-switching or are written entirely in English. When Spanish is used, it is always as quotations from monolingual speakers, and these are not instances of code-switching as such. Code-switching does occur in poetry and drama. We chose to focus on the latter in this paper because the interactions on the stage do to a certain extent reflect interaction in real life where, as we have seen, code-switching is an appropriate variety and forms part of the Chicano linguistic repertoire.

We looked at five plays: Luis Valdez' "Bernabé," "Las Dos Caras del Patroncito," and "Los Vendidos," and Ysidro R. Macías' "Mártir Montezuma" and "The Ultimate Pendejada."

2.1 An Overview of Code-Switching in the Plays

These five plays are different in regard to external characteristics but the main concern underlying all of them revolves around the Chicano identity. "Bernabé" has a Spanish title and is basically written in Spanish, but code-switching is used in a couple of scenes. The title in "Mártir Montezuma" is itself an example of code-switching. Mártir is a Spanish noun but Montezuma is an English adaptation of a Spanish name. This play is written in English and only one-word-switches are used. The other two plays by Valdez have Spanish titles but the texts are written primarily in English with code-switching into Spanish. In "The Ultimate Pendejada" we have another title which is itself a code-switch. The text is basically English with code-switching into Spanish.

238

In Table 1. we give an overview of the use of code-switching in each of the plays.

Table 1.: Instances of Code-Switching Types in Five Plays

	Single Lexical Items						Phrases	Sentences/ Clauses	Total number of switches	Use of Proper Names
	a)	b)	c)	d)	e)	f)				
Bernabé	3	8	10	3	7	0	9	27	67	6 Spanish
			31							4 English
Mártir Montezuma	99	89	0	10	2	3	22	9	234	9 Spanish
			203							4 English
Las Dos Caras del Patroncito	19	12	2	0	1	3	21	6	64	1 English
			37							4 Spanish
Los Vendidos	8	35	0	3	1	4	25	8	84	5 English
			51							2 Spanish
The Ultimate Pendejada	57	51	5	1	4	3	26	38	185	9 English
			121							12 Spanish

a) appellations
b) substantives
c) verbs
d) adjectives
e) conjunctions
f) interjections

As stated in the first part of this paper, clauses together with substantives are the most common switches in natural discourse. If we compare the figures for substantives (under b) and the clauses to the total number of switches, frequencies are somewhat different from the findings in natural discourse. Particularly the figures under "Clauses" are considerably smaller. In "The Ultimate Pendejada" and in "Bernabé" they account for 21% and 40% of the total amount of switches, respectively. In the other three plays, clause-switching accounts for less than 10% of the total. It is quite obvious that these percentages are considerably lower than the ones found in investigation of natural discourse (63%, Huerta-Macías, 1981, see page 27). If we turn to the column for substantives (under b), we have a range between 12% and 42% of noun-switching, and this is a bit more similar to the 16% found in natural discourse, although in "Mártir Montezuma" and in "Los Vendidos" the percentages are higher, 38% and 42% respectively. One sort of switch which is very common in these five plays, for which we do not have figures from natural discourse investigations, are the appellations (under a). We see that the number of appellations in "Las

Dos Caras del Patroncito" (30%), "The Ultimate Pendejada" (31%), and in "Mártir Montezuma" (42%) is quite high. Only in "Bernabé" and in "Los Vendidos" the number of appellations accounts for less than 10% of the total number of switches.

Perhaps another interesting point to make in Table 1. is the column "Use of Proper Names." In spite of the fact that these plays are primarily written either in English or in Spanish, both Spanish and English names are used throughout all the plays, in a more or less balanced way.

2.2 Chicano Identity as a Theme

Although different on the surface, there is an attempt in each of the five plays to define who is a Chicano. The Chicanos are a group of people who could identify either as Americans since they live in the United States, or as Mexicans because, to a greater or lesser degree, Mexican blood runs in their veins. In fact, they do not want to identify fully with either of these two groups. This concern about belonging to the United States or to Mexico causes an identity problem which Chicanos resolve in different ways throughout these five plays.

Their concern over self-identity is also reflected in the languages Chicanos use. Because they live in the United States, they speak English, but because they have a Mexican background, they speak Spanish. And the mixing of the two languages, that is, code-switching, as we have seen in part 1, has come to be seen as the true Chicano means of communication among Chicanos.

The search for a self-identity is also reflected by the continuous reference to Mexican history. Most of the time, such allusions are to a distant, mythicized glorious Mexican past. It is not, however, a simple attempt to identify with that Mexican past. When Aztec gods and emperors are mentioned, the intention of this retrospective view of Aztec life as cultural roots is to illuminate the distinction between Chicanos and Mexicans on the one hand and between Chicanos and the other peoples living in the United States on the other. Thus, as means for preserving this needed distance, history and historical names are manipulated. For instance, in "Mártir Montezuma" Emperor Moctezuma becomes Mártir Montezuma, and in "The Ultimate Pendejada" Emperor Cuautémoc and Porfirio Díaz become Cuahtemoc "Porfirito" Díaz, bringing together a Mexican dictator and the Aztec emperor. This character, in fact, seems to be proud of his Mexican name:

(6) C: *Me dicen Porfirito.* My name is *Cuahtemoc "Porfirito" Díaz.* My nickname comes from a Mexican hero.

(CMM, II,1, p. 143)

But instead of being proud of his Aztec name, the last emperor who is considered a hero in Mexico, this character is proud of his nickname, although the dictator Porfirio Díaz is not usually considered a hero in Mexican History.

Other names, both Aztec and Spanish, are mentioned: Maya Xochimil, Padre Miguel Hidalgo, Emiliano Zapata and Pancho Villa; at one time the latter two appear as Emiliano Villa and Pancho Zapata.

In the next sections we will look at each of the plays, one by one, in more detail.

2.3 "Mártir Montezuma"

"Mártir Montezuma" provides a curious mixture. The action should take place in 1524, the Indians living at this time are Aztlecas (not Aztecs) under Spanish rule. They work for a plantation owner named Hernán Gimarra (Hernán Cortés conquered Tenochtitlán in 1521) but the Viceroy is called Rigan. In placing the play in 1524 the author is looking at this mythicized although not so glorious Mexican past. But the situation is so conceived that it becomes very easy for the reader or for the audience to identify these Aztlecas, who boycott the sale of chilis, with the Chicanos, who strike in California during the 1960s. Between the second and third acts there is a lapse of 300 years, and in this third act Padre Miguel Hidalgo leads the Aztlecans' fight for independence from Spain. The Aztleca leader is Mártir Montezuma who has learned a non-violent philosophy from Gandi, and he has some liberal politicians as friends (like senador Roberto Quinadi and his wife Hy-Tol Quinadi) who help him out of prison. The only consequences for the Aztlecans of this philosophy of nonviolence are prison and death. At the very end of the play, the Chicanos are mentioned as a "lost tribe of *Mexicanos*" who should rise together with Mexico against "this monstrous system."

The use of Spanish in this play is almost ornamental. Of the 234 switches, 203 are only one word long; 97 of them are only appellations like *Mártir* or *hermana* as in examples in (7):

(7) M: What do you mean, enjoy
pressuring the *mercados?*

What do you mean, enjoy
pressuring the markets?

A: Wh ... Why, of ... course,
Mártir. We're going to have
to get tough with the *mercados* in order to stop the
chiles, no?

Wh ... Why, of ... of course,
Mártir. We're going to have to
get tough with the markets
in order to stop the chilis,
aren't we?

M: No! *Hermana,* how many times
do I have to tell you ...
no violence!

No! Sister, how many times do
I have to tell you ... no
violence!

(MM, I,2, p. 170)

The most common switches to Spanish are the words *chile, indio, gachupín, español*, also one word long. These switches are not character-specific. Not only do the Aztlecas and Mártir use them, but also Hernán Gimarra, Juan Hantle, Francisco Marrano, the Spanish policeman, Viceroy Rigan, and Quinadi as shown in the examples in (8):

(8) R: ... after a while we'll   ... after a while we'll
         let him "win" there too,   let him "win" there too,
         as long as he does it   as long as he does it
         the *español* way ... ha,   the Spanish way ... ha,
         ha, ha ... no violence ...   ha, ha ... no violence ...

    G: ... I can just see the   ... I can just see the head-
         headlines ... ha, ha,   lines ... ha, ha, ha ...
         ha ... Aztlecas win *Chile*   Aztlecas win Chili Boycott
         Boycott ... Everyone will   ... Everyone will be eating
         be eating *chiles* even if   chilis even if they like them
         they like them or not ...   or not ... ha, ha, ha ...
         ha, ha, ha ... and we'll   and we'll make more money ...
         make more money ... ha,   ha, ha, ha ...
         ha, ha ...

    R: ... make more money, and the   ... make more money, and
         indios will be convinced that   the Indians will be convinced
         Montezuma was right ... ha,   that Montezuma was right ...
         ha, ha ...   ha, ha, ha ...

    (MM, I,4, p. 176)

In this play, then, code-switching plays a minimal symbolic role, perhaps comparable to the use of costumes appropriate to the 16th century.

2.4 *"Las Dos Caras del Patroncito"*

In "Las Dos Caras del Patroncito," the role of code-switching into Spanish has a clearly different role. The two main characters represent types: on the one hand, a Mexican farmworker and on the other, an Anglo owner. Each of them clearly belongs to a different stereotypic social class, the former working for the latter. This difference is also linguistically codified in the ways of addressing each other. The owner calls the worker "boy" in English and the worker code-switches most of the time to *patrón* in Spanish. The first clearly establishes the superiority of the owner and the status of English and the dominant language in the interaction, while the second alludes to the inferiority of the worker and thus, the status of Spanish as the dominated language in the interaction. Thus, in this play language choice and code-switching help depict this asymmetric relation between the characters, and the diglossic situation in the USA as conceived by Fishman. The farmworker is supposed to have arrived in California from Mexico only recently:

(9) P:	You're one of the new ones, huh? Come in from ...	You're one of the new ones, huh? Come in from ...
F:	*México, señor.*	Mexico, Sir.

(LDCdP, p. 47)

If all his answers were of this type, misunderstandings could arise quite often through the play. But in fact, the worker turns out to have a fair command of English. In fact, he introduces the play with a speech in English, in which he switches to Spanish 5 times, each time just for one word, in example (10):

(10) P:	Good morning, boy!	Good morning, boy.
F:	*Buenos días, patroncito.*	Good morning, boss.
P:	You working hard, boy?	You working hard, boy?
F:	Oh, *sí patrón! Muy* hard!	Oh, yes, boss! very hard!
P:	Oh, you can work harder than that, boy. Harder! Harder! HARDER!	Oh, you can work harder than that, boy. Harder! Harder! HARDER!
F:	*Ay*, that's too hard, *patrón.*	Oh, that's too hard, boss.

(LDCdP, p. 47)

At the beginning of this first contact between the two characters, the worker speaks Spanish switching only momentarily to English: *"hard."* Most of these two first lines however, could be regarded as formulaic utterances: *buenos días*, or appellations: *patroncito; oh, sí, patrón.* But then he is able to make it clear that the boss is asking too much, so he utters a whole sentence in English.

It becomes quite clear that the Patroncito, as Anglo, speaks only English, but having Mexicans work for him, he knows some Spanish words which are important for him:

(11) P:	Well lemme tell you, you don't have to be afraid of him, AS LONG AS YOU'RE WITH ME, *comprende?* I got him around to keep an eye on them *huelguistas.* You ever heard of them son? Ever heard of *Huelga?* Or Cesar Chávez?	Well lemme tell you, you don't have to be afraid of him, AS LONG AS YOU'RE WITH ME, do you understand? I got him around to keep an eye on them strikers. You ever heard of them, son? Ever heard of strike? Or Cesar Chávez?

(LDCdP, p. 48)

The question form *comprende* is very important, it helps him in getting his orders across to the workers and assuring himself that the excuse "I did not understand" be eliminated. The fact that he knows these words might lead the reader or the spectator to think that he does speak some Spanish, but that is not the case as we see in (12):

(12)P: ... don't I let you live in my labor camp -nice, rent-free cabins, air conditioned?

... don't I let you live in my labor camp -nice, rent-free cabins, air conditioned?

F: *Si señor, ayer se cayó la puerta.*

Yes sir, yesterday the door fell down.

P: What was that? ENGLISH.

What was that? ENGLISH.

F: Yesterday the door fell off, *señor.* And there's rats *también. Y los escusados,* the restrooms *-ay, señor, fuchi* (holds fingers to his nose).

Yesterday the door fell off, sir, and there's rats too. And the restrooms, the restrooms, -oh sir, phooey (holds fingers to his nose).

(LDCdP, p. 49)

As soon as the farmworker utters a complete sentence in Spanish, the owner demands that English be spoken, so in his next intervention the worker tries to use less Spanish. And when he gets to a point he cannot describe in English, he resorts to mime.

At the end of the play, where both characters interchange their roles the farmworker stops switching to Spanish and adopts those terms linked with superiority, for instance "boy":

(13)F: Because I felt like it, boy! You hear me, boy? I like your name, boy! I think I'll call you boy boy!

(LDCdP, p. 52)

This emphasis on the word "boy" at this point of the play not only reinforces the change of role undergone by the character. It also brings to the reader's mind that the owner had never called the worker by his real name. Either had he used "boy" or "son," or he had made one name up, like Pancho. In this way it is underlined that for the Anglos, all Mexicans are the same; they are only work-machines, and they are all called Panchos or Juanes.

Also at the end of the play, while the farmworker masters his second role as patroncito, it becomes clear that the owner cannot do the same. For one thing, he does not speak Spanish, so he is unable to code-switch:

(14)F: Come 'ere boy.

Come 'ere boy.

P: (his idea of a Mexican) *Sí, señor,* I theenk.

(...) Yes, Sir, I think.

(LDCdP, p. 52)

P: Charlie! Stop it! Some-   Charlie! Stop it! Somebody
    body help me! Help! Where's   help me! Help! Where's those
    those damn union organizers?   damn union organizers? Where's
    Where's Cesar Chávez? Help!   Cesar Chávez? Help! Strike!
    Huelga! HUELGAAAAA!   STRIKE!

(LDCdP, p. 53)

In his role as farmworker, the owner can use only a few words in Spanish. The fact that they are only a couple of words, would not strike the reader so much, were it not for the fact that *Cesar Chávez* and *Huelga* are exactly the same words he had already used in his role as the patroncito. Also noteworthy is the fact that these two words *Huelga* and *Cesar Chávez* are fully emotionally charged: they are vital terms for a Chicano farmworker who tries to do something against exploitation.

2.5 "Los Vendidos"

In "Los Vendidos" also, common stereotypes of the Chicano are presented. The action occurs in a shop where Chicano models are for sale. Each model has certain characteristics: external outfit, food taken, qualities, place of birth, and language(s) spoken.

For instance the "Farmworker" is presented as carrying a *sombrero* and *huaraches,* he eats beans, *tortillas* and *chile,* he is friendly and hardworking, his place of birth seems not to play an important role but he doesn't speak English. The "Revolucionario" carries a *sombrero* and a *carabina*; he eats raw meat and tequila; he is a movie and TV star, he is a lover, and he was born in Mexico. The "Johnny Pachuco" model wears mag shoes and dark glasses; he eats hamburgers, tacos, beer, wine, marijuana, coke...; he knife-fights, he dances, he has an inferiority complex, he can be beaten and kicked, and he is bilingual. The "Mexican American" model wears a business suit; he eats steaks and dry Martinis, he is acculturated, college-educated, ambitious, and also bilingual.

In fact, what the author is trying to do here is present types of Chicanos from the Anglo point of view. For this reason, characteristics like food are important, or the fact that English be spoken or not. It is noticeable that both the "Farmworker" and the "Revolucionario" models use only Spanish when they are activated. Nevertheless, at the end of the play, as soon as they return to their normal identities, both of them speak some English. The farmworker makes one-word-switches into Spanish, but the revolucionario does not even do that. Perhaps what the author is trying to convey through the last scene, as soon as the secretary is driven out by the models, is that the Chicanos' picture of themselves is quite different from the picture Anglos have.

The secretary herself also belongs to a certain group of Chicanos, different from any of those represented by the models. She insists on speaking English all the time, and she even makes a remark about her name:

(15)S: Good morning. I'm Miss   Good morning. I'm Miss Jimé-
        Jiménez from –   nez from –

HS: ¡*Ah, una chicana!* Welcome,   Oh, a Chicana! Welcome, wel-
    welcome *Señorita Jiménez.*   come Miss Jiménez.

S: (Anglo pronunciation)   (Anglo pronunciation) Jim-
    JIM-enez.   enez.

HS: ¿*Qué?*   What?

S: My name is Miss JIM-enez.   My name is Miss Jim-enez.
    Don't you speak English?   Don't you speak English?
    What's wrong with you?   What's wrong with you?

(LV, p. 17)

Members of this group of Chicanos share the fact that they reject everything that reminds them of their origin: they change the spelling or the pronunciation in their names and they avoid using Spanish. This proves very difficult, though. Even Miss Jim-enez cannot help it at a particular moment and she utters some Spanish. She is so impressed by the Farmworker's working abilities that she forgets she has to keep up speaking only English, as shown in (16):

(16)S: ¡*Chihuahua!* ... I mean, good-   Goodness – I mean goodness,
        ness, he sure is a hard worker.   he sure is a hard worker.

(p. 19)

She reacts very quickly, though, and resumes her Anglo attitude immediately afterwards.

In this play, thus, we have found a hint at the existence of at least two sorts of Chicanos: those who identify with their *chicanismo*, and those who try to reject as much as possible their Mexican background. We will be discussing this issue in a deeper way in the next section.

2.6 *"The Ultimate Pendejada"*

In this play the author makes a clear distinction between different groups of Chicanos. Chicanos in this play do not only behave characteristically but are distinct also in terms of language choice and in the use of code-switching.

Linguistically speaking, this is the most interesting of the five plays we have looked into. This play tells the story of two Chicanos in search of their own identities and in this process they go through several phases. Except for one, all of the characters in this play are university students.

In the first act the two protagonists identify themselves as "Americans of Spanish descent." Their friends are an Anglo couple; they speak only English; in fact, they have totally assimilated to the Anglo society. This becomes clear not only through their way of discussing topics in their conversation, or the fact that they call each other Robert and Mary, but also in their pronunciation of certain words, which in their speech seem to have the status of Spanish loan words, integrated into their English, as in (17):

> (17) R: Here's a story in the paper
>   about a *Checano* [CHi-ka-no] from the
>   *bear-eo* who was caught
>   smoking *mary-juana*, Mary.
>
> (UP, I,1, p. 137)

> M: What's this I hear about   What's this I hear about
>   Caesar Shaavez? That awful   Cesar Chávez? That awful
>   man! Everytime I hear about   man! Everytime I hear about
>   them *wellgistas* ...   them strikers my blood boils
>   my blood boils over!   over!
>
> (UP, I,2, p. 142)

Both Robert and Mary seem satisfied with their acculturated lives, but in the second act of the play they meet another group of Chicanos.

This group of Chicanos tends to identify with an ideal Mexico which is becoming an industrial power and where people live happily. This does not exist in reality, but this second group of Chicanos identifies with this made-up idea of Mexico. These people code-switch from English into Spanish. The most usual of the switches is a form of appellation, as in (18):

> (18) C: Wait a minute, *ése.*   Wait a minute, man.
>
> C: I don't know exactly,   I don't know exactly, man.
>   *ése.*
>
> C: Well, what do you think,   Well, what do you think, man,
>   *ése,* ...?   ... ?
>
> (UP, II,1, p. 144)

When switches are longer, they usually are inter-sentential, as in (19):

> (19) C: *Bueno, ésos, vamos a comenzar.*   Well, guys, we are
>   Let's begin.   going to begin. Let's begin.
>
> (UP, II,3, p. 149)

> P: *Está de aquéllas, ése.* I   It is very good, man. I didn't
>   didn't know you could speak   know you could speak Spanish.
>   Spanish.
>
> (UP, III,2, p. 156)

> E: *Órale* ... There's nothing to   Yes, O.K. there's nothing to
>   it ...   it ...
>
> (UP, III,2, p. 155)

The use of dirty words in Spanish seems to be highly accepted within the group, especially at moments of high emotion, in order to warn or challenge:

(20) F: *¡Hijo de tu chingada madre!*   You son of a b ...! Just
       Just let me catch you with   let me catch you with an
       a *gringa!*   Anglo girl!

    M: *¡Sí, cabrón! ¡A ver si te*   Yes, bastard! I would like to
       agarro con una gringa!   catch you with an Anglo girl!

(UP, III,2, p. 159)

The leader of this group is Cuahtemoc, the Chicano who is proud of having been named after a Mexican dictator. He is the only one who, at one point (in 21), seems to be code-switching from Spanish into English:

(21) C: *Me llamo Cuahtemoc 'Porfiri-*   My name is Cuahtemoc 'Por-
       to' Díaz y vengo de Sacra.   firito' Diaz and I come
       Mi estación es sophomor-*e*   from Sacramento. My class is
       and *mi vocación es revolu-*   sophomore and my profession is
       cionario.   revolutionary.

(UP, II,3, p. 149)

Here Cuahtemoc even tries to hispanize the English word "sophomore," which does not have a translation into Spanish, adding a vowel at the end of the word.

Cuahtemoc's code-switching is quite smooth, he even makes intra-sentential switches as in (22):

(22) C: *A ver, que vamos a* talk   Let's see, what are we going
       about at the meeting.   to talk about at the meeting.

(UP, II,1, p. 145)

    C: Look *ése,* a *macho* is a man!   Look, man, a man is a man.

(UP, II,1, p. 146)

There are a few points, though, in which he makes slight mistakes, as in (23):

(23) C: *Te pregunte, ares Chicano?*   I asked you, are you Chicano?
       (...) *lo que sayas,* whatever   whatever you are, whatever you
       you want to be called.   want to be called.

(UP, II,1, p. 143).

    C: Yeah, *ése,* I think *que ésta*   Yeah, man, I think it is very
       de aquéllas.   good.

(UP, II,1, p. 144)

Cuahtemoc makes two sorts of mistakes: first, mistakes in stress placement like *pregunte* instead of *pregunté* and *ésta* instead of *está*. These mistakes, not normally characteristic of natural code-switching, make his code-switching a bit choppy. Secondly, he produces two nonstandard verbal forms: one of them could be the result of a doubt, whether to code-switch at that moment or not: *Te pregunte are you/eres Chicano?*

We think the doubt is legitimate, because in this case both forms are somewhat similar, but nevertheless, it is a verbal form which is not part of the code-switching system. The other nonstandard form, *sayas,* could be seen as a mixture of the English verb *say* plus the regular present subjunctive in Spanish *-as*, (which would not make much sense in the context), or else as the Anglo pronunciation of the standard form *seas*. In any case, these mistakes signal Cuahtemoc as nonmember of the real Chicano community, because his code-switching does not perfectly match the system. In fact, all the members of this group are waiting to finish college and get their degrees to start helping other Chicanos during the weekends. And this idea of helping other Chicanos in the future once they are in top positions fits with the idealized Mexico they want to reproduce. In one word, everything is unreal, even their code-switching.

As the protagonists of the play, Mary and Robert, have contact with Cuahtemoc, they decide to accept the fact that they are of Mexican descent. In order to enter the group, they also decide to speak Spanish, but due to their lack of proficiency, when they code-switch, they make mistakes continuously – so that a humorous effect is produced. In order to signal mistakes in pronunciation, the author misspells words "essa" *ésa* (=women); "sena" *cena* (=dinner); "kerido, a" *querido, a* (=dear); "carnalees" *carnales* (=brothers); "ka tall" *qué tal* (=hello); "match-o" *macho* (=man). Proper names suffer curious transformations on their lips: *Cuahtemoc Díaz* becomes "Cooactemoc Di-as"; *Guadalajara* becomes "Guadalahara." Their own names are included: Robert becomes *Robert-o* and Mary becomes *María*.

Only Cuahtemoc tries once to correct their pronunciation:

(24) R: What's this about Checano time?　　　　　　　　What's this about Checano time?

　　 C: *Chicano, ése, Chicano,* not Checano.　　　　　　Chicano, man, Chicano not Checano.

(UP, II,1, p. 145)

But he does not succeed, it is only at the end of the play that this sort of mistake disappears from Robert's and Mary's speech. They also try to make intrasentential code-switches, also without much success as shown in (25):

(25) R: *Dónde* you get recipe for *sena, kerida?*　　　　Where you get recipe for dinner, dear?

　　 M: *Flor darme* recipe, *kerido.*　　　　　　　　　Flor give me recipe, dear.
　　　　Ella decir recipe *para chili*　　　　　　　　She say recipe for chili comes
　　　　es de Guadalahara.　　　　　　　　　　　　from Guadalajara.

　　 R: *Que bu-a-no. Esper-o estar* good.　　　　　　Fine. I hope it be good.

(UP, III,1, p. 152)

Their use of Spanish verbs is totally ungrammatical. The use of infinitives definitely proves that they are nonproficient speakers of Spanish. There is only one tense marker throughout the whole sequence, and articles are avoided. These features provide a sort of primitive Tarzan-like sort of speech in which only content words are used. In one word: their attempts to render the Chicano code-switching speech variety fails completely due to their lack of command of the Spanish language.

It is also remarkable that the auxiliary "do" is missing in Robert's question in (25). The same thing happens a little later in Mary's question in (26):

> (26)M: Yes ... *que pensar* we   Yes ... what you think we
> do to become more Mexican,   do to become more Mexican,
> *kerido?*   dear?
>
> (UP, III,1, p. 153)

In this case "we can do" would be much better than "we do." This sort of mistake would signal them as noncompetent speakers of English, and we know that this is not the case, since we have seen them speaking English only throughout the first act. In fact, these mistakes only emphasize the other mistakes in Spanish. One of them is the omission of *que* after the verbs *esperar, decir,* and *pensar,* which becomes very obvious in Roberto's second line in (25) because he decides not to switch after *espero* where *que* is obligatory in Spanish, and thus, also obligatory in the code-switching system.

In their effort to speak Spanish, a language they do not command, Robert and Mary make pragmatic mistakes in addition to the syntactic mistakes we have talked about so far. For example, Mary greets her Chicano guests saying (27):

> (27)M: *Bu-a-nas tardes, siniores*   Good afternoon, gentlemen
> *y sinioritas.* Oh, *carnalees*   and ladies. Oh brothers of
> *mios, pa-sen a mi casa!*   mine, come in to my house!
>
> (UP, III,2, p. 155)

Besides the mispronunciation signals, which drive us to laughter the whole greeting is ridiculous. Mary is using too many things at once. She opens her line with a normal greeting, *buenas tardes,* and changes afterwards to a totally different speech style: *señores y señoritas.* This is a formal appellation one would use at a banquet or at the beginning of a lecture. At any rate, Mary also modifies the usual form of this appellation, moving the masculine form to the first place and introducing a diminutive which is never used in these cases. Then comes a Chicano appellation, *carnales,* together with a typical Anglo interjection, *oh.* At the end of her line, Mary uses a phrase which, at least in Mexico, would be totally impolite. Mexican hosts would never emphasize the fact that guests come to their place. For them to feel at home, guests should feel like they are at *their* own place. So hosts would rather say: *pasen a la casa de ustedes* than *pasen a mi casa.*

Another strange collocation is the use of Spanish apellations with an introductory English "Oh." These appear several times in this third act as in (28):

(28)M: Oh ... Flor! *Tu bestido*   Oh, Flor! Your dress be so
         estar tanto bo-nito ...   beautiful ... Margarita ...
         Margarita ... *ka* you have   what you have to say?
         to *decir?*

(UP, III,2, p. 156)

Besides the appellation, Mary uses an English construction with an intra-sentential switch into Spanish which makes it very awkward. Using a literal translation from the English expression "what do you have to say" as a switch is completely inadequate in the code-switching system. In Spanish, one would ask for an opinion with ¿*Qué te parece, Margarita?* in which case the addressee comes after the question about the opinion, not before.

At the third scene of the third act, we notice that the two protagonists have moved into a different phase in their process of search for identity. They no longer try to speak Spanish, but they do switch for nouns in Spanish, and at this point the author spells all names in Spanish correctly, so that they talk about *Cuahtemoc,* the *Chicanos,* their *carnales,* and even *Robert-o* has become *Roberto* by this time. This more adequate Spanish pronunciation well suits their concern, quite serious by now, about their own identity as Chicanos and the best way to do something for the Chicano community. They realize that Cuahtemoc's group believe either in dreams or in lies and the activities of the group (writing proposals and exploiting the system by becoming a part of it) cannot really help the Chicano movement.

The last scene of the play introduces a new character: Chuey. He belongs neither to the university Chicanos nor does he reject his Chicano background. On the contrary, he is conscious of being a Chicano and he is happy with his identity.

His code-switching is very smooth, it includes appellations, single lexical items, intra- and intersentential switches as in (29):

(29)C: Sure, *ése* ... I was calling   Sure, man ... I was calling
         you. Relax. *Aliviánate.* I   you. Relax. Relax. I thought
         thought you were a *placa.*   you were a cop.

   R: A *placa?* What's a *placa?*   A cop? What's a cop?

   C: ¡*Ay qué vato!* ... ¿*no sabes*   Oh, man! ... Don't you know
         que es un placa? A *placa*   what a cop is? A cop is a cop
         is a *juda* ... I mean, a police-   ... I mean, a policeman.
         man.

(UP, III,3, p. 163)

In contrast to Cuahtemoc, who is sometimes very aggressive towards Robert, Chuey's attitude is helpful. He does not at any point want to take advantage of Robert. So if Robert does not understand the word *placa,* he gives him another word, *juda,* and when he realizes he has been using only Spanish terms, he switches into English in order to get the idea across to Robert. As Robert explains his story about his and Mary's changes from "American of Spanish descent" into a "Mexican American" and his disappointment with those college "Chicanos," Chuey's attitude is compassionate:

(30)C: *Sabes que, ése,* we all   You know what, man, we all
go through changes like   go through changes like that.
that. *Es nuestra vida;* it's   It is our life; it is our
our life. *Tenemos que evolu-*   life. We have to develop.
cionar. And that causes much   And that causes much pain,
pain, much heartache and hard-   much heartache and hardship.
ship. Your ultimate *pendejada*   Your ultimate mistake was
was that you changed on the   that you changed on the
outside only, *pero no en donde*   outside only, but not where
cuenta, not inside where it   it counts, not inside where
really counts.   it really counts.

(UP, III,3, p. 164)

Chuey does not criticize Roberto and María, he rather tries to convince them their concern is legitimate and they should go on their search for identity.

Ysidro Macías himself probably belongs to this third group of Chicanos. At least linguistically speaking, there would be some evidence in this direction. For example, there are short switches into Spanish in the stage directions such as those in 31 which are not, like most of the short switches, nouns, but adjectives.

(31) — They (Robert and Mary) are   They are very Anglo-like
very *agringado* in speech,   in speech, behavior, customs,
behavior, customs, etc.   etc.

(UP, I,1, p. 137)

— A young *gringolofico* college   A young Anglo college couple
couple enters.   enters.

(UP, I,2, p. 139)

— He (Robert) assumes   He assumes a "macho" pose.
macho pose.

(UP, II,1, p. 145)

The syntax the author uses is always English. In several cases, though, he takes Spanish adjectives which do not follow the morphemic Spanish rules. That is, he uses the *-o* ending without regard to the reference noun or pronoun with which an adjective in Spanish should concord. The first example in (31) would be: *Ellos son muy agringados*, if we were to use only Spanish, in which case the predicate adjective would concord in plural with the subject *ellos*. In the second case we would have something like: *una pareja universitaria gringolófica*, in which the adjective would concord in feminine with the noun. In the third case, the noun *macho* should take the ending *-ista* in order to be used as an adjective. In all three cases, however, the author follows the English conventions: anteposition to a noun transforms automatically any word to an adjective. Thus, his switches fit in the code-switching system.

In introducing Chuey he makes a strange mixture:

Standing around is a	Standing around is
local *vato loco,* Chuey	a local grazy guy, Chuey

Here he combines both Spanish and English conventions in order to qualify the Spanish noun *vato.* First he supplies an English adjective, "local", which is placed before the noun, and then a Spanish adjective, "loco" (=crazy), placed after it with the appropriate concord.

3. Conclusion

In conclusion, we can say that code-switching, as observed in these five plays does not perfectly mirror code-switching in natural discourse, but it does bear an important relationship to it. First, there is much less code-switching in the works we examined than in natural discourse and it is of a much more limited nature. Appellations together with culturally bound items are the most common single lexical items.

Intra-sentential switching is also less frequent than in natural discourse, and when it does occur, like in "The Ultimate Pendejada," it clearly has a symbolic function because some of these switches do not conform to the syntactic constraints that govern switches in natural discourse. Intra-sentential switching provides a cue to the falsity or incompletely attained Chicano identity in some of the characters, like Cuahtemoc, Robert, Mary and Miss Jim-enez, while smooth switching indicates that the character has achieved the status of a real Chicano, like Chuey.

In general, we can state that the use of code-switching in Chicano drama supports the findings of the studies of natural discourse, that is, that "code-switching" is a speech variety in its own right. Further, that it is the variety which covertly, if not yet overtly, represents the true Chicano identity — drawing on both Anglo and Mexican culture — but a distinctive blend on its own.

References

Linguistic Sources

Amastea, John, and Lucía Elías-Olivares, eds. *Spanish in the United States: Sociolinguistic Aspects.* Cambridge, Mass.: Cambridge University Press, 1982.
Durán, Richard P., ed. *Latino Language and Communicative Behavior.* Norwood, N.J.: Ablex, 1981.
Elías-Olivares, Lucía. "Ways of Speaking in a Chicano Community: A Sociolinguistic Approach." Unpublished Ph.D. Dissertation. University of Texas, Austin, 1976.
Ferguson, Charles A. "Diglossia." *Word,* 15 (1959), 325–40.
Fishman, Joshua A. *Language Loyalty in the United States.* The Hague: Mouton, 1966.

Fishman, Joshua A. "The Sociology of Language: An Interdisciplinary Social Science Approach to Language in Society." In Joshua A. Fishman, ed., *Advances in the Sociology of Language*, Vol. I. The Hague: Mouton, 1971, pp. 217–404.

Fishman, Joshua A., Robert Cooper, Roxanna Ma, et al. *Bilingualism in the Barrio*. Bloomington: Indiana University Press, 1971.

García, Maryellen. "Preparing to Leave: Interaction at a Mexican-American Family Gathering." In *Latino Language and Communicative Behavior*. Ed. Richard P. Durán. Norwood, N.J.: Ablex, 1981, pp. 195–215.

Grosjean, François. *Life with Two Languages. An Introduction to Bilingualism*. Cambridge, Mass.: Harvard University Press, 1982.

Gumperz, John, and Eduardo Hernández-Chávez. "Cognitive Aspects of Bilingual Communication." In *El Lenguaje de los Chicanos*. Ed. Eduardo Hernández-Chávez, Andrew Cohen, and Anthony Beltramo. Arlington, Va.: Center for Applied Linguistics, 1975.

Haugen, Einar. *The Norwegian Language in America. A Study in Bilingual Behavior*. Bloomington: Indiana University Press, 1969.

Hernández-Chávez, Eduardo, Andrew Cohen, and Anthony Beltramo, eds. *El Lenguaje de los Chicanos*. Arlington, Va.: Center for Applied Linguistics, 1975.

Huerta-Macías, Ana. "Codeswitching: All in the Family." In *Latino Language and Communicative Behavior*. Ed. Richard P. Durán. Norwood, N.J.: Ablex, 1981, pp. 153–68.

Kloss, Heinz. *The American Bilingual Tradition*. Rowley, Mass.: Newbury House, 1977.

Pedraza, Pedro, Jr., and John Attinasi. "Rethinking Diglossia." In *Language Policy Task Force 9*. New York: Centro de Estudios Puertorriqueños, 1980.

Peñalosa, Fernando. *Chicano Sociolinguistics: A Brief Introduction*. Rowley, Mass.: Newbury House, 1980.

Pfaff, Carol W. "Functional and Structural Constraints on Syntactic Variation in Code-Switching." In *Papers from the Parasession of Diochronic Syntax*. Ed. S. Steever, C. Walker, and S. Mufwene. Chicago: Chicago Linguistic Society, 1976.

Pfaff, Carol W. "Constraints on Language Mixing: Intrasentential Code-Switching and Borrowing in Spanish/English." *Language*, 55 (1979), 291–318.

Poplack, Shana. "Syntactic Structure and Social Function of Code-Switching." In *Latino Language and Communicative Behavior*. Ed. Richard P. Durán. Norwood, N.J.: Ablex, 1981, pp. 291–318.

Poplack, Shana. "Bilingualism and the Vernacular." In *Issues in International Bilingual Education: The Role of the Vernacular*. Ed. Beverly Hartford, and Albert Valdman. New York: Plenum Publishing Co., 1982, pp. 1–23.

Sánchez, Rosaura. Spanish Codes in the Southwest. Typescript, 1976.

Weinreich, Uriel. *Languages in Contact*. The Hague: Mouton, 1953.

Anthologies of Chicano Literature

Anaya, Rudolfo A., ed. *Cuentos Chicanos*. Albuquerque, New Mexico: New America, 1980.

Cárdenas de Dwyer, Carlota, ed. *Chicano Voices*. Boston: Houghton Mifflin Company. 1975.

Castañeda Shular, Antonia, Tomás Ybarra-Fraustro, and Joseph Sommers, eds. *Literatura Chicana, Texto y Contexto*. Englewood Cliffs, N.J.: Prentice-Hall Inc., 1972.

Empringham, Toni, ed. *Fiesta in Aztlán, Anthology of Chicano Poetry*. Santa Barbara, Ca.: Capra Press, 1982.

Garza, Roberto J., ed. *Contemporary Chicano Theatre*. Notre Dame, Indiana: University of Notre Dame Press, 1976.

Harth, Dorothy E., and Lewis M. Baldwin, eds. *Voices of Aztlán. Chicano Literature of Today*. New York: The New American Library, Inc., 1974.

Valdez, Luis, and Stan Steiner, eds. *Aztlán: An Anthology of Mexican American Literature*. New York: Random House, Inc., 1972.

Source Texts

Macías, Ysidro R. "Mártir Montezuma." In *Contemporary Chicano Theatre*. Ed. Roberto J. Garza. Notre Dame, Indiana: University of Notre Dame Press, 1976, pp. 165–89.

254

Macías, Ysidro R. "The Ultimate Pendejada." In *Contemporary Chicano Theatre*. Ed. Roberto J. Garza. Notre Dame, Indiana: University of Notre Dame Press, Inc., 1976, pp. 135–64.

Valdez, Luis M. "Bernabé." In *Contemporary Chicano Theatre*. Ed. Roberto J. Garza. Notre Dame, Indiana: University of Notre Dame Press, Inc., 1976, pp. 29–58.

Valdez, Luis M. "Las Dos Caras del Patroncito." In *Literatura Chicana, Texto y Contexto*. Eds. Antonia Castañeda Shular, Tomás Ybarra-Frausto, and Joseph Sommers. Englewood Cliffs, N.J.: Prentice-Hall, Inc., 1972, pp. 46–53.

Valdez, Luis M. "Los Vendidos." In *Contemporary Chicano Theatre*. Ed. Roberto J. Garza. Notre Dame, Indiana: University of Notre Dame Press, 1976, pp. 15–27.

Self-Determined Chicano Adult Education in the California Central Valley: D–Q University

Hartmut Lutz

In the Treaty of Guadalupe Hidalgo (Feb. 1848) the Mexican Americans were guaranteed their cultural integrity, including that of language.[1] However, as early as 1855 a California State Law forbade the use of Spanish for school instruction. This law marks the beginning of a process of Eurocentric, Anglo-oriented education for the Californios that has rightly been termed "de-education" by Stan Steiner[2] or been described as a "colonizing mechanism" by Carlos H. Arce.[3] It has led to a "culture of silence" in the sense of Paolo Freire,[4] and it would clearly be in violation of the United Nations Convention on Genocide of 1948.[5] Ostensibly, the rationale of such educational policy was "assimilation," and even though there is general agreement that the melting pot has never worked for non-European ethnic groups, there is a marked tendency in recent years to question multiethnicity and cultural self-determination and to return to older assimilationist practices.[6]

A historical perspective shows quite clearly that over a century of enforced acculturation of Mexicans through Anglo educational institutions has had devastating effects on the Chicano people as a whole. Educational statistics indicate that Mexican Americans are far behind the majority,[7] and the de-education process intensifies considerably the higher up we move in the educational ladder. Moreover the gap has widened in the last couple of years. In 1979 it was estimated that only 68% of the Mexican American students graduated from High School, as opposed to 87% of non-Hispanic Americans.[8] A more recent comprehensive study by Alexander W. Astin, *Minorities in American Higher Education*, analyzed the last years of the Carter administration and the first year of Reagan's presidency, and it came to the conclusion that only 55% of the Chicano cohort graduate from High School as compared to 83% of the whites.[9] (See: "The Educational Pipeline for Minorities"; overleaf) According to the Astin study, the greatest leakages in the educational pipeline are in High School itself, in the transition from High School to college, and then during the first undergraduate years: whereas 22% of Chicano students enter college, only less than a third of them, 7%, earn a degree. Next to Puerto Ricans and American Indians, Mexican Americans are educationally the most deprived group in the United States — and statistics do not even consider the million or so migrant workers entering the U.S. every year, who did or did not

256

Figure 1. The Educational Pipeline for Minorities

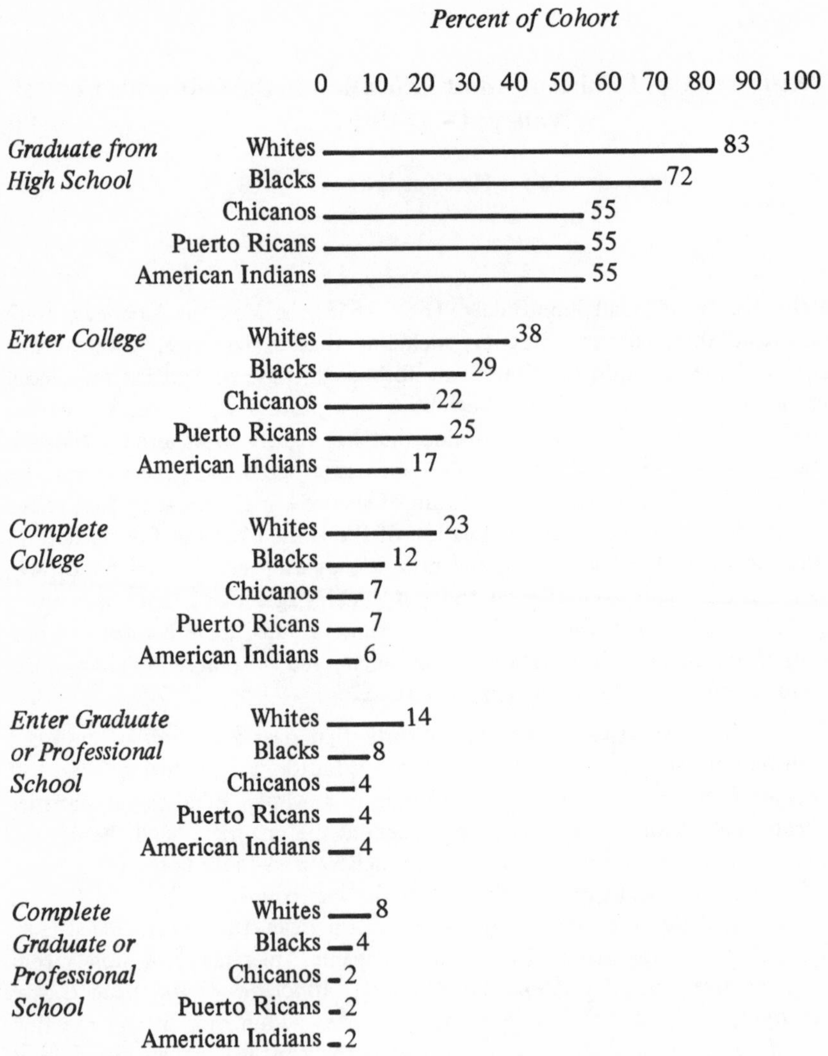

Percent of Cohort

0   10 20 30 40 50 60 70 80 90 100

Graduate from   Whites ————————————————— 83
High School   Blacks ——————————————— 72
               Chicanos ——————————— 55
       Puerto Ricans ——————————— 55
  American Indians ——————————— 55

Enter College   Whites ————————— 38
              Blacks ——————— 29
          Chicanos ———————22
      Puerto Ricans ——————— 25
 American Indians ————— 17

Complete   Whites ————— 23
College   Blacks ——— 12
           Chicanos —— 7
     Puerto Ricans —— 7
 American Indians —— 6

Enter Graduate Whites ———14
or Professional   Blacks ——8
School   Chicanos ——4
      Puerto Ricans —— 4
 American Indians —— 4

Complete   Whites ——8
Graduate or   Blacks ——4
Professional   Chicanos —2
School   Puerto Ricans —2
 American Indians —2

[from: Alexander W. Astin, *Minorities in American Higher Education*
(San Francisco, 1982), p. 175.]

receive an education in Mexico, most of them never getting anywhere near High School.

However, in order to function independently in Anglo society and to be able to combat racism and job discrimination, Chicanos need not only possess certain language skills to communicate with the Anglo world but also enough general knowledge about the dominant society in order to know how to obtain and defend the rights and liberties their Anglo peers enjoy, or should enjoy, or think they enjoy. Without a positive self-identity, minority students in general tend to fail, and a positive self-concept is closely linked with the acceptance of and a certain pride in one's own cultural and ethnic heritage. Such concepts are not developed in Eurocentric, Anglo-dominated educational institutions, and it is for that reason that Chicanos — like other minorities in the U.S. and elsewhere — need to control their own educational institutions, particularly on the secondary and post-secondary, adult education level.

Deganawidah-Quetzalcoatl University, near Davis, Ca. was founded in Winter 1970/71, as a joint effort of the Chicano and Indian communities in the Sacramento Valley and the staff and students of the Chicano Studies and Native American Studies Programs at UC Davis.[10] Their aim was self-determined culture-based education for all students over 18 willing to learn, regardless of schooling previously received. By opening the college to all persons interested it was hoped to reach even those educationally most deprived groups who would otherwise be excluded from further education due to the mechanisms characteristic of the colonial situation, where it is in the power of the dominant group to select a few individuals from out of the subordinate group while excluding the vast majority, without that group having a say in the selective process.[11]

The overall objective of DQU was, is, and will remain, self-determination. This, in itself, is a political goal, pursued by means of education in the widest possible sense. Besides, the founders of DQU formulated four more specific objectives, which can be briefly summarized as:

(1) general education (like other community colleges), but in a culture-based context,
(2) practical training in the skills needed by the communities for their respective developments,
(3) documenting and disseminating traditional knowledge and wisdom, including the spiritual (e.g. American Indian religions),
(4) making resources available to the communities and training "students who will serve as agents of social change when they leave the university."[12]

The last objective, in particular, has met with much governmental concern and opposition, but even objective number three, practising the spiritual heritage, has recently been slandered as "savagism," not fit for a college. Likewise, the community-development objective, running counter to paternalist measures in a colonial situation, is in contrast to mainstream education. So, with three objectives running counter to the interests of the dominant group, DQU's success as a college is measured solely according to its achievements in general education by the outside-world, i.e. are courses and standards comparable to other community colleges in dominant society? But even here, given the special educational background of the Chicano and Indian students, their lack of formal schooling and lack of resources, DQU is at a disadvantage when compared to mainstream institutions. Nevertheless, auditors and accreditation committees judge the college according to their Euro-American cultural bias, and under the Reagan administration, the cultural base of the curriculum has come under attack as being more "cultural" than "educational"[13] — whatever that may mean. Despite these odds, DQU has survived. It is a fully accredited two year college, providing Associate of Arts and Associate of Science degrees. Despite having to go without pay ever so often, administrative staff, teachers, and students have cleared an average of two to three audits per year, which is about five times as many as for mainstream institutions, and the survival of DQU for almost fifteen years has justly been called a "miracle."[14]

In the beginning DQU had a board of directors consisting of equal numbers of Chicanos and Indians, and in its history, there have been more Chicano than Indian presidents. Factionalism, which seems to haunt all comparable minority institutions, has also occurred at DQU, but rifts did not run along ethnic lines — as might perhaps be expected — but rather along political and ideological lines cutting across ethnic barriers. It is important to know this, because in 1978 the Chicano board members resigned to give way to an all-Indian board of directors. This was a move to ensure the survival of DQU, making it officially an Indian-controlled community college — similar to 18 tribally controlled community colleges on reservations throughout the U.S. — thus qualifying both for membership in AIHEC (American Indian Higher Education Consortium) and for funds allocated through the Tribally Controlled Community Colleges Assistance Act.[15] Regardless of such "official Indianness," DQU continues to offer courses for Chicano students, both in Spanish and English, and its present president, Carlos Cordero, is a Chicano himself.

The courses and programs offered specifically for Chicanos at DQU are manifold and varied. In the past there have been seminars on Latin American and Mexican history, culture and literature in Spanish, as well as vocational training programs in agriculture and community development etc. Extracurricular events have included Third World philosophy symposia and joint programs with the United Farm Workers' Union and other local Chicano groups,[16] and there have been — and still are — special "College Survival Courses" in which students were given opportunity to fill the gaps left open by previous colonialist de-education, or in which they are offered English language instruction geared to their most urgent needs.

Out of a great variety, two such programs are presented here. First, the federally funded "Migrant Farm Worker Project" of 1972/73, and secondly the unspectacular routine of teaching English to Mexicans in 1979/80. Both reflect the colonial situation of Chicanos in California on a structural and on a personal level.

In 1972/1973 DQU was given nominal charge of a 3.1-million-dollar migrant farmworker training project. This federal program, sponsored by the Department of Labor (DOL) had previously been offered to Ronald Reagan's California State Department of Human Resources Development, who had declined the offer. Then, DOL decided to hand it over to DQU to serve as the roof organization. Politically, the program was part of Nixon's campaign for reelection to the presidency, hoping to catch Chicano votes, and undoubtedly it did benefit many migrant farmworkers in California, giving staff training in manpower development to 130, rendering vocational training to 650 campesinos and helping about 300 persons to be placed in new jobs.[17] With DQU as the administrative center, it reached fourteen outlying training sites throughout California. All the time, it was supervised by a permanent government representative on the DQU campus as project officer, and part of the time by two DOL full-time auditors, who stayed on site for months. In the end, however, the project proved too big and too complicated for a small institution like DQU. Inconsistencies in handling the program through DOL officials and conflicting policies between the Department of Health, Education, and Welfare (DHEW), responsible for the DQU campus, and DOL, indicate that the program was probably meant to serve a double political function, i.e. (1) to attract pro-Nixon votes while at the same time (2) disrupting the Chicano community, splitting them into factions fighting for their share of the cake, thus "neutralizing" radical Mexican American groups opposed to Nixon. The Watergate hearings brought to light that CREEP – the Committee for the Re-Election of the President – was active in many DOL programs in California at the time, and names of people occur which were also connected with the migrant farmworker project.[18] However, it is virtually impossible to fully prove this allegation because most of the records of so called "responsiveness" and "politicizing"[19] programs planned by CREEP were burned at the White House in 1972, and even the local California files of the State Office of Economic Opportunity relating to DQU were apparently destroyed by the parting staff of the then governor of California, Ronald Reagan, before Brown succeeded to the office – an extended search for the files in 1982 through the State Archives and the State Office of Economic Opportunity did not turn them up.[20]

The critical stage came for DQU when, at the end of the program, DOL ruled that all equipment bought under the project, including tractors and heavy machinery, be brought to the DQU campus instead of returning it to local DOL offices or leaving it to follow-up programs. No funds were allocated for transporting and collecting the materials, and when some outlying centers refused to return the equipment, DQU in turn refused to accept the overseer function over local campesino groups throughout the state. As a consequence DQU was accused of having mismanaged government funds. None of all later DOL and DHEW charges against DQU did ever stick, but it has taken DQU years to overcome the feuding and factionalism sparked off by the project. So, while helping and training many individuals, structurally the program weakened Chicano political and cultural unity, and instead of promoting real self-determination, it resulted in the in-fighting of the colonized over the crumbs dropped them by the colonizer.

Despite earlier plans to make DQU a large university, including a Medical and a Law School plus a Chicano Studies and Indian Studies college each, DQU is now a very small institution, serving not many more than 200 students, both on campus and in off-campus programs. Being situated in rich farmlands, migrant workers and resident Mexican Americans live in that region, and many come to DQU for the education they have previously been denied. In 1979/80, while doing research as an ACLS-fellow with the Native American Studies Tecumseh Center at UC Davis, I taught two terms at DQU, and I would like to conclude by introducing you to two of the students I worked with — who, incidentally, gave me their permission to take their materials and present their cases to inform people in Germany about Chicano situations. Hereby, this is partly done.

Mrs. Anita Robles, a then 37-year-old mother of eight children had had only three winters of schooling in Mexico as a child (see appendix I). She came to DQU in order to improve her spoken English and to develop reading and writing skills in that language. At first, when coming to classes, she brought relatives as chaperons, but then came by herself. In the second term, Mr. Ezequiel Robles, her husband, also joined our course, and we eventually developed it into a three-person-tutorial, moved off campus and met in our private homes or my office, and started a continuous dialog in which students and teacher learned from each other about each other's cultures and experiences. For me as a teacher it was a most rewarding experience because Ezequiel and Anita were exceptionally diligent students who at the same time gave me more insights into the Chicano migrant situation than I could have gathered theoretically from books.

Anita, as a Mexican, a woman and a poor person, had to battle racism, sexism and class barriers, in order to overcome her culture of silence.[21] Writing words in English, then sentences, then paragraphs and eventually a two page curriculum vitae, cost her immense work and effort, but also gave her pride and growing confidence in her own skills — it was the first time she ever produced materials in writing, and in this case materials about her own experiences, the memories of which were often painful. The importance was in the learning process per se, not in the finished project, and so we took all the time we needed. While battling with questions of spelling, grammar, sentence structures, punctuation, etc., we were also discussing questions of geography, law, history, trade unionism, colonialism, etc. Anita finished lines 1–34 of her paper in the first term, with me helping quite often with the sentence structure and stylistic questions, but lines 35–64, composed in the second term, were entirely her own. She had learned to form short but coherent sentences, expressing in English her own thoughts.

By contrast, Ezequiel, her husband, had had six years of schooling, and he was more fluent in spoken English and also in reading and writing, but he too decided to write down the story of his life, which he did in less than a term. Observing me as an "Anglo" with a reserved dignity at first, Ezequiel soon grew more and more interested in our discussions and our dialog grew more and more symmetric. Noticing that at the time I was working mainly with the Indian people at DQU and UC Davis, he eventually offered to take me on a tour of Chicano sites around Davis, from which tour I am now showing a few slides. (Here slides were shown.)

During that one year exchange, Anita's and – to a lesser degree – Ezequiel's command of English grew considerably. This could easily be observed by dictations and reading exercises. It is more difficult to measure, however, in how far their self-confidence grew in relation to acquiring more general knowledge about the dominant society and how to cope with it. Things were made easier in that I was undoubtedly an "Anglo" but not a U.S. citizen and also a stranger in California. In all our teaching and learning, Anita's and Ezequiel's needs and interests determined the subject matter, whereas it was my function to provide necessary skills, find material or serve as a reference for background information. Using a curriculum vitae as the central project forced us to relate everything to Anita and Ezequiel and their own experiences, which, in English and in a written, filtered and reflected form, acquired a new objective dimension and quality. I think that in this case, the use of English did not serve to alienate, but to rediscover what had seemed almost natural and organic before, as influenced and determined by social and political conditions that are characteristic of the colonial situation and that are not haphazard outgrowths of personal fate but occur elsewhere and are rooted in a general structure dominating Mexican-American or Third World-U.S. relations.

It is difficult to ascertain in how far this understanding was reached and became rooted, but we definitely moved in that direction, and if emancipation is seen as a process liberating individuals from limitations forced upon them by societal restraints by making conscious the restrictions and turning them into objects of change, then DQU has helped, in this instance, to let people move towards greater self-determination, who would otherwise be totally excluded from any further educational services. It is for this reason that DQU must survive.

262

Notes

[1] Pastora San Juan Cafferty, "The Language Question: The Dilemma of Bilingual Education for Hispanics in America," *Ethnic Relations in America*, ed. Lance Liebman (Englewood Cliffs, N.J.: Prentice-Hall, 1982), pp. 101–127, 111. Also: Rodolfo Acuña, *Occupied America: The Chicano's Struggle Toward Liberation* (San Francisco: 1972), pp. 27 ff.

[2] Stan Steiner, *La Raza: The Mexican Americans* (New York: Harper and Row, 1970), pp. 280–81.

[3] Carlos H. Arce, "Chicano Participation in Academe: A Case of Academic Colonialism," *Grito del Sol: A Chicano Quarterly*, 3 (1978), 75–104, 86.

[4] Paulo Freire, *Pädagogik der Unterdrückten: Bildung als Praxis der Freiheit* (Reinbek: Rowohlt, 1970), pp. 10–11.

[5] Article II of the United Nations Convention on Genocide lists as one possible form of genocide: "(b) Causing serious bodily or mental harm to members of the group," – and bereaving a people of their language, does cause severe mental harm. The U.S. is not a contracting party to the convention, c.f.: Jack Norton, *When Our Worlds Cried: Genocide in Northwestern California* (San Francisco: 1979), p. 141.

[6] Cafferty, pp. 125 ff; Nathan Glazer, "Politics of a Multiethnic Society," in *Ethnic Relations in America*, ed. Lance Liebman (Englewood Cliffs, N.J.: Prentice-Hall, 1982), pp. 128–49, 148–49.

[7] John W. Moore with Alfredo Cuellar, *Mexican Americans* (Englewood Cliffs, N.J.: Prentice-Hall, 1970), pp. 67 ff.

[8] Cafferty, p. 118.

[9] Alexander W. Astin, *Minorities in American Higher Education. Recent Trends, Current Prospects, and Recommendations* (San Francisco: Jossey-Bass. Inc., 1982).

[10] For the history of the foundation of DQU see: Jack D. Forbes, Kenneth R. Martin, and David Risling, Jr., *The Establishment of D–Q University: An Example of Successful Indian-Chicano Community Development* (Davis: D–Q University Press, 1972). For a history of DQU up to 1980 see my own book: Hartmut Lutz (author & editor), *D–Q University: Native American Self-Determination in Higher Education* (Davis: 1980). Originally published by the Native American Studies Tecumseh Center of the Dept. of Applied Behavioral Sciences, Univ. of California Davis, the book is now available on microcard or as a xerox from: ERIC Clearinghouse on Rural Education and Small Schools, Las Cruces, N.M.; for an abstract see: *Resources in Education*, 17, No. 3 (1982), 149. More recent developments regarding DQU are rendered by: Jack D. Forbes, *Education, Culture, and Academic Freedom: The Reagan Administration's Attack on an American Indian-Chicano College* (Davis: D–Q University Press, 1983).

[11] Carlos H. Arce defines "academic colonialism" as: "...the selective imposition of intellectual premises, concepts, methods, institutions, and related organizations of other groups by selected members of a subordinate group, with the selection processes not being in the control of the subordinate group." Arce, p. 77; also: Carlos H. Arce, "Chicanos in Higher Education," *Integrated Education*, 14, No 3 (1976), 14–18, 14.

[12] Lutz, p. 27.

[13] Forbes, *Education, Culture* ..., pp. 1–2.

[14] This term was repeatedly used by Sarah Hutchison, a Cherokee instructor at Native American Studies Tecumseh Center, UC Davis, and the first woman on the DQU board of directors.

[15] For further details see Lutz, pp. 29 ff.

[16] Besides, there are many extracurricular political events organized by and for the Indian community, e.g. The Longest Walk (1978) and the Walk for Survival (1980), cross-continental marches to Washington to protest anti-Indian legislation; the pan-Californian 500-Mile-Run held each year, the First International Indian Tribunal in 1982, besides religious activities such as the Annual Sun Dance, see Lutz, pp. 40 ff., 105–118, 133–138. See also: Bernd C. Peyer, "D–Q University. A Native American Institution of Higher Learning Struggling for Existence," *Zeitschrift für Ethnologie*, 106, No. 1 & 2 (1981), 139–48.

[17] Ch. Burkhard, "David Faces Goliath Again: D–Q University and the Bureaucracy," unpubl. typescript, 21 pp. (Davis, 1982), 8.

[18] United States Senate, *Hearings Before the Select Committee on Presidential Campaign Activities of the United States Senate, 93rd Congress, 1st Session: Watergate and Related Activities*, vol. 13 (Washington: 1973), 5289, 5321, 5396 *et passim;* Burkhard, *passim.*

[19] Burkhard, p. 6.

[20] Burkhard, pp. 18–19.

[21] See: Dieter Herms, "La Chicana: Dreifache Diskriminierung als Drittweltfrau," *Gulliver: Deutsch-englische Jahrbücher* 10, Argument Sonderband 72 (Berlin: Argument Verlag, 1981), pp. 79–93.

Appendix 1

CURRICULUM VITAE
Anita R., Mexican, Student at DQ-University, Cal.

I was born in Potrero de Callegos, State of Mexico, on June 2, 1943. My father was a poor man. He had to work in the fields every day of the week. I had to help him so we could have food in the house. We used to go by donkey or horse to sell vegetables, chicken, and jugs at the small towns or ranches. We rode to a different ranch every day. We were three sisters, but I would go with my father every day.

When I was about 9 years old my father took us to Texas. We had to cross the Rio Grande by night. My father built a raft because I could not swim at that time. We went to Texas every summer for 6 month periods, and we had to cross the river each time. In the river many people drowned. At one time my sister got lost in the woods and we could not find her for three hours. We were very much afraid of the Mexican people, too, because we had to cross the land they owned.

I remember one time we were working the fields when the border patrol came to ask for our legal papers. When they found out that we didn't have papers they took us back across the border to Mexico. When we got there some rich Mexican ranchers were waiting for us. The American told us that we had to go to the Mexican people and work for them. They put us in big trucks and took us to their ranch. They put all the men in one big shack and our family was put in the hen-coop. My mother talked to one family living there, and they told her that the owner was going to make us work without pay. After that my parents decided to leave. About three in the morning we ran away from them, crossed the river and went back to work for the same American farmer. During that time I was between 9 and 12 years old (1952–1955).

During the winter I went to school in Mexico for three years. At that time there was no public school in our area. The people got together and hired a private teacher for the kids. We were 50 children of all age groups. We were taught reading, writing, and some mathematics.

In 1956 we got the good papers. We lived in La Jolla, Texas, for three months. After that we travelled to Idaho to work in the sugar beet and potatoe fields. We had to wake up at three in the morning every day. Every day I made nine or twelve dollars. After that we moved to Arizona and we worked in the cotton fields. Then we came to California and worked in the orange and cotton fields. And in the vineyards.

In 1959 I wanted to become a nun. I went to Mexico City to a convent. I stayed for one year. I didn't like it. I came back.

After that I married in 1961. I was 18 years old. I have three sons and five daughters. The first one came in 1963 the last one in 1973.

In 1974 the Farmworkers Union came to Yolo County. My husband was working for a farmer in Davis. When the people came and talked to me and my husband, we went with them and helped. We had to go every day at 3.00 a. m. to the boycott line and stayed until 10.00 p. m. Sometimes we had something to eat, sometimes we didn't. We stayed for three months. They gave us one hundred and fifty dollars every two weeks.

In 1971 we moved to Clarksburg, because my husband found a good job. We lived in a garage house for six years. In 1976 my husband got hurt in his back in the job. We went to the doctor. The doctor put him in the hospital. And my husband got an operation. The doctor removed one disk from his back. I went to talk to the boss. I told him: "I need your help because I don't know nothing where I am supposed to go and ask for help." He answered me, "Well, the only way I can help is to loan you money". I went to a friend she told me that I have to go to the F.W.U. office in Sacramento. We went and asked for a man. His name was Morco Lopes. We told my problem. I found out that the boss lied to me. We don't have to pay the doctor or hospital. The insurance pays the bills for my husband. They have to give us a cheque for $ 35.00 dollars a month. They go up at $ 145.00 monthly. In 1978 we moved to Woodland because the boss told my husband, "I don't want you to work for me! I don't want problems. You are sick. I need my house for another worker. You have 45 days to move."

On June 15, 1978 I started to work for the farm worker service center. I worked without pay. I was the director, Richard Johnson was my teacher. He was a good man at that time. I left the work because of too much problems. Nobody wanted to listen to nobody. They do whatever they want. Now I study at DQU. I am learning something.

Appendix 2

CURRICULUM VITAE
Ezequiel R., Mexican student at DQ-University, Cal.

I, Ezequiel R., was born in the Estate of Mexico. I grew up on a ranch taking care of the animals.

When I was six years old my father put me in the public school. Then, in the vacation time I had to go back again to the ranch to plant corn, beans and squash and all the family had to go to the forest ranch. My mother had to milk the cows by hand, and she got very tired. She made much cheese. The cheese was very delicious. In winter time my parents had many things to give to us to eat, like cheese, corn, beans and my father sometimes killed one cow to eat meat. In other words, we had a lot to eat the whole year.

Then, when the vacation time was over we had to go back to school again to study hard. I went to school in Mexico for six years. Then when I was 18 years old, I came to the United States to work for three years from 1959 to 1961. Then I met my wife and we got married and we came to Tijuana, Mexico, to have the visa. It took only about one month to get the visa. Then in 1961 we came here to Davis I started to work with one farmer in the field. I worked for him for four years. When the farmer don't have nothing to do we had to go to another place to look for another job and we found one job picking oranges.

In that time my wife helped me picking oranges to make a little more money. Then we had to come again in the summer with another farmer in Clarksburg, California. And I worked with that farmer for almost seven years. Then I left the job because I went to help the people around Chavez. At that time it was very hard to live because we got $35.00 in strike benefit. After the strike was over my boss refused to give me work again. Then I started to work again two years. Then I hurt my back. I was feeling very sick, the pain was very hard. Then I went to see the doctor and the doctor gave me about 30 tablets to drink, I drank all in one time. Then, after I drank all the tablets, I feel no change. Then I went to see another doctor and the doctor operated on my back. I have been in the hospital for a long time, sixteen days. I was very sad because I was alone without my wife and my family. After when I was feeling well, I returned to my work but not too long because my boss did not want to take anymore chances about my sickness. Then after two or three months, we received one letter from my boss, the letter said you have to go out from the home because I have other plans for the house. Where we were living was free. There where a lot of problems but at last we moved to Woodland. We lived there for two years. Then we found another boss.* He is in construction and he is a very good person. He gave us a chance to build a house to live in. My son and me we took six months to finish the house now we are living here in it. Now we feel happy because we are living in a good place. and my wife and we are going to school to take an English class to learn the English language to try to find other jobs.

* Mike Corbett, architect specializing in solar and earth energy homes, living at Davis and teaching courses in alternative energy construction at DQU.

267

References

Arce, C.H. "Chicanos in Higher Education." *Integrated Education.* 14, No. 3 (May–June 1976), 14–18.
– "Chicano Participation in Academe: A Case of Academic Colonialism." *Grito del Sol: A Chicano Quarterly,* 3, No. 1 (Jan.–Mar. 1978), 75–104.
Astin, Alexander W. *Minorities in American Higher Education. Recent Trends, Current Prospects, and Recommendations.* San Francisco: Jossey-Bass Inc., 1982.
Brown, Peter G. & Henry Shue, eds. *The Border that Joins. Mexican Migrants and U.S. Responsibility.* Maryland Studies in Public Philosophy. Totowa, N.J.: Rowman & Littlefield, 1983.
Burkhard, Ch. "David Faces Goliath Again: D-Q University and the Bureaucracy." Davis, Ca.: unpubl. typescript, 1982; 21 pp.
Cafferty, Pastora San Juan. "The Language Question: The Dilemma of Bilingual Education for Hispanics in America." In *Ethnic Relations in America.* Ed. Lance Liebman. Englewood Cliffs, N.J.: Prentice-Hall, 1982; pp. 101–27.
Forbes, Jack D., Kenneth R. Martin and David Risling, Jr. *The Establishment of D-Q University.* Davis: D-Q University Press, 1972; 10 pp.
– and Howard Adams. *A Model of 'Grass-Roots' Community Development: The D-Q University Native American Language Education Project.* Davis, Ca.: Native American Studies Tecumseh Center, 1976.
– *Education, Culture, and Academic Freedom: The Reagan Administration's Attack on an American Indian-Chicano College.* Davis, Ca.: D-Q University Press, 1982.
Freire, Paulo. *Pädagogik der Unterdrückten: Bildung als Praxis der Freiheit.* Reinbek: Rowohlt, 1970.
Glazer, Nathan. "Politics of a Multiethnic Society." In *Ethnic Relations in America.* Ed. Lance Liebman. Englewood Cliffs, N.J.: Prentice-Hall, 1982, pp. 128–49.
Herms, Dieter. "La Chicana: Dreifache Diskriminierung als Drittweltfrau." In *Gulliver: Deutsch-englische Jahrbücher* 10. Argument Sonderband 71. Berlin: Argument Verlag, 1981.
Liebman, Lance, ed. *Ethnic Relations in America.* Englewood Cliffs, N.J.: Prentice-Hall, 1982.
Lutz, Hartmut (author & ed.). *D-Q University: Native American Self-Determination in Higher Education.* Davis: Dept. of Applied Behavioral Sciences/Native American Studies Tecumseh Center, 1980.
Moore, John W. with Alfredo Cuellar. *Mexican Americans.* Englewood Cliffs, N.J.: Prentice-Hall, 1970.
Peyer, Bernd C. "D-Q University: A Native American Institution of Higher Learning Struggling for Existence." *Zeitschrift für Ethnologie,* 102, No. 1&2 (1981), 139–48.
Steiner, Stan. *La Raza: The Mexican Americans.* New York et. al.: Harper & Row, 1970.
Thernstrom, Stephen. "Ethnic Groups in American History." In *Ethnic Relations in America.* Ed. Lance Liebman. Englewood Cliffs, N.J.: Prentice-Hall, 1982; pp. 3–27.
United States Senate, *Hearings Before the Select Committee on Presidential Campaign Activities of the United States Senate, 93rd Congress, 1st Session: Watergate and Related Activities.* Book 13. Washington D.C.: U.S. Government Printing Office, 1973.

Multicultural Education
– Education for a Multiethnic Society:
A Comparative Survey of the German and American Experience

Manfred Zirkel

1. The Background

The starting point of this paper is a joint study project undertaken by the Pä-dagogische Hochschule Schwäbisch Gmünd (West Germany), The Teesside Poly-technic at Middlesbrough and the City of Birmingham Polytechnic (Great Bri-tain). The project has been running for three years and has been sponsored by the European Institute of Education and Social Policy of the European Cultural Foundation, Brussels. Its objectives are the production of modules to be inte-grated in the respective multicultural study courses and teaching materials to be used in multiethnic classes at elementary school level.

The types of programs undertaken in the United States, Britain, and the Fed-eral Republic of Germany to cope with the multiethnic situation in these countries, and in many others that cannot be dealt with here, show a great deal of similarity and prove that the problems are indeed international. A comparison of the different national approaches therefore seems a useful means for achieving a more profound understanding of the problems involved and for enlarging the scale of possible solutions to them.

At present about 4.6 million "guestworkers" live in the Federal Republic of Germany. One third of them are Turks. The "guestworkers" make up 6 percent of the total population of the FRG. In some cities the percentage is considerably higher. In Frankfurt nearly every fourth person is a foreigner, in Stuttgart al-most every fifth.

By comparison, the British situation is very similar to that of the FRG in that the importation of labor from the 1950s onwards has resulted in an immigrant population that makes up about 3 percent of the total population with great differences in regional distribution.

In the U.S. an estimated 30 million citizens or residents speak a mother tongue other than English and most of these could be considered non-indigenous. They make up about 16 percent of the total population, with regional averages four or five times that much.

270

In both countries children make up a considerable proportion of that group. And it is here that the preparation for life in a multiethnic society must begin with education being, if not the "great equalizer," at least a potential harmonizer in the relationships of man to man.

2. Multicultural Education

2.1. The German Experience

The policy of the German Federal Government is largely geared towards integration of the migrant families. The Government's basic position is that the FRG is not a country of immigration. The original legal measures taken by the Government were almost exclusively guided by economic and occupational interests and were aimed at provisional integration of the migrants for a limited period of time. It was only through the prolonged residence of migrants in this country as well as family unification and a high birth rate among migrant families that the Government was induced to include humanitarian considerations in its legal measures with a focus on improving the learning conditions and job opportunities of migrant children. The position of the Federal Government can be exemplified by quoting from a paper on the "Equality of Opportunities for Second Generation Migrants" issued by the Baden-Württemberg government in the form of 11 theses.

Theses 1—3 read:

Migrant policy is social policy and must be guided by the social-ethic principles of equal opportunities, social justice, political responsibility and partnership.
This policy requires self-determination on the part of the migrant, i.e. to decide whether he/she wants to stay in Germany or return to his/her native country; thereby excluding all forms of tutelage.
This government assumes that the greater part of children of migrants born in Germany will stay here.[1]

Further on, theses 6—7:

A policy aimed at improving the opportunities for migrant children has to state its priorities. It is an illusion to believe that migrant children could be optimally trained for both a life in Germany and in their country of origin. Integration is not thinkable without at least a partial loss of identity.
An effective improvement of the opportunities for migrant children in the FRG is only conceivable on the basis of a policy of integration, i.e. a policy which gives clear priority to measures integrating migrant children in German society.[2]

Thesis 9 states the Government's position with regard to bilingualism:

The following consequences must be drawn from the integrationalist priorities for our educational policies: no bilingualism in playschool; learning German is to be given priority; as far as the parents want it, additional instruction in the mother tongue will be offered on the basis of voluntary participation in order to maintain the migrant's cultural identity.[3]

The blow which is dealt bilingualism in the education system, as the above mentioned policy does not entitle a German child to participation in the instruction of any of the migrant languages, is to some extent softened by the statement in thesis 11 that:

The integration of foreigners in our society is a task that concerns all social groups and requires their joint involvement. Integration cannot be ordered from above. It has to materialize out of a long process of mutual adaptation between Germans and foreigners. The whole of the population has to be sensitized for it.[4]

The educational consequences of the German Government's adherence to a concept of integration with the option of maintaining the migrant's identity on a voluntary basis are:
— comprehensive schooling of the migrant children from the earliest date possible (from playschool to vocational school)
— joint instruction of German and foreign children with remedial teaching to make up for the migrant children's learning difficulties and problems arising from socio-cultural identity crises
— inclusion of the migrant's family and home environment in educational work
— training German and, where possible, teachers from the migrants' countries of origin for teaching in multiethnic classes.

The results of the educational measures taken so far are on the whole not satisfactory. Two central issues have to be dealt with more effectively: firstly, the migrant children's educational and job opportunities must be improved; and secondly, the programs for strengthening their ethnic identity must be systematized and included in the schools' curricula and syllabuses.

The first issue needs to be dealt with, because the majority of migrant youths can be expected to spend their professional careers in the FRG and they have to be enabled to perform in their jobs and in German society as well. The second issue needs serious consideration and involvement, because the migrant child has a right to learn his/her mother tongue properly and be immersed in his/her own culture in order to communicate with and interact in his/her native community in Germany or, in case of repatriation, in the country of origin.

In the field of employment the FRG has been, due to its membership in the EC and its economic policy since the 1950s, de facto, if not de jure, a multiethnic/multinational nation. This situation will only be solidified by Turkey's expected entry into the EEC in 1986, Turkey being the country of origin of the largest group of migrants in the FRG. In the long run coexistence of the different nationalities seems only possible on the basis of mutual acceptance and respect for each group's identity and ethnicity. Integration is then possible on the basis of partnership, and it is here that education plays its important role by imparting knowledge about the various cultural backgrounds, by giving the pupils the opportunity to experience the intercultural situation in the classroom, to find common ground but also to learn to solve conflicts resulting from the multicultural situation in actual involvement.

2.2 The British Experience

The British experience parallels the German experience and must therefore be mentioned in brief. With the immigration of increasing numbers of West Indians and Asians from the 1950s onwards, the British authorities successively developed two concepts to cope with the joint education of majority and minority group children.

The first concept of immigrant education was assimilation, i.e. the belief that all immigrants irrespective of cultural heritage or skin color could and should be fully assimilated into British society. The implementation of this concept in schools did not allow for the cultural diversity of the different language standards of the minority group children, since the only acceptable culture and standards were to be the British ones.

The concept failed in two respects: first, because the white majority was unwilling to accept the immigrants' attempted assimilation, and secondly, the minority groups rejected it after a while, because the expected acceptance by the larger society did not come and in their view the assimilation attempt only left them with a loss of their cultural identity.

The next concept, proposed by Roy Jenkins as early as 1966, was integration. In Jenkins' words it was meant to be "No flattening process of assimilation, but as equal opportunity accompanied by cultural diversity, in an atmosphere of mutual tolerance..."[5] The idea of social and political integration on the basis of equality was implemented in the schools by introducing non-English ethnic elements into the curricula of a number of subjects. Ideally the entire school life should reflect the multicultural situation. The concept succeeded in a few schools, but was largely in contrast with social reality and was rejected by both groups for the same reasons as the previous concept.

No identifiably new concept has replaced it. Instead, the more flexible didactical principle of 'permeation' was introduced in the 1980s, which means that all teaching materials and the teaching itself should contain elements from the various ethnic groups or reflect the multiethnic situation of the community. Its aim was and is not only to help improve the learning situation of the minority group children by introducing mother tongue teaching as part of the curriculum, but also to heighten the majority group's awareness of the multiethnic character of the society they live in and of the constant need to come to terms with it on a mutually acceptable basis.

2.3 The American Experience

Due to its character as a country of immigration from the very start, the U.S. has had an early awareness of multilinguism and multiculturalism. Keller and van Hooft report that as early as 1774 (Continental Congress) "The Congress provided for the publication in German of a number of documents in order to make them accessible to the German-speaking minority, which was quite sizeable. In addition federal laws were printed in French for the first time in 1806, and the government later mandated that all laws applying to the Louisiana territory be printed in both English and French."[6]

Bilingual education in public schools can be traced back to the time after the annexation of Upper California, New Mexico and the Southwest through the Treaty of Guadalupe Hidalgo in 1848 with sporadic cases of instruction in Spanish and English in that region. In Ohio a law was passed in 1840 providing for the establishment of schools where instruction was in German and English. Other nationalities like the Poles, Lithuanians, Slovacs and Italians first established private non-English parochial schools and in the latter part of the 19th century exerted political pressure for the initiation of bilingual programs in their public schools. While all immigrant groups at one time or another had bilingual schooling, the instruction in American Indian schools was until recently in English only.

The period between the two world wars, in which isolationism and nationalism were very prominent, was characterized by "the almost complete abandonment of bilingual education in the United States and by a declining interest in the study of foreign languages."[7] Many states adopted an English-only policy for instruction in public schools, and the Nationality Act of 1940 required spoken English and in 1950 amendments to the Nationality Act required English literacy, i.e. reading, writing and speaking, as a condition for naturalization.

The trend of an English-only policy for instruction was reversed from the 1950s onwards, starting with the promotion of foreign languages in elementary schools (the Earl J. McGrath Program) and the "Little Schools of the 400" — preschool classes set up to help Chicano children learn the 400 most common words in American English — and culminating in the Bilingual Education Act of 1967/68, officially Title VII of the ESEA of 1965, authorizing the funding of programs for "children from environments where the dominant language is other than English,"[8] and in the Equal Educational Opportunities Act of 1974, which states in Section 204:

> No state shall deny equal educational opportunity to an individual on account of his or her race, color, sex, or national origin by ... the failure by an educational agency to take appropriate action to overcome language barriers that impede equal participation by its students in the instructional program.[9]

In a memorandum DHEW attempts to clarify the goals of Title VII ESEA by stating that:

> The fundamental goal of a federally supported bilingual education program is to enable children whose dominant language is other than English to develop competitive proficiency in English so that they function successfully in the educational and occupational institutions of the larger society.[10]

The legal measures are followed up by regular funding of the programs, by the development of a Language Assessment Battery in Spanish and English (New York City Board of Education, Aspira) from kindergarten through 12th grade, by the creation of regional Bilingual General Assistance Centers or "Lau Centers," by vocational training programs for the purpose of teacher training, materials development, and actual training of students in accordance with the procedures of vocational bilingual education and by the creation of a new education department, the Office of Bilingual Education and Minority Language Affairs.[11]

A survey by the National Center for Educational Statistics issued in 1978 indicated that "28 million citizens or residents of the United States speak a mother tongue other than English or live in households where a language other than English is spoken. About 5 million of this population are children" and that "one out of every eight Americans has had a non-English language background" and that "one-third of the adults and 60% of the school-age children have a Spanish language background."[12]

3. The Philosophy of Multicultural Education

A review of the educational situation of minority group children in these countries has shown that considerable efforts have been made to come to terms with the majority — minority conflicts. A closer examination will reveal, however, that the situation in these countries, given their differing frameworks, falls short of the goals of multicultural education.

For the purpose of clarity a definition of terms seems necessary. Multicultural education does not mean teaching English or German as a second language, though it plays an important role in any multicultural program. It can be synonymous with bilingual education provided bilingual education means that instruction does not only take place in two languages but includes the teaching of two or more cultures. In other words, we can speak of multicultural education when the public school system reflects full recognition of the country's cultural and linguistic diversity by teaching the relevant cultures and languages to both minority and majority group pupils, i.e. both groups learn essential skills in both languages. The goals of multicultural education are then to produce a pupil who is reasonably competent in at least two languages, who has retained a positive individual and cultural self-esteem and whose intercultural socialization has made him or her a competent member in a pluralistic society.

3.1 A Rationale for Multicultural Education

There are a variety of reasons for the promotion of multicultural education in the above mentioned countries. All three of them have de jure or de facto multicultural societies with a national percentage of minorities varying from about 3% in Britain to about 7% in West Germany and about 16% in the United States. These national averages can reach 70% and more in regional distribution. The social, economic, and other problems that are bound to result from a neglect of these groups are so obvious that for political reasons alone solutions have to be found. But a rationale for multicultural education must above all be based on the pedagogical consideration of what is best for the children involved, i.e. the minority group child in particular but the majority group child as well.

Of the reasons collected for bilingual schooling in the United States by Andersson and Boyer (1970) some are applicable to any other national context:

- American schooling has not met the needs of children coming from homes where non-English languages are spoken; a radical improvement is therefore urgently needed.
- Such improvement must first of all maintain and strengthen the sense of identity of children entering the school from such homes.
- The self-image and sense of dignity of families that speak other languages must also be preserved and strengthened.
- The child's mother tongue is not only an essential part of his sense of identity; it is also his best instrument for learning, especially in the early stages.
- Preliminary evidence indicates that initial learning through a child's non-English home language does not hinder learning in English or other school subjects.
- Closely related to bilingualism is biculturalism, which should be an integral part of bilingual instruction.
- Bilingual education holds the promise of helping to harmonize various ethnic elements in a community into a mutually respectful and creative pluralistic society.[13]

Lastly, the growing self-awareness of the child, furthered by the multicultural context in which he grows up, will initially strengthen his perception of the differences that exist between the different cultural groups.

He will then come to a consideration of the different but also of the often very similar values of the two groups and will inevitably arrive at a synthesis of different views and values resulting in a sense of identity that might be called intercultural in that the child no longer identifies with one group or the other, but with both and comes to see his identity as a new one that incorporates elements of both cultural groups bound to the new social and cultural context in which he lives, i.e. as a Turk in Germany, as an Asian or West Indian in Britain or as a Mexican in the United States.

3.2 Models for Multicultural Education

The countries involved in educating minorities along with its majority group have tried various approaches and implemented their ideas in many different programs and models.

Among those programs which come close to or actually achieve multicultural education in the sense defined above, one can distinguish two basic types, each with a different emphasis.

The first type has been called the "transfer-oriented (transitional) program."[14] It is a type of bilingual education program whose ultimate goal is to assimilate the minority pupil in the majority culture and society. Von Maltizt notes that this type of program is "aimed at helping students, usually new arrivals in a school system, over the difficult language hurdle, making it possible for them to keep up in their academic work while they are learning enough English to function successfully in regular English classes."[15] All TESL and TESOL programs belong to this type as well.

The second type has been called "maintenance-oriented," and is aimed at preserving the pupil's ethnic language and culture (Baratz et al., 1973) and is therefore the genuinely multicultural type of educational program. Its characteristic is that it "encourages pupils from various ethnic groups to perfect and maintain their knowledge of the mother tongue while also mastering English — in other words, it aims to develop truly and competently literate bilinguals."[16]

A study carried out by Sally D. Tilley of the University of New Orleans which involved the rank ordering of 57 goals and objectives relating to bilingual education by 14 directors of bilingual education programs representing a cross-section of the United States showed that "both adapting to mainstream society through the teaching of English and the preservation of ethnic ties through the teaching of native language and culture" were considered "important goals of bilingual education."[17] All programs then stressed both assimilationist and preservationist goals.

While it is acceptable that a multicultural program should contain both goals one must be aware, though, of the differences and their underlying tendencies. A program with assimilationist features tends towards the fastest possible transfer from the minority group child's native language to the language of the majority group, or it offers the majority language only with additional remedial instruction and separate instruction in the child's native language. It relegates the child's native language thereby to an inferior or secondary position. The assimilationist program also assumes that there is a superior and an inferior culture. It further assumes that there is a mainstream society that is homogeneous in its values and practices. This, however, is never so. They are only the values and practices of one section of the social spectrum, namely that of the middle class. Assimilation thus means adaptation of the minority group to majority group values and patterns of behavior and is in its aims identical with integration.

The preservationist goals are prominent in two models, the separatist model and the pluralistic model. The separatist model is based on the conviction that the public schools have altogether failed the minority child in his educational needs. As a consequence the minority group organizes alternative schooling which either excludes the majority culture and language completely or relegates it to a subordinate position and makes the teaching of its own culture and language the exclusive content of its curriculum.

In its uncompromising exclusion of the majority culture the separatist model is unacceptable as a viable alternative. It does nothing to promote the minority child's opportunities in the mainstream society and breeds hostility among the two groups.

The pluralistic model expresses equal recognition of the minority as well as the majority culture. Bilingual and bicultural instruction is considered an enriching experience for the children of both groups. The model implies instruction in both languages, "initially through the presentation of a lesson in the student's strongest, or native, language, followed by presentation of the same materials in the second language. Later, ..., the class may alternate from one to the other without doubling or repeating the same materials in the second language."[18]

This model is obviously ideally suited to achieve the goals of multicultural education and belongs to the maintenance-oriented type, with continuity in bicultural schooling and active participation in the program by both communities being an integral part of it.

4. A Comparison of the National Approaches

An evaluation of the different approaches to the joint education of minority and majority group children in the FRG, Britain, and the United States in the light of our closer analysis of multicultural education shows that the approaches and practices vary considerably owing to the inherent differences in the national context, the legal situation, and general attitudes.

278

4.1 The Federal Republic of Germany

The description of the German situation has shown that the programs instituted here are at best transfer-oriented programs. It is necessary, though, to mention the contrast that exists here between academic opinion which largely favors the implementation of maintenance-oriented multicultural programs and public opinion which favors transfer-oriented programs with the aim of integration or repatriation.

The two decisive factors which have shaped the German approach and which make up the major differences between the British and the American approaches are the legal status of the migrants in the FRG and the open question of their return to their countries of origin.

The legal status of migrant workers in Germany, in particular from non-EC countries, is such that they are usually not eligible for German citizenship and that their residence permits extend only as long as they have jobs. If they are out of work for a longer period of time they may have to face involuntary repatriation. The second factor, the profession of a high percentage of migrant workers to want to return to their countries of origin at an unspecified time in the future creates a situation that is unfavorable to any maintenance-oriented multicultural program. It also keeps the involvement of both communities in a joint program, which is an essential part of any multicultural program, at a low level.

A more successful multicultural program can only be achieved in the given German context, if the legal status of the migrant and his family is improved, possibly through a European solution securing all migrants from European countries the unlimited right of residence. In addition, measures have to be taken to strengthen the migrant children's cultural and intercultural identity.

The cooperation between both school and communities has to be improved, and the migrant community has to be encouraged to take a more active part in their children's school life. The migrants' native languages will have to be integrated in the German school curriculum and offered to all children in order to raise their status, but also to make use of them to facilitate learning on the one hand and to improve the migrant children's performance in both their native and their second languages on the other. To conclude, measures have to be taken to further mutual understanding and to overcome racism and ethnocentricity.

Judging from the amount of materials produced for use with migrant children or for use in mixed ethnic classes and the growing willingness of the education authorities, educators, and teacher trainers to develop new programs that are increasingly multicultural in character, there is reason to believe that multiculturalism will become an integral part of every school's curriculum but rather in the form of permeation than bilingual-bicultural education.

4.2 Great Britain

The British experience has shown that multiculturalism cannot be achieved through majority-dominated concepts that are imposed upon a multiethnic society. It can also not be achieved by addressing the minority community only.

Although the legal framework is there, West Indians and Asians are British passport holders and have citizenship, and only a few immigrants return to their countries of origin to stay there permanently, all minority groups have chosen to remain ethnically separate, though accepting British citizenship.

This is then the situation Britain has had to accept and politicians and the education authorities have accounted for it by giving up any assimilationist-integrationist concepts in favor of the more flexible and less rigorous approach of permeating the curricula with multicultural elements and thereby enabling a gradual acceptance of the social reality by all groups involved.

The type of education achieved through permeation is different from say the American model of bilingual-bicultural education, but it must also be ranked as a maintenance-oriented program in that it does not try to bridge a time until full integration is achieved, but tries to preserve the ethnic groups' identities throughout. It is multicultural in that it exposes both majority and minority group pupils alike to the teaching of various ethnic contents, although overall, the implementation of multiculturalism is far less stringent than in the American models.

4.3 The United States

The United States must be credited with the most comprehensive legal framework to implement multicultural education and possibly the largest resources to carry out the respective programs.

Its position with regard to multicultural education is more felicitous than that of Britain or West Germany in that it has a long history of immigration and is in its essence multinational; its majority culture has not been shaped exclusively by one ethnic group and is therefore more international from the start; its minority groups are larger and therefore form more powerful pressure groups; the question of repatriation seems largely irrelevant unlike in Britain or West Germany, where repatriation programs exist that are either run by the country of immigration or by the country of origin.

All in all the chances for multiculturalism achieved through maintenance-oriented programs are very good. While the national context and the legal situation are favorable, the problems seem to lie in the area of general attitudes, if a critic of the education system maintains: "Public education, moreover, is not the great social equalizer it is thought to be. For every child who has succeeded there are many more who have failed."[19] The list does not only include minority groups but all those groups whose learning has been impaired by what Padilla calls "extracurricular rules" and of which he says:

> These rules have little to do with that set of principles laid down by psychologists and educators about the most efficient ways to learn in the classroom. Rather, these 'extracurricular rules' have to do more with the correct language to speak in the classroom, grooming, ..., etc. There is a degree of racism, sexism, ageism and anti-intellectualism in all of this.[20]

The latter applies to all the countries involved in attempts at multicultural education and constitutes an omnipresent factor always to be reckoned with.

The American experience of only very moderate success or even failure of bilingual-bicultural education points to the same conclusion that can be drawn from the British experience, namely that the problem does not only lie with the minority group but to a considerable degree with the majority group's unwillingness to even accept an only partial involvement in the minority group's language and culture. Far greater attention has then to be drawn to the majority group's involvement in multicultural education and some form of 'permeation' seems unrenounceable in all multicultural programs.

Notes

[1] *Baden-Württembergischer Staatsanzeiger* Nr. 10, 2.2.1980.
[2] *Baden-Württembergischer Staatsanzeiger*
[3] *Baden-Württembergischer Staatsanzeiger*
[4] *Baden-Württembergischer Staatsanzeiger*
[5] The Open University, *Race Children and Cities*, Educational Series: A Third Level Course, E 361, Education and the Urban Environment, Block 12 & 13, prepared by Rosalind Street-Porter, Milton Keynes, The Open University Press, 1978, p. 80.
[6] Gary D. Keller and Karen S. van Hooft, "A Chronology of Bilingualism and Bilingual Education," in *Bilingual Education for Hispanic Students in the United States*, ed. J.A. Fishman and G.D. Keller (New York, London: Teachers College Press, Columbia University, 1982), p. 4.
[7] Keller/van Hooft, p. 7.
[8] Keller/ van Hooft, p. 12.
[9] Keller/ van Hooft, p. 14.
[10] Keller/ van Hooft, p. 14.
[11] cf. Keller/ van Hooft, p. 17.
[12] Keller/ van Hooft, p. 15.
[13] cited by A.M. Padilla, "Bilingual Schools: Gateways to Integration or Roads to Separation," in *Bilingual Education for Hispanic Students in the United States*, p. 53.
[14] Joan C. Baratz, et al., *Development of Bilingual-Bicultural Education Models* (Washington D.C.: Education Study Center, 1973)
[15] S.D. Tilley, "Goals and Objectives of Bilingual Education," in *Bilingual Education for Hispanic Students in the United States*, p. 38.
[16] Tilley, p. 38.
[17] Tilley, p. 46.
[18] Padilla, p. 56.
[19] Padilla, p. 48.
[20] Padilla, p. 48.

Ecos de la Cultura y de la Literatura chicanas en Italia

Lia Tessarolo Bondolfi

La literatura, la poesía, el arte lo mismo que la filosofía y la ciencia, aparecen siempre enlazados con una situación objetiva creada, a su vez, por las transformaciones socio-políticas, tecnológicas y económicas.

Toda doctrina debe tener en cuenta la realidad, es decir, los hechos reales que, al fin y al cabo, son su verdadero sustentáculo.

Remontándonos a la teoría de Carlos Bousoño[1] podemos hablar de visión del mundo o cosmovisión, inherente a un período que determina, entre otras cosas, la forma literaria: " ... Todo ser humano y no sólo todo artista, está situado y se yergue, (...) desde un entramado cosmovisionario en el que se realiza como hombre, (...), en el que vive."[2]

Esta cosmovisión vincula a los demás y sobre todo a los que forman parte de un mismo grupo étnico, ya que están ligados por una *raíz genetica* o *motor cosmovisionario* o *foco irradiante.*[3]

Si se habla de cultura chicana y de modo especial del hecho literario hay que evidenciar este *foco* dictado por la potencial desintegración de la identidad del méxico-americano por parte de la sociedad anglosajona. *Foco* que podríamos llamar, paradójicamente, individualismo de grupo, individualismo como crecimiento y afirmación de la personalidad humana, como autosuficiencia del hombre cualquiera que sea el grupo étnico al que pertenezca, como liberación frente al sometimiento y a las imposiciones injustas.

"Hay un movimiento lento de la Historia, una toma de conciencia del hombre por el hombre;"[4] parafraseando esta afirmación de Jean-Paul Sartre diríamos que el motor cosmovisionario que da vida al fenómeno cultural y literario del que estamos hablando resulta ser: *una toma de conciencia del chicano por el chicano.* Es, por lo tanto, esta toma de conciencia unida a las causas históricas que produce el individualismo de grupo, causas como la supresión de la cultura mexicana y las convivencias culturales. En nuestro caso no debemos olvidar que las raíces culturales mexicanas ahondan en aquellas civilizaciones mesoamericanas pre-clásicas como la olmeca y la de Monte Albán en Oaxaca, civilizaciones que sobreviven durante el período clásico hasta la plenitud de la teotihuacana, llegando paulatinamente hasta la fusión con lo español ya mezcla, él mismo, de una serie de culturas como la hispánica, la árabe y la judía durante varios siglos. Todo ello dio como resultado el individuo mexicano y este último, fundiéndose, a su vez, con el mundo anglosajón, produjo *el chicano*. Chicano es una palabra que, además de sus más que aceptables significaciones e interpretaciones filológicas dadas por parte de unos autores, puede tener su origen, también, en la palabra portuguesa *cigano*, es decir *cíngaro, cañí, calé, caló*, haciendo referencia a un grupo étnico nómada, abundantemente mezclado con los pueblos de distintos países.

Claro está que estas convivencias y superposiciones culturales nos inducen a pensar en las dificultades que hay en la formación y transformación del individuo.

La pregunta ontológica y antropológica al mismo tiempo es: ¿cuál es la identidad del chicano? ¿qué papel desempeña ese hombre? Es, sin duda alguna, una pregunta legítimamente filosófica a la cual el chicano contesta intentando encontrar la solución a su problema, dando vida a una serie de actividades culturales comprometidas con el fin de conocerse y dar a conocer a los miembros de su mismo grupo étnico sus exigencias y el derecho a la supervivencia de sus raíces culturales, reconstruyendo las manifestaciones de su propio yo y los fragmentos de una o más culturas superpuestas. Este es el caso de la tradición musical donde convergen elementos españoles y neo-latinos con las golondrinas, pastorelas, aguinaldos, alabados y los corridos "que representan uno de los más populares vehículos de información"[5] igual que los *cantastorie* del sur de Italia. Como es el caso también de la válida propuesta del Teatro Campesino que, ya sabemos, fue fundado en 1965 por Luis Valdez, desarrollándose después durante las luchas sindicales de César Chávez y de la National Farm Workers Association, el Great Grape Boycott. "Teatro de comunidad o teatro político," según lo define Michele Bottalico, teatro que "... por una parte no se puede encerrar en una definición asfíctica que limite sus tareas con intentos propagandísticos, por otra presenta la exigencia de una búsqueda de nuevos y distintos rumbos que, en modo mejor, puedan contribuir (...) para incrementar el proceso de cambio social."[6] Y es también el caso de la representación de los *mitos* y de los *actos* que une las creencias ancestrales de los rituales mayas y aztecas con las funciones didáctico-religiosas de la Iglesia católica, junto al aspecto folklórico de origen mexicano, al teatro político americano en general y, algunas veces, a la *commedia dell'arte*. También la dramaturgia sirve para educar al chicano a través de las representaciones en que se satirizan los vicios del enemigo de la Raza, dramaturgia en que se expresa la filosofía india del Universo: "In lak'ech" que significa: "tú eres mi otro yo," palabras por medio de las que se entrevé un repertorio cultural denso de implicaciones filosóficas y antropológicas pero, sobre todo, sociales.

El *mito* llega a ser, en la mayoría de los casos, el fulcro de este arte nuevo, se diría casi la estrategia de la moderna política chicana.

Escribe Tino Villanueva: "Nuestros teatros han intentado reflejar ese concepto para reeducar a la Raza en la unidad social, y *este abrevar en nuestros antepasados* es una vía importante para dar a los chicanos una mayor liga con sus raíces; el ayudarnos nos identifica con lo cósmico."[7]

Expresiones éstas, por lo tanto, de los aspectos sociológicos e ideólogicos del contenido teatral y no sólo teatral, ya que bien en la prosa bien en la poesía la voz chicana intenta evidenciar su realidad como el éxito que subraya un proceso cultural donde la función comunicativa trata de responsabilizar al chicano de su propio ser hasta la raíz.

El hombre chicano no debe considerarse prisionero de una identidad vacía; la suya no es una cultura ocasional. El quiere recomponer las manifestaciones del yo y los fragmentos de una civilización de la misma manera que hicieron sus antepasados por medio de la tradición oral que, como ya sabemos, es una forma de resistencia cultural.

Las prácticas literarias indican una unidad de intentos cuya finalidad es que converjan los chicanos, los pachucos y los pochos hacia una dirección única y, claro está, que las expectativas tendrían que ser las mismas ya que todos son fruto de los mismos acontecimientos históricos, de los mismos procesos evolutivos teniendo una misma ascendencia.

La literatura, entonces, en todas sus manifestaciones y expresiones, llevada a cabo con una óptica y una visión nuevas, con el fin de poner en evidencia la historia y la intrahistoria de la Raza. De todas formas se ha intentado conducir al chicano hacia la autodeterminación a través de la revaluación cultural y, por consiguiente, a su autodefinición y adquisición de su identidad.

Hemos formulado esta premisa bastante larga y, desde cierto punto de vista, obvia puesto que deseamos afirmar que estamos de acuerdo con lo que ha sido el primer arranque unificador que ha empujado al espíritu chicano hacia una cultura y una literatura políticamente comprometidas y que las dos permitan un conocimiento más adecuado y una exacta toma de conciencia del problema.

Conocemos bien la espesa red de normas que envuelve el *sistema* que no permite autodeterminarse y al mismo tiempo intenta sofocar y anular lo que estima incómodo, pero tenemos la convicción de que si no se amplían los puntos de partida, si no se traspasan las barreras del provincianismo cultural se corre el riesgo de no divulgar su propio *Mensaje*. No hay que dejar a parte el triángulo: remitente, vehículo, destinatario y, de la misma manera, no se pueden ignorar las expectativas del potencial fruitivo.

El chicanismo abarca todo un universo ideológico, proclama un sincero afán por cambiar estructuras socio-políticas pero, al mismo tiempo, contempla una verdadera pasión humanística, por lo tanto podemos hablar no sólo de autodefinición y autodeterminación, no sólo de impulso regenerador y toma de conciencia política, factores, lo repetimos, determinantes para la formación y el desarrollo del Movimiento, sino que podemos hablar también de un verdadero empuje literario.

Por lo que se refiere a los estudios sobre el hecho cultural chicano no se han obtenido en Italia la atención y el vigor necesarios por parte de las editoriales — esto, quizá, porque ya desde el comienzo de la estructuración del Movimiento, los complejos matices culturales siempre han desembocado, por razones socialmente válidas, en la que podríamos definir una aventura política. Es decir que en el proceso evolutivo que abarca el renacer y el florecer cultural chicano, la línea de conducta ha sido pura y simplemente social.

La editorial Jaca Book de Milán ha hecho sus primeras publicaciones al final de los años sesenta cuando, también en Europa, empezaban a cuajar las contestaciones políticas juveniles y la inteligentzia de todos los países favorecía el conocimiento de las problemáticas innovadoras.

El primer libro introducido por la Jaca ha sido: *La Raza: i Messicoamericani — L'occidente a confronto* de Stan Steiner, traducción de Pier Paolo Poggio — 1969, 1970, 1972. La introducción al texto es esquelética y muy reducida y no pone de relieve lo que ha sido la odisea espiritual de la Raza. La lectura resulta fluida, pero no hay elementos necesarios para sopesar la compleja experiencia artística chicana. Además, de la misma casa editora, se publica en 1976 *¡Macho!* de Villaseñor, traducido por Carla Muschio, autora también de la presentación en la que intenta, en pocas páginas, informar al lector de esa experiencia de marginalización del chicano a causa de los prejuicios educacionales y raciales. Pero Carla Muschio no considera útil proporcionar datos históricos con la finalidad de comprender la novela, en cambio encuentra interesante resaltar, a nivel de estructuras narrativas, el doble plano de la narración, es decir, el de la información histórico-ideológica en contraposición con el cuento real y propio. Ella afirma que: "Esta doble descripción basada en los dos planos distintos de la misma realidad permite duplicar la posibilidad de comunicación bien sea de uno bien sea del otro, en una competición de ecos entre narración y datos históricos."[8]

Mario Maffi, para la editorial Universale Laterza, en el texto *La cultura underground*, hace referencia en pocas líneas al Teatro Campesino, en el que afirma que éste constituye " ... uno de los sectores más estimulantes en el cuadro de las organizaciones políticas."[9]

En 1976 sale: *¡Chicanos! Cultura e politica dei Messicoamericani*, Marsilio editori — a cargo de Alessandro Gebbia en que el autor subraya que esta antología "... no pretende ser una colección completa de los documentos y textos del renacimiento México-americano, sino ofrecer (...) un panorama general de las múltiples expresiones políticas y culturales del Movimiento chicano" y espera "que ellas contribuyan para que los lectores italianos se sensibilicen, empujándolos hacia una aportación constructiva y solidaria en la lucha para la autodeterminación ..."[10]

Hablando todavía de las editoriales oficiales nos queda señalar de: *Novecento Americano,* Lucarini ed. 1981 — el compendio de Michele Bottalico en el que el autor, en la parte introductiva, pasa brevemente en reseña la historia y la tradición chicana haciendo referencia al " ... desarrollo de un cuerpo literario con una fisonomía más autónoma,"[11] mencionando también los trazos que emergen de la dúplice matriz cultural de los autores. Por lo tanto da a conocer al lector los rasgos esenciales del teatro, de la poesía y de la narrativa ahora puestos en tela de juicio.

Después de esta breve exposición se deduce que en Italia oficialmente no se ha realizado mucho y lamentamos que la literatura chicana no ha obtenido la acogida que nosotros hubiéramos deseado, quizá todo ello causado por su carácter estrictamente didáctico y también por su sabor diaspórico enlazado, claro está, con un contexto histórico-social-político muy poco conocido en nuestro país.

Afortunadamente en el interior de las Universidades hay nuevos fermentos por medio de los que se trata de poner en conocimiento de los estudiantes y de los colegas, especializados en otras disciplinas, el complejo mundo chicano. Nos duele admitir que hasta ahora todo ello ha ocurrido casi exclusivamente en los departamentos de anglística y nosotros, como hispanistas, no nos sentimos satisfechos con esta solución.

Alessandro Gebbia de la Universidad de Roma; Michele Bottalico de la Universidad de Bari; Monica Berretta, Gabriele Morelli, Bruno Gallo de la Universidad de Bergamo; Luisanna Fodde de Cagliari, han contribuido y aún contribuyen con aportaciones significativas.

Gebbia ha tenido una serie de cursos articulados en dos años, cursos que abrazan las lecturas de algunas obras como *Bless me, Ultima* o *Barrio Boy* hasta la focalización de algunos aspectos importantes como las relaciones entre cultura chicana y norteamericana o el papel de la mujer en la literatura chicana. Junto a esto, Gebbia tiene en programa la traducción de *Bless me, Ultima* mientras que están para publicarse: *La literatura chicana entre homologación y diversidad* y *El chicano en la literatura norteamericana.* Este último es un análisis específico de lo que ha sido la progresiva imagen del méxico-americano; desde la visión romántica del suroeste hasta llegar a algunos ejemplos en la literatura más congenial a nosotros. En el próximo número de *Studi Americani* saldrá el ensayo: "Il corrido come ballata di frontiera" que será una lectura de los textos efectuada desde un punto de vista histórico.

Un acontecimiento sobresaliente ha sido el primer Coloquio de Antropología Histórica que ha tenido lugar en Roma en octubre de 1983 sobre *Cultura planetaria: ¿Homologación o diversidad? La relación entre los pueblos indígenas del continente americano y el occidental,* con la participación de numerosos estudiosos. Dicho Simposium, en que se espera " ... hayan brotado las sugerencias capaces de influenciar las elecciones colectivas útiles para todas las minorías del humano consorcio,"[12] ha sido patrocinado por la *Camera dei Deputati,* la *Regione Lazio Assessorato alla Cultura,* la *Provincia di Roma Assessorato alla Cultura,* el *Comune di Roma,* la *Università degli Studi di Roma,* la *Opera Universitaria.* La participación de entes tan calificados nos permite suponer que realmente se esté haciendo algo para que el Viejo Continente conozca las realidades de etnias desconocidas.

Monica Berretta del IUB ha dirigido, junto con Alessandra Marzola, la tesis doctoral de Nicoletta Cereda sobre el *Cambio de Código.* El trabajo consta de tres partes:

1) Rasgos históricos
2) *Bilingüismo* y *diglosía, interferencias* y *préstamos*
3) Cambio de código verdadero y propio con definición, reglas morfosintácticas, reglas probabilísticas y grado de bilingüismo.

Michele Bottalico es, sin duda, el más fecundo entre los escritores italianos que están interesados en este problema; además del extracto ya citado ha escrito: *The Rebirth of Mexican American Theatre in the United States: towards an "old" poetics of new performance,* publicado en *Estudios de Filología Inglesa*[13] y, además, ha escrito en las Revistas *Metaphorein, Quaderni del Cut di Bari, Sipario*[14] y también ha comentado y traducido *Los Vendidos,* pero ha tenido que imprimirlo pagándose él los gastos. A este propósito merece la pena dar a conocer por medio de sus palabras, sacadas de una carta del 8 de abril de 1984, cuáles son las dificultades que se encuentran en Italia para recorrer el áspero camino de la editoría: "... el primer trabajo que contiene la traducción de *Los Vendidos* — afirma Bottalico — había sido aceptado por *Il lettore di Provincia* pero sin embargo, en el último momento ha preferido dar espacio a otros argumentos y, por consiguiente, he debido publicarlo pagándome los gastos (cosa que no volveré a hacer jamás), también porque es obvio que el texto del Teatro Campesino no ha tenido alguna difusión. Lo mismo dígase de la comunicación, presentada por mí en un Coloquio en Bélgica, que ha obtenido hospitalidad solamente en una revista española mientras que a mí me interesaba difundir el argumento en Italia."

Estas palabras nos hacen reflexionar y todavía una vez más nos hacen pensar en los obstáculos que se encuentran en Italia en el sector de la publicación y de la difusión de un producto literario.

Yendo adelante en la disquisición emprendida sobre los trabajos efectuados en nuestras Universidades, nos parece un deber citar la contribución de Loredana Burini que está presente en este Simposium. Ella, sin duda, con su tesis *Documentación y estudio sobre la cultura y la literatura chicana* — director Bruno

Gallo, codirector Gabriele Morelli — escrita después de un período transcurrido en los Estados Unidos en la New Mexico State University de Las Cruces, N.M., ha puesto en luz las peculiaridades del Movimiento, pasando en reseña obras y autores. Es un documento de recopilación que podrá ser utilizado por aquellos que piensan tener un primer contacto con este mundo cultural tan lejos de nosotros los italianos.

Por último, de Cerdeña, un trabajo efectuado por Luisanna Fodde que ha elaborado el ensayo *Alienación y conciencia cultural: el florecimiento de la literatura chicana.*[15]

Luisanna Fodde declara que está de acuerdo con las nuevas corrientes del pensamiento que afirman la exigencia de una total renovación de la escritura de la Historia de la Literatura de los Estados Unidos, basándose en el carácter multiétnico de dicha literatura. La autora del ensayo especifica, además, la importancia de una serie de elementos que caracterizan este tipo de escritura como objeto de investigación histórico-crítica, elementos como: alienación y conciencia. El concepto de conciencia o *cultural consciousness* está extractado de un artículo de Wayne Charles Miller, aparecido en *MELUS* (the Journal of the Society for the Study of the Multi-Ethnic Literature of the United States) en el que se hace patente que la "literatura sirve como medio para ulteriores desarrollos de la conciencia cultural de un específico grupo de personas ya sea nacional, regional o étnico."[16]

Luisanna Fodde avala también el concepto de *Locus of self-hood* (el lugar de sí mismo) de Carlota Dwyer[17] en el que no se habla de un solo protagonista en búsqueda de su propia identidad, se habla, en cambio, de la "... voluntad de englobar en la narración la historia pasada y actual de la gente y de los sitios a los que los autores, junto con los protagonistas, pertenecen."[18]

La escritora cagliaritana afirma que la literatura chicana saca ventajas de la continua renovación del patrimonio originario que exalta y valoriza las obras de varios autores, y añade también que el pertenecer a una etnia es fundamental, lo mismo que el deseo de reproducir la propia experiencia étnica.

En fin, para llevar de nuevo esta disquisición hacia la tesis sostenida por nosotros a lo largo de esta ponencia subrayamos, como ha dicho Gebbia durante el Coloquio de antropología desarrollado en Roma, que se pueda hablar de "... un punto de llegada y un punto de partida en el proceso de conocimiento del complejo y articulado universo representado por las culturas indígenas de Norte América."[19]

A nosotros nos gusta pensar en un punto de partida con el fin de que la literatura chicana no se quede, en Italia, relegada en una zona de silencio. Para obtener cualquier posibilidad de acceso en el mundo editorial es indispensable un gran esfuerzo por parte de todos.

288

Los autores chicanos tendrán que alejarse, en parte, de la óptica primaria socio-política, cosa que por lo demás ya se está verificando, dando lugar a una producción más reflexiva y estilísticamente más cuidada de la que puedan emerger las tradiciones culturales indo-hispánicas y también los contextos socio-lingüísticos, de otra manera se corre el riesgo de una embalsamación ideológica. Según escribe Raymund Paredes: "Political literature, of course, is a tradition in Latin America and among Chicanos, but the danger lies in the abandonment of esthetic principles for purely political consideration."[20]

Por nuestra parte nos empeñaremos más en la difusión y en el conocimiento del mundo chicano ya que, a pesar de la competencia de los estudiosos italianos, se ha visto que las investigaciones hechas prefieren poner de relieve, sobre todo, el aspecto político. Hasta ahora se ha tratado de informar al lector italiano sobre las publicaciones y sobre las actividades teatrales sin formular juicios críticos, dejando, por lo tanto, al lector la interpretación de los textos.

Nosotros deseamos férvidamente que, por medio de esfuerzos comunes, la literatura chicana pueda soportar la fuerza del tiempo colocándose al alcance del público italiano; y que esto se realice tratando de armonizar la orientación ideológica con la universalidad de la palabra.

Quizá entonces la tierra mítica de Aztlán pueda llegar a ser también nuestra tierra prometida puesto que: "Tu sueño es contagioso hermano..."[21]

Notas

[1] Carlos Bousoño, *Epocas literarias* 1 (Madrid: Editorial Gredos, 1981).
[2] Bousoño, p. 11.
[3] Bousoño, p. 12.
[4] Jean-Paul Sartre, *El País,* 17 de Abril, 1980, p. 29.
[5] Alessandro Gebbia, *¡Chicanos! Cultura e politica dei messico-americani* (Venezia: Marsilio Editori Collettivo, 1976), p. 75.
[6] Michele Bottalico, "Cultura di base e ricerca d'identità di una minoranza etnica americana," *Metaphorein,* 2 (1979), 6.
[7] Tino Villanueva, *Chicanos: Antología histórica y literaria* (México, D.F.: Colección Tierra Firme, 1980), p. 141.
[8] Carla Muschio, introduzione a *¡Macho!* di Edmund Víctor Villaseñor (Milano: Jaca Book, 1976), p. 9.
[9] Mario Maffi, *La Cultura Underground* (Roma: Universale Laterza, 1980), p. 194.
[10] Gebbia, p. 5.
[11] Michele Bottalico, *Novecento Americano* (Roma: Lucarini Editore, 1981), p. 696.
[12] Teodoro Cutulo, *Cultura planetaria: omologazione o diversità?* (Viterbo: Union Printing, 1983), p. 12.
[13] Michele Bottalico, *The Rebirth of Mexican American Theatre in the U.S.,* Estudios de Filología Inglesa, 9 (Granada: Enero), E 1981.
[14] Michele Bottalico, varios artículos: *Metaphorein,* 6 (1979), 6; *I Quaderni del Cut di Bari,* 23 (Dicembre 1981); *Sipario* 34 (1979).
[15] Luisanna Fodde, *Alienazione e consapevolezza culturale: l'emergere della letteratura chicana* (Roma: Il Centro di Studi Americani di Roma, 1983).

[16] Wayne C. Miller, "Cultural Consciousness in a Multi-Cultural Society: The Uses of a Literature," *MELUS*, 8, No. 3 (1981), 30.

[17] Carlota Dwyer, "Cultural Nationalism and Chicano Literature in the Eighties," *MELUS*, 8, No. 2 (1981), 46.

[18] Fodde, p. 20.

[19] Alessandro Gebbia, *Cultura planetaria: omologazione o diversità?* (Viterbo: Union Printing, 1983), p. 15.

[20] Raymund Paredes, "The Evolution of Chicano Literature," *MELUS*, 15, No. 2 (1978), 104.

[21] Abelardo, *25 Pieces of a Chicano Mind* (n.p.: n. p., n. d.), p. 19.

Contributors

Alurista was born in Mexico City in 1947 and received his Ph.D. in Spanish Literature from the University of California, San Diego in 1982. He is one of the most significant and widely known Chicano poets. He has published six collections of poetry, including *Floricanto en Aztlán* (1971), *Timespace Huracan* (1976), *Spik in Glyph* (1981), and *Return* (1982). Many of his other poems, plays, short stories, and essays have appeared in various publications. He has recited his poetry throughout the U.S., Mexico, Germany, and Holland as a participant in the III Annual International One World Poetry Festival. He is currently editor-in-chief of Maize Press and teaches in the Romance Languages Department at The Colorado College.

Renate von Bardeleben was born in Eisenach, Germany in 1940. She received her Ph.D. in American Literature from Mainz University in 1967 and completed her habilitation there in 1977. In 1978 she followed a call to the Free University of Berlin and taught in the Division for North American Culture at the John F. Kennedy Institute. Since 1980 she has held the chair in American Studies at the University of Mainz in Germersheim. Her main research areas are American colonial literature, autobiography, minority writing (Jewish American, Black, and Chicano), social and regional dialects, bilingualism. She has been a recipient of a Dissertation Award and of an ACLS fellowship. Besides publishing various articles and reviews in both German and American journals, coediting and coauthoring two festschrifts (1969, 1975), she has also contributed to collections, handbooks, and guides. Her major publications include *Das Bild New Yorks im Erzählwerk von Dreiser und Dos Passos* (1967) and *Studien zur amerikanischen Autobiographie: Benjamin Franklin und Mark Twain* (1981).

Wolfgang Binder was born in Esslingen, Germany in 1941 and received his Ph.D. from the University of Erlangen-Nürnberg in 1973. He is presently teaching at the American and British Studies Institute of the University of Erlangen-Nürnberg in Erlangen. He has written numerous articles on Puerto Rican, Chicano, and Black American Literatures and on Caribbean literature. His major publications include *Europäisches Drama und amerikanische Kritik, 1890– 1914* (1974), *„Anglos are Weird People for me."* *Interviews with Chicanos and Puerto Ricans* (1979), and *"America is my Home."* *Interviews with Young Blacks from Georgia* (1983). Dr. Binder is currently editing a volume with the papers of the First Symposium on Caribbean Cultures held at the University of Erlangen in 1985, and completing his habilitation study „Puerto Rican Literature since 1952."

Gustav Blanke was born in Bad Salzuflen, Germany in 1914. After studying German and American literature, history, and art history at several German universities and as a fellowship recipient at various American universities, he received his Ph.D. from the University of Münster in 1942. After the second World War he worked for the United States authorities as teacher and interpreter.

Following further research in the U.S., he completed his salient sociolinguistic studies *Der amerikanische Geist* (1956) and *Der Amerikaner* (1957). He is a founding member of the German Association for American Studies. He earned his habilitation at the University of Münster in 1960 with a study entitled *Amerika im englischen Schrifttum des 16. und 17. Jahrhunderts* (1960). From 1968 to 1979 he was one of the two chairpersons of the English and American Studies Institute of the Department of Applied Linguistics at the University of Mainz in Germersheim. His teaching and research focus on American culture and politics and on linguistic studies (*Methoden der semantischen Analyse*, 1973). His research interests include sociolinguistic approaches to the American mind and character, semantic analysis, and the history of political ideas. Among his publications are numerous articles on such topics as American literary theory, the semantics of political terms, the rhetoric of America's world mission, the American Indians, and ethnicity.

Lia Tessarolo Bondolfi was born in Rome in 1939. She received her doctorate in Foreign Languages and Literatures at the Istituto Universitario di Lingue Moderne in Milan and is presently teaching Spanish Culture and Literature at the Istituto Universitario di Bergamo and at the Scuola Superiore per Interpreti e Traduttori in Milan. She has done research on the *Monserrate* (1978), the epic poem by Cristóbal de Viruès, and has also published the manual *Guida al dettato, apporto didattico per l'apprendimento della lingua spagnola* (1982). Her study on Antonio Buero Vallejo is forthcoming.

Melba Joyce Boyd was born in Detroit, Michigan in 1950. She earned a Doctor of Arts in English at the University of Michigan in 1979 and has been on the faculty at the University of Iowa since 1983. She has published three books of poetry, *Song for Maya* (1983), *Cat Eyes and Dead Wood* (1978), and *Thirteen Frozen Flamingoes* (1984). Other poems have appeared in Black and feminist publications. She has also done research on the application of perceptual theory to the teaching of compositional skills. She has served as assistant editor for the Broadside Press and was a Senior Fulbright Lecturer at the University of Bremen, West Germany in 1983–1984.

Dietrich Briesemeister was born in Altena, Germany in 1934. He has held the chair for Spanish and Portuguese Studies in the Department of Romance Languages and Literatures at the University of Mainz in Germesheim since 1971. He has conducted research and published articles on Hispanic, Portuguese, and Neo-Latin literature of the Middle Ages and the 16th and 17th centuries, comparative literature, and the history of translation and criticism. He is a member of the editorial boards of *Criticón, Portugiesische Forschungen*, and *Biblioteca del 36*, serves as managing editor of *Iberoromania* and consulting editor of *Lexikon des Mittelalters* and *Kindlers Literaturlexikon*. His major publications include *Camões na Alemanha* (1983), *Das Bild des Deutschen in der spanischen und das Bild des Spaniers in der deutschen Literatur* (1980), and *Aureum Saeculum Hispanum* (1983).

Juan Bruce-Novoa was born in Costa Rica in 1944. He obtained his Ph.D. in Mexican contemporary literature at the University of Colorado at Boulder in 1974. His main research interests include the contemporary Mexican and Chicano novel and Hispanic theater. He has taught at several major universities, including the University of California at Santa Barbara and Yale, and is affiliated with Trinity University in Texas since 1985. He has published widely, especially in the area of Latin American Studies and Chicano literature. Among his publications are *Chicano Authors: Inquiry by Interview* (1980) and *Chicano Poetry: A Response to Chaos* (1982). He has also developed his reputation as a literary critic and poet. Along with various other poems and short stories, he has published a collection of poetry entitled *Inocencia Perversa/Perverse Innocence* (1976).

Heiner Bus is a native of Gydgoszcz, Poland, where he was born in 1941. He earned a Ph.D. in American literature at the University of Mainz in 1970 with a study on Saul Bellow, *Die Figur des 'Helden' in Saul Bellows Roman 'Herzog'*, and received his habilitation in 1978. He is presently teaching in the American Studies Department of the University of Mainz and has conducted research in U.S. minority literatures, the relationship between literature and history, and the cultures of the American Southwest. His publications include articles on Chicano Literature and the Black American heritage as well as a study of Washington Irving, *Studien zur Reiseprosa Washington Irvings* (1982).

Laura Chávez was born in Mexico City in 1953. Since 1979 she has been on the faculty at the Universidad Autónoma de México where she also obtained the Licenciatura in English. She is currently conducting research on bilingualism at the Free University of Berlin under Carol Pfaff and working towards a Master's Degree.

Sergio D. Elizondo is a native of Mexico, where he was born in 1930. He received his Ph.D. from the University of North Carolina at Chapel Hill in 1964 and is presently on the faculty at New Mexico State University. As well as having written numerous articles on Chicano literature, language, and culture, he is also a writer and a poet in his own right. He is a founding member of the *Journal of Ethnic Studies* and was for several years its corresponding editor. He has also given numerous lectures on Hispanic topics and has produced various plays at the University of Texas. His publications include *Perros y Antiperros*, a collection of poetry (1972), *Rosa, La flauta*, a selection of short stories(1980), and the novel *Muerte en una estrella* (1983). He is presently working on a second novel: "Cuadrados, Redondos y Marrano Blindado."

Geneviève Fabre was born in Paris in 1936. She completed her Doctorat d'Etat at the University of Paris III in 1978 and is presently teaching at the University of Paris VII. She has published widely in the field of American Studies and has specialized in the areas of Afro-American theatre and Black women writers. Her publications include: *The Restless Journey of James Agee* (1977), *Le Théâtre Noir aux Etats-Unis* (1982) and *Drumbeats, Masks and Metaphors* (1983). She has also coauthored several works including *F.S. Fitzgerald* (1964) and *En Marge: Les Minorités aux Etats-Unis* (1970). She has published numerous articles in *American Quarterly, Caliban, Black World*, etc. She received a Fulbright Fellowship, an ACLS grant and fellowship and she was a DuBois Fellow at the Afro-American Center of Harvard University in 1984–85.

Yves-Charles Grandjeat was born in 1957 in Paris. He has just completed his doctorate in Anglophone Studies at the University of Paris VII and is presently a faculty member of the English Department of the University of Bordeaux. His dissertation topic was "Aspects du Mouvement Culturel Chicano: l'historien, le politicien et l'artiste" (1985). He has given various lectures and published several articles on Chicano culture.

Dieter Herms was born in 1937 in Hannover, Germany. He received his Ph.D. in English and American Studies from the University of Regensburg in 1968 with a study entitled "The Humorous Adaption of Arthurian Materials in Recent English and American Fiction." He has held the chair in American literature at the University of Bremen since 1975. His major research areas include U.S. ethnic literatures and working class literature, "second culture" in the U.S., the political theater, and the works of Upton Sinclair. His major publications include a book on Upton Sinclair, *Upton Sinclair – Amerikanischer Radikaler* (1978), and a textbook for American Studies (1982). He has published a study on the political theater in the U.S. *Agitprop USA* (1973) and has coauthored two books on the same topic, *Politisches Volkstheater der Gegenwart* (1981) und *Ein Vierteljahrhundert San Francisco Mime Troup* (1984). He is the editor of Upton Sinclair's work in German and of *Gulliver*, the German-English Yearbook, and has published various articles on Chicano literature.

José Alfonso Huerta was born in Los Angeles in 1942. He received his Ph.D. in the field of Theatre Arts from the University of California, Santa Barbara in 1974, and is presently teaching in the Drama Department of the University of California, San Diego. His published works include *El Teatro de la Esperanza: An Anthology of Chicano Drama* (1973), and *Chicano Theatre: Themes and Forms* (1982). He founded El Teatro de la Esperanza in 1971, has directed numerous Chicano plays, and has received various grants to further his work with the Chicano theatre. He also serves as contributing editor for several periodicals dealing with Chicano culture.

Alfred Jung was born in 1955 in Elz, Germany. He has received research scholarships to the Free University of Berlin and the University of Texas at Austin and is presently working on his dissertation on the novels of Rudolfo A. Anaya at the University of Mainz. He is also teaching night classes and secondary school classes in Mainz.

Nicolás Kanellos was born in New York City in 1945. He received his Ph.D. in Spanish and Portuguese from the University of Texas at Austin in 1974 and is now a faculty member in the Department of Hispanic and Classical Languages at the University of Houston. He has received broad acclaim for his achievements in the area of publication of Hispanic works and for his research on Hispanic literature, especially theatre. He has received numerous awards and fellowships, including grants from the National Endowment for the Arts and the Outstanding Editor Award from the Coordinating Council of Literary Magazines. He is an editorial board member for the *Latin American Theatre Review*, *Explorations in Ethnic Studies* and the *Puerto Rican Journal*. He is also the editor/publisher of Arte Público Books and of the *Revista Chicano-Riqueña*. His publications include *Essays on Hispanic Theatre in the United States* (1984) and numerous articles on Hispanic literature and theatre.

Juanita Luna Lawhn is a native of Sabinal, Texas, where she was born in 1945. She received an M.A. in Spanish and English from Southwest Texas State University and an M.A. in Bicultural-Bilingual Studies from the University of Texas at San Antonio. She is currently teaching English at San Antonio college. She is coeditor of *Mexico and the United States: Intercultural Relations in the Humanities* (1984), and is presently working on several research projects dealing with the Spanish language newspaper, *La Prensa*.

Francisco Lomelí was born in Sombrerete, Mexico in 1947. He received his Ph.D. in Romance Languages from the University of New Mexico, and is presently teaching in the areas of Spanish, Portuguese, and Chicano Studies at the University of California at Santa Barbara. His research focuses on Chicano literary history, Chilean literature, and the Latin American novel. His publications include *Chicano Perspectives in Literature* (1976) and *La Novelística de Carlos Droguett* (1983). He is coeditor of *A Decade of Chicano Literature (1970–1979)* (1982) and *Chicano Literature: A Reference Guide* (1985).

Hartmut Lutz was born in Rendsburg, Germany in 1945. He received his Ph.D. from the University of Tübingen in 1975 and completed his habilitation at the University of Osnabrück in 1982, where he is now teaching English and American Studies. He has published various articles on Native American studies, minority and cultural studies, and regionalism. He also received an ACLS fellowship at the Tecumseh Center for Native American Studies, University of California-Davis and at D-Q University, Davis. His publications include *D-Q University: Native American Self-Determination in Higher Education* (1982) and *"Indianer" und "Native Americans": Zur sozial- und literarhistorischen Vermittlung eines Stereotyps* (1985).

José Montoya was born in 1932 in El Gallego, New Mexico, but has spent most of his life in California, where he studied at the California College of Arts and Crafts. He earned a Master of Arts degree at California State University in 1971 where he has been teaching art since 1970. He must be counted among the most prolific and most widely acclaimed Chicano artists and poets. His art has been exhibited at various universities, cultural centers, and galleries, and he has been invited to read his poetry and lecture on Chicano art and poetry at major universities in the U.S. and Puerto Rico. Collections of his poetry have been published in *El Espejo* (1969), *Rascatripas* (1970), and *El Sol y los de Abajo* (1972). Other poems have been published in *The Nation, Aztlan, Maize* and in various community and university newspapers. His work has been the subject of numerous studies on Chicano literature. He helped found the Royal Chicano Air Force, a collective of cultural workers who have been instrumental in bringing international attention to the Chicano movement.

Carol Wollman Pfaff was born in San Francisco in 1944. She received a Ph.D. in Linguistics from the University of California at Los Angeles and has been teaching linguistics at the John F. Kennedy Institute for North American Studies of the Free University of Berlin since 1977, where she is the Head of the North American Language Department. Her major research areas include bilingualism, second language acquisition, minority psycho- and sociolinguistics. She has published numerous articles on such topics as: Black English, Pidgin, and Creole languages, "Gastarbeiterdeutsch," and sociolinguistic problems of immigrants.

Her articles have appeared in *Language, General Linguistics, Language in Society, Studies in Second Language Acquisition,* and other journals.

Marcienne Rocard   was born in 1931 in Paris. She received her Ph.D. from the University of Lyon (France) in 1978. She is on the faculty at the University of Toulouse – Le Mirail. Her research focuses on Anglo-Canadian literature, Mexican-American history and literature, and Caribbean literature. Her publications include *Les Fils du Soleil: La minorité mexicaine à travers la littérature des Etats-Unis* (1980), as well as articles in *Canadian Studies* (Université Bordeaux), *Caliban* (Université Toulouse), and *Caravelle: Cahiers du monde hispanique et luso-brésilien* (Université Toulouse).

José David Saldívar   was born in Brownsville, Texas in 1955. He completed his Ph.D. at Stanford University in 1983 and is presently teaching in the English Department of the University of Houston. His main research interests include Chicano and ethnopoetic American literature, Latin American literature, and critical theory. He has also published various articles on Chicano topics and several reviews of Chicano works. He is editor of the *Revista Chicano-Riqueña* and served as contributing editor to *Mango: A Journal of Multi-Ethnic Literature* from 1979–1980. He is also the editor of "The Rolando Hinojosa Reader" (forthcoming) and is presently working on a book entitled "Claiming the Americas: The Making of Third World and Ethnopoetic American Literature, 1949–1985."

László Scholz   was born in Budapest, Hungary in 1948. He obtained his Ph.D. in Hispanic Philology at the Eötvös Loránd University in 1975. He is presently teaching in the Spanish Department of the same university and has been involved primarily in research on the Latin-American essay, the modern short story in Latin America, and 20th-century Latin American fiction. In addition to several textbooks, he has published *El arte poética de Julio Cortázar* (1977) as well as translations of several Latin American novels. He has also written critical anthologies of the modern Peruvian short story (1982) and of the classical Latin American Essay (1984) and is now preparing an anthology of Borges' essays.

Horst Tonn   was born in 1953 in Oldenburg, Germany. He is presently finishing his Ph.D. thesis in the area of the Chicano novel written in English. He is the coauthor of a book on the farm worker movement in the United States and has published a translation of Rudolfo A. Anaya's *Bless Me, Ultima* (1984) in German. He is currently teaching at the American Studies Institute of the Department of Applied Linguistics at the University of Mainz in Germersheim.

Annick Tréguer   was born in Pau, France in 1940. She obtained the Agrégation in Spanish in 1964. After spending five years in California, she began teaching in the Spanish Department of the University of Paris III in 1982. Her major area of research is the Hispanic theater in the U.S. and she has published several articles on Chicano topics. She is also a founding member of A.D.E.C.L.A.N. (Association pour la Diffusion et l'Etude des Cultures Latines en Amérique du Nord).

Donald W. Urioste   was born in 1947 in Trinidad, Colorado. He has taught at the University of New Mexico and the Colorado College and is presently an instructor in the Foreign Language Department of California Lutheran College. He expects to receive his Ph.D. in 1985 from the University of New Mexico. Mr. Urioste served as counselor for the Mexican American Educational Program at the University of Colorado at Denver for four years. He has written several articles on Chicano writers and literature, and is coauthor of *Chicano Perspectives in Literature: A Critical and Annotated Bibliography* (1976).

Manfred Zirkel was born in Gelsenkirchen, Germany in 1942. He completed his Ph.D. in American Literature in 1976 at the University of Münster and is presently on the faculty at the Pädagogische Hochschule at Schwäbisch Gmünd. His primary areas of research are American literature, language testing, and the teaching of English and German as foreign languages. His publications include *Mensch und Mythos: Der Mittlere Westen im Romanwerk von Wright Morris* (1971), and he has coauthored *Deutsch Aktiv. Ein Lehrwerk für Erwachsene* (1979).

Index